PADRE PIO

PADRE PIO

MIRACLES AND POLITICS
IN A SECULAR AGE

SERGIO LUZZATTO

TRANSLATED BY
FREDERIKA RANDALL

METROPOLITAN BOOKS
HENRY HOLT AND COMPANY
NEW YORK

Metropolitan Books
Henry Holt and Company, LLC
Publishers since 1866
175 Fifth Avenue
New York, New York 10010
www.henryholt.com

Originally published in Italy in 2007 by Giulio Einaudi editore s.p.a, Turin.
Revisions to this English-language edition have been made with the approval of the author.

Library of Congress Cataloging-in-Publication Data

Luzzatto, Sergio, 1963–
  [Padre Pio. English]
  Padre Pio: miracles and politics in a secular age / Sergio Luzzatto; translated by
Frederika Randall.—1st U.S. ed.
      p. cm.
  "Originally published in Italy in 2007 by Giulio Einaudi editore s.p.a, Turin"—T.p.
verso.
  Includes bibliographical references and index.
  ISBN 978-0-8050-8905-9
  1. Pio, of Pietrelcina, Saint, 1887–1968.   2. Christian saints—Italy—Biography.
I. Randall, Frederika.   II. Title.
  BX4700.P7755L8913 2010
  282.092—dc22
  [B]   2010020198

First U. S. Edition 2010
Designed by Meryl Sussman Levavi
Printed in the United States of America
10 9 8 7 6 5 4 3 2 1

All flesh is not the same flesh.

—ST. PAUL, THE FIRST EPISTLE TO THE CORINTHIANS

CONTENTS

PADRE PIO

PROLOGUE: SEPTEMBER 20, 1918

For a Capuchin friar hidden away in the half-empty San Giovanni Rotondo monastery on the remote Gargano Peninsula in southern Italy, September 20, 1918, was a fateful day. Around nine that morning, while Padre Pio of Pietrelcina was praying before a crucifix in the monastery chapel, "a mysterious personage" materialized before him, a figure bleeding from his hands, his feet, and his side. Alarmed, the thirty-one-year-old priest begged for God's assistance. The figure disappeared immediately, but Padre Pio's alarm only grew when he saw that Jesus's stigmata were now visible on his own body. "I look at my hands, feet and side and see they are wounded and blood is pouring out," he wrote to his spiritual adviser.[1] "All my innards are bloody and my eye must resign itself to watch the blood gushing out," so much of it that "I fear I will bleed to death."[2]

Over the next ninety years, the minuscule Capuchin monastery in San Giovanni Rotondo would become a leading place of pilgrimage in Europe, as crowded with worshippers as Santiago, Lourdes, Fatima, or Medjugorje. Padre Pio would become the most venerated saint in twenty-first-century Italy, more popular than St. Anthony of Padua and St. Francis of Assisi, more popular even than the Virgin Mary or Jesus of Nazareth.[3] And questions about the meaning—if there was one—that the Lord intended to transmit to mankind with the friar's five stigmata would trouble believers and nonbelievers alike.

Was the Capuchin friar from this remote corner of Puglia a holy man capable of inspiring other Catholics? Was he a throwback to an archaic version of faith untenable in the twentieth century? Was he merely a fraud? Authorities within the Church and outside it, high prelates and clever con men, leading intellectuals and committed Fascists would all take sides on the matter. The Holy Office—what was once called the Inquisition—would ponder the matter of Padre Pio's legitimacy at length. This book is one historian's attempt to disentangle the skeins of old and new, of sacred and profane, that made Padre Pio a twentieth-century legend.

❖

Padre Pio's stigmata did not appear at just any moment. Although the friar had long been telling his superiors that Christ's Passion was renewing itself in his body,[4] the timing of the event was powerfully cued to the public sphere. The autumn of 1918 was a special moment in collective awareness, a time heavily in need of the sacred. The immense trauma of the Great War—a war so unbearable that everywhere around Italy there abounded rumors of young maidens with mysterious powers to end the fighting[5]—had ripened into the conviction that the conflict was a never-ending crucifixion, in which the soldiers' unspeakable suffering would providentially save mankind.[6] The equally unspeakable suffering of the soldiers' mothers was likewise represented by the figure of the *Mater dolorosa*, the Holy Mother holding the dead Christ in her arms in the supreme act of grief.[7]

The ultranationalist Italian poet Gabriele D'Annunzio captured this theme of the soldier as Christ, the war as his Passion, in his *Songs of the Latin War*, which was crammed with biblical citations.[8] And it was not only poets who took to interpreting the war in Christian terms. Deep in the trenches, the rude material world of the soldiers teemed with crosses, nails, and crucifixes; between the boom of the cannons and the blast of the grenades, Jesus was ever-present in an immediate, ambiguous set of symbols.[9] Was this an end or a rebirth, destruction or resurrection? Trench warfare had confounded the very notions of life and death.[10] Soldiers at the front had an obsessive fear of being buried alive; they had recurrent fantasies of being the living dead. The Italian poet Clemente Rebora thought that the Great War had begotten a new existential dimension, *vitamorte*, "death-in-life."[11] All across Europe, millions of disfigured and wounded veterans testified to that condition, men upon whose faces and bodies devastating military technology had impressed its indelible mark, the cruel stigmata of modernity.[12] After the war, some of these men would brandish their injuries like patriotic slogans. In Italy, their ranks included wounded veterans like Giuseppe Caradonna and Carlo Delcroix, soon to be leading Fascists.

Padre Pio's wounds, meanwhile, had no patriotic significance. Although the Capuchin friar was enrolled as a soldier-priest, he managed to live out the entire conflict far from the front lines. Nevertheless, some of the words he wrote in autumn 1918 curiously echo the thoughts of the trench fighters. In November, just after the victory of Vittorio Veneto, Padre Pio wrote to his spiritual adviser that he considered himself among the "living dead."[13] In a sense, he too counted himself a survivor of the greatest of wars. In the inferno of the Dolomites trenches and on the cruel heights of the Carso, Italian soldiers had won their battle against the Teutonic devil, but they had been scarred in body and in spirit. And in the inferno of a monastery cell in Puglia, the Capuchin friar had won his battle with Satan, but he too had been wounded, in spirit and in body.

Of course, the wounds of the veterans were different from those of Padre Pio. The first were metaphorical stigmata: they were the "tattoos" that the Great War had inscribed on an entire generation, as one war-wounded poet, Nicola Moscardelli, so memorably put it.[14] The second were literal stigmata, the marks that the Lord had placed on one specific individual. From metaphorical stigmata, only profane happenings could come. Padre Pio's literal stigmata promised amazing, sacred developments.

The Great War was not the only affliction that set the stage for the dramatic events in the remote Capuchin monastery. As the summer of 1918 drew to a close, a new horror arose: the "Spanish" flu, which began its grim harvest in August and which in just seven months would kill more Italians than all of World War I.[15] While the war had decimated the men, the *spagnola* attacked mostly women, particularly where hygiene and nutrition were poor. Among these places was Puglia, and especially the province of Foggia. There, in the town of San Giovanni Rotondo, home to fewer than ten thousand people, some two hundred died between September and October 1918.[16]

Padre Pio thus received his stigmata as death was knocking on the doors of San Giovanni Rotondo, of the Gargano Peninsula, of Puglia, of Italy, and of Europe. It was a moment when believers everywhere were saying heartfelt prayers for clemency and protection. Of course, a man of God could try the argument used by one priest in a ravaged Veneto town, who told his faithful that death had come because "the Carnival went on too long, so now perhaps we'll have a long Lent."[17] Still, as the war drew to an end, Christian men and women could reasonably expect something more than the usual moralizing. As good Christians, they could hope that some exceptional individual—a saint—would come along to rescue them from all the evil in their midst: from disease, from destitution, from grief. They might even, as in other apocalyptic moments in the history of Christianity,[18] convince themselves that the Lord had made himself flesh a second time, so that sinning humanity could once again be redeemed.

The unknown friar in his Gargano monastery who, praying one morning, receives the five wounds of Christ on his body must therefore be situated in the spiritual climate of Italy and Europe at the end of the war's slaughter and the epidemic's devastation. Many centuries earlier, the arrival of the Black Death had stirred a kind of faith that was more anxious than before, more impatient and imploring.[19] Something like this, too, happened after the Great War when Padre Pio's fame as a holy man began to spread.[20] From the point of view of the friar and his superiors, the stigmata were merely the last step in a mystical journey that he had embarked on years before. From the point of view of the war-weary faithful, however, the stigmata were of immediate import, and it would not be long before crowds appeared at the friar's door.

❖

Saints exist mainly to perform miracles.[21] The story of Padre Pio cannot escape being, among other things, a history of these miracles—the healings, the apparitions, the conversions. Telling it requires approaching these events as an anthropologist would, making no distinctions between reality and myth—or perhaps the way that medieval historians, those professional agnostics, would do it.[22] Let me be clear right away that this study does not intend to establish once and for all whether Padre Pio's wounds were *genuine* stigmata, or whether the works he did were *genuine* miracles. All those seeking answers—affirmative or negative—as to whether the stigmata or the miracles were "real" had better close this book right now. Padre Pio's stigmata and his miracles interest us less for what they tell us about him than for what they tell us about the world around him: the many-colored world of priests and friars, of clerics and laymen, of believers and atheists, of the cultivated and the unlettered, of the good and the bad and the shrewd and the simple, of those who believed in the stigmata and the miracles and of those who refused to believe. Sainthood is a social custom made up of rites of interaction; saints matter as much for how they appear as for what they are.[23]

It is not easy to find the appropriate way to tell Padre Pio's story, and that helps to explain why there exists no proper historical study of the man that the Italian newspaper *Il Manifesto* once called, half seriously, "the most important Italian of the twentieth century."[24] There are, of course, countless hagiographies of Padre Pio,[25] all of them utterly lacking a critical perspective (though two French biographies and one by an American, written in a devout spirit, do provide some useful documentation).[26] There are also several good works of cultural anthropology and religious sociology on the "Padre Pio phenomenon," the cult that exploded in the later years of his life and in the decades after his death.[27] But no historian has ever written about the world of Padre Pio, almost as if there were something shameful about elevating the friar and his followers to the level of historic actors. Apparently what scholars of the Middle Ages take for granted—that studying beliefs is not the same as being a naive believer oneself—remains to be accepted by scholars who deal with the present.

At the close of the nineteenth century, secular intellectuals hurriedly proclaimed the end of religion and the disenchantment of the world. Yet today, a century later, a deep need to find some transcendent poetry in prosaic everyday life is still evident all around us. Were it not so, twentieth-century popular religiosity might simply be dismissed as the sad relic of an all-but-extinct sensibility. But secularism hasn't destroyed religion, because political, cultural, and scientific progress has not eliminated the dimension of evil from our lives, nor the need, for many, to see misfortune as part of a providential plan. The story of Padre Pio cannot be understood without keeping in mind the shrewd observation once made by writer and politician Ignazio Silone: having a labor union doesn't mean you can do without the saints, because "the poor are always afraid."[28] Especially among the most humble, material progress does not destroy piety, that is, the spiritual need for reassurance and the wish to be protected.

But Padre Pio's story also cannot be seen simply as part of a long continuity, as if a man could be a saint in the twentieth century in the same way as in the Middle Ages. The stakes of sainthood have changed. As long as Christian faith was unquestioned, the portentous methods—mysterious healings, bodily marks, celestial apparitions—by which the divine appeared to man were seen as *signs* of the existence of God, and theologists, notaries, and doctors could debate their authenticity without shaking the whole house of the Christian supernatural.[29] Even the detractors of St. Francis in the thirteenth century, for example, could doubt that his human wounds were the true stigmata of Christ's divinity without in any way bringing into question the message of the Savior.[30] But in the contemporary era, once Christian faith became a choice, the same portentous events started to be seen as something more: they became *proof* of the existence of God.[31] Those who questioned whether Padre Pio's stigmata were divine were often ready to reject Christianity altogether, while those who saw his stigmata as a fresh revelation of Christ were emboldened in their faith, ready to proclaim to all the world that the crucifixion was still very much alive.

❖

A story of piety must necessarily also be a story of impiety—of execration, blasphemy, and just plain denial.[32] To reconstruct Padre Pio's tale and that of his advocates we must also tell the story of his opponents, who didn't hesitate to speak up soon after the events of September 20, 1918. There were some secular adversaries, obviously: skeptics and anticlericals, liberals and socialists. But also, and above all, Padre Pio had his clerical adversaries. Men of religious orders and not, modest church officials and powerful Vatican insiders—they ranged across twentieth-century Italian Catholicism's many worlds and its many kinds of faith.[33]

For some fifty years, until his death in 1968, Padre Pio never moved from San Giovanni Rotondo. His material horizons coincided with those of the monastery where he took shelter during World War I and where he earned the terrible prize of the stigmata. But while Padre Pio did not move, all around him men of the church did. They acted from far and near, by choice or out of duty. Among those who came to concern themselves with the Capuchin friar were Cardinal Pietro Gasparri and Father Agostino Gemelli, Pope Pius XI and Pius XII, Don Luigi Orione and Don Ernesto Buonaiuti, Pope John XXIII and John Paul II. In a twentieth-century Church still brooding over the humiliating fall of the Papal States in 1870 and vowing a Catholic *reconquista* of Italian society, both Padre Pio's opponents, like Father Gemelli, and his advocates, like Pius XII, were mindful of the humble friar's role in that fateful historical battle. Measuring themselves against Padre Pio, leading men of the Church also had to face tough questions about the material nature of faith, about the proper limits of pastoral duty, about the direct or indirect routes to sainthood.

And behind these was a question even more serious and troubling: could a good Christian ever accept the existence of an *alter Christus*, a living Christ figure? Didn't even contemplating such a possibility suggest that Jesus's Incarnation and his Passion had only partially redeemed mankind, that there might be more chapters still to come in the story of salvation?[34] Though St. Francis's contemporaries had also faced this problem, it became more complicated in Padre Pio's case.[35] St. Francis had received the stigmata near the end of his life, and he had kept them hidden; Padre Pio, on the other hand, was young when the wounds appeared, and he would display them for half a century. What's more, while Francis of Assisi was never ordained, Padre Pio was a priest who performed all the public functions of that office. When he said mass, the stigmata that marked him as a bleeding *alter Christus* were so boldly evident they could only be judged as either sublime or sacrilegious.

Such concerns help to explain the caution, reticence, and suspicion with which the Church of Rome treated Padre Pio. Between 1923 and 1933, the Holy Office imposed sharp limits on his pastoral role. And for decades, while the friar's reputation rose and fell (not because he changed his personal or priestly behavior, but because a variety of figures came and went at the top of the Capuchin hierarchy and on the papal throne), the Holy Office kept Padre Pio firmly in its sights. The Holy Office archives—used here for the first time in reference to the period 1919–39—document the prolonged and often dramatic confrontation between the Church as an institution and its other central and peripheral forces, the friar with the stigmata and the community of the faithful. Indeed, for more than half a century the cult of Padre Pio represented the pressure of a "low" Church that mobilized the faithful not only *for* the Capuchin friar of San Giovanni Rotondo but *against* the representatives of the Church of Rome, whether they were ordinary priests of the diocese, emissaries of the Holy Office, or cardinals from the Apostolic Palace. At the same time, the movement behind Padre Pio would never have overcome institutional resistance had there not also been high-ranking Vatican officials who were enthusiasts about the Capuchin with the stigmata. Ultimately, it was only the ascendancy of one of these admirers—Karol Wojtyla, who was elected Pope John Paul II ten years after Padre Pio's death—that ended the decades of internal Vatican wrangling over the friar and assured his canonization.

❖

Saints are always at the center of a kind of stage where they interact with other figures in society: with assorted suppliers of religion of varying degrees of orthodoxy; with consumers of religion from the skeptical to the credulous; and, in recent times, with enemies of religion who may be more or less pugnacious.[36] Padre Pio was not exempt from this rule, and his personal story must thus be read alongside many other stories. To understand why the Capuchin friar merited the title of "the most important Italian of the twentieth century," even if only ironically, we must step back from the geographic particulars of San Giovanni Rotondo and from the specifics of one mystic's biography. A study of Padre Pio's life will only tell us something about twentieth-century Italian history if it tells us about collective experiences and practices, if it is able to illuminate landscapes larger than a place of pilgrimage and circumstances broader than a case of sainthood.

Arguably the most important phase of Padre Pio's life came in the 1920s and '30s, when haughty prelates and distinguished doctors, converted Freemasons and enterprising fixers, leading writers and blackshirted Fascists all took sides in the matter of the Capuchin friar with the stigmata. It was then that the small story of Padre Pio met the larger stream of Italian history—from the abstract ideals of "Soviet-style" socialism to the concrete brawling of the Blackshirts, from the Giolitti government's stolid inertia to Mussolini's crafty maneuvering. The 1920s, in particular, saw the emergence of what must be called *clerico-fascism*, a term that has sometimes been abused but remains the right one to mark the cultural and political "change of climate" that took place after the war.[37] Although the interests of the regime and the Church did not always coincide, the ancient alliance between throne and altar found new expression in the fasces and the cross, the nightstick and the holy water.[38] (Even before Benito Mussolini and Pius XI signed the Lateran Treaty of 1929, the clergy had found common ground with the Fascists on a number of matters, such as the need to restore social order after the Great War, the all-out battle to defeat the "reds," and a plan to encourage Italian women to have more children.)[39] In the 1930s, meanwhile, in intrigues worthy of a spy novel that have lain hidden under the dust of the archives, Padre Pio's destiny became intertwined with international politics: the Italian war in Ethiopia, the League of Nations, France's Popular Front, and Hitler's New Order.

It was only in the years after World War II, however—the era of media-savvy Catholicism promoted by Pius XII—that most Italians learned of Padre Pio's existence. By the 1950s and '60s, the little Capuchin monk had become a tabloid saint, a bona fide star with stigmata. In 1957 Padre Pio asked for and was granted a special dispensation from his vow of poverty, so that he could personally manage the wealth connected with the hospital he had founded in San Giovanni Rotondo. Against the order's pauperistic rhetoric, the aging Capuchin friar thus revived a concrete and economically realistic concept of charity toward the sick that had been part of the early Franciscan creed—charity that was all the more effective because it was market-minded and unashamed of itself.[40] And after the Second Vatican Council reformed the liturgy in 1963 by introducing the vernacular mass, Padre Pio asked for and got another dispensation, permitting him to continue to celebrate mass in Latin. To the end of his life, the Capuchin monk continued to treat the mass as an arcane rite, whose mystery was guaranteed by the use of an incomprehensible language.[41] The fascination of this strange man of faith, who combined mystical religiosity and capitalist entrepreneurship, was no small part of his attraction to the crowds of believers.

All these connections—the way that adventures of the Capuchin friar and his followers were closely interwoven with political matters and diplomatic affairs, police work and espionage, celebrity and atavism—must be kept in mind if we want to make sense of Padre Pio's story. Otherwise, it risks being no more than a petty tale of friars' quarrels, suspicious stigmata, and feats of illusionism.

❖

A historian who wants to enter the world of Padre Pio and his followers—particularly his female followers—must get to know "Donna Bisodia," as the Communist intellectual Antonio Gramsci called her. "Donna Bisodia" represents a world of superpious country women who, reciting the Paternoster in Latin without understanding the words, heard *da nobis hodie* ("give us today") as "Donna Bisodia," a lady they imagined was a model of Christian piety.[42] At the same time, a historian investigating Padre Pio must not just *descend* into the depths of peasant society and popular religion—he must also *climb*.[43] He must head up the Italian peninsula, as the cult of Padre Pio spread rapidly from the Gargano mountains of Puglia to the rest of Italy; up the social ranks, as Padre Pio's following began to include all social classes; and up the ladder of education and cultivation, for the Capuchin friar impressed not only the uncouth and the unlettered but Christian souls of distinguished learning and enviable wisdom.

Secular culture has not done much more than lampoon what non-believers see as "the imbecility of the poor in spirit" and the "doltishness of the perfect admirers of Padre Pio."[44] The Livorno satirical rag *Il Vernacoliere* regularly announced the Capuchin friar's latest miracles.

> Miracle n° 31: There's this nun who breaks her leg and it's another miracle of Padre Pio because she could've broken both of them. A-men.
>
> Miracle n° X: There's a guy who's going to the barber and he's about to step in some shit and Padre Pio appears in front of him and he dodges to miss him and he doesn't step in the shit.[45]

Such ridicule can be a way to affirm the scientific view of the universe, to insist that science is not simply a mythology like any other.[46] But to see the cult of Padre Pio only through the peephole of satire risks blinding us to the social and political significance of the collective experience that blossomed around him. Nor has Catholic culture done much better, leaving the story of their *alter Christus* to the hagiographers, who in their hundreds of volumes piled one upon another have given us a narrative that is spiritually prodigious but intellectually impoverished.

This book aims to restore Padre Pio of Pietrelcina to the place he deserves in twentieth-century history. It means to measure, in the friar's success story, the surprising vitality of the saint figure that the Middle Ages and the ancien régime have bequeathed to the modern world—a creature with many lives, a personage able to move from the lower registers to the high, from the here and now to the hereafter.[47] Above all, it intends to show how Padre Pio's life speaks of us as much as of him. At nearly every moment between 1918 and 1968, the adventures and disasters, the epiphanies and eclipses, the triumphs and the defeats of the humble friar point to a broader, deeper story, a particular path toward modernity. It is a path of holy oil and charismatic power, a path on which the premodern and the postmodern, the reasonable and the improbable, the institutional and the homegrown, the religious and the political tend to merge as often as they stand as opposites. And it is not by chance that we meet along it, in addition to Padre Pio, so many other charismatic figures of the twentieth century, and other crowds ready to worship that quality—whatever it is—that makes certain ordinary people into extraordinary figures.

1. A LIVING CHRIST

In the years just after the Great War, the Gargano Peninsula was a forbidding place. From the city of Foggia on the plain up to San Giovanni Rotondo in the hills, there was no railroad, no bus, no taxi, only—as a reporter of the period put it—"a fast horse trot" for hours and hours across the "silent and seemingly endless plain of the Tavoliere." Arriving at the foot of the mountains, the traveler faced "an exhausting climb up a series of switchbacks" to the little cluster of huts that answered to the name of San Giovanni. The landscape was gray, stony, and barren. Only those who had seen the carstic mountains of Italy's northeast front during the war, "the terrible, bloody Carso, Italy's grievous Calvary," could imagine this place, the visiting reporter wrote.

> A narrow alley, almost unbelievably filthy and muddy, flanked by a row of poor, squat, miserable huts out of which burst gangs of runny-nosed children and pigs wallowing and snorting in the mud; houses with primitive furnishings, men and women who stare at you with sorrowful, unsmiling, suspicious faces; nowhere a flower: this is San Giovanni Rotondo.[1]

To this corner of Puglia punished by nature as well as by history, with no other vegetation but "the rare spindly olive tree" like on the "hills of Palestine,"[2] Padre Pio of Pietrelcina had come in July 1916, on leave from military service in a war he had been fighting with a barrage of medical exemptions while others fired mortar shells.[3] The friar had been to Puglia before. He knew the city of Foggia, where he had spent

time in the monastery of Sant'Anna; he knew the town of Serracapriola, at the northern border of the region, where he had completed his theological studies. But most of his ecclesiastical training and his first experiences as a priest had taken place elsewhere: in little settlements near Benevento in Campania, where he had been born in 1887 to a peasant family in the village of Pietrelcina,[4] and near Campobasso, in the neighboring region of Molise. Places like Morcone, Montefusco, Gesualdo, Venafro, Sant'Elia a Pianisi, San Marco la Catola—the geography of the Capuchin monasteries in which young Francesco Forgione grew into Padre Pio maps out the close-knit network of religious institutes that the Catholic Counter-Reformation had built all over southern Italy. These institutes had flourished under the activism of the regular religious orders, the confraternities governed by monastic rules, and even the Savoy conquest—the secular Kingdom of Italy— had not eliminated them altogether.[5]

By the spring of 1918, Padre Pio had settled into the monastery of Santa Maria delle Grazie in San Giovanni Rotondo. It was a place where the Capuchin order could boast some distinction: just a few years after the monastery's founding in 1540, the pure air of the cloister had tamed the dissolute soul of a no-account soldier, Camillo De Lellis, who went on to found the order of St. Camillus.[6] During the centuries

to follow, the Capuchin friars of San Giovanni had sometimes been scattered by anticlerical forces—the Kingdom of Naples under Joseph Bonaparte, the unification of Italy in the nineteenth century. But they had reconstituted their community in 1909, part of a movement that the southern bishops had promoted since around 1900 to combat a growing lack of belief in the rural south.[7]

Like most religious communities in southern Italy,[8] the Capuchin order at San Giovanni did not engage in social outreach of the kind that was practiced farther north following the teachings of the encyclical *Rerum Novarum*.[9] In the Gargano mountains in the early twentieth century, the Church merely offered the people what the southern Church had been offering for centuries. On the one hand, an understanding of devotion as suffering and penitence: statues of the *mater dolorosa* and paintings of Jesus crowned with thorns, figures of saints carried in processions, flagellations in the main square on Good Friday. On the other, a vision of faith as asceticism and mysticism: remote hermitages in the most inaccessible places, where friars who were half sorcerers, half gurus would show off their miraculous powers to the rare pilgrim[10]—sanctuaries that to the eyes of the young Gabriele D'Annunzio seemed "a terrible spectacle," peopled with "fanatics" who arrived "in huge mobs" and committed assorted "atrocities," with "shrieks, cries, sobs, whining, tragic fainting spells, blood, tears . . . all kinds of wretchedness."[11] Among the towns of the Gargano mountains, San Giovanni Rotondo was one of the very few that did not have a sanctuary. From 1918 onward, however, it had Padre Pio.

In the End, They Will Have a Saint

The religious vocation of the young Francesco Forgione—as the future Padre Pio was baptized—grew out of a beard. The beard belonged to Fra Camillo of Sant'Elia a Pianisi, a Capuchin friar whom Forgione had first met around 1898, when he was eleven years old. Fra Camillo was a wayfaring friar who traveled from one town to another in the territory around Benevento, living off the alms he received. He was never in a hurry. He would go from house to house, chatting with the women, smoothing the brow of the sick, reciting prayers with whoever wished to join him. Sometimes he would go up to the pastures where the shepherd boys were and get them together for some catechism, or recite some of St. Francis's precepts, or give out holy cards and medals. During the harvest, he could be seen bent over the fields, working side by side with the same farmers from whom he begged his alms. But in Padre Pio's later recollection, the thing that struck him most as a boy was the friar's facial hair, the beard that every member of the Capuchin order had to wear. "Fra Camillo's beard stuck in my head," he said, "and no one could dislodge it."[12]

That remark, made by Padre Pio as an adult, cannot be dismissed as mere whimsy, for it suggests the role that imagination—iconic figures, devotional stereotypes, social images—plays in the construction of sainthood. It points, especially, to the appearance of the Capuchins, an order that defines a powerful current in modern Italian religious identity. The beard, the hood: that physical mark and that unique vestment heighten the order's powerful presence among their lay brethren, a presence so strong the Capuchins have at times had a reputation for being intrusive, excessive.[13] Between the two quintessential Capuchins that Alessandro Manzoni depicted in his novel *The Betrothed*—Fra Cristoforo, so fiery and willful he is almost violent, and Fra Galdino, his jolly, obtuse, and greedy antithesis[14]—young Francesco Forgione

seems to have chosen a little of both. His religious vocation drew on the easygoing pastoral manner of Fra Galdino but also on the fierce and restless style of Fra Cristoforo—not just a soldier of Christ but a man cut out for Calvary, an actual Christ figure.[15]

In the first years of the twentieth century, when Padre Pio was a seminarian, the Eucharist—the body and blood of Christ—was at the height of its importance in Catholic practice. Communion was celebrated frequently and became a mass phenomenon.[16] At the same time, asceticism was interpreted in ever more physical terms. Body language—ecstasy, levitation, the stigmata—was held to be the only real mystical language.[17] These trends had no difficulty finding followers in the seminaries and the monasteries of the Capuchin order, an order that right from its beginnings in 1528 had based its religious identity not only on the Eucharist but on the contemplation of Christ on the cross, on the consuming love of the brothers for "the stigmata of their father."[18] In the centuries after the order was founded, the enthusiasm for the crucifixion had made St. Francis the supreme model for Capuchin spiritual life. Theirs was a Franciscanism so concrete it was positively theatrical, baroque.[19] During the years of Padre Pio's training, the order was zealous in promoting the beatification of friars like Charles

of Abbiategrasso and Innocent of Berzo: nineteenth-century Capuchins whose passion for Christ on the cross had led them, the hagiographies say, to weep tears of blood and levitate in ecstasy.[20]

As the twentieth century drew near, on June 8, 1899, stigmata had
appeared on the hands of Gemma Galgani, a twenty-year-old woman
from Lucca who dreamed of becoming a nun and who was extremely
devoted to the Sacred Heart. Every Friday, those wounds bled—the
most explicit mark of saintliness the Lord could deliver.[21] In the following four years, various doctors saw the young woman, and many of
them diagnosed the cause of her wounds as hysteria. But her spiritual
adviser, Germano Ruoppolo, a leading official in the Passionist order,
disagreed. He had no doubt that Gemma's condition was imposed
from on high. Against the advice of the Lucca priest who served as her
confessor, he persuaded Gemma to keep a diary of her saintly life.
After her death in 1903, the Passionist father would use that diary to
press for her beatification.

Spiritual suffering on the part of women, often vulnerable women
who bore the physical marks of extreme mysticism, has frequently
been exploited by men of the cloth hoping to promote themselves or
their religious congregations.[22] But Father Germano's zeal was extraordinary by any measure. Gemma Galgani's corpse was already in the
casket and had been lowered into the grave when a telegram arrived
from the Passionist brother ordering a full autopsy to determine whether
some divine sign had been left on Gemma's heart.[23] No such sign was
found, but that did not stop this salesman of sainthood. In 1907, as the
archbishop of Lucca was opening beatification proceedings, Ruoppolo
published his *Biography of Gemma Galgani, A Virgin of Lucca.* The
work was an immediate success, running to six editions and selling
more than twenty thousand copies.[24]

In 1909 Father Germano published a second book devoted to the
young mystic, *Letters and Ecstasies of God's Servant, Gemma Galgani.*[25]
This second volume, containing Gemma's letters to Father Germano
and other writings, also found a wide public, selling 8,200 copies—
including one that ended up on the desk of Pope Pius X.[26] Another
copy of *Letters and Ecstasies* would reach the as yet unstigmatic hands
of the young Capuchin Padre Pio, who, though he had been ordained a

priest in August 1910, would spend the years until 1916 far from his order, at his family's home in Pietrelcina. Each time Padre Pio approached the monastery, it seems, his health would begin to fail, and he would get permission from his Capuchin superiors to return home. Between 1911 and 1913, while his father, Grazio Forgione, and his brother, Michele, briefly emigrated to the United States, he was effectively the man of his family.[27]

These were in fact very intense years for Padre Pio's psyche,[28] as attested by the dozens of letters he sent to his spiritual directors, Father Benedetto and Father Agostino.[29] His letters spoke the language of asceticism and mysticism: he wrote of Jesus's infancy, of the heavenly bodies of the Savior and the Virgin, of the blood of the Crucifixion, of sin, suffering, redemption, and expiation, of himself as the passive object of divine action, of offering himself as a sacrifice.[30] In one letter, written to Father Agostino on March 21, 1912, he spoke of an absolute passion for the body of Christ and his intuition that he would one day receive the stigmata. After mass the previous day, he wrote,

> My mouth savored all the sweetness of the immaculate flesh of the son of God . . . But I become confused and am unable to do anything but weep and say 'Jesus, my nutriment!' . . . What afflicts me most is that so much love from Jesus is met with so much ingratitude from me . . . I would like, were it within my power, to wash with my own blood those places where I have committed so many sins, where I have scandalized so many souls . . . Thursday evening until Saturday and then again Tuesday have been a painful drama for me. My heart, my hands and feet seem to have been pierced with a sword, the suffering is so great . . . And meanwhile the devil never ceases to appear before me in his hideous guises and to beat me in a terribly frightening way.[31]

We do not know whether Father Agostino, reading these words, realized that Padre Pio had copied them verbatim from a letter by Gemma Galgani.[32] Nor do we know whether he or Father Benedetto were aware that a dozen other letters by Padre Pio, written between September 1911 and May 1913, reproduced word for word—without citing it—items from her *Letters and Ecstasies.*[33] Certainly Padre Pio's behavior was disingenuous, to say the least. Not only did the young Capuchin friar not tell his spiritual directors that the words he used to describe his mystical experiences were not his own, but, to confuse matters further, he sought to make them believe that he did not even possess Gemma's book. And so, on May 2, 1912, he wrote to Father Benedetto to ask for "a good deed." "I would very much like to read the book titled *Letters and Ecstasies of God's Servant, Gemma Galgani,*" he said, "along with another work by that same servant of God, *The Holy Hour.* Confident you will find this desire worthy and procure me these books, I glorify you and ask your benediction."[34] For months, Padre Pio had been copying out sentences from books he claimed not to have—and he would continue to do so for another entire year.

Yet even if they were aware of his borrowings, his spiritual advisers would not necessarily have taken Padre Pio for a plagiarist or an imposter. In Christian tradition, mysticism is by definition an experience that has been lived by another, an experience both mundane and outlandish.[35] Had Father Agostino or Father Benedetto known that Padre Pio had copied page upon page, they could have attributed that fact—as the Jesuits do today[36]—to the intensity of his psychological identification with Gemma and her stigmata. And of course, we cannot exclude the possibility that the two men had something else on their minds. Even before Padre Pio's stigmata appeared, might Father Benedetto and Father Agostino not have reasoned that the young friar's piety was so exceptional as to make him, one day, a candidate for sainthood? Like Germano Ruoppolo, who saw the potential in Gemma Galgani, the two Capuchin friars from San Marco in Lamis may have felt it was their job to support Padre Pio's possible future claims.

Among the religious orders founded during the Counter-Reformation, nearly every one saw its founder elevated to sainthood during the seventeenth century.[37] But that rule did not hold for the Capuchins, who, because of a series of sixteenth-century misadventures, had no founder-saint.[38] Yet even early on, the Capuchins held that their order would achieve the prophesied last stage of Franciscanism. As a chronicle of the order put it, while the Capuchins "did not have a saint at the beginning, and experienced abundant tribulations, there is no doubt that in the end, they will have a saint."[39] More than three centuries later, when the two friars of San Marco in Lamis weighed Padre Pio's spiritual heft—in 1915 they went so far as to declare him *their* spiritual guide[40]—they might well have imagined he was the saint "promised in the aforementioned prophecy."[41] If that were the case, it mattered little that in some of Padre Pio's letters his imitation of Christ was a mere imitation of Gemma Galgani. Padre Pio was no young pupil who had to show his teachers he knew his lessons; he was a mature soul whose *Short Treatise on the Dark Night*, written during the Great War, could be compared with some of the most important mystical voices of Catholic tradition, from St. John of the Cross to St. Teresa of Avila.[42] And after September 20, 1918, when the five wounds of the Savior appeared on Padre Pio's body, Father Benedetto and Father Agostino would have known they were not mistaken.

Bloody Fridays

Padre Pio's first reaction to the stigmata was a mixture of confusion, fear, and shame. For several weeks after that fateful September day, he did not even tell his spiritual directors what had happened. At the time the two friars were lodged at the monastery of San Marco la Catola, far to the other side of the city of Foggia on the plain, and both were ill with Spanish flu. By mid-October both had recovered, and it was then that Padre Pio decided to tell Father Benedetto, who held the title of Capuchin "minister provincial," about the disturbing appearance of the stigmata. Seeking to describe his reaction to his "crucifixion," he wrote that he was experiencing humiliation. "My Lord, what confusion and humiliation I feel in having to manifest what you have imposed on me, your wretched creature!" he complained in a letter dated October 22.[43] Several times in those days he came back to that same concept: the stigmata made him feel humiliated before God and man.[44]

As far back as St. Augustine, Christian thought has struggled with the conflicting notions of *humilitas* and *humiliatio*—"humility" that emanates spontaneously from a person of goodwill, and "humiliation" imposed from without, but that in some cases may have a divine significance.[45] Whether or not he was aware of the theological question, Padre Pio obviously suffered on account of the outward visibility of the stigmata. Father Benedetto sought to convince him there was nothing shameful in those visible signs of grace, and that they should be welcomed as a miraculous gift from on high.[46] Father Benedetto also made sure to inform the order's minister general, Father Venance of Lisle-en-Rigault, who advised the utmost prudence and reserve about the matter.[47]

Yet it wasn't clear how to put the minister general's advice into practice. Padre Pio's stigmata were a secret that could not be kept. Even supposing it had been possible to maintain silence among the Capuchin friars at San Giovanni Rotondo, Padre Pio's condition was sure to be disclosed when, following the rules of the liturgy, he celebrated mass with his bare hands—and thus without any gloves covering his wounds. On March 5, 1919, following a visit to Padre Pio's monastery, Santa Maria delle Grazie, Father Benedetto brought Father Agostino up to date on this astonishing matter.

> It is not that his skin is spotted or marked; he has true wounds that perforate his hands and his feet. When I looked closely at the one on his side, I could see it was a real gash from which there flows a continuous stream of blood or bloody matter. On Fridays, he bleeds. When I went to see him he could barely stand up, but when I went away he was able to celebrate mass, and when he does, his gift is exposed to all, for he must hold up his bare hands.[48]

Gestures are full of significance in Christian practice.[49] The Gospels teach how to recognize and interpret Christ's symbolic acts: his soothing touch on the bodies of the sick; his hand raised in benediction toward men of goodwill; the final meal of bread and wine; his death on the cross. The priest's gestures during the mass—the elevation of the chalice, the consecration of the wafer, genuflection—are likewise charged with the meaning of salvation. And there is no other moment in pastoral practice when the priest is as much Christ's alter ego as during the Eucharist. He alone is worthy enough to touch the wafer, the body of the Savior. He alone may drink the wine, the blood of Jesus who has died and risen. Only he may place the host in the mouths of lay churchgoers, for them to partake of the wondrous body.

At San Giovanni Rotondo, the symbolic meaning of the Eucharist was, to say the least, greatly enhanced when Padre Pio was officiating; in the minds of many believers, the stigmata are the highest gesture, the ultimate sign.[50] In the history of the Church, Christ's wounds had never before been inscribed on one of God's ministers.[51] St. Francis, who earlier bore the stigmata, was a layman, and he never celebrated the Eucharist. Padre Pio, on the other hand, was a priest—a priest with stigmata. When he said mass, he did not merely commemorate Christ's sacrifice by way of the liturgical metaphor of the bread and the wine. As the blood ran from his wounds and mixed with the wine, the metaphor became fact. Padre Pio was reliving Christ's sacrifice.[52]

So, at any rate, thought the Capuchin friar's followers. The news of his crucifixion quickly spread, first within the borders of the Gargano Peninsula, and then to all of Italy and Europe.

The Wonders of the Possible

The first miracle attributed to Padre Pio to be reported in the mainstream Italian press took place on May 30, 1919. It concerned one Antonio Colonnello from Orsara di Puglia. In the final days of World

War I, this "ninety-niner"—a soldier born in 1899, the youngest cohort called up—had been struck in the right foot by grenade shrapnel, an injury that according to unanimous medical opinion meant he would be permanently lame. But after months of suffering, his wound still open, and walking with a crutch, the 140th Infantry veteran had made his way to San Giovanni Rotondo to see the "Saint"—as people there had begun to call Padre Pio once the word of his stigmata, and of his reputed special powers, got out. Merely by raising his hand in benediction, the friar cured the young man "instantly and completely." There was great jubilation, such as the brothers in the monastery had become accustomed to ever since groups of pilgrims began to climb up to San Giovanni to ask Padre Pio for blessings. A "delirious crowd" poured into the cloister to celebrate the miracle. Antonio Colonnello, leaving behind his crutch and the purulent dressing from his wound, meanwhile went happily home to Orsara.[53]

It probably wasn't by chance that the first report in the national press about Padre Pio involved his healing of a lame ninety-niner. Postwar Italy suffered from a widespread feeling of impotence regarding the suffering of injured and mutilated young veterans, adults who, in the trenches, had been reduced to the status of needy children.[54] Whatever the reason, the Naples newspaper *Il Mattino*—where leading journalists like Edoardo Scarfoglio and Matilde Serao had an almost seismographic sensitivity to popular religiosity[55]—saw in Colonnello's healing the perfect occasion to tell all of southern Italy about Padre Pio's astonishing powers, powers that the people of the Gargano had already learned about in previous months. The *Mattino* article deserves to be quoted at length, for it is a prototype of the story of Padre Pio as Christ incarnate—with all the elements that would go into a tale both hagiographic and evangelical.

Padre Pio was "a very sympathetic figure," the Neapolitan newspaper said. He was pale-skinned, almond-eyed, aquiline-nosed, dark-haired, emaciated, and slightly hunched over. It was impossible, unfortunately, to procure a photograph, because "he shuns the photographer's lens." But luckily there was a great deal of information about his style of life, his physical condition, and his good works. His education was meager, and he hardly ever read anything. He ate only vegetables

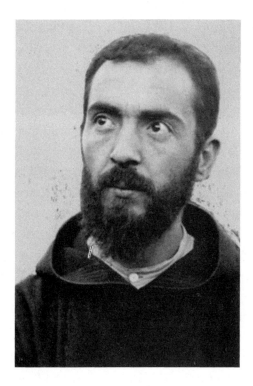

dressed with oil, for his body refused meat and other rich foodstuffs. He drank no wine, but he took water, coffee, beer, "and also a special drink called 'ginger birr.'" More often than not, after he ate a meal in the refectory, he would vomit up the small amount he had ingested. He slept little, for at night, praying in his cell, he would fall into an ecstatic state.[56]

The editor of the article in *Il Mattino* saw fit to distinguish, by means of subtitles within the story, between the friar's *physiological phenomena* and *empathic phenomena*. The paper's reporter from San Giovanni Rotondo, Adelchi Fabroncini, filled readers in on the details. Padre Pio's corporal peculiarities included a number of marvelous features, including a tendency to hyperthermia and the gift of ubiquity. But it was naturally the stigmata that most astonished those who met him. Not that it was easy to see the wounds, for the friar was reticent about them. ("He blushes when these wounds are spoken of and is ashamed to let his hands be seen. He always wears black half-gloves, which cover the hands to the base of the fingers.") But the paper's reporter, Fabroncini—an elementary school teacher who, as it happened, was closely related to Nina Campanile, Padre Pio's preferred "spiritual daughter"[57]—evidently had an inside track when it came to the stigmata.

> In the center of his hands, both on the palm side and on the back, is a reddish spot, almost blood-stained, that looks like the scab of a wound. The spots are the size of a large coin. Taking the spot between thumb and index finger and pressing the two fingers together, one has the impression that there is a void under the skin, so much so that one's fingers go deep into the hand. One feels nothing, no obstacle, in this void, yet all the joints of the Padre's fingers work.

For obvious reasons, it was more difficult to assess the wounds on Padre Pio's side and on his feet. But the reporter from *Il Mattino* informed the readers that the good friar's undershirt was patched over the breast, "on the left side, near the heart." On Fridays, Padre Pio's sufferings were more intense: "He looks paler and more run-down."[58] In the friar's arduous calendar, every Friday was Good Friday.

Such were the physiological phenomena, and the empathic phenomena were no less impressive. Those who went to Padre Pio to make their confession often found that he knew their sins in advance, "as if this 'Saint' had been present at the scene and knew all secrets." Outside the confessional, too, the good friar could foresee exactly what his interlocutor was going to say. And, above all, Padre Pio could perform miracles. Not just the healing of the soldier Colonnello but many others! Like the time when the daughter of Vincenzo Gisolfi, a mechanic in San Giovanni, lay sick in bed and the doctors did not know how to cure her: the friar appeared to her, he stroked her arm, he disappeared, and the next day the young woman was completely well. Or that time when Filomena Cristofaro, a widow from the Great War, had received in her home the ghost of Padre Pio, who assured her that her husband was at peace in the hereafter. Or when the doctors despaired of saving a town landowner, Giuseppe Pazienza: his wife went to the monastery, took away a handkerchief soaked in blood that had come from Padre Pio's breast, and pressed it all night long to the breast of the sick man, who then recovered in just a few days. These were "simple, but power-ful episodes" that "could not be just the product of popular fantasy."[59]

In the half century between the appearance of Padre Pio's stigmata in September 1918 and his death in September 1968, how many devout souls did as Signora Pazienza did, stroking the body of a sick relative with a relic from the living Christ? How many of the infirm were visited by Padre Pio in their suffering? How many men and women entrusted their earthly lives and their hopes for loved ones' eternal sal-vation to an image of the good friar? One thing is certain: between 1918 and 1919, Padre Pio's reputation for sainthood spread so quickly that it defied the geographic isolation of San Giovanni Rotondo, not to mention the poverty-stricken condition of a great many Italians after the war. "Every day hundreds of people of all classes and places of ori-gin come to visit Padre Pio the Saint," observed the editor of *Il Mattino*. All day long the monastery was buzzing with the "huge influx" of believers.[60] Something important was happening, and the editors of both local and national papers—the *Corriere delle Puglie, La Nazione* of Florence, *Il Tempo* of Rome—joined *Il Mattino* of Naples in spread-ing the word. Padre Pio was not just any ordinary guru, not just the latest miracle worker to come forth from the fervid imaginations of the

southern masses. He was something more profound, more mysterious.[61]

But there were some in San Giovanni Rotondo who saw the matter differently in that spring of 1919. Even as the press was trumpeting the miraculous recovery of Antonio Colonnello, some local citizens who signed themselves "a group of the faithful" sent a letter to the Holy Office in Rome. Filed there on June 14 in a folder titled *Devozioni varie* ("Worship, miscellaneous") under the heading "Capuchins," this letter is the very first of the many hundreds of documents that for decades would swell the inquisitorial dossier on Padre Pio.[62] Although it is anonymous, the letter is not just pure and simple slander. Rather, it belongs to a long tradition of complicity between the people of the Mezzogiorno and the authorities of the Inquisition, a complicity based on the spoken and the unspoken, on genuine scruples as well as outright lies, a complicity reflecting both personal and collective interests. Matters of faith often concealed opportunism, and in many denunciations sent to the Holy Office it is not easy to distinguish the sincerity of the good Catholic from the animosity of the sworn enemy.[63] In that sense, the letter from the San Giovanni faithful is a small classic. And it is also a kind of urtext of the arguments and sentiments, reasons and passions, suspicion and malice that would inflame the counterhistory of Padre Pio.

The only thing the writers of the letter did not seem to doubt was the veracity of the five wounds on the friar's body. All the rest, to them, was the product of overheated imaginations. The reported miracles needed to be judged by the light of reason rather than abandoned to the propaganda of "a few sick, pathetic little women" in questionable liaisons with the more astute friars in the monastery, who in turn were shrewdly promoting this incipient saint. Padre Pio himself was above reproach; he was good, obedient, humble, patient. But there was a "band of other friars . . . that is spinning tales out of trifles, and a band of female fanatics who publicize facts and fairytales that the humble greet with fetishistic zeal. Meanwhile the clergy and the cultivated are also forced to believe, if they care for their lives." And the problem was not confined to San Giovanni, nor even to the Gargano. By now outsiders were coming by the thousands from every part of Italy, prostrating themselves before Padre Pio and imploring from him every sort of grace and favor. According to the "fervent and aware" Christians who wrote to alert the Holy Office, the creed being practiced in that little Gargano town was an idolatrous cult, and, as such, the worst possible threat to the true religion of the Holy Roman Church. "For these fanatical visitors, neither God nor the Holy Virgin exists," they reported; "there is only Padre Pio, the 'Saint' who predicts, reads minds, heals the sick, and transports himself from place to place."[64]

A few weeks later the Holy Office received a new warning from "some of the faithful" in the archdiocese of Manfredonia, whose jurisdiction included the monastery of San Giovanni Rotondo. The illustrious cardinals based in Rome, this missive said, must not—not even for an instant—allow themselves to be deceived by the foolish tales being spun by newspapers like *Il Mattino* of Naples! Was it possible that the whole world could be "duped by four friars" who were "profiting from this moment the way many had profited from the war?" Sharks of sainthood, they had made the monastery into a genuine brothel! Day and night, in fact, Padre Pio was surrounded by his so-called spiritual daughters, "the twelve apostles" who did not hesitate to enter the monastery and even the friars' cells, hoping to claim the leftovers from Padre Pio's meals and nattering with him well after sundown. "The miracles being publicized are all the work of these twelve apostles and the other friars. But the people believe them, and woe to anyone who tries to say it isn't true!" As for Padre Pio, he seemed disoriented. He was too weak a character to repulse the conspiracies of his treacherous Capuchin colleagues, and too susceptible to female charms to resist the assault of the falsely pious lay sisters.[65]

The senders of this letter did not rule out that what was taking place at San Giovanni Rotondo might really be miraculous. "We do not deny the possibility that a Saint may arise in the Church," they wrote to the Holy Office. But the matter was too serious to be left in the hands of the little clique that ran Santa Maria delle Grazie. The dishonest friars must be immediately replaced with more reputable men, or the Holy Office must summon Padre Pio and carry out a proper examination of his person. In any case, the Church must act prudently, because the risks were great. "The friars seek to give events the appearance of a miracle because they know that they are playing the ultimate game—life or death... They will end up inciting the populace, which is unbelievably fanatical, and they will be responsible for a terrible carnage between those who believe in the 'Saint' and those who do not."[66]

Just a little more than a year later, that sinister prediction would prove a terrible prophecy. On October 14, 1920, San Giovanni would be the setting for the worst massacre of the *biennio rosso*, the "two red years" of 1919–20 when Italy was seized by numerous strikes and farmers' revolts.[67] And the events, if not directly caused by Padre Pio, would certainly be linked to him.

The Padre Pio Problem

The good friar with the stigmata had already become a problem of public order during the summer of 1919. It is possible that behind such complaints as those presented by the faithful of Manfredonia, accounts were being settled among the ecclesiastical community. Rumor had it that the archbishop of Manfredonia, Pasquale Gagliardi, was himself a man of sexual appetites,[68] and perhaps he had the same suspicion toward the Capuchins of San Giovanni Rotondo that lay friars sometimes felt toward their religious brothers. And then there were the economic considerations: the cult of Padre Pio threatened to channel resources toward Santa Maria delle Grazie that might otherwise have gone to the whole of the Gargano. Whatever the reason, the rapid expansion of the Padre Pio cult soon involved the civil authorities as well as the ecclesiastical ones. Around the same time that the Holy Office received the first anonymous letters, the prefecture of Foggia registered the arrival of a statement signed by "a group of citizens" from San Giovanni, asking for an investigation of Padre Pio's reputed miracles and his reported stigmata. The prefect was also asked to guarantee that in light of the arriving droves of believers, the police were taking measures to deal with those exploiting this "lurid industry," and doing something to ensure public health—for many pilgrims came from towns "infected with smallpox and perhaps also with typhus," and when the faithful gathered around Padre Pio, himself ill with tuberculosis, "they gathered up his bloody sputum."[69]

Losing no time, the prefect of Foggia asked the subprefect of San Severo to investigate the matter in loco, while noting that the state was not in the business of judging whether the feats attributed to Padre Pio were genuine ("the right to freedom of conscience and the statutory recognition of the Catholic religion do not permit the state to deny or confirm miracles"). The subprefect quickly prepared a report. Padre Pio's stigmata, the report said, were nearly circular spots, of a dark yellow color "like that produced by tincture of iodine." The friar's fame, it went on, had initially been confined to San Giovanni Rotondo and nearby towns like San Marco in Lamis and Monte Sant'Angelo; then, articles such as the story in *Il Mattino* began to appear in the local and national press, drawing attention from all over. By now, the average number of pilgrims arriving in San Giovanni was estimated at between three hundred and five hundred people per day. There was no threat to public order, because those skeptical about Padre Pio's sanctity were a tiny minority. The public health situation, however, was more delicate, because it was true that smallpox and typhus were present in various towns in the area. The subprefect of San Severo recommended controls of the "few hotels" and "many improvised sleeping places" into which pilgrims crowded in unhealthy proximity.[70]

Despite the subprefect's reassurances about public order, the prefect of Foggia was soon obliged to write to the minister of the interior in Rome about a clash at the Foggia railroad station. On June 28, 1919, the station's platforms were thronged with people—travelers, as the prefect reported, "belonging mostly to the humblest classes," who had just arrived in town for a visit to San Giovanni or were returning from visiting the monastery. That evening, the northbound troop train B 7-8 of the Royal Army had stopped in the station, an unidentified lieutenant colonel in command. When he learned that the crowds on the platforms had collected because of a friar with stigmata reputed to be a saint, the army officer began to shout for the policeman on duty. How could they permit such a display of ignorance? Where was the prefect whose job it was to put an end to such appalling mystification? In his report to the minister of the interior, the prefect of Foggia argued, as before, that religious questions were outside his purview: the 1848 Albertine Statute, the Savoy constitution,

explicitly stipulated that the civil authorities were to play no role in religious practice beyond protecting public health and order and making sure that credence did not become a pretext for fraud. The prefect deplored the scene staged by the lieutenant colonel in front of those "poor souls," whose only fault was the guilelessness of their own faith.[71]

Meanwhile, the day before the unpleasant incident, a *santino*—a holy card—depicting Padre Pio with the stigmata had been issued by a photographic studio not far from Foggia.[72] It was the first product from one of those workshops making Padre Pio cult objects that would prove so very industrious over the coming years. The images of Padre Pio from 1919, which soon began to circulate as normal postcards,[73] show him to be less shy in front of the camera than his reputation suggested. And if most of those photos show him wearing half gloves that hide the wounds on his hands, in at least one portrait his hands are purposefully uncovered, so that the wounds of Christ are clearly visible in a close-up. This is not to say that Padre Pio was always an active part of the devotional factory that had begun to spring up around him. If we can believe a certain Enrico Morrica, a teacher in Foggia, writing in *Il*

Mattino on June 30, Padre Pio sometimes regretted the zeal with which many promoted him as an *alter Christus*, a Christ figure. "I am nothing but what the Lord wishes," Morrica reports him saying, "and they make of me something I am not."[74]

That quotation from Padre Pio may well be closer to the truth than many others, if only because Morrica did not belong to the devout followers of the good friar. On the contrary, he had approached *Il Mattino* to express his doubts as a scientist about the supernatural nature of Padre Pio's condition.[75] Wounds resembling Jesus's were not particularly unusual, he pointed out; even the lay Franciscan "Auntie Minnona" of Via Fragatella in Bisceglie had them! Meanwhile, Padre Pio's visible wounds had a halo around them "of the characteristic color of tincture of iodine applied to a normal epidermis." Not only that, but the friar's person and his cell smelled distinctly of lysoform or iodoform. As for the discovery in the friar's cell of a bottle of "black commercial carbolic acid (which recalls the color of the stigmata)," could one really believe the explanation of the father guardian that Padre Pio used it "for the purposes of humility" to attenuate his own scent of sainthood? The various tales of his miraculous powers were also not to be taken at face value, for "the miracle of the lame soldier of Ascoli

Satriano, the deaf and dumb man of Carapella, and the hunchback of Foggia were all false."[76]

In a comment posted at the end of Morrica's article, the editor of *Il Mattino* argued that it was too soon to say whether the mysterious phenomena taking place in the Gargano mountains were supernatural.[77] One such phenomenon had been reported just a few days before in a Rome newspaper: it seems that Padre Pio knew neither French nor English, and yet he was able to reply to letters in those languages![78] Without probing further into the arcane, we can nevertheless use this report to take stock of how quickly Padre Pio's fame was spreading beyond his own country. Various clues suggest that the diffusion was rapid. In France, news of Padre Pio appeared in religious publications, both in modest provincial bulletins and in the prestigious *Annales franciscaines*, even before he was well known in much of Italy.[79] The fact that the Capuchin order had an international organization helps to explain, probably, the prompt spread of information.

In Spain, the fame of the Capuchin with the stigmata also spread rapidly—not surprisingly, for Spanish Catholicism had long had a penchant for the spectacular. In March 1919, for example, in the church of the Basque village of Limpias, a life-size statue of Christ on the cross called Cristo de la Agonía began to sweat just after two Capuchin friars held an intense prayer session. Within a few months, pilgrims would be coming to Limpias from all over Spain, hoping to see the miraculous event happen again.[80] There was nothing new about this in the long history of Iberian Catholicism; for centuries the veneration of more or less sweaty crucifixions had been a part of popular spirituality.[81] But from 1919 on, the enthusiasm for Cristo de la Agonía was linked to a special interest in the news from Italy about the Gargano Christ.[82] It was in Spain that the very first biographies of Padre Pio were published in 1921—two hagiographic studies, almost impossible to find today, both written by a certain Friar Peregrino da Mataró.[83]

At the Age of Thirty-three

In Italian literature and in religious experience, the Capuchin friar had a dual stereotype: he was placid but fiery, kindly but ferocious, earth-bound but heavenly. Padre Pio, however, seemed to embody this synthesis to a rare degree. During the long hours he spent behind the screen of the confessional, he took part in the Christian notion of mercy as *zelus animarum*, a compassion for his fellow man, addressed to human beings; while through his body, in that dramatic event that was the celebration of the mass, he took part, more than any other priest anywhere, in the Christian notion of mercy as *imitatio Christi*, a mystical communion addressed to God. In the eyes of his followers, Padre Pio was thus the unattainable fusion of two fundamental elements of Christianity: the divine in human form and the human made divine.

It's almost impossible to overstate how much all of this had to do with *blood*. The bishop of the city of Melfi in Basilicata, Monsignor Alberto Costa, visited San Giovanni Rotondo at the end of August 1919 and wrote to the new Capuchin minister provincial, telling of his impression of Padre Pio ("I have spoken to a Saint") and of the unequivocal sign that God had stamped on the friar's body. The stigmata—on which the bishop had planted "warm kisses"—were, he said, "all too eloquent mouths" for anyone to doubt the sacred nature of Padre Pio, "an angel made flesh."[84] And yet, because all this had to do with blood, the subject was more complicated than Monsignor Costa seemed to want to admit. Aside from their eloquence, or rather because of their eloquence, Padre Pio's stigmata were by no means self-explanatory; and the blood that flowed from them was actually the heart of the matter.

For a thousand years after it was established in the West, Christianity suffered from the harrowing divide between the glorious blood of Christ and the impure blood of human beings—infected blood, menstrual blood, and so on. The turning point came in the thirteenth century, when St. Francis of Assisi made the epochal gesture of approaching and touching a leper, overcoming his disgust and fear of contamination.[85] At the end of his life, St. Francis's own body had been contaminated in another way. The stigmata had made him—to his great embarrassment[86]—an *alter Christus*, the first in Western history. From then on, the ancient Christian custom of maintaining contact with the Savior's body had a new form of expression. Beyond the metaphor of the Eucharist, beyond the bones of the relic, there were the stigmata, a sort of relic incarnate.[87]

For the pilgrims of San Giovanni Rotondo, just as for the cardinals of the Church of Rome, this was what it meant to face Padre Pio. It meant coming to terms—awed or suspicious, enthusiastic or skeptical—with a second St. Francis, a twentieth-century Christ. Here was not merely a man who, like many saints, gave off a "delicious scent" that made the entire monastery of Santa Maria delle Grazie a "house smelling of balsam";[88] not merely a man who already in his youth had the gift of tears, a sure sign of sainthood.[89] Padre Pio presented a figure even more extraordinary: from his ever-open wounds, wounds of the dead-in-life, his body wept blood. "While he was celebrating the mass it was necessary to send up some cotton to dry his hands because they were covered in blood," a witness wrote,[90] and it was impossible to tell the blood from the wine, to distinguish the good friar's martyrdom from that of the Good Lord.

We should not be surprised, then, that the vox populi of 1919 had something else to say about Padre Pio: that the time he had available to perform miracles was running out. "The friar is young, not yet 33 years old, but they say he has predicted he is soon to die, and precisely when he turns 33."[91] The "two young deaf-mute girls" from a town somewhere near Foggia who hoped to get their speech back had better hurry up.[92] In fact, anyone who needed some intercession or some grace had better hurry. Padre Pio was not going to live longer than Jesus Christ.

2. NEUROSIS AND BEATITUDE

Bound Hands, Bloody Hands

"The etiology of Padre Pio's lesions cannot possibly be of natural origin," wrote Dr. Luigi Romanelli, chief surgeon at the Barletta public hospital. "The agent that produced them must assuredly be sought in the realm of the supernatural."[1] Dr. Romanelli, the first in a long series of doctors to offer his opinion, had no doubts about the causes of the stigmata when he sent a May 1919 report about the Capuchin friar's wounds to Church authorities. The only way those wounds could be explained was by divine intervention, he concluded. As it happened, Providence had already brought the friar's superhuman nature to Dr. Romanelli's attention. The previous summer the good doctor had twice prayed to Padre Pio without receiving the desired blessings, so Romanelli had traveled from Barletta to San Giovanni to ask Padre Pio why his prayers had not been acted on. But as he approached the friar—even before he got the question out of his mouth—Padre Pio brusquely interrupted him and called him to account for two recent occasions on which he had taken the Lord's name in vain.[2] Nothing, it seemed, escaped the "Saint" when it came to the fatal weaknesses of the human soul.

Padre Pio's stigmata were a gift from God—or so newspapers like *Il Tempo* and *La Nazione* decreed based on Dr. Romanelli's report, a document they were able to consult thanks to the helpful intervention of Adelchi Fabroncini, the elementary school teacher of San Giovanni who had profiled Padre Pio for *Il Mattino*.[3] The ecclesiastical authorities, however, preferred not to depend on an opinion that might

subsequently be proven fanciful. And so in July 1919, the Capuchin order called on an authority from a hospital far more illustrious than Barletta's: Amico Bignami, professor of pathology at the University of Rome, a malaria specialist widely respected in international scientific circles.[4] An evaluation of the stigmata by Bignami was certain to be reliable, especially because the professor was well known for his freethinking beliefs and was even rumored to be an atheist.

Despite the sympathy Bignami seems to have felt on meeting Padre Pio (he wrote of "his high, serene forehead; his lively, sweet, sometimes darting gaze; an expression on his face of goodness and sincerity"), when it came to the causes of his condition, the pathologist's judgment was stern. Bignami ruled out any suggestion that the wounds were purely self-inflicted, but suggested that two factors—one natural, one artificial—had played a role. The lesions of the epidermis on Padre Pio's hands were compatible with a diagnosis of "multiple neurotic necrosis," he wrote. However, that diagnosis did not explain why the wounds were so perfectly symmetrical, nor why they persisted unchanged over time. Here, the expert pathologist suggested, there was a willed component to the wounds. "We can in fact hypothesize that the lesions we have described began as a pathology . . . and then were, either unconsciously or by means of suggestion, filled out in their symmetry and artificially maintained by chemical means, for example with tincture of iodine."[5]

As for the other reported stigmata on Padre Pio's body, Bignami found no necrosis of the epidermis on his feet or his ribs. There was merely a brown pigmentation to the skin, which seemed to have been irritated by the repeated application of a caustic substance, perhaps tincture of iodine that had been allowed to evaporate. In order to clarify once and for all a clinical picture that was evidently being influenced by external factors, Professor Bignami suggested to the new Capuchin minister provincial, Father Pietro of Ischitella, that Padre Pio not be allowed to dress his own wounds. At least for a few days, he suggested, it would be a good idea if the father guardian of the monastery bound the wounds with sealed bandages so that the friar from Pietrelcina could not take them off himself. Left alone, Bignami believed, the wounds would quickly begin to heal.[6]

Such a translation of Padre Pio's mystic poetry into chemical prose— God's tattoos replaced by mere tincture of iodine—had tempted skeptics even before Amico Bignami made his confidential report. There was Professor Morrica's article in *Il Mattino*, the report of the subprefect of San Severo, and who knows how many comments destined to escape the historian's net—morning chatter at the newsstand, evening debates at the Socialist Club. But such views did little to squelch the enthusiasm of those who saw in Padre Pio a new Christ figure. In fact, by offering the prospect of a great battle between two opposing concepts of the world, they probably only whetted that enthusiasm. Just after Professor Bignami left the monastery, the father guardian of Santa Maria delle Grazie, Father Paolino of Casacalenda, sent the minister provincial a message to say that Padre Pio was now the object of a relic cult. When the friars sent out their dirty linens to the laundresses of San Giovanni Rotondo, the shirts believed to belong to Padre Pio, or sometimes just the bloodied parts of those shirts, would often disappear. The devout, both locals and outsiders, were so determined to come away with something vaguely resembling a relic that they would sometimes come into the monastery armed with scissors. "The crowd . . . slashed chasubles, shirts, girdles, even the chairs where Padre Pio had sat," reported Father Paolino.[7]

In a 1919 report to the minister general of the Capuchin order, the

minister provincial, Father Pietro of Ischitella, told of his efforts to contain the flow of pilgrims toward the Gargano Peninsula. Couldn't Padre Pio dispense his blessings without the faithful having to come all the way to San Giovanni Rotondo? "For some time now it's been evident that those who've been blessed by the intercession of God's servant are not the ones who undertake the disastrous voyage, but those who pray to the Lord from afar," he wrote. The proof was the recent return to health of a certain Signora Cozzi of Florence, who had an ailment of the tongue and was healed directly without moving from her local hospital. Father Pietro told the order's minister general that he sought to dissuade as many people as possible from making the pilgrimage to San Giovanni, instead inviting the faithful to appeal to Padre Pio directly through their prayers. At the same time Father Pietro warned the hierarchy in Rome that it would be unwise to try to "transfer Padre Pio elsewhere." He explained that when he arrived to serve as minister provincial in early September, he had undergone "a nasty half-hour" when the people of San Giovanni decided his arrival was a sign that the friar with the stigmata was about to be transferred.[8]

Father Pietro gave stern orders to the Capuchin monks of Santa Maria delle Grazie aimed at containing the cult of Padre Pio. He forbade lay persons to enter the refectory. No journalists or photographers were to be permitted to meet Padre Pio. The cult of Padre Pio relics was also to be discouraged ("no one may take objects that belong to him, and it is equally forbidden to give them to third parties"). The only concession Father Pietro made was to permit the faithful to bring holy cards to Padre Pio, cards on which he was allowed to write little homilies.[9] But all his orders, Father Pietro admitted in his report to the minister general, held little weight against the factors that motivated the people of San Giovanni with regard to Padre Pio: "their fanaticism, their pride, and let me even say, their business acumen." There were also other factors: as Father Pietro noted, the enthusiasm for the friar with the stigmata was not confined to those who lived near the monastery or those who exploited the cult for money. Every day, as many as seven hundred letters and telegrams arrived at the monastery from all over: from Tuscany, from Liguria, from the Marches, from Sicily, even from France and England, Malta and America. And at times, Padre Pio really did seem to act as the hand of Providence. "Just recently that young Florentine Jew was baptized here, the one who had previously gone to Rome [without deciding to convert]," Father Pietro told the minister general with some satisfaction.[10]

Padre Pio's sphere of action seemed to have no limits, nor were there limits to the marvelous way that the body of the friar could speak. At the end of July 1919, the father guardian of Santa Maria delle Grazie, Father Paolino of Casacalenda, had agreed, in accordance with Father Pietro, to follow the advice of Professor Bignami and remove all medicines, "including the tincture of iodine," from Padre Pio's cell. For a week the friar's wounds were bound one by one by Father Paolino himself, with the help of Father Basilio and Father Ludovico. There was no change in the appearance of the wounds until Thursday, when they took on a brighter, blood-red color; and then the blood began to flow more copiously than ever, so abundantly that it was necessary to wipe the blood off Padre Pio's hands even as he stood before the altar to celebrate mass. "I have preserved in my room all the dressings from the very first day so that you will have them at your disposition for any necessities," Father Paolino told Father Pietro.[11] Even while bound, the friar's hands had begun to bleed.

Among those who were soon convinced that Padre Pio had very special powers were some influential Roman cardinals. In November 1919 the head of the San Giovanni Rotondo monastery received a letter from the office of the Vatican secretary of state, signed by the secretary himelf, Cardinal Pietro Gasparri. The letter advanced several requests. First, the cardinal urged the monastery to consider the plea of a certain Rosi family from the Marches region: despite the crowds thronging to San Giovanni to see Padre Pio, the family aspired to take communion directly "from his hands." Cardinal Gasparri also asked that the Rosi family be given "some personal object" belonging to Padre Pio, which the cardinal intended to pass on to his niece. Finally, the Vatican secretary of state added: "Tell Padre Pio to pray fervently every day during mass for the Holy Father and for myself, that the Lord may illuminate us and guide us through the many troubles in which we find ourselves."[12]

It would be a mistake to make too much of a document like this; in his long career as a priest and as a prelate of the Vatican, Gasparri must have written many similar letters. But it does demonstrate that, early on, authorities in the Church of Rome disagreed on the Padre Pio question. On the one hand, there was the Capuchin order, whose leaders were cautious about—even reluctant to take advantage of—the friar's reputation for holiness. On the other hand, high-ranking Vatican officials like Cardinal Gasparri and Bonaventura Cerretti, archbishop of Corinthus and secretary of the Congregation for Extraordinary Ecclesiastical Affairs, openly expressed their personal devotion to Padre Pio.[13] Between them was the Congregation of the Holy Office, which during the following year would decide to investigate the matter further.[14]

At the end of April 1920, the crucial document arrived at the Holy Office. It was a letter from Father Agostino Gemelli, a Milanese Franciscan who was making a name for himself at the time both within and outside the Church for his determination to found a Catholic university in the secular kingdom of Italy—what would become the Catholic University of the Sacred Heart.[15] Father Gemelli had also made a pilgrimage to San Giovanni Rotondo, where he had met Padre Pio. And he was determined to have his say.

The Whole Truth

The mystery of the stigmata was the perfect subject for a perpetually curious priest and scientist such as Agostino Gemelli. Histological evidence and psychological secrets, the limits of positivism and the frontiers of spiritualism, the clues of saintliness and the hard evidence of fraud—for Father Gemelli, delivering an opinion on Padre Pio's stigmata meant gathering reflections, experiences, and research in vastly different fields of scientific knowledge, religious experience, and even military practice. Although no ecclesiastical official had asked him to investigate and although he traveled to the Gargano Peninsula on his own initiative, Gemelli's personal letter to the Holy Office would become a quasi-official report on the question of Padre Pio.[16]

Given the powerful influence that the Franciscan's letter would have on Padre Pio's life, we must first take a step back to comprehend the man who sent it. For we cannot fully appreciate Gemelli's logic, nor the reactions of the Holy Office, unless we understand the Milan of Gemelli's youth and his conversion to the Catholic faith. Indeed, we must follow Father Agostino almost step by step through the fifteen years between his baptism and his visit to San Giovanni. They were years brimming with history, during which the Milanese doctor

became a genuine religious activist—became, in fact, Italy's foremost friar.

If the road from Francesco Forgione to Padre Pio began with a beard,[17] the ordination of Dr. Edoardo Gemelli as Father Agostino can be traced to a book: a *Life of St. Francis* that he read in September 1903 as he was approaching the end of his military service.[18] This was not merely one of the thousand lives of St. Francis that centuries of hagiography had furnished. The book that so struck Gemelli was the first biography of the saint based on the methods of positivist historiography.[19] Published in 1894 in Strasbourg by the Protestant minister Paul Sabatier, the book had excited a wave of questioning, criticism, and enthusiasm across Europe. What appealed to Gemelli, among others, was the critical intelligence that Sabatier brought to bear on the medieval sources, an approach far from the hagiography of the day. Rationalists were astonished that such a serious scholar would accept that St. Francis's stigmata were genuine, and define them expressly as the wounds of Christ. Catholics were disturbed that a Protestant minister could co-opt the figure of a revered Catholic. Protestants were annoyed that one of their own had written a celebration of a Catholic saint.[20] Because Sabatier was neither orthodox nor Catholic, Vatican officials put his book on the Index Librorum Prohibitorum, the official list of literature forbidden by the Church, but that did not stop readers everywhere from picking up the *Life of St. Francis*. It was even rumored that Sabatier was on the short list for a Nobel Prize for literature.[21]

Two months after reading Sabatier's book, Edoardo Gemelli was on his own road to Damascus. In November 1903 came the illumination, the call, the monk's habit tossed over the lean body of the twenty-five-year-old. It was something of a scandal, both for his family and for his ex-companions. Gemelli came from a solidly secular environment. He had studied medicine at Pavia with Camillo Golgi, a future Nobel Prize winner;[22] he had done laboratory research on brain histology; the intellectual circles he frequented included the elite of Milanese and Italian socialism.[23] When his parents learned of his conversion, they had Gemelli seen by two Milanese psychiatrists, on the grounds that only an attack of madness could account for his religious passion. The Socialist press wrote of "a phenomenon of sudden mysticism" and suggested that Gemelli's "mental balance had always been unstable."[24] The *Corriere della Sera*, deploring the uproar around Gemelli, struck a softer note, suggesting that the young man ought to be "pitied," not hunted down by friends and family ready to inscribe the "stigmata of the madman" on his forehead.[25]

In the years following Gemelli's conversion, Sabatier became a crucial figure for Italian Catholics, both lay and clerical, who were tempted by the modernist way.[26] For Catholics, modernism meant questioning aspects of the faith that were hard to reconcile with science and progress, especially faith based on icons, relics, and dramatic miracles. Implicitly, it also meant questioning religious authority, as expressed in the hierarchical command of the Holy Roman Church. At the same time, however, Catholics and non-Catholics alike shared a yearning for prophecy and a mystical language.[27] Antonio Fogazzaro's best-selling 1905 novel *The Saint* offers a deft summary of that modernist Catholic sensibility and its ambiguities.[28] The novel's protagonist, Friar Benedetto, a reluctant saint living in a rural village, is considered a miracle worker by his humble fellow townsmen. But Benedetto, true to a modernist creed, refuses to perform the spectacular miracles of curing the sick,[29] unwilling to use the healing powers attributed to him by the masses. Meanwhile, the author's alter ego, the intellectual Giovanni Selva, is forced to reflect that the faith of the peasants who live alongside

Benedetto—a faith that to Selva seems mere credulousness—is, however, genuine. "It was, inside a rough vessel of brittle ignorance, the perception denied to more superior minds of the hidden Truth that is Life, mysterious radium beaming inside a mass of impure minerals."[30] The half-willing saint, the humble believers, the skepticism of the educated—in many ways *The Saint* prefigured all that would unfold in San Giovanni Rotondo, the history and the antihistory of a Padre Pio in twentieth-century Italy. It was a time when a man like Padre Pio could be called a saint even as one like Edoardo Gemelli was considered deranged because he had converted.

At the end of 1906, Gemelli wrote to Sabatier for the first time. The correspondence brought together the French Protestant pastor—well along in years, recognized by all (whether they liked him or not) as the world authority on Franciscan affairs—and an impatient young Italian seminary student, far less well known, but with the advantage of a first-class medical education. It is no wonder that their letters came to focus on St. Francis's stigmata. "If only you were to carry out a study on St. Francis's ailment!" Sabatier immediately proposed to Gemelli.[31] The implications of such a study would by no means be limited to the causes of some centuries-old wounds. As both men saw it, the question involved exploring a strategic frontier of contemporary life. It meant coming to terms with a possible—or necessary—conciliation between scientific truth and Christian truth.

From Gemelli's very first letter it is clear that he meant to bring together both sides of his character as friar-scientist, that he wanted to inhabit two worlds and make them one—reconciling Catholic ontology with positivist science and making the interest of the Church coincide with the interest of humanity. Although his French is somewhat uncertain, his letter brims with moral energy and intellectual determination: "I am a poor clergyman with the idée fixe of pursuing my studies of natural science (especially histology, embryology, etc.) so as to be able to tell my confrères the truth—*the whole truth*—and by this route labor for the Church."[32]

Three months after Sabatier wrote telling the young Italian doctor to pursue his studies on the *maladie de S. François*, Gemelli replied that yes, he intended to study the Franciscan stigmata. And he meant to do so freely, without regard for any philosophical, theological, or mystical constraints. *Je ne sais pas où j'arriverai*, the young seminarian wrote.[33] But he meant to arrive at the truth, the whole truth.

David's Memory

Father Gemelli's determination to pursue the truth would rapidly collide with his Catholic faith, however. If, just a year or two previously, Gemelli had experienced modernism's restless questioning as a personal crisis that called even his faith into doubt,[34] by the end of 1907 he had made an unacknowledged about-face, becoming a stubborn spokesman for a new kind of Catholic orthodoxy. Rather than "the whole truth," he would now pursue a far less radical course—scientifically informed but distinctly neoscholastic, politically flexible but culturally pugnacious. Even as Gemelli explored his scientific interests (writing more than one hundred papers in biology, psychology, and pedagogy in the year 1907 alone),[35] he was on his way to becoming one of the greatest standard-bearers for the Church of Rome's *reconquista* to come. When Paul Sabatier came through Milan in late 1907, Gemelli, now circumspect, made no effort to meet the man whom the Jesuits of the review *Civiltà cattolica* were calling the black sheep of international modernism.[36] Just a few months later, Gemelli was ordained a priest. His detailed study of St. Francis's stigmata would have to wait almost twenty years.[37]

In 1910, Gemelli turned his attention to the work of Cesare Lombroso, the most famous scientist of the late nineteenth century. Lombroso's pathbreaking *The Man of Genius* had portrayed some of the most noted saints of the Catholic Church—Paul of Tarsus, Francis of Assisi, Ignatius of Loyola—as "half-mad" men, afflicted by various pathologies traceable to hysteria or epilepsy. Their hallucinations and telepathy, anesthesia and self-destructive behavior were, in this telling, typical symptoms of madness. In these ranks of the "half-mad" Lombroso also included David Lazzaretti, the mystical leader of a small messianic-communistic movement in the Amiata mountains who had sacrificed himself in a battle with a police squadron in 1878. According to Lombroso, Lazzaretti's particular case was one of a "Christomimetic" mania; this

explained the fact that he had begun to prophesize at the age of thirty-three, as well as the *C*'s tattooed on his forehead, which served as a stigmata of a social contract with God. The poor, ignorant, geographically isolated mountain folk of the Amiata hills had done the rest, bringing to Lazzaretti's personal mental disorders their own collective derangement.[38]

In Lombroso's scheme of things, "degenerative stigmata"—somatic or psychic anomalies found both in geniuses and the unbalanced, in criminals as well as in saints—was a key theory.[39] But soon after Lombroso died in 1909, Gemelli seized on the concept of "degenerative stigmata" to mount a frontal attack on Lombrosian thought. In the maliciously titled *Funeral Services for a Man and a Doctrine*, the pugnacious Catholic doctor was able to show that the concept of "degenerative stigmata" had no solid scientific basis.[40] But Father Gemelli didn't stop there. He went on to argue that Lombroso represented the utter failure of the positivist ideology. Lombroso's mortal sin had been to insist on studying only the material sphere, ignoring completely the spirit. "The good Lombroso," Gemelli wrote, "a doctor who did not heal souls or study thought, who merely inspected skulls and observed urine, never thought about one little problem: he never studied the genius of the geniuses or the criminality of the criminal, but only their bodies."[41]

In his own studies of psychopathology, Father Gemelli wanted to do precisely what Lombroso had not: to inspect the psychic reality rather than its organic manifestations, to look at the inner life, not the body—and, above all, never confuse the two. He intended to shatter materialism, using the new science of psychology to probe the old problems of mystical experience and miracles.[42] Nevertheless, in spite of these intentions, Gemelli continued to think and write like a positivist. He would merely graft—onto the empiricist bases of the medical education he had received before his conversion—some artificial shoots of piety. The result was less the hoped-for conciliation between scientific and Catholic truth than an embarrassing confusion.

Fin de siècle secular culture seemed intent on equating beatitude with mental illness.[43] Apparitions of the Virgin, wounds of Christ, female ecstasy, and male levitation—most of the phenomenology of mysticism had been labeled psychosomatic pathology.[44] In Gemelli's view, a Lombroso-style "medical materialism" had taken hold, in which Jesus was diagnosed as an ecstatic, St. Paul a sort of epileptic, St. Francis a depressive, St. Teresa a hysteric. Furthermore, the theory of suggestion—the notion that many hysterical symptoms were produced by *psittacism,* a mindless parroting of words and gestures—was then preeminent, thanks to the enormous influence of the Parisian school of Jean-Martin Charcot and especially Félix Babinski. Accordingly, it seemed that nervous disorders led to hysteria, and imitation of hysteria produced mystical experience. In his lengthy 1912 work on *Neurosis and Beatitude,*[45] Father Gemelli sought to demolish this logic with a scientific demonstration that some mystical experience was indeed supernatural in nature. At most, he argued, psychopathology could link the "inferior phenomena" of mystical experience (physical manifestations like visions, lights, sounds, ecstasy) with neuropathies, but it was helpless to explain the inner, spiritual "superior phenomena"—the perception of the divine, or at least of the transcendent.[46]

Beatitude and neurosis were not synonymous, Gemelli insisted. To prove it, one merely had to restrict the sample to "true mystics," excluding those " 'psychiatric hospital mystics' who are merely the caricature of the first category." He argued that in order to discredit mysticism (and religion in general), the Lombroso school psychiatrists had made a point of confusing the two categories—mixing up the rare "great mystics" who had "discovered a new form of life and realized it" with the legions of "inferior, degenerate mystics who lacked genius, neurotics without intellectual and will power." Once the distinction was reestablished, all became clear. Catholic culture had to acknowledge that the true mystics were not immune from nervous frailty; secular culture, in turn, had to admit that a true mystic was "a potent creator of life, a logical force that builds and consummates—in short, a genius—a quality that is absolutely lacking in the hospital mystic."[47]

If that does not sound entirely convincing, it is because Gemelli was getting bogged down in his contradictory mélange of empiricism and dogmatism, flailing in his attempt to combine reason and faith. But the Franciscan doctor was certainly not the only one, there in the closing years of the belle epoque, to be struggling to accommodate the mystical side of human experience. In the decade prior to the Great War, Italian and European culture, ever more disturbed by the telluric shocks of modernity, was undergoing a crisis,[48] and the revolt against positivism and the search for new moral and spiritual fundamentals suddenly brought Catholic thinkers and the secular intelligentsia closer together. Young writers of the Florentine avant-garde, such as Giovanni Papini, combined the vigor of a new language with the draw of mysticism and a fascination with theosophy.[49] Along with Gemelli, they were among the principal critics of Lombrosian thought.

Cowards and Imposters

Gemelli probably first learned of Padre Pio's existence in late 1911, not long after Pio had begun to copy extensively from Gemma Galgani's *Letters and Ecstasies* in his own correspondence with his spiritual advisers. One of those advisers, Father Agostino of San Marco in Lamis, had moved to the monastery at Venafro to instruct young priests in sacred elocution, and Padre Pio went to see him there between October and December of 1911. For those several months, Father Agostino experienced at first hand the extremes of Padre Pio's mysticism: his stigmatic pains, his ecstatic visions, the vexations visited on him by Satan. During these bouts, Father Agostino more than once called a local doctor to the monastery, so that a clinically trained eye could

observe the spectacle and perhaps offer a diagnosis.[50] Although we cannot be sure, it's likely that a similar consideration induced Father Agostino of San Marco in Lamis to bring the restless, prolific clergyman Agostino Gemelli—by now well known to many Italians as a scientist, an intellectual, and an opinion maker—into the picture as well.

It may be that the Capuchin friar decided to turn to the Franciscan because of his reputation as an expert on the relationship between neurosis and beatitude—that is, because he wanted to get the doctor's opinion on Padre Pio's psychological state. A note in Gemelli's hand points to contact between the two in January 1912: "Reverend Father, do write to me in as much detail as you like and I will try to reply in terms of what I know, as I can."[51] There seems to have been, however, no follow-up to that particular letter.

The paths of the two Agostinos would veer toward each other again, without ever actually crossing, during the First World War. In the spring of 1916, Padre Pio's spiritual director was mobilized as a military chaplain. He was sent not to the front but to several military hospitals, first at Palazzolo sull'Oglio near Bergamo, then to Orzano near Udine, then back to Palazzolo from March 1917 to September 1918, when—having fallen ill with Spanish flu—he returned south to convalesce at the monastery of San Marco la Catola.[52] In those same years Father Gemelli moved back and forth between Milan and the war zones, earning a reputation with the supreme command, the soldiers, and the general public as an eloquent spokesman for the anti-Teutonic cause.[53] The diaries of various military chaplains provide marvelous snapshots of Gemelli's patriotic-religious exploits—the sermons delivered "dressed up as a captain with gloves, spurs and even a horsewhip";[54] the infantrymen waiting for hours in front of the confessional to receive the absolution from him, the communion wafer directly from his hands;[55] the mass celebrated just behind the front lines, with the sacred host divided up "in minuscule fragments" for the crowds of soldiers whose sins had already been absolved in the heat of the battle.[56]

The mystical anti-Teutonic crusade of certain priests like Gemelli did puzzle some believers. One infantry officer, writing to a friend, remarked that "here, *De Imitazione Christi* brings to mind precepts of which we are acting out the contrary."[57] Worse, Father Gemelli's patriotic fervor disturbed the minister general of the Franciscan order, Brother Serafino Cimino, who let Gemelli know as early as September 1915 that the Franciscan hierarchy—up to, he suggested, the pope—had a "disastrous" impression of his opinions. "Could a hardened warmonger write worse? Could a secularist be more vicious and less Christian in promising ruin to the enemy, whoever he may be?" Gemelli should be more cautious in his preaching and his writing, Cimino suggested. He should remember that his job as a soldier was to heal wounded bodies, as a priest, wounded spirits. Nothing else was needed from him, especially not when Benedict XV was doing all he could to "shorten the tremendous worldwide calamity."[58]

Father Agostino of San Marco in Lamis was distinctly more cautious about his role in the war: apart from a few formal expressions of hope that the nation would survive unscathed and victorious, the letters he exchanged with Padre Pio throughout the European conflict simply recounted a hospital routine of wounds to dress, minds to comfort, deaths to endure. By contrast, just a few kilometers away from Father Agostino's hospital at Palazzolo sull'Oglio, Sergeant Angelo Roncalli (the future Pope John XXIII) was carrying out his duties as chaplain in a bellicose spirit worthy of Father Gemelli.[59] "Annoyed" by the "silly prattle" about peace from various "layabouts," untouched by the "boring, repetitive womanish lamentations" and the "ready tears" for the fallen, Roncalli was eager to see "our green young soldiers"—the "boys of '99"—off to the front with the others.[60] Like him, some two-thirds of army chaplains were ardently militaristic; Father Agostino of San Marco in Lamis, meanwhile, belonged to the pacific one-third.[61] His wartime letters to Padre Pio during the war never used the language of the rifle, but always the language of the ministry.[62]

And what of Padre Pio himself? His Great War would involve precious little war. Called up as a priest-soldier (not, that is, as a chaplain) despite a diagnosis of TB, he was first admitted for observation to the military hospital at Caserta, then assigned to the Tenth Company of the Army Medical Corps, based in Naples. He was there only briefly, however, because—with the help of a good word put in by an influential acquaintance—he was granted a year's leave on health grounds, which he spent between his hometown of Pietrelcina and the Capuchin monasteries at Foggia and San Giovanni Rotondo. In 1917, judged again to be able-bodied for service in Italy, Private Forgione was sent

from San Giovanni to the Sales barracks in Naples. (A group photograph from the time shows him at the far right of the front row, seated
on the ground with a rifle in his lap.) He was there from September to
November, perpetually complaining, in his letters to his spiritual
advisers, about the foolish doctors who paid no heed to his many ailments. Finally given another leave, he returned to San Giovanni
Rotondo.

"The Army Medical Corps is more like the Camorra than any other
association in Naples," one interventionist intellectual wrote in 1915
after a brief experience at the front.[63] The accusation was probably
unfair when it came to the medical teams just behind the battle lines,
but the farther away from the Dolomites and the Carso one went—and
especially if one descended the Apennines down to southern Italy—
the more truth there was to the comparison between the medical
corps and Naples's organized crime gangs.[64] When Italy entered the
war the medical corps had been assigned just about all the priest-
soldiers, who, not having got the title of chaplain, had to wear the gray-
green battle uniform.[65] Many of them conveniently found a way to
work in military hospitals near their hometowns or their dioceses;
in short, they were not what could be called model soldiers. Just in
the Sales barracks in Naples, where Padre Pio was assigned, there

were some nine hundred priest-soldiers, and even their chaplain brothers thought they were lazy and selfish—"especially . . . the Capuchins."[66]

If Italian patriots had their doubts about the Army Medical Corps, it was partly because military hospitals had a reputation for being full of malingerers. In Italy, as in other countries involved in the First World War, the battle against the enemy was accompanied by a creeping civil war of soldiers against doctors.[67] Foot soldiers would rely on the old-fashioned expedients of popular wisdom, or on the latest tricks learned in the trenches, to remove themselves from the front with a medical certificate: they would simulate bodily illness, pretend to be insane, injure themselves. On the other side, doctors developed a special eye for unmasking the fakers, learning that certain symptoms—varicose veins, hemorrhoids, eczema, laryngitis, blennorrhea, colics, rheumatism, sciatica—were typical ruses of infantrymen eager neither to fight nor to die.[68] Officers were often divided between affection for their men and annoyance at their deceit. "All of them moaning about their arthritis, pains, indigestion," noted Carlo Emilio Gadda up on the front near Asiago in 1916. "Some legitimately, others despicably, from cowardice." He wrote of his "fitful rage" against "the cowards and the imposters."[69]

Self-inflicted injuries, doctors thought, demonstrated the moral and mental inferiority of certain foot soldiers, expressing the primitive, savage form of humanity to which they belonged.[70] And military law was very strict with soldiers found to have purposely injured themselves: beginning in 1916, the penalty was death before a firing squad selected from the man's own detachment.[71] Nevertheless, the ways to procure false injuries were almost infinite: pus-filled swollen limbs simulated by injecting petroleum, turpentine, and gasoline; abscesses caused by injecting a solution of dissolved feces; mutilations with knives and swords, wounds from guns and rifles.[72] Most frequent were injuries to hands and feet, seemingly ideal for obtaining the desired noncombatant certificate were it not for the fact that doctors were especially suspicious about damage to the back of a hand or missing toes.[73]

The most important book that Father Gemelli found time to write during the Great War was *Our Soldiers: Studies in Military Psychology*.[74] In it he provides a list of various simulated and self-inflicted injuries, reflects on the relationship between self-destructive tendencies and popular culture, and develops a scientific hypothesis about the link between simulation and neurosis.[75] Gemelli was convinced that soldiers who injured themselves stood somewhere between rogues and psychopaths. The good doctor shows not a hint of the mercy displayed, for example, by the writer Aldo Palazzeschi, who wrote of military hospitals that "the true wounded suffer alongside the bogus wounded, who suffer even more than the first and are more compassionate."[76] There was nothing at all like this in Father Gemelli. He pointed the same accusatory finger at those who had procured their own injuries that he pointed at the soldiers suffering from shell shock, and employed the same jargon for both: the listless, the slackers, the overscrupulous, the hallucinators, and the "emotionally predisposed," the victims of suggestion and of self-suggestion.[77]

It was in one of those hospitals in Italy's Mezzogiorno, the south, far from the battlefields—where the slackers from the front and the shirkers from behind the lines took refuge, or so said the patriots—that the soldier-priest Francesco Forgione lived out the most dramatic months of Italy's Great War. When the rout at Caporetto came, Forgione was hospitalized in Naples Trinità Hospital, and in his letters to Padre Agostino he offered not one word of comment on that historic defeat.[78] The previous weeks, which he had spent at the Sales barracks, had been a trial for Padre Pio, and he was much more worried about his own health than about Italy's military debacles. He felt so sick he was sure that the end was at hand: "If Jesus does not hold me up and come to my aid, I shall most certainly succumb."[79] Padre Pio's body and soul were far too absorbed in the battle against evil to register the battle against the Austrians. "I would be most displeased to depart this world via the barracks, not the cloister, with these accursed rags on my back," he wrote to his spiritual adviser.[80]

Traces of the ruses employed by these priest-soldiers—the hundreds of them who roamed the halls of the Sales barracks in Naples, performing no work at all except perhaps to write letters to Rome complaining about their lay colleagues and begging to be designated as clerks or orderlies—can be found in the archives.[81] But unfortunately the archives have not preserved any memory of how the priest-soldier Forgione was viewed by his fellow soldiers in Naples in the months running up to the wondrous events of the stigmata. We must use a little imagination to fill out the picture. Perhaps he was a figure something like the fellow depicted by Ernesto Rossi—then an officer of the Royal Army, later to be an important anti-Fascist intellectual. Rossi, disabled in the war and hospitalized near Gorizia,[82] had noted, among "the brouhaha of priests" in the ward, "one very particular aesthete" named Teadina. Thin and wan, Teadina wandered through the wards "as if permanently in another world," his nose stuck in the greasy pages of a breviary that he jealously concealed from the view of others. He would only come into the barracks when the others were already asleep, or pass the night in a little church nearby, rapt in mystical contemplation right up until 7 a.m.

In a letter to his mother, Rossi apologized for going on at length about this peculiar figure but could not resist a few more words. "I assure you he's a type well worth studying. In earlier times he would have been a candidate for sainthood, but a modern psychiatrist wouldn't think twice about sending him to the asylum."[83] Luckily for Teadina, the thin, wan priest would never meet the modern psychiatrist Agostino Gemelli.

A Psychiatric Hospital Mystic

On April 19, 1920, Father Gemelli arrived at the Capuchin monastery of San Giovanni Rotondo. He departed the following day, April 20, having spent no more than a few hours with Padre Pio in person. As Gemelli himself acknowledged, he did not examine the friar physically; there was no histological study of the wounds and no neurological exam. The Franciscan conducted only a "psychiatric examination" of Padre Pio—carried out "without him being aware of it, by means of harmless artifice."[84] Yet we can confidently say that Gemelli did not need more time with Padre Pio in order to write up his evaluation and send it to the Holy Office. Long before that fleeting encounter, he had developed a pretty good notion of what he thought of the Capuchin friar.

It would be too much to say that Gemelli's judgment of Padre Pio was identical to what Cesare Lombroso had made of the "half-mad"

David Lazzaretti, the would-be "saint" of the Amiata hills. Still, it was a verdict founded on the conviction that some kinds of mysticism were connected with hysteria, a conviction that sprang from the late nineteenth-century positivism on which early twentieth-century psychiatric science was founded. It was a verdict, furthermore, grounded in the suspicion of bogus and self-inflicted injuries that Gemelli had developed during the First World War. And finally, it was a verdict based on the methods of persuasion he thought the Catholic Church should use to impose itself in postwar Italy—methods more advanced than the worship of saints. The saints had been useful during the Great War, when soldiers depended on them almost superstitiously; but saints, Gemelli thought, belonged more to the Church's past than to its future.[85] All this, combined with his firsthand experience at San Giovanni Rotondo, had made up Gemelli's mind. There was nothing less seductive than the archaic spectacle of a living saint and the crowds enchanted by his wounds—not, in any case, for a priest who was determined, with his Catholic University of the Sacred Heart, to pursue Catholic cultural hegemony and political power.[86]

In the letter he sent to the Holy Office after his visit to San Giovanni Rotondo, Gemelli said that he had gone there drawn by reports that Padre Pio was a saint, with the idea of asking for some prayers of intercession. But after a brief introduction in these terms, Gemelli's letter rapidly shifts tone. Reports of Padre Pio's miracles circulating in Puglia were "uncontrolled tales and legends," he said. The propaganda that the Capuchin brothers had mounted about the stigmata was spreading "superstitious practices." The ecclesiastical authorities were thus right to have Padre Pio seen by medical experts; indeed, they should go further. Because neither clinical pathology nor biological research in general was capable of distinguishing true mystics from false, the Padre Pio question could not be resolved by recourse to "crude medical materialism"; what was needed were the techniques of experimental psychology.[87]

Father Gemelli had no complaints about Padre Pio's religious life, which he thought was exemplary. But he was very troubled by the hypnotic "atmosphere of suggestion" that surrounded the Capuchin friar, with Father Benedetto of San Marco in Lamis, Padre Pio's adviser, and the ex-minister provincial of Foggia, "he who testifies to extraordinary happenings that ought to be investigated," zealously fanning the flames. Given the state of affairs and the "incessant stream" of pilgrims both Italian and foreign, Gemelli had little doubt about what the Church ought to do. "Padre Pio [must be] removed for some time from the artificial environment he is in," he concluded, and be examined by a mixed board made up of a doctor, a psychologist, and a theologian. This last wasn't likely to be of much use, however, because the friar with the stigmata demonstrated "none of the elements typical of the mystical life."[88]

Not a human being inhabited by the supernatural but rather an impoverished soul, Padre Pio was "a man with a restricted field of knowledge, low psychic energy, monotonous ideas, little volition"—so the members of the Congregation of the Holy Office read in Father Gemelli's report. These were harsh words. A decade previously, battling against the school of the French doctor Charcot, Gemelli had ridiculed the notion that the symptoms of mysticism derived from psittacism, the hysterical imitation of words and gestures.[89] Yet after he met Padre Pio, Father Gemelli's diagnosis of the Capuchin seemed right out of Charcot's book. "The case is one of suggestion unconsciously planted by Father Benedetto in the weak mind of Padre Pio, producing those characteristic manifestations of psittacism that are intrinsic to the hysteric mind."[90]

A few weeks after he sent his first letter to the Holy Office, Father Gemelli sent a second brief message, spelling out what had to be done to achieve a secure diagnosis. Some of what he said coincided with what Professor Bignami had advised the previous year: to rid Padre Pio's cell of any suspect materials and forbid him access to medicines coming from outside the monastery; to wrap one of his limbs in plaster ("or even better, one of his arms and one of his legs") long enough to allow the wounds to heal, making sure that the plaster was tight enough so that no substances could be introduced beneath it.[91] Other measures that Gemelli proposed had less to do with the pharmacological and dermatological aspects of the case than with psychological and environmental factors. Padre Pio must undergo a rigorous psychiatric exam to explore the diagnosis of "hysterism" or "psittacism." The "coloring

agent" that marked Padre Pio's skin must be examined under a micro-
scope. A systematic check must be made of what he ate and what he
vomited up. The aromatic substance that emanated from Padre Pio's
hands must be identified, and he must not be allowed access to ordinary perfumes.[92] And, not least, Father Benedetto of San Marco in
Lamis must be transferred from San Giovanni Rotondo.

When, not long after this, the Vatican hierarchy decided to deal
with the Padre Pio problem using the ancient instruments of inquisitorial power,[93] the spirit of Gemelli's medical report would hang heavily over the men of the Holy Office. Many of their actions would be
determined by the conviction that they were not dealing with a living
saint, and certainly not with a Christ figure—but rather, in the cruel
words of *Neurosis and Beatitude*, with a "psychiatric hospital mystic."[94]

An Italian Jesus

It is still possible today to see the memorial plaque posted a mile and a
half up on the Dolomite rockface of Tofana di Rozes near Cortina
d'Ampezzo.

> EACH ONE HAD THE FACE OF CHRIST
> INSIDE HIS HELMET'S DARK HALO
> EACH ONE WORE THE MARK OF PAIN
> ON HIS BAYONET'S CROSS
> IN HIS POCKETS, CRUMBS OF THE LAST SUPPER
> IN HIS THROAT, TEARS OF FAREWELL.

Historians haven't been able to determine exactly when this inscription
was placed at the mouth of the Castelletto tunnel, excavated in 1916 by
Italian Alpine troops in order to blow up the entrenched Austrian forces.
Nor do they know who wrote the words on the plaque.[95] To some, they
suggest the fancies of an unknown soldier, carving words on a stone
inside his tent. Others have thought they sensed the hand of Giuseppe
Ungaretti, a war veteran who would soon be crowned a major poet.
More convincing is the attribution to the *grande mutilato*—severely
disabled veteran—Carlo Delcroix, a Florentine officer who, having lost

his hands and his sight in battle on the high Dolomite peak of the Marmolada, became a leading figure in the veterans' movement (and later a high Fascist official and keen promoter of the cult of Mussolini).[96]

Way up there on that Dolomite rockface, the epigraph at Castelletto proclaimed the creed of Gabriele D'Annunzio, for whom the Great War was a kind of Passion endlessly reincarnating the Redeemer: the sacrifices of the "poor Jesuses," the "poor kids" in their gray-green uniforms, would newly save humanity. But it was one thing to hold that view when the fighting was still going on and every poetic fancy served propaganda purposes. It was another to think that way after the war's end, when the words *Poor Jesus*—the title of a 1920 novel by Mario Mariani[97]—evoked not as much the poetry of salvation as the dreadful prose of a postwar existence too mean for soldiers who had escaped hell in the trenches, soldiers now condemned to an Italy that neither understood nor loved them. For D'Annunzio and his followers, this distressing postwar Passion-without-Redemption led to irredentist political action: the 1919 invasion of the city of Fiume (now Rijeka) on the Istrian coast.[98] Others, less inclined than D'Annunzio to translate ideas into deeds, merely wrote jeremiads about what the war's "poor kids" merited and were not getting.

For Kurt Suckert (later Curzio Malaparte), the "poor kids" were "damned saints," as he called them in an unforgettable, if overblown, tribute to the soldiers of the Dolomites and the Carso.[99] Less magniloquent, more believable, was Aldo Palazzeschi's portrait of these "holy creatures" in his *Two Empires . . . Unconquered*. Palazzeschi, who for health reasons never served at the front, but who worked behind the lines distributing provisions and later helping to return personal effects to the families of war dead, brought genuine kindness and mercy to bear on the soldiers, emboldened by his recent return to Christianity. For Palazzeschi, the foot soldiers were "victims" on whom "all the weight of the injustice, the lies, the cowardice, the lack of responsibility, all the evil in the world" had fallen. The terrible rout at Caporetto "was merely the warning of what must be their justice," he wrote.[100]

Palazzeschi's avant-garde confrere Giovanni Papini, himself a reborn Catholic, was enthusiastic about *Two Empires . . . Unconquered*; their friend Ardengo Soffici called the work "a holy book."[101] Papini said that he had felt closer than ever to Palazzeschi, because the latter had not fallen, between 1914 and 1915, into the trap of interventionism; he had not been fooled into thinking that war would offer the world salvation. Papini himself had believed that all too much. "But from 1916 on my repugnance and my disillusion have been growing enormously," he wrote to Palazzeschi in July 1920. "Today, like you, I curse and condemn that which I exalted . . . The horror has taught us what we really are." He meant: we're Christians; we can only find salvation through Christianity, not war. In the same letter, he referred in modest terms to a work he was rapidly bringing to a conclusion. "My next book is no more than a modern, impassioned transcription of the four evangelists," he wrote to his friend.[102]

It was false modesty: Papini, along with the publisher Vallecchi, was in fact carefully crafting that book to be a huge best seller. He even looked after the most minute typographical details, suggesting the printer use American linotype, requesting a more glossy paper than usual, demanding a Bodoni font.[103] Above all, Papini had sniffed the air, divined the zeitgeist of the immediate postwar years. He managed to convince Vallecchi that this was the most important book he had ever written and the most exciting that the publisher had come across. As early as July 1919, Papini was predicting "an immense and lasting success" not only in Italy and in Europe, but far across the ocean in the United States of America.[104] And he was right: released in Italy just before Easter 1921, translated within a few years into all the most important languages, Papini's *Life of Christ* would indeed be an astonishing best seller.[105]

At the end of September 1920, having written 2,400 pages, Papini came to the final chapter, the crucifixion, "the last cry in earth's darkness."[106] In a letter to his friend Domenico Giuliotti, Papini vigorously denied rumors that he was about to submit the *Life of Christ* to the Congregation of the Index in the hopes of getting the Vatican's imprimatur and keeping the book off the list of forbidden literature.[107] In fact, he did something very much like that, arranging with the Jesuits (in particular with Father Enrico Rosa, the influential editor of *Civiltà cattolica*) to review the proofs together.[108] The vast distance between Papini and his *Life of Christ* and a writer like Fogazzaro, author of *The Saint*, could not be more evident. Fogazzaro had thought of his novel as a thorn in the side of Pius X's Church—an effort to stem the reactionary tide, if not actually push it toward modernism and reform;[109] Papini, on the other hand, delivered his version of the story of Christ to the Church of Benedict XV as if he were delivering a war machine. With all the zeal of the new convert, Papini offered his services to the Church's hoped-for restoration: a society in which faith would dissolve politics and modernity in the making of a new Middle Ages.[110]

"To recover some of the lost" was how Papini defined his goal for the *Life of Christ*.[111] We do not have any way of knowing how many of the readers of the two ponderous tomes had always been Catholics, and how many were lost souls brought back to the Church thanks to Papini's book. We do know that fifty thousand copies were sold in the first three months after publication, and twenty thousand more by the end of the year.[112] For the times, those were astonishing figures. "The *Life of Christ* has been bought and read by almost every priest in Chianti," a friend wrote to Papini in May 1921.[113] In August, another friend, enjoying a holiday near Arezzo, informed him, "My hotel possesses only two books: Artusi* and the *Life of Christ*."[114] And outside the hotel, his friend joked, among the firs and the beeches, under the pines and in the thickets, along the woodland paths and by the streams, in the hands of Gentiles, in the hands of Jews, among Christians, among skeptics—everywhere there were copies of the *Life of Christ*! "I see your satisfied, vindictive smile behind those thick, thick lenses."[115]

Papini had reason to be vindictive: the most important reviewers had quickly fallen on his book, tearing it to shreds.[116] Nor did critics change their tune in the following years. Few significant books published in Italy between the First World War and the Second got such unanimously negative reviews as the *Life of Christ*. Papini's longtime colleague Ardengo Soffici merely complained about the book's "bad taste."[117] But other, less friendly readers (Gramsci among them) were repelled by what they saw as Papini's phony Christianity and his hypocrisy.[118] Yet others pilloried the wild expressionism of the entire tale, right down to

---

Translator's note: Pellegrino Artusi's cookbook *La Scienza in cucina e l'Arte di Mangiar bene,* first published in 1891, was a classic thirty years later, as it still is today.

the grand finale of the Crucifixion, with "Jesus's muscles straining and his joints dislocating on the cross."[119] Even among Catholics there was a certain reserve, although it was mostly rather quietly expressed, for the overall reaction among ecclesiastical authorities was generally enthusiastic.[120] Although Papini was offered a professorship of Italian literature at the newborn Catholic University of the Sacred Heart as well as the editorship of the review *Vita e Pensiero*,[121] Father Gemelli himself disliked the "industrialism" of the *Life of Christ*[122]—that is, the marketing logic that inspired the book, as we would say today.

Not even the sharpest minds of that generation understood that Papini's expressionism and his "industrialism" were themselves signs of the times, and that Papini's genius lay in his intuition that an unthinkable (yet strangely contemporary) theme—the life of Jesus—could be given stylistic pizzazz and commercial appeal. Where that was understood, oddly enough, was in the Protestant United States of America, which Papini had predicted would be a fertile market for his ever-so-Catholic book. Charlie Chaplin immediately grasped the entertainment potential of the *Life of Christ*,[123] and in 1923 urged his producers to make a film of the story, starring no less than Chaplin himself as Jesus. The little tramp with bowler hat and cane? Charlie Chaplin, whom many thought to be Jewish, as Papini's Christ? It was all too much for Hollywood to digest, and in the end nothing was done with the proposal.[124]

On the Italian market in 1921, there was only one book that could challenge the success of the *Life of Christ*: Pitigrilli's novel of sex and sin, *Cocaine*.[125] And despite the huge differences of subject, style, and literary value (not to mention the fact that Papini was famous while Pitigrilli was a mere beginner), the two books drew on a common culture. Both sought to engage the reader with moral scandal. Both focused on the body as a way to arouse the senses. Above all, both books reflected, on the literary front, the deepest scars of the trauma of the Great War. The profound repugnance of any idea of historical progressivism; the morbid attraction of the putrid, the rotten, the filthy; the obsessive need for an enemy with which to do battle; the obsession, too, with a conspiracy that must be unmasked, the rage against the traitor who must be punished—all these were themes that Pitigrilli played out in

mawkish detail, while Papini gave them a furious, and in his own way splendid, interpretation.[126]

In a note to readers at the front of his book, Papini wrote that he would like to create the conditions for a "second coming."[127] At the end of the book he goes even further, praying that Jesus will return to earth "if only briefly, a sudden appearance followed immediately by a sudden departure": "We pray that you will return once more among the men who killed you, among the men who continued to kill you, to bring all of us, assassins in the dark, the light of true life."[128] Words like these—as rhetorical as they were—could not but seem to evoke the wonderful news that had begun to circulate in southern Italy beginning in the winter of 1918–19. How could they not make readers think of Padre Pio, the living Christ? And what about the prophecy that the Capuchin friar would not live beyond his thirty-third year—which, as it happened, would be 1920? Although Giovanni Papini never mentions Padre Pio (and perhaps did not yet know of his existence),[129] he certainly spoke the same language as the pilgrims streaming by the thousands down to the Gargano Peninsula.

Just as he was about to send the *Life of Christ* to press, Papini had received a particularly poignant letter in the mail from Paris. The letter came from a war veteran with ambitions to be a poet, who, before taking a job at the Italian foreign ministry, had worked for a while as a correspondent for *Il Popolo d'Italia*—in part because he admired Mussolini, the editor, in part to pay the rent. From Paris, the young Giuseppe Ungaretti wrote to Papini about Christianity and love. Postwar Italy, so fractured, so little victorious, needed very badly to hear someone say: make of your love a God! Whoever that someone might be, he would himself be a new Christ figure: "He will be Jesus . . . who is an Italian creature." No people in the world were as capable of love as the Italians. "This love which is a wound, a balm, a yoke," a love that puffed them up, that strangled them, that burst their hearts like a curse, love that roared like a tiger and mewed like a kitten—theirs was a love that no one should ever be allowed to transform into a mere "knickknack for the sitting room." "If that were to happen," Ungaretti wrote, "peace might enter our hovels. But this land of ours would be as empty as a monastery full of friars."[130]

Ungaretti's words were not just poetical, but also political.[131] Historians ought to bear them in mind as they seek to reconstruct the mixture of disappointment and hope, premonitions and fears, sensibilities and faiths that came together in the 1920s to make Mussolini a charismatic figure[132]—so charismatic that finally an entire nation was draped in clerico-fascist garb. But Ungaretti was wrong about at least one thing. In the fall of 1920, not all monasteries were empty. Certainly not the Capuchin monastery of San Giovanni Rotondo, where a complex game of love and hatred was being played out.

3. JESUS'S SHOCK TROOPS?

In the fall of 1920, little San Giovanni Rotondo would find itself scrutinized in newspapers up and down the Italian peninsula, drawing attention even inside the great hall of Parliament in Rome. The reason for this newfound notoriety was far more bloody than Padre Pio's stigmata: on October 14, a massacre took place in San Giovanni's main square. It was the most deadly of the many massacres of Italy's *biennio rosso*, the "two red years" of 1919–20 when labor struggles erupted all over the country.[1]

The dynamics of the San Giovanni massacre were much like those of all the others in that dramatic period, when Italy, nominally governed by the Liberals, was in fact a no-man's-land torn between "Soviet" revolution and Fascist revolution. There had been local elections earlier in October, and the people of San Giovanni were riled up, their political passions at a fever pitch. On one side were the Socialists, who had won the elections but not by much. On the other was the conservative bloc of the so-called Fascio d'Ordine, which in San Giovanni was composed of the Popular Party (the Catholics) allied with the Liberals and the veterans' association. Caught in the middle, as often happened in Italy in those times, were the men of the institutions: the special commissioners, the carabinieri, and the ordinary police officers, all of whom could appreciate the grave threat to public order yet were unable to prevent the explosion of violence. On the morning of October 14, the massacre they were expecting arrived. There was a Socialist march, flanked by an anti-Socialist march; a knife was unsheathed; two bombs went off; the troops fired—and eleven farmhands were left dead on the ground, all of them belonging to the side of the reds.

At the other end of town, a kilometer from the main square, the Capuchin monastery of San Giovanni was physically removed from the deadly events. As for Padre Pio, the massacre that took place not far from his cell did not seem to affect him at all—just as the Great War scarcely seems to have grazed the priest-soldier Francesco Forgione. Nowhere in his correspondence with his spiritual advisers is there any mention of the events of October 14. Yet the San Giovanni massacre did have two crucial connections with Padre Pio. In August, a public gesture by the "Saint" had sealed the alliance of the parties in the Fascio against the Socialists. Then, just a few weeks after the massacre, the chief of the Fascio's militiamen in Foggia joined Padre Pio's entourage. It was a trial run for what clerico-fascism would eventually become on a national scale.

The Anchorite Dispensing Blessings

It was August 15, 1920, the feast of the Assumption of the Virgin. An automobile escorted by the *mutilati*—the war-wounded—and other veterans was slowly making its way along the road that separates the Capuchin monastery from the main square of San Giovanni. Crowds thronged the way, hoping to get a look at Padre Pio. What had motivated him to leave his cloister? He had not come to take part in a liturgical function; he had ventured out merely because he felt like doing so, a decision that would never be explained in all the letters he exchanged with his advisers at the time.[2] When the car arrived at the square, it stopped so that the "holy one" could get out, and the war veterans gathered around Padre Pio, pushing their veterans' association banners toward him. The friar raised his right hand—gloved, as always, to hide the stigmata—and made the sign of the cross over the banners.[3]

In Italy's overheated political climate during the summer of 1920, there was nothing innocent about Padre Pio's gesture. At a time when most of the clergy tended to be cautious about politics, confining their role in holiday celebrations to the liturgical,[4] the Capuchin friar with the stigmata was taking sides in a very bold way. The political microcosmos of San Giovanni had recently suffered a serious split. As late as the fall of 1919, local Socialists had marched alongside the veterans'

associations as they took over and occupied untilled fields and state lands. These occupations by landless farmers and veterans amounted to a huge social uprising—and in the towns around Foggia, particularly in San Giovanni Rotondo, the revolt was bigger and more heartfelt than anywhere else in Italy.[5] But by the summer of 1920, a bitter conflict between the groups had arisen, and moderate newspapers had begun to depict San Giovanni Rotondo as the epicenter of anarchy. The landowners, not content with the efforts at mediation by the prefect, were turning more and more to private militias to defend their property,[6] while the local veterans, led by the *mutilato* Giuseppe Caradonna, switched to the side of the landowners and began to organize the first Fascist *squadre*.[7] When Padre Pio blessed the pennants and flags of the veterans in the town's main square, he was announcing— within the small horizons of San Giovanni Rotondo—a preference in the epochal battle between the veterans' movement and the Socialists, a battle that would have national implications.

Elsewhere in Italy, that August 15 was a bloody day. At the little town of Abbadia San Salvatore on Mt. Amiata (the very same place where David Lazzaretti had been gunned down a half century before),[8] a Socialist demonstration degenerated into an antireligious frenzy. A small procession of Catholics following a statue of the Virgin—most of them women, most of them elderly—was savagely attacked by the "reds." They had no trouble overwhelming the few carabinieri present and didn't hesitate to kill a priest, Angelico Galassi, whose body was left in front of the church. According to a later reconstruction of the events by a Fascist author, "a mob of thousands" assaulted other priests and law enforcement officials. At the end of the day, the death toll, in addition to Galassi and one of the "drunken demonstrators," included a carabinieri officer, a clerk, a field hand, and a two-year-old child.[9]

The dramatic events at Abbadia San Salvatore were not the only occasion on which the Socialists made violent antireligious and anticlerical attacks. In rural Italy, the Socialist antagonism against the Catholic Popular Party frequently took the form of physical aggression against the priests, who were seen as covert soldiers of the Church in the political arena.[10] At San Giovanni Rotondo, as we have seen, this covert influence had been made overt. Right after the massacre of October 14, the *Corriere delle Puglie* would note that the "electric atmosphere" in San Giovanni was partly due to the bitter struggles for land, but also to the Socialists' aversion to Padre Pio, "an anchorite from these parts who is considered a holy man and whose hermitage is visited by pilgrims."[11] Was this emphasis on Padre Pio merely the slant given to events by a newspaper that openly supported the conservatives? Probably not; the Socialist national party paper *Avanti!* took a similar angle, describing the "little village" on the Gargano as a place "well-known in Italy for the would-be miracles of Padre Pio," miracles that had enriched "numerous speculators."[12] All the evidence suggests that the presence of the Capuchin friar and the unending influx of his followers helped to radicalize the local political conflict.

As the October 3 municipal and provincial elections approached, Socialist propaganda rose to a paroxysm of anticlerical hatred. According to a witness who spoke to police after the events, people in the streets of San Giovanni were heard to say that proletarian knives would shed the blood not only of the bourgeoisie but of the priests, and that once the clergy had been eliminated churches would be converted to barns for the animals.[13] Of course, such rhetoric was common among the hard-liners during the *biennio rosso* and didn't necessarily imply that the threats would be carried out. As the Socialist leader Filippo Turati once put it, the Socialists were particularly good at carrying out "revolutions of words" while the Fascists excelled at "revolutions of blood."[14] Still, outbreaks of violence like that at Abbadia San Salvatore showed that the Socialists, too, could hurt people when they wanted to.

Like other nearby towns on the wide, flat plain of the Tavoliere and on the Gargano Peninsula—San Severo, San Marco in Lamis, San Nicandro—the town of San Giovanni Rotondo was a stronghold of the Socialist extremists, led by the fiery figure of national MP Leone Mucci.[15] In a particularly provocative gesture just a few days before the elections, Mucci decided to drive through the town in a car draped in red at the precise moment when the supporters of the Fascio were holding a rally. "Some fistfights broke out," *Corriere delle Puglie* reported, and when the Socialist MP tried to escape he was dragged out of his car and beaten by the hostile crowd.[16] After such treatment, Mucci must have savored his party's triumphant victory in the elections. The province of Foggia was then one of the reddest in Italy, and the Socialists obtained a majority in twenty-nine towns out of forty.[17] San Giovanni Rotondo was one of these, although the Socialist victory was not overwhelming: 1,070 votes to 874. It was enough to make the winners a little high-handed, ready to deride their adversaries in public, but not enough to keep the losers from acting pugnacious and charging that the vote had been meddled with.

The new city council was due to be seated for the first time on October 14, and the Socialists—perhaps in revenge for the attack on Mucci a few days before, or simply because they appreciated the power of a symbol—let it be known they intended to fly the red flag, rather than the Italian *tricolore,* from the balcony of city hall. Leaders of the Popular Party and of the veterans' association warned they would punish anyone who so dishonored the national flag. Neither the prefect's office nor the chief of the local carabinieri barracks thought that this threatened war of the flags was to be taken lightly. The prefect's office telegraphed the subprefect of San Severo, and the barracks chief got in touch with the carabinieri lieutenancy to sound the alarm and call for reinforcements. PARTY OF ORDER THREATENS TO FIRE WEAPONS, warned the man from the prefect's office.[18] EXPECT ARMED VIOLENCE

BY PARTY OF ORDER, wrote the carabinieri inspector, too worried about what was happening to note the paradox in his message.[19] The carabinieri had no more than eleven officers in San Giovanni, and the local chief's telegraph message called for reinforcements of thirty officers plus a functionary from the Ministry of the Interior to take charge of public order.

As often happened during the *biennio rosso*, the men charged with order by the Liberal state foresaw tragedy but could not prevent it—or rather, they chose not to.

A Revolution of Words

The guardians of law and order in San Giovanni were convinced that the threatened war of the flags was a serious matter. Indeed, it *was* serious, not only because it reflected deep divisions within the community but also because the material objects themselves—those pieces of colored fabric—were precious vectors of identity. As historians have observed, the most virulent conflicts of those years took place when a mayor or a municipal government decided to run up the red flag, or simply not to run up the *tricolore*.[20] Illiteracy, which was still widespread, especially in the countryside, meant that a flag could become a veritable icon. Monuments to the war dead were another nexus of conflict between 1918 and 1922, the sites of innumerable battles and scuffles for the symbolic conquest of public space.[21] The scars of the Great War and developments on the international front had only made people more acutely sensitive to the value of these symbols. In the eyes of the Socialists, the red flag was all the more potent in light of the extraordinary news coming from the East, filling them with hopes of "doing as they did in Russia."[22] As the Fascists saw it, to show contempt for the Italian flag was to profane the sacred fatherland, while the "red rag" revealed the human and political squalor of the Bolshevik "rabble."[23]

As October 14 approached, the Socialists of San Giovanni made it clear that when the new city council was seated, not only would they hang the red flag from the balcony, but "the soviet system would commence."[24] According to the noisiest local Bolshevik hard-liners, the town was not to be, as the queues of pilgrims outside the monastery thought,

the first in Italy to welcome a new Christ, but the first to welcome the New World. The Bolsheviks of San Giovanni bragged they would storm the carabinieri barracks and redistribute the weapons among the "red guards," then attack the houses of the rich, dividing up the spoils equally—"including the women of the bourgeoisie." At any rate, this was the version of their plans that the local chief of the carabinieri gave to investigators after the massacre. If they won the elections, he said, the Socialists intended to govern "in the manner of the soviet councils": "in other words, they would have no regard for law and authority."[25]

What is striking about the propaganda of the Bolsheviks of San Giovanni Rotondo is its fundamentally religious language.[26] From the late nineteenth century, Socialist propaganda had often used much the same imagery as Catholic proselytizing,[27] and the "Sovietism" espoused by the rural Socialists of San Giovanni was rife with the local Italian traditions they knew. In their cosmology, decidedly more anticlerical than anti-Christian, the enemy was not Jesus but the priest—that is, a church establishment they perceived to be aligned with conservative forces. Their goal was the victory of Good (peace, progress, brotherhood) over Evil (war, reaction, selfishness). Speaking at the Italian Socialist Party national congress in Bologna in October 1919, one delegate declared that in Lenin's Russia "the word has been made flesh." He got more applause than the Socialist luminary Filippo Turati, who urged his comrades not to think of *soviet* as a "magic word."[28] Even the hard-liners' most revolutionary goal in the years just after the Great War—to socialize land—could take on Christian colors. At San Severo, twenty miles away from San Giovanni Rotondo, the headquarters of the farm-workers' league were decorated with red-draped portraits of Marx, Engels, and Jesus Christ.[29]

In the little world of San Giovanni in the fall of 1920, Socialists and anti-Socialists were far more like each other than either side would have wanted to admit. Socially, both parties sprang largely from the same stratum: the rural masses, the demobilized army of soldier-peasants. Anthropologically, too, they were similar, two communities whose core beliefs were held with a religiously intense fervor. The Socialists expected that the Bolshevik system would miraculously heal the world and make it right; the anti-Socialists expected their miracles to come from Padre Pio; and both lived in what Father Gemelli would have called "an atmosphere of suggestion." Completely alien to secular cul-ture (the percentage of active laborers in San Giovanni who could not read or write was 92 percent),[30] the marching troops of the two tiny armies were equally distant from Max Weber's rational, "disenchanted" modern world.

The fact that both sides came from the rural masses would harden the conflict. The farmworkers who dreamed of miracles and rebirths had historically shown themselves capable of terrible acts of violence. The main square of San Giovanni Rotondo was called the Place of the Martyrs after the tragic events that had marked southern Italy's pas-sage from Bourbon rule to that of the new Savoy king Victor Emman-uel II in 1860. On October 21 of that year, the day of the vote that would decide whether the south joined Italy, a mob of farmhands back-ing the Bourbon crown attacked the supporters of Victor Emmanuel and of Garibaldi and killed twenty-two "gentlemen" and members of the national guard. When the Garibaldini regained control of the town, their revenge was similarly savage: they killed ten Bourbon supporters.[31] Sixty years later, the memory of the two slaughters was still fresh. After the October 14, 1920, massacre, a local doctor explained to a police inspector sent from Rome that "the population, of Saracen origin, easily rises to violence" and "once they begin, they kill without measure . . . as happened in 1860 in this same month."[32]

Francesco Morcaldi—an army lieutenant working at the Ration Board of San Giovanni who was active in the Popular Party, and who will play an important role in the story of Padre Pio to follow—later said that the most responsible members of the Fascio had tried to cool down their followers, telling them not to worry about the Socialist threat to raise the red flag at city hall, but that many militants of the Popular Party "and above all the members of the veterans' association" were ready to "get out their carbines" to prevent the "reds" from putting up their flag.[33] Another witness of the events, a sergeant with the municipal guard, told the police that it was the local clergy, adept at controlling the Fascio's political mood, who took the most intransigent positions,[34] and then left town on the night of October 13. "The priests are leaving because they're scared" was the verdict of the farmworkers on the other side.[35]

As if in slow motion, the actors on the scene thus prepared themselves for the coming conflict. The carabinieri got their reinforcements, but right from the start they were not really impartial, having been placed under the command of a certain commissioner Matteo Bevere, known for backing the landowners and hostile to the Socialists.[36] The Fascio, composed of the Popular Party supporters and the veterans, was led by the landowner Ettore Fiorentino, who as the boss of the veterans' cooperative was handing out arms to his men—including hand grenades, the fetish-weapon of the Arditi shock troops.[37] The Socialist forces, meanwhile, were barely armed but made up for it with their verbal braggadocio. Their ranks included not only men but also women, in the best anarchist-unionist tradition. "The women were the most threatening, talking about what their husbands would do," the carabinieri inspector reported.[38] The husbands, meanwhile, didn't hold back in their revolution of words. "Just you wait, by tomorrow I'll be having three chickens a day," one Socialist militant declared, according to a witness. "He meant that he'd be deflowering three girls a day."[39] "When they talked about having chickens, they meant they intended to rape young women of the bourgeoisie," explained Reverend Giovanni Miscio, a section leader of the Popular Party.[40] It was a kind of retaliation for the legendary prerogative of the *jus primae noctis*, the right the landowners claimed to bed the daughters of the farmhands.[41]

Having heard threats of such crimes and such punishments, is it any surprise that the local police and the carabinieri stood a priori with the Fascio, even pretending to believe that the Socialist women would have been thrilled by the extramarital exploits of their men? On the plain of the Tavoliere and the Gargano Peninsula, the inhabitants had a reputation for ferocity so extreme it could sound like a biblical scourge. "The population here is blood-thirsty, especially the shepherds and farm hands, so any threats coming from those elements are to be believed," Reverend Miscio stated.[42] On the one side, there were promises of a world turned upside down; on the other, vows to restore order and authority. Is it any wonder that the guardians of the law suspected the Socialists, sympathized with the Fascists, and always aimed their guns first at the militants on the left?[43] By the end of 1920, the total dead in political disorders nationwide numbered 172 Socialists, 10 members of the Popular Party, 51 bystanders, 51 police officers, and just 4 Fascists.[44] The results of the massacre at San Giovanni Rotondo—eleven "reds" dead out of eleven— reflected, on the local level, the unwritten national rule.

A Revolution of Blood

> When it became clear that the Socialist Party intended to launch its program of tyranny and violence, and members were heard to say that they planned to break into the houses of the bourgeoisie and rape their women and loot and kill, as they did in 1860, it was thought to be wise not to let them take the first step, but to keep them under control from the moment they began to talk . . . The Socialist Party needs to know that the middle classes do not intend to suffer the same fate as those slaughtered in 1860.

Giovanni Giuliani—public notary and ex-Liberal turned Popular Party man who had helped create the Fascio d'Ordine in San Giovanni

Rotondo—spoke loud and clear when he took the witness stand to talk about the October 14 massacre. The Socialists had terrorized the good people of the town, he said, raising the specter of revolution. During the election campaign, MPs like Leone Mucci and Michele Maitilasso had pumped into San Giovanni the corrosive ideas of communism and Leninism. After they won, local Socialists had spread the word among farmworkers and shepherds that a revolution would take place the very instant they took over in city hall. Their plans had included not just occupation of the land and the creation of soviet councils, but much more. "The women had publically declared they would sack the houses of the wealthy," Giuliani testified, and had said that "their husbands would wear red neckties dipped in the blood of the bourgeoisie." The Fascio had merely acted in self-defense.[45]

That was also the line taken by the moderate press in the days after the massacre. In *Avvenire delle Puglie*, for example, the events of the Piazza dei Martiri were reconstructed with such heavy-handed bias as to be almost caricature. The crowd that assembled in front of city hall had been a "drunken mob" of Socialists waving their red flags and singing "idiotic subversive anthems," the newspaper wrote. The police had done what they could to contain the wild crowd, but then suddenly, "with the flash of a dagger, a carabiniere fell" and two hand grenades were thrown. The "red rag" was dragged toward city hall. The support- ers of the Fascio, who had come out onto the piazza to stand behind the Italian colors, decided it was better to withdraw to the headquarters of the veterans' association in order to avoid any further violence. The police, needless to say, had applied only the minimum force necessary.[46]

The Socialist paper *Avanti!*, on the other hand, saw the massacre of San Giovanni Rotondo as the consequence of a malign political, social, and religious alliance among "landowners, artisans and priests, monks and nationalists." In the period leading up to the elections, this alliance had generated "an organization new to the civilized world" called the Arditi di Cristo—"Christ's Shock Troops"—"complete with a black flag and papal insignia." In spite of these paramilitaries of the Arditi di Cristo and the incessant efforts of the priests and the friars "who are abundant in that town," the Socialists had won the election on October 3, so the leaders of the Fascio had decided to take their revenge

on the very day the new city council was to be seated. They had a helping hand from the man in charge of law and order, the "infamous Commissioner Bevere," who had already carried out anti-Socialist maneuvers
in the nearby towns of San Marco in Lamis and San Nicandro. All was
set for Piazza dei Martiri to become a new place of martyrdom.
When the two groups of demonstrators approached each other, *Avanti!*
reported, several bombs were heard to go off, and the rioters on the side
of the Fascio quickly withdrew, opening the way for the police to fire
on a helpless bunch of Socialist field hands.[47]

That the police did fire, and that they only hit militants of the left, is
undisputed. According to a October 20 report by the prefect of Foggia
to the minister of the interior, the carabinieri fired only as a last resort
after the Socialist militants—some six hundred people—attacked them
first with knives, then with hand grenades. "The forces showed restraint
and then forbearance to the point of self-sacrifice," the prefect of Foggia
told his superiors in Rome. "Weapons were used only when some officers were disarmed and others were about to undergo the same, and
after many of their companions had been wounded and even lay dying."
As the prefect described it, the police had been forced to fire on the
crowd to save themselves.[48]

As we shall soon see, this first account of the events was by no
means unbiased. But first let us look at the eleven dead of San Giovanni
Rotondo: name, gender, age, and in the words of the Foggia prefect, "a
brief social description." As the prefect listed them, there was Michele
Fiore, 23, "poor peasant." Giuseppe Santoro, 37, "poor peasant." Giovanni
Cassano, 63, "poor peasant." Francesco Crifa, 65, "farmer, well-off."
Michele Musciale, 50, "peasant with small income." Michele Pinnelli,
40, "poor peasant." Antonio Santoro, 75, "poor peasant." Giovanni
Siena, 22, "poor peasant." Filomena Tortorelli, 23, female, "poor peas-
ant." Maria Miglionico, 23, female, "small income." Paolo Gorgolione,
35, "small income."[49]

The list is both telling and poignant. It confirms beyond doubt that
women were present in the Socialist ranks at San Giovanni Rotondo. It
bears witness to the fact that there were militants in all age groups. It
confirms that hard-line ideas appealed to the most dispossessed of the
rural masses. From other information sent to Rome by the prefecture,

we can deduce the collective identity of the Socialist militants involved in the incident. This was, overwhelmingly, the rural proletariat of San Giovanni, with only a rare middle-class participant. Among the twenty-nine wounded militants, the prefect counted twenty-two "poor peasants," one "poor shepherd," one "poor carter," one "poor housewife," three peasants "with small incomes," and one "shoemaker." Ever so slightly up the social scale were the militants arrested for having provoked the disorders—all these, too, from the Socialist camp: fourteen peasants (including three women), three students, two masons, a baker's wife, a shepherd, a "pyrotechnician," a guard, a property owner, a doctor, and a law graduate. As for the nineteen carabinieri injured in the course of the conflict (the ones the prefect had said "lay dying"), one did indeed die that day, but none of the others required more than a few days of medical treatment.[50]

The massacre at San Giovanni Rotondo was such a serious event that news of it soon traveled beyond the Gargano mountains. In Rome, the government immediately moved to investigate what had happened. On October 25, Don Luigi Sturzo, the founder and political secretary of the Popular Party, wrote a letter to the man effectively responsible for public order in Italy, Interior Undersecretary Camillo Corradini,[51] in which he denied that the Popular Party of San Giovanni Rotondo had played any part whatever in the massacre.[52] Popular Party adherents, he insisted, had taken not even "the slightest" role in the events, which were to be blamed exclusively on the Socialists, both the "town hotheads" and the "local members of parliament."[53] But it seems the government was not entirely convinced by Don Sturzo's claims, for the police service's very best investigator was sent to carry out an inquiry on the massacre.

Vincenzo Trani was an honest cop[54]—as different as he could be from the anti-Fascist stereotype of police as reactionaries and sell-outs to Mussolini. The son of small landowners from south of Rome, an officer with some thirty years of service, now nearing sixty, Trani was a faithful servant of the Italian state. In his long career he had earned many honors, from a gold medal for aiding the victims of the devastating 1908 Messina earthquake, to a knighthood in the Saints Maurice and Lazarus hospitaller order. Arriving in San Giovanni Rotondo just six days after the massacre, Trani sought neither to reassure nor to please anyone, but merely to understand what had happened.[55] After the obligatory visit to the injured in the hospital and a quick meeting with local officials, Trani shook off all those keen to explain the events to him from their own party perspective. Going out alone, he explored "the streets, even the most remote corners of town, to question ordinary people incognito."[56]

Inspector Trani's report lets us follow his walk through the town after tragedy had bloodied those streets. Like the protagonist of a crime novel, Trani was a man with a ponderous step, a sleepy, slightly foolish air about him, the public employee's threadbare clothes—but also a rare grasp of how the world works.[57] He first questioned the humble people of town, then talked to the elite, from the public notary to the local doctor, and finally consulted the records of the prefect and carabinieri. Today the most precise picture of the massacre of San Giovanni, of those dead who lay so near and yet so far from Padre Pio, comes to us not from the tendentious newspaper articles of the time, nor from the obsequious rhetoric of the prefect's reports, but from the dry and bureaucratic yet also honest and perceptive prose of that near-invisible witness, Inspector General Vincenzo Trani.[58]

The first thing that Trani's report makes clear is that the group of about a hundred San Giovanni veterans who went to Piazza dei Martiri that day were intent on provocation. Just when the Socialist throng had decided that they would not, after all, raise their red flag on the city hall balcony, the leader of the veterans came out and challenged them, and a fight broke out. The Socialist arsenal was mostly made of sticks and stones; if someone did have a knife or a revolver, it went unused, and "no harm was done to the Fascists or the forces of order." As for the detonations heard by everyone in the square, the sounds assumed to be the explosions of hand grenades, "they seem to have been caused by ordinary fireworks often set off during festivals." In fact, as Trani pointed out, a pyrotechnician was among those arrested.[59]

In his meticulous reconstruction of the gunfire that followed, Trani writes that "a large part of the responsibility" belonged to Deputy Commissioner Carmelo Romano, who first fired on the Socialists.

Commissioner Matteo Bevere—who had been busy trying to prevent the red flag from going up instead of keeping the two factions apart—was almost as much to blame. Trani didn't think that either side present in the square had come with a premeditated plan to provoke a massacre, but he did not completely exclude the possibility that there had been an unholy pact between the police and the veterans—the first ready to shoot if the second group created the circumstances. And perhaps this was why, reasoned Trani, the Fascists were able to rapidly withdraw from the square "which was supposed to become a bloodbath." Perhaps that was why "none of them were killed or wounded, while all the dead came from the Socialist ranks, as did the injured."[60]

Trani's report thus supported the Socialists' version of what had happened. He did, however, categorically deny the Socialist allegation that the clerico-fascists of San Giovanni belonged to a paramilitary organization called the Arditi di Cristo. Such a charge was not entirely unthinkable in those turbulent postwar years. In addition to the genuine shock troops of the Great War, the Arditi d'Italia (who would provide many of the Fascist movement's violent *squadristi*), the country had already seen the emergence of the Arditi del Popolo, dedicated to the anarchist cause,[61] and the Arditi Bianchi, linked to the Popular Party and active around the northern city of Treviso in the spring of 1920.[62] However, Inspector Trani, who had investigated the matter, told the minister of the interior that he had found no trace of the Arditi di Cristo. There were many red flags in San Giovanni Rotondo; there was a white flag belonging to the Popular Party; there were two green, white, and red Italian flags belonging to the veterans; and, in the local headquarters of the Arditi d'Italia, there was a black standard embroidered with a silver eagle. But there was no flag at all with a papal insignia. The fabled "shock troops of Christ," Trani concluded, were probably a legend that grew out of the events, "well-known to all," that had taken place in the Piazza dei Martiri the previous August, when Padre Pio had blessed the Italian flag and the standard of the Arditi veterans "in a solemn patriotic celebration." Beyond that episode, he could find no more substance to reports about Christ's shock troops.[63]

On December 4, 1920, Interior Undersecretary Corradini appeared in the Chamber of Deputies to answer questions from Socialist MPs Mucci and Maitilasso about the "premeditated massacre" at San Giovanni Rotondo.[64] There is no reason to think that by this point Corradini had not seen at least a summary of Trani's report. And yet, rather than openly confront the political implications of the affair, Corradini withdrew behind a bureaucratic defense of the ministry's response. The police reinforcements that local authorities had requested in advance of October 14 had been deployed in good time, he said. On the day of the demonstration, apart from a few small technical errors, the forces of order had discharged their duties well. The blame for the massacre must therefore rest entirely on the Socialist agitators, who were determined to raise the red flag at city hall, inciting the fury of the veterans and exacerbating a political conflict that had already been poisoned by the recent electoral campaign.[65]

When Corradini finished his remarks, the Socialists took the floor to dispute the undersecretary's version of the events. That day, for the first time, Padre Pio of Pietrelcina was mentioned in the hall of Parliament. MP Michele Maitilasso, summoning up all the courtroom eloquence that an attorney could muster, described to the chamber the desolate rural town of San Giovanni Rotondo and its dubious Capuchin friar with the stigmata. It would take "hours and hours by carriage" or by car on terrible roads to reach this wretched place, he said, "known in Italy, if at all, for a certain Padre Pio, a monk who attracts men and women with his fame as a miracle worker." In Maitilasso's telling, the massacre had been followed by "a reign of terror" in the town, with Inspector Gigante "walking up and down like Napoleon with his saber in hand," Commissioner Bevere hunting down the remnants of the Socialist militants, and the Arditi di Cristo ready to unsheathe their daggers once again.[66] A second Socialist deputy, Domenico Majolo, rose to blame the Fascio d'Ordine of San Giovanni for the violence— "that bloc that runs from the patriotic veterans to Padre Pio and the Arditi."[67] In the ferocious Italian climate of late 1920, such speeches were inevitably tinged with propaganda. But in pointing to the political pact between the friars and the Fascists, they also contained a kernel of truth.

"If You Don't Know Who We Are . . ."

On the same day as the massacre in San Giovanni Rotondo, an episode of violence shook the city of Bologna. At an anarcho-Socialist demonstration called to commemorate the proletarian victims of the *biennio rosso* and to show solidarity with the soviet councils in Russia, militant extremists attacked a barracks housing the royal guard, killing a sergeant and an inspector.[68] From then on, Bologna's local political conflict would turn dramatically more brutal, and it would profoundly influence political developments on the national level.[69]

All around Italy, the ceremonies to celebrate the November 4 anniversary of the war's end were turning into pitched battles between nationalists and Socialists about whether to hoist the red flag or the *tricolore*.[70] The atmosphere was particularly tense in Bologna. After the barracks killing of October 14, there had been local elections on October 31. Just as in San Giovanni, the Socialists won, but the veterans also racked up a sizable number of votes; and, just as in San Giovanni, the two sides in Bologna were threatening a war of the flags. The Socialists promised that they would run up their red flag not only from the balcony of the city hall, the Palazzo d'Accursio, but also from the top of the Asinelli Tower. The veterans warned that they were ready to use force to defend the green, white, and red. As before, the police noted the danger but could not, or would not, prevent the conflict. On November 21, the day when the new city council was supposed to convene, veterans and Fascists attacked the Palazzo d'Accursio and fired on the Socialists. Not wishing to be shown up, the carabinieri and troopers also fired on the left-wing militants. The "red guards" responded with hand grenades. When the bitter fight was over, ten Socialists lay dead.[71]

The massacre in Bologna was thus virtually a carbon copy of the one in San Giovanni Rotondo. And at Palazzo d'Accursio, as in San Giovanni, the other side also had one victim: Giulio Giordani, a lawyer and interventionist in the years before the war, an officer wounded in battle and sent home with medals—a figure whom the Fascists would quickly elevate to the level of martyr to Mussolini.[72] Carlo Delcroix, the national leader of the Association of Disabled Veterans, was among the first to commemorate Giordani in specifically pro-Fascist terms.[73] Later, when the regime had solidified and its list of martyrs had grown,[74] there were worshippers of Giordani who saw him as much more than a hero: they saw him as a Christ figure. "Just as Christ died on the cross to redeem men, so he went to his death for the spiritual redemption of his country," one of his war buddies and political comrades, Alberto Del Fante, would write of Giordani in 1934.[75]

Giordani as Christ: a little piece of propaganda that wouldn't be worth mentioning here were it not for the fact that its author, Del Fante, would turn up again in the story of Padre Pio, first as a secular critic denouncing a scandalous fraud, then as a devout entrepreneur promoting the Capuchin friar's sainthood.[76] The link between Christian martyrology and Fascist martyrology, in fact, lies at the heart of the clerico-fascist alchemy. We've seen that the Socialists, although fiercely anticlerical, spoke a language steeped in religious imagery of brotherhood and peace. The Fascists, meanwhile, embraced the militant, physical side of Christian suffering. Centuries of Christian writing and iconography had blended faith and sacrifice, ecstasy and agony,[77] and after the Great War fascism inherited these traditions, adjusting them to its own ends. The martyred bodies of men mutilated in battle were particularly suited to their purposes.[78]

Carlo Delcroix was not the only famous wounded veteran to build a career as a Fascist official on his own injuries. Giuseppe Caradonna—captain in the grenadiers at the front, decorated with one bronze and three silver medals, twice wounded, an attorney in the Puglia city of Cerignola—quickly climbed the steps of postwar veterans' activism to become, first, a leader in the Association of Disabled Veterans, then a local Fascist potentate, and then, in the national elections of 1921, the sole Fascist deputy elected in the entire south of Italy.[79] And only a few weeks after the San Giovanni Rotondo massacre, Caradonna already had the bright idea of visiting that little town in the Gargano to celebrate with local Fascists.[80]

When the festivities were coming to a close, a young woman, Angela Serritelli, approached the illustrious veteran and invited him to the monastery of Santa Maria delle Grazie to meet Padre Pio, who was Angela's spiritual adviser. To a devout Catholic and fervent nationalist like Caradonna, the Capuchin friar's stigmatic wounds must have seemed very much like his own war injuries, one single ache of suffering and redemption. In any event, Padre Pio gave Caradonna a warm welcome. If we can believe an enduring Fascist legend, the friar told the Fascist boss that he approved of his activities with the veterans' association and added, "God always loves the strong and he galvanizes them when necessary."[81] What's certain is that the meeting inaugurated a solid relationship between the Capuchins of San Giovanni and the rising Fascist leader of the province of Foggia. Throughout the 1920s, Caradonna's wife, a Franciscan lay sister like Angela Serritelli, would often be a guest at the monastery, and Caradonna himself would visit San Giovanni as a pilgrim.

Caradonna's visit to Padre Pio helps to account for something that would otherwise be difficult to explain: how the friar with the stigmata attracted something more (and something worse) than a mere adoring mass of the faithful. Beginning in 1922, a genuine Praetorian guard would be mounted at San Giovanni Rotondo to prevent any attempts to remove Padre Pio from the monastery and transfer him elsewhere. This menacing presence, combined with memories of the massacre of October 14, made the authorities—both civil and ecclesiastical—so cautious about provoking any disorder that in fact they did virtually nothing. The prolonged impotence of both the Vatican hierarchy and the Italian state in dealing with the problem of Padre Pio can therefore be partly attributed to the unwritten pact sealed by the local Capuchins with Caradonna, who was destined with the rise of the Fascist regime to become the supreme boss of Foggia.[82]

Se nen ci canuscit' / uhè! pe la mala donna / nu sim' i fascist / de Peppin' Caradonna! "If you don't know who we are / hooray for the raunchy lady / we are the brave Fascists / of Peppino Caradonna!" So sang the *squadristi* of the Foggia plain during the run-up to national elections in the spring of 1921,[83] elections those militiamen would transform—thanks to police inaction—into a manhunt against the Socialist-Communists of the Tavoliere plain. (It would also be a personal duel between Caradonna himself and the most pugnacious of his adversaries, Giuseppe Di Vittorio, leader of the Cerignola farmhands and later Italy's foremost labor leader.)[84] Indeed, Caradonna's militiamen went so far as to field *squadre* mounted on horseback, the so-called cavalry of Puglia. In theory, these *squadre* were supposed to protect the landowners from the supposed Communist threat; in practice, they served to terrorize the rural population.[85] The wounded Great War hero received by Padre Pio in his monastery would thus play a decisive role in transforming Puglia's political conflicts into a civil war. And Caradonna's cavalry would parade again in October 1922, when they turned out enthusiastically for the March on Rome that brought Mussolini to power.[86]

More than one contemporary would remark on the way events in San Giovanni Rotondo took a political turn after the massacre of October 14, 1920. What attracted notice was not so much Caradonna's visit to Padre Pio—that remained private—but the determination with which the Fascio d'Ordine sought to overwhelm and destroy the Socialists. The Popular Party and the Fascists of San Giovanni even tried to overturn the 1920 election results, arguing that the Socialist Party wasn't fit to lead the town, that its "Sovietistic" propaganda had discredited it. They failed in that effort because they met with adamant resistance from Inspector Trani, who didn't intend to let the clerico-fascists circumvent the rule of law.[87] Meanwhile the Socialists went to Parliament to denounce the Fascio d'Ordine's attempt to cheat them out of the elections. They argued that this was proof that democracy was under threat not only in a remote town on the Gargano Peninsula but all around the country. "The massacre at San Giovanni Rotondo, in terms of the number of dead and wounded and the way it took place, is far more serious and significant than the recent events in Bologna," a Socialist deputy told the chamber.[88] It was serious because there had probably been a connivance between the militants of the Fascio and the official police forces. It was significant because Inspector Trani had been forced to impose his authority on the chief of the carabinieri and the judge, insisting they seat the city government that had been elected at the polls. The local authorities, it appeared, had been ready to sacrifice democratic procedure to the rule of the local tyrants.[89]

Beginning in the winter of 1920–21, the Fascist *squadre* all over Italy moved from defense to offense, from protecting landowners' property to attacking Socialist property.[90] These campaigns of conquest went on until they had totally annihilated the political and cultural edifice built up by the Italian left in twenty years of struggle.[91] While the police looked on, largely passive, the Fascists systematically destroyed the meeting halls of the leagues and cooperatives, burned down the party headquarters and employment boards, and attacked and humiliated union leaders and party officials. In some parts of the peninsula, such as Ferrara and the Po River delta, Fascist violence was played out as a display of virility: the Socialist adversary was to be reduced to the condition of an animal, physically degraded, sodomized. Defeated, diminished, and helpless, several "comical" left-wing militants could find nothing else to do but show up at the headquarters of the Fascio with the red flag rolled up under their arm, a "despicable offering" of an unconditional surrender.[92]

There were few left-wing activists willing to contradict their essentially pacific Socialist principles and reply to Fascist violence blow for blow—few, in short, ready to exchange a revolution of words for a revolution of blood. One exception was a clash that took place in Sarzana in July 1921, when the left-wing Arditi del Popolo took up arms against a punitive raid by some Tuscan *squadristi*. The *squadristi*, forced to flee, were pursued through fields and ditches, and a dozen of them were killed by local farmers.[93] Prime Minister Ivanoe Bonomi, who had replaced Giovanni Giolitti, ordered Inspector General Vincenzo Trani to carry out an inquiry into the events. Trani was every bit as evenhanded in Sarzana as he had been in San Giovanni Rotondo. He traced the terrible violence of the anti-Fascists to a widespread state of exasperation—not only among left-wing militants but among ordinary people—about the way the *squadre* ignored the rule of law, spread panic, and wantonly shed blood.[94]

For his report, Trani received death threats from the Fascists, who called him an "anti-Italian piece of junk," and was criticized by the prefect of Genoa, who went so far as to accuse him of colluding with the "subversives." Soon, he was jettisoned by the Bonomi government, which decided it preferred a more accommodating investigator.[95] Forcibly retired in February 1923, the inspector general would die, eight years later, without ever having been granted a pension.[96] The fate of the honest cop, in Mussolini's Italy, could be bitter.

4. HOLY MAN, HOLY OFFICE

In his anti-Fascist classic *March on Rome and Vicinity*, Emilio Lussu provides a vivid description of the moment when Italian democracy began to fail. The date was June 13, 1921. Lussu, just elected with the Sardinian Action Party, was in the halls of Parliament, passing through the great sitting room outside the Chamber of Deputies. Seated with two colleagues on a nearby banquette was the Communist Francesco Misiano—a Turin railway workers' union leader of Calabrian origins, a conscientious objector who had gone abroad to avoid fighting in the war and was then elected to Parliament as an antimilitarist. For the Fascists, Misiano was nothing more than a deserter, a coward of the worst sort. Exhorting the crowd from his balcony in occupied Fiume, Gabriele D'Annunzio himself had asked for his head.[1]

Suddenly a small platoon of Fascist MPs led by Roberto Farinacci, the boss of Cremona, headed toward Misiano with guns in hand and invited him to leave Parliament—for good. As the frightened Communist MP walked toward the exit, not a single other deputy nor any of the staff made the least move in his defense.[2]

Lussu then noticed the Fascist MP Giuseppe Caradonna, "pale and immobile, with his pistol in hand, as if lying in wait for someone," standing in the "narrow side hallway" through which Misiano could be expected to leave the building. Incredulous but unafraid—both Lussu and Caradonna had received medals for bravery at the front[3]—Lussu shouted at the Fascist boss from Puglia: "What are you doing? What are you doing?" "There was no reply. But it was clear: he was waiting for the Communist deputy to come through . . . I was in time to inform some of my colleagues and Misiano was able to leave by another door."[4]

From the time of the massacre in San Giovanni Rotondo, Caradonna and his mounted peasant militiamen had been regularly lining up outside the town's little Capuchin church to confess their sins to Padre Pio.[5] The Holy Roman Church, though, was not much interested in hushed meetings at the confessional between a Capuchin friar and a Fascist boss, nor in Caradonna's activities in Parliament. For Vatican authorities, it was far more urgent to find out the facts about Padre Pio's performance as a priest and mystic, about the five wounds inscribed on his body, and what his confreres and the lay sisters around him were up to. In that last year, a large and worrisome pile of documentation had been growing on the desks of the Holy Office, too large and worrisome for the tribunal of the faith to ignore.

And so while Caradonna and company strolled around Parliament, pistols in hand, settling accounts with Communists, a dignitary from the order of the Discalced Carmelites was traveling down to the Gargano from Rome to settle some very different accounts. The Holy Office had asked him to carry out what was being called an "apostolic visit" to San Giovanni Rotondo. In fact, his job would be to conduct no less than an inquisitorial review of the friar with the stigmata.

The Little Chemist

Serious suspicions had begun to collect around Padre Pio not long after the Holy Office received Father Gemelli's report that spoke of "a man whose field of knowledge is limited," a man of "infirm mind," a "psychiatric hospital mystic."[6] In sworn statements before Monsignor Salvatore Bella, the bishop of Foggia, two good Christians of that Puglia diocese had suggested there were sinister aspects to that stigmata-ridden body. Instead of the sweet perfume of violets, the scent of holiness that was supposed to issue from Padre Pio's cell, there were hints of acid and poisons, the smell of fraud and deceit.

The first statement was signed by Dr. Valentini Vista, the owner of a pharmacy in the center of Foggia. The pharmacist explained how he had come to know of Padre Pio after his brother had died in September

Foggia - Piazza Lanza

of 1918, and how he had hoped that the friar—who just in those very days had first received the stigmata—could intercede on behalf of his brother's soul. He had exchanged letters "frequently" with the Capuchin until, "as the rumors about the holy friar and his miracles spread widely" and a huge number of pilgrims began arriving in San Giovanni Rotondo, Padre Pio became too busy to keep up with his personal mail. And so, the pharmacist told Bishop Bella, he had traveled to San Giovanni himself in May 1919. He had met Padre Pio, "a very affable figure, very humble, very pious," and undertaken the sacred rites of penitence; yet the experience had left him feeling oddly puzzled and disappointed. He was struck by the "enormous . . . press of the crowds" in the vestry, and the "hasty," "utterly wrong" way Padre Pio conducted the confession. He thought there was nothing very special about the way the Capuchin behaved: "He asked me the same questions that all confessors do; in fact he asked me whether I was a Freemason or not."[7]

Dr. Valentini Vista then told the second part of his story. In the late summer of 1919, his cousin, twenty-eight-year-old Maria De Vito, "a very good young woman, and very religious," who herself was the owner of a pharmacy, had made a pilgrimage to San Giovanni. The young woman had stayed in the Gargano town for an entire month, sharing Padre Pio's daily routine, joining the circle of other devout women who had gathered around him. After De Vito returned home, she made a disconcerting request.

> When she came back to Foggia, she brought me greetings from Padre Pio and asked me, on his behalf and in sworn secrecy, to supply her some pure carbolic acid that he needed. She showed me a little bottle containing 100 grams, a bottle given to her by Padre Pio himself, to which was attached a seal with a poison sign (a skull and crossbones). I was supposed to fill the bottle with pure carbolic acid, which, as is known, is a poison that burns and has grave caustic effects when used in pure form. When I heard this request, it occurred to me that carbolic acid in that form could be used by Padre Pio to procure or irritate those wounds on his hands.[8]

Rumors of acids in Padre Pio's cell had already begun to circulate in Foggia in the spring of 1920, when Professor Morrica had published his own scientific doubts about the Capuchin's stigmata in the Neapolitan newspaper *Il Mattino*,[9] so Valentini Vista had been particularly struck by the friar's request for pure carbolic acid. Nevertheless, "because the friar in question was Padre Pio," the doctor convinced himself that Pio's need for the chemical must be based on innocent motives, and he gave his cousin the bottle with the acid. But his concerns widened into suspicion a few weeks later when Padre Pio made another request, once again under a vow of secrecy. This time, Padre Pio asked for four grams of veratrine.[10]

In his testimony before Monsignor Bella, Valentini Vista explained the chemical composition of this second product, a mixture of alkaloids derived from the medicinal plant hellebore (*Veratrum album*). It was, he noted, a highly caustic product. "Veratrine is so poisonous that only a doctor can decide whether to prescribe it," the pharmacist said, citing from a manual on drugs published in Naples in 1883. The manual indicated a dose of veratrine between one and five milligrams in tablet or liquid form for therapeutic purposes. "He writes of milligrams!" Dr. Valentini Vista exclaimed. "Padre Pio's request, instead, was for four grams!" And the friar had requested that "enormous quantity" of the poisonous material "without presenting any medical prescription whatsoever" and "in great secret." At that point Valentini Vista had decided to confide his doubts to his cousin Maria, asking her not to accept any more requests for medicines from Padre Pio. In the following year and a half, the pharmacist had not told anyone else of his grave suspicion that the friar was using one or both of the caustic substances "to procure or make more visible the stigmata on his hands." But when he heard that Monsignor Bella was soon to be transferred to the diocese of Acireale, the pharmacist, "spurred by conscience" and "in the interests of the Church," had decided to tell the bishop of his suspicions.[11]

The second statement taken by Monsignor Bella was sworn by Dr. Valentini Vista's cousin Maria De Vito, and it matched what the pharmacist had said. De Vito confirmed that she had spent a month at San Giovanni Rotondo in the summer of 1919, and that when she was about to leave, Padre Pio took her "to one side" and spoke "in great secret," "imposing on me the same vow of secrecy as the other monks in his monastery were sworn to." The friar had given De Vito an empty bottle, asking her to fill it with pure carbolic acid and send it back to him "by means of the driver who works for the bus line between Foggia and San Giovanni." As for what Padre Pio intended to do with the carbolic acid, he had told her it was "to disinfect the syringes he used to give injections to the novice friars under his supervision." "At the same time, he asked me to supply Valda tablets, Nasalina, etc., which I sent along with the carbolic acid," the young woman told Monsignor Bella. The request for four grams of veratrine had arrived about a month later, via one of the penitents returning from San Giovanni. De Vito spoke to Dr. Valentini Vista, who advised her not to send any more medicines to Padre Pio. He also told her not to speak to anyone else about the matter, "for it is possible our suspicions are rash."[12]

Were they rash, the suspicions of the good pharmacist and his devout cousin? The bishop of Foggia does not appear to have thought so, for he sent the two depositions to the Holy Office in Rome.[13] As a matter of fact, most of the local ecclesiastical hierarchy was skeptical about Padre Pio's reputation for saintliness. Father Pietro of Ischitella, the Capuchin minister provincial, had warned the minister general about the "fanaticism" and the "appetite for business" of the monks in

San Giovanni.[14] Meanwhile, the archbishop of Manfredonia, Monsignor Pasquale Gagliardi, had described the religious life of San Giovanni as being totally out of control, with lay sisters circulating in the streets with photographs of Padre Pio tied around their necks, and selling the photos and bloody handkerchiefs and other relics to the pilgrims. Monsignor Gagliardi had personally discovered a young woman—"between 17 and 20 years old," estimated the archbishop, who himself had a reputation for rather liking the fair sex—spending the night in the Capuchin monastery, supposedly to assist a friar who was "ill in bed." Which friar? Padre Pio, of course.[15]

Right from the start of Padre Pio's story, his detractors had deployed those time-honored accusations—sex and lucre—that crop up again and again over the centuries whenever a holy man is charged with fraud.[16] For forty years, the celestial perfume issuing from Padre Pio's cell and from his body would stink of sulfur to all those who saw his cult as a source of profit and his charisma as a carnal matter. But the first question that seemed urgent to the Holy Office, in light of the sworn depositions by Valentini Vista and De Vito, was the problem of the stigmata. The depositions had all the more weight because the bishop of Foggia had also enclosed a document that the twenty-first-century historian cannot pick up without a real twinge of excitement as he sits paging through the files of the Vatican archive for the Congregation of the Doctrine of the Faith (as the Holy Office is called today): the sheet of paper on which Padre Pio, at the time perhaps concerned he might not be able to speak privately to Maria De Vito, had written down, in black and white, his request for carbolic acid.

To the inquisitors of the Holy Office, this was the genuine "smoking gun," the clue the little chemist had left at the scene of the crime. "For Marietta De Vito, personal," Padre Pio had written on the envelope. Inside, on a single handwritten page, there is a briefer message than the kind of letter the Capuchin friar would usually send to his spiritual daughters.

> My dearest Maria,
> May Jesus comfort you always and bless you! I come to ask you a favor. I need to have from 200 to 300 grams of pure

carbolic acid to sterilize. Please send it to me Sunday by way of the Fiorentino sisters. Sorry to bother you.[17]

The Fiorentino sisters were members of that little circle of pious ladies closest to the friar with the stigmata.[18] If Padre Pio really needed carbolic acid to disinfect the syringes he used to give injections, why would he go about procuring it so indirectly? He could have simply asked the doctor of the Capuchins for a prescription rather than sending the request in secret to the cousin of a pharmacist-friend, and then having it transported to him in such a roundabout fashion. There was plenty to pique the curiosity of the Holy Office, which was probably already suspicious after receiving Father Gemelli's report. The prelates of the congregation certainly did not doubt the testimony of Dr. Valentini Vista and Maria De Vito, especially backed up by the handwritten note from Padre Pio. The records of the Holy Office also include the transcription of a second note written by Padre Pio to Maria De Vito, matching precisely what she had testified. "I shall need 4 grams of *veratrine*," wrote the friar. "I would be very grateful if you could procure it for me and send it to me quickly."[19]

The secretary of the Holy Office at this time was Cardinal Rafael Merry Del Val, and Cardinals Gaetano De Lai, Pietro Gasparri, and Willem Van Rossum were among the theologians charged with verifying the orthodoxy of one or another doctrinal stance. But the job of opening an inquisitorial review of Padre Pio fell to a man lower down in the Vatican hierarchy, the French priest Joseph Lemius. At sixty, Lemius had been for some years the procurator general of the Oblates of Mary Immaculate, as well as an adviser to the Congregations of the Propaganda Fide, of Rites, and of Education.[20] He went to work on the case of Padre Pio in the fall of 1920, as the shots fired by the police at the Socialist farmhands in San Giovanni Rotondo were echoing around Italy. On January 22, 1921, Father Lemius put his signature to the conclusions of his *Voto* on Padre Pio of Pietrelcina.

Close the Gates

Although he was little known outside the Vatican, inside the Church Father Lemius had a reputation as a big thinker. That reputation was well deserved: in 1907 he had written, on behalf of Pius X, the doctrinal passages of the *Pascendi dominici gregis*, an encyclical that would have a huge effect on the modern Catholic clergy.[21] In a display of real theological genius, Lemius had pulled together the scattered ideas of various reformers who were arguing that church doctrine and practice must be brought into the twentieth century, amalgamating them into a coherent doctrine that the encyclical labeled "modernism."[22] When the Church then closed its doors to reform, the threat of this modernist monster—which Lemius himself had, in a sense, created—was used to justify persecution of the reformers, now considered heretics.[23]

One of the few things that the modernists *had* worked out clearly, even without Lemius's help, was that they rejected all charismatic and miracle-working versions of Christianity. "Miracles are immoral," Paul Sabatier had gone so far as to assert in his *Life of St. Francis*, even as he was also writing that he considered the stigmata of St. Francis to be authentic wounds.[24] The Church of Rome, too—although it had responded very harshly to modernism[25]—had clearly understood the danger to its authority of popular enthusiasm for miracles and grace. The fact that someone as learned as Father Lemius was asked to conduct the investigation suggests that the Vatican was aware how sensitive the whole matter of popular cults could be.

At the same time, there was nothing new in the figure of the *consultor*, the adviser to the Holy Office. Lemius, part master theologian, part police inspector, belonged to a tradition that went back to the sixteenth century, in which the inquisitor, seated at a comfortable table in the papal palaces in Rome, passed judgment on the faith of a nun in Novara or a shoemaker in Pistoia by consulting written documents forwarded to him.[26] There was nothing new in the fact that the Vatican hierarchy wanted to contain popular religiosity; nothing new in the use of scientific arguments to combat the excesses of popular belief. As far back as the seventeenth century the clergy had been allied with medical doctors in studying simulated mystics, and while "feigned beatitude" had sometimes been judged to be pure imposture, it was more often traced to mental illness.[27]

All this helps to explain the report Father Lemius gave to the Holy Office in January 1921, in which he noted his skepticism about the miracles attributed to Padre Pio and expressed his view that the stigmata were of psychopathological origin. He compared the evaluation of Professor Bignami from Rome, who had concluded the stigmata were attributable to both somatic and artificial causes, with that of Dr. Romanelli from the hospital in Barletta, Puglia, who had argued for a supernatural cause.[28] "I would say I stand fully behind Dr. Bignami," Lemius wrote. In certain cases, it was "possible to produce, via the imagination, an accumulation of blood in a particular part of the organism" with "consequent lesions and even breakage of arterial and venous capillaries." The wounds produced by such a process were defined by positivist science as hypnotic stigmata, while Lemius preferred the term *auto-stigmatization*. As for the wound that Padre Pio claimed to have on his side, the *consultor* agreed with Professor Bignami's diagnosis of "dermographism" or "autographism." "If Padre Pio is genuinely neuropathic," Lemius wrote, "it would be enough that he traced a cross on his ribs with his fingernail to produce the phenomenon in the precise shape of a cross."[29]

Like Professor Bignami, Father Lemius did not believe that Padre Pio had deliberately provoked the stigmata with some physical or chemical instrument. That would be pure and simple charlatanry, while Lemius, based on the documentation, thought that the case was more complex. Like the doctor, Lemius was inclined to think that Padre Pio, "meditating profoundly on the wounds of Our Lord with the wish to deeply explore His pain," had first produced via such meditation "a trace of the stigmata," which had then been "filled out by chemical means." The depositions of Maria De Vito and Dr. Valentini Vista supported this conclusion. It was clear that bottles of carbolic acid and other caustic substances circulated inside the monastery of Santa Maria delle Grazie. "Padre Pio is far from ignorant about pharmaceutical matters," added the Holy Office's *consultor*, with a hint of practiced innuendo.[30]

However, what was the Church to do about Padre Pio? In his report to the Holy Office, Father Lemius discarded the expedient that ecclesiastical authorities had used for centuries every time the faithful had become overexcited about some "living saint" in some convent or monastery around Italy. The standard remedy was to transfer the friar or nun to a faraway place, to break the ties that linked the holy man or woman to his or her territory; in short, to aim a well-placed kick to the middle of the anthill.[31] But it would be "impossible" to remove the friar with the stigmata from San Giovanni Rotondo, Father Lemius believed. "There are simply too many Padre Pio fanatics down there, too many people who have an interest in seeing pilgrims continue to arrive." As for Father Gemelli's practical suggestions, the *consultor* thought it would be impossible to wrap the friar's arm or leg in plaster so as to allow the wounds to heal. What might the "fanatics" do "if the doubts about his stigmata were made visible with that plaster covering"? Gemelli's other suggestion, to send an evaluation committee made up of a theologian, a psychologist, and a medical doctor, would also rile the faithful. "What would happen if they saw those three experts around Padre Pio for many days?"[32]

To control the epidemic of popular belief in San Giovanni Rotondo, Lemius suggested a less invasive therapy. The Holy Office should identify a man of the Church who was both an expert theologian and a cautious fellow, he said. That man should be sworn to loyalty by the Holy Office and sent to San Giovanni as an apostolic visitor. Once on the scene, taking care not to be drawn into "the atmosphere of suggestion," the envoy from the Vatican should carry out an "accurate inquiry" but "without calling too much attention to himself." Padre Pio must be studied from all angles, especially from the point of view of humility and obedience. His way of behaving with women should be observed; so should his use of pharmaceutical products. His cell should be inspected, if necessary; and it should be determined whether he really used carbolic acid to disinfect needles and give injections to the novices. Finally, Padre Pio's spiritual director, Father Benedetto of San Marco in Lamis, should be kept away from the monastery for the entire duration of the apostolic visit. "Perhaps such an inquiry could lead to the conclusion that certainly the stigmata are not of divine origin," noted Father Lemius. His choice of words (*perhaps* followed by *certainly*)

may have been wobbly, but his determination to resolve the doubts about Padre Pio once and for all was not.[33]

An intense exchange of notes among the advisers of the congregation of the Holy Office shows how Lemius's report was discussed in the first few months of 1921. From today's perspective, those comments, carefully preserved in the archives, are striking because we know how the story ends: the skeptics were brushed aside, the Capuchin with the stigmata was canonized, and San Giovanni Rotondo became one of the most hallowed destinations for pilgrims from around the planet. But in 1921, not a single one of the religious advisers inside the hushed palace of the Holy Office saw any merit in Padre Pio's pastoral style. No one suggested there was anything good about the streams of pilgrims coming to visit him, and no one envisioned him as a Christ figure in the Gargano mountains. In fact, the advisers considered measures to isolate the friar and totally wipe out his cult—measures far sterner than those suggested by Father Lemius.

The Dutch priest Joseph Drehmanns of the Most Holy Redeemers proposed the most draconian solutions, but Father Luigi Santoro of the Friars Minor Conventuals and Father Filippo Maroto of the Sons of the Immaculate Heart of Mary were nearly as severe. "Pay no attention to

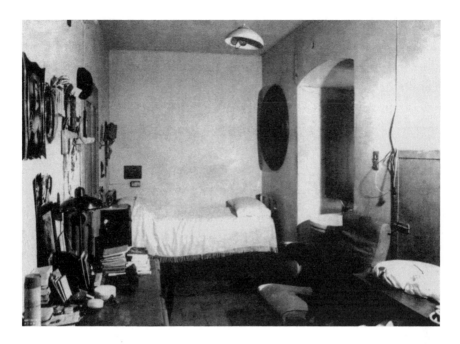

the tales told about him," suggested Father Drehmanns; "show no inter-est whatsoever," "let there be silence around the figure of Padre Pio." An unsigned note suggested the Church just ignore the stigmata ("they'll heal by themselves, and if they itch, that can be soothed with an oint-ment") and focus on measures to stop the flow of pilgrims and the cor-respondence: "close the gates of the monastery and do not reply to any of the letters." Others thought that it would not be impossible, after all, to transfer Padre Pio to another location; it would merely be necessary to take precautions to maintain public order "via direct negotiations between the Holy See and the head of the government" and by "trans-ferring him in secret, using an automobile, by night, etc." Father Maroto wanted to publish a notice in the Vatican press forbidding the faithful to gather around the monastery and obliging Padre Pio "to lead a reserved and hidden existence," while Father Santoro suggested that the friar Pio's toughest critic, Agostino Gemelli, should take part in activities to repress the cult. And someone pointed out that, should the wheel of fortune turn in Padre Pio's favor, the members of the Holy Office could always justify their actions to God and history because "these measures will constitute a proof of Padre Pio's virtue."[34]

The hierarchy of the Holy Office, however, did not follow up on the advice to repress the cult immediately. Between April and May 1921, the congregation decided instead to follow the course laid out by Father Lemius: to send an apostolic visitor to San Giovanni Rotondo to study the personality of Padre Pio, sort out the matter of the stigmata, observe the friar's relationships with women, and evaluate the spiritual leadership of Father Benedetto of San Marco in Lamis. It was a demanding mission, and Father Lemius had advised that the envoy chosen be intellectually prepared and diplomatically shrewd. The Vatican chose Pisa-born Raffaele Carlo Rossi, a forty-five-year-old Discalced Carmelite who had served for a while as a young *consultor* to the Holy Office and who had just been named bishop of Volterra.[35] The very same day that Caradonna and the Fascists were brutally expelling the Communist deputy Misiano from Parliament—June 13, 1921—Monsignor Rossi climbed the hills of the Gargano from the Tavoliere plain, an inquisitor in the land of Padre Pio.

Padre Pio's Oath

An inquisitor, Monsignor Rossi? Well, not quite. There was a difference between the Holy Office in its role as a tribunal ruling on the doctrine of the faith and simple inquiries about a *publica voce et fama*.[36] What took place in 1921 was an inquiry about Padre Pio, not a trial against him. Nor, in the decades to come, would the Capuchin friar ever be formally put on trial by the Holy Office, which would instead several times send apostolic visitors to San Giovanni Rotondo. And yet an apostolic visit had some things in common with an inquisitorial trial: there was the preliminary review of the documentation, the depositions of witnesses in loco, and the forceful way the person in question was interrogated as if he or she were guilty.

Monsignor Rossi's 150-page report "On Padre Pio of Pietrelcina," dated October 4, 1921, tells us that this apostolic visitor stayed at San Giovanni Rotondo for precisely one week. He questioned the archpriest, Doctor of Canon Law Giuseppe Prencipe, the parish superintendent, Don Domenico Palladino, and a number of Padre Pio's confreres at the monastery of Santa Maria delle Grazie—Father Lorenzo of

San Marco in Lamis, Father Ignazio of Jelsi, Father Luigi of Serracapriola, Father Romolo of San Marco in Lamis, Father Lodovico of San Giovanni Rotondo, as well as the minister provincial of the order, Father Pietro of Ischitella. Many of these friars had come from towns where the Capuchins had monasteries, and their vocation was often less a heartfelt choice than a stifling destiny; their experience of life spanned no more than the one hundred kilometers as the crow flies between the mountains of Campania and those of Gargano. As for Padre Pio, he gave six depositions before Monsignor Rossi between June 15 and 20 and underwent an examination of the stigmata. Each time the reputed saint or his fellow friars were questioned they had to take two oaths on the Bible, swearing beforehand to tell the truth, and then afterward that they would keep their testimony secret.

Except for the one-on-one encounter with the Divine Mystery when he received the stigmata in 1918, the one-on-one meetings with Bishop Rossi were certainly the most dramatic events in Padre Pio's entire life. After the terrible gift of the five wounds, what could be as intense and painful as placing his right hand (wearing a half glove to hide the stigmata) on the holy book and replying to a Holy Office messenger come down from Rome to investigate whether those marks of Christ were supernatural or artificial, divine or sham? Like the doubting apostle Thomas, Monsignor Rossi would almost literally put his finger in the wound, using a tailor's meter to measure the depth of "the *injuries* that Padre Pio is supposed to have on his hands, his feet and his chest," and inspecting each one to see whether the wound on the palm of the hand or the sole of the foot corresponded to the one on the back of the hand and the top of the foot, as they would if made by a nail. The emissary from the Holy Office was no less scrupulous about the wound on Padre Pio's side and included a drawing of it in his report.[37]

Padre Pio's interrogations revolved around how closely his experience mirrored that of Christ. At one point Monsignor Rossi, having heard that the friar occasionally displayed marks on his head like those left by a crown of thorns, mentioned to him: "There are those who say that sometimes you have signs on your head, too." Padre Pio, laughing, replied: "Oh for the love of God! What can I say?" Bishop Rossi also asked the friar about the rumors that he would live no longer than Jesus Christ. "About this matter that you will die when you are 33 years old, etc., have you said anything about that?" "I wouldn't dream of it" was Padre Pio's straightforward reply. The friar often replied to the bishop in surprisingly colloquial terms, so that the transcript of his interrogations can sound as fresh as an audiotape. Had the friar, perhaps when ill, ever been looked after by women "at night, in the visitors' rooms"? Padre Pio's irreverent reply, in something like his native dialect, was: "Your excellence, I'm hazy on that." And to the following question, whether the women had behaved impeccably or not, the friar's response was: "Your excellence, I was under the weather, what can I say?"[38]

The transcripts of Padre Pio's depositions include a long list of "I don't know," "I couldn't say," "I don't remember," "I can't recall anything about that," "it's all hazy to me," "my memory is vague on that precise point."[39] This may have been because the Capuchin friar was genuinely unable to bring up one episode or another from the depths of his memory, or it may have been deliberate evasiveness before the toughest questions. However, Padre Pio's replies were more precise when Monsignor Rossi asked him about various miracles attributed to him by the vox populi, including his miraculous healings and episodes of bilocation, when he appeared in two places at once. In these cases, the Capuchin friar often replied with the phrase "non mi consta" ("not so far as I'm aware"), borrowed from the judicial Latin *non constat*, "not proven." Asked whether he had really once been in Foggia at the military command at the same time as he was inside the monastery at San Giovanni Rotondo, Padre Pio's reply, although perhaps running on a bit, was very clear.

> Your excellency, not so far as I'm aware. There have certainly been rash acts on the part of people who have named me in connection with things I would never dream to talk about or to make known. It's enough to make a person crazy and I have to thank the Lord that the greatest grace he's blessed me with has been, in fact, that I haven't lost my reason or my health for all the nonsense that has occurred.[40]

"For all the nonsense": it was Padre Pio himself, before the emissary of the Holy Office, who played the role of devil's advocate with regard to his own sanctity. Less explicit, but much the same, were his replies when he was questioned about the miraculous effects of his intercession on the incurably ill: the hunchback of Lucera, the cripple of San Giovanni Rotondo, the two young deaf and dumb girls, the lame chancellor at the magistrate's office, and all the rest of the suffering humanity that had turned to Padre Pio for help. Padre Pio insisted that he had done no more than pray; it was the faithful who engaged in "rash acts" and announced miracles. "I pray for the needs of those who have been sent to me, the poor, the needy, etc. That's all I'm aware of." "The results obtained I don't know about." "I said, as usual, something like: confide in the Lord, I will pray on your behalf, etc. That's what I'm aware of. As for the rest, I don't know." "Did anyone ever make them that promise? Even from the human point of view, who would want to make a promise like that without having any certainty?" "Yes, I prayed. The effects are something they know; I don't."[41]

The climax of Padre Pio's inquisitorial review came at 9 p.m. on June 17, 1921. Earlier that evening, Bishop Rossi had inspected the stigmata and had asked the Capuchin friar a long list of questions about his use of cosmetic, chemical, and pharmaceutical products. What did the man in question think about the sweet smell that the faithful said emanated from his wounds? Padre Pio had heard about this from people who came to kiss his hand, but otherwise, he said, he knew nothing. "I don't know, I can't distinguish. I only have soap in my cell." As for other products, the friar admitted that he had procured some carbolic acid "for the use of the Community," and he maintained that he had acquired it in secret because he didn't have a medical prescription. The carbolic acid, he said, was used to sterilize syringes, "which in a seminary of young men are often needed." As for the veratrine, he had acquired it "for recreational purposes": to play a joke on his confreres, he would mix the substance with snuff in order to make the other friars sneeze uncontrollably.[42] Hard to believe as that explanation was, Monsignor Rossi made no comment. The apostolic visitor was busy preparing a coup de théâtre.

Here, it's worth citing the transcript of the inquiry at some length, for this was a decisive scene in the tale of Padre Pio; a scene that, though it took place in the twentieth century, also feels distinctly archaic, or at any rate anachronistic. An update of a painting by Francisco de Zurbaràn—or the anticipation of a novel by José Saramago.

At this point I the undersigned Visitor—even though the reverend Padre Pio has already sworn an oath—remind him of the holiness of that religious act, I point out how serious it is and ask him, in fact, what he thinks of that oath. And he replies: It is the most solemn action that man can carry out because it means calling on God to testify to the truth.

That said, I invite him to reply under the sanctity of that special oath to the following questions, him kneeling and with his hands on the Bible.

Your Fatherhood, do you swear on the Holy Bible that you have never used perfumes and that you do not now use them on your person?

And Padre Pio swears he has not and does not, adding that apart from being a clergyman, he has always found such a thing repugnant.

Does Your Fatherhood swear on the Holy Bible that you have never procured, encouraged, cultivated, exacerbated or preserved, directly or indirectly, the signs that you bear on your hands, your feet and your side?

Reply: I swear.

Does Your Fatherhood swear on the Holy Bible that you have never used dermographism on your person, that is, that you have never exerted a form of self-suggestion in which you made signs on your body that could then become visible by means of compulsive thoughts?

Reply: I swear, for goodness sake, for goodness sake! If instead the Lord would free me of them, how grateful I would be![43]

Padre Pio on his knees, his hands on the Bible, swearing before God that he has not interfered with his stigmata, and actually begging the Lord to free him from his torment—it was a striking, vaguely baroque image, powerful enough to dazzle a pious man like Raffaele Carlo Rossi.[44] Not that the apostolic visitor was ready to join the cult of Padre Pio; throughout his visit and in the final report he gave to the Holy Office, Rossi remained skeptical about the miracles attributed to the friar in local lore, and was rather sarcastic about the friar's local promoters. Nevertheless, on that day in June 1921, when he inspected the stigmata and then invited Padre Pio to take a special oath, Monsignor Rossi was convinced that the divine was manifest in the friar's body—or at least in his hands.

Hands, of course, are the symbolic center of a priest's body. It is with his hands that the minister of the Father speaks the language of the Son—a language of gestures as much as a language of words. When a priest is ordained, the liturgy of the Church of Rome prescribes that the officiating cleric anoint the *hands*—specifically, the palms—of the initiate with oil, making the sign of the cross with his index finger: *Pontifex cum oleo catechumenorum inungit unicuique ambas manus simul junctas, in modum crucis, producendo cum pollice suo dextero in dictum oleum intincto duas lineas . . . ungendo mox totaliter palmas.* Then the officiator binds the two joined hands of the initiate with a white cloth and presses them between his own hands: *sic clausas, et alligatas manus tenet.* And finally, the two men unite their hands around the chalice of wine and the paten holding the host: *ipsi illam accipiunt inter indices et medios digitos, et cuppam Calicis et Patenam simul tangunt.*[45] So the Catholic liturgy has specified for centuries. Add to that the miraculous power Jesus exercised in laying on hands, as told in the Gospels, and the symbolic value of the wounded, bound hands of Padre Pio is clear.

As for the Capuchin's body, however, Monsignor Rossi did not find any marks on his feet or his side that corresponded to the usual idea of stigmata. On his chest, there was only a triangular, "wine-red" spot and some other, smaller marks—but no sign of the upside-down cross described by Dr. Romanelli. On his feet, Bishop Rossi noted "no more than two spots like buttons on which the epidermis was whiter and more delicate" than the surrounding skin. But on Padre Pio's hands, wrote Monsignor Rossi to the congregation of the Holy Office, underlining to make himself perfectly clear: "*There are* stigmata. We have before us a fact, impossible to deny." And so the issue was no longer the existence of the stigmata but their origins. Monsignor Rossi ruled out "any diabolical interference and all human imposture." He could eliminate the possibility of diabolical interference (it was an ancient obsession of the inquisitors that stigmata were a sign of fraudulent holiness, a mark of the devil)[46] because Padre Pio's "extremely upright" life was proof that Satan had not possessed him.[47] And he could be confident that the stigmata were not caused by human interference because Padre Pio had given sufficient justifications for the business about the carbolic acid and the veratrine.

The third hypothesis—that the wounds on the friar's hands were of divine origin—seemed to Monsignor Rossi the most likely, given the uninterrupted flow of blood, the way the wounds were localized on the palms of the friar's hands, the fact that no medicine seemed to heal them, and the "powerful and very agreeable" smell of perfume that emanated from the bleeding flesh. "Should this manifestation be not only exceptional, but also miraculous, the Lord will demonstrate as He sees fit," concluded Monsignor Rossi of the stigmata.[48] Although this judgment might sound equivocal, it was in fact a vote of confidence in Padre Pio. For the first time since the friar had come into the sights of the Holy Office, an official voice was dissenting from the chorus of censurers. Prudent, but sure of himself, the bishop of Volterra was writing the first page of a counterhistory of Padre Pio, in which not all was hysteria or psittacism, hypnosis or suggestion, dermographism or self-inflicted damage. For Monsignor Rossi, not all was neurosis—there was also some beatitude.

The Army of Hope

Convinced now that Pio's were the "real wounds" of Christ[49] and that his interviewee was an honest man, the emissary from the Holy Office divested himself of the police inspector's uniform and put on that of the Discalced Carmelite. "To tell the truth, Padre Pio made a rather favorable impression on me," he wrote, "even though I had gone there fairly convinced of the opposite." Both the other friars and the lay

brothers questioned by Monsignor Rossi spoke of Padre Pio as an excellent man of the cloth, and the visitor himself was impressed by the way that the friar upheld the vows of humility and obedience—"in spite of the many vain words that had projected this poor Capuchin in such an unhappy light!" Ignoring the rumors he must have heard in the palace of the Holy Office before leaving for the Gargano mountains, Bishop Rossi had the courage to write that Padre Pio "was anything but a commercial miracle-worker, anything but a wild agitator of the people." Fun-loving with his confreres, loyal to his superiors, charismatic with the faithful—what more could one ask in a pastor of human souls?[50]

Yet the final report by Monsignor Rossi was by no means an enchanted account of Palestine on the Gargano. To the contrary, the apostolic visitor was both scrupulous and severe in describing just how the backward town of San Giovanni Rotondo had turned into a sort of *cour des miracles* around Padre Pio. As he told it, in the middle of the Great War, Father Paolino of Casacalenda, then the father guardian of Santa Maria delle Grazie, had been willing to do almost anything to try to reverse the fortunes of his empty monastery. When rumors first began to circulate that there was a "living saint" in Foggia who communicated directly with the Lord, Father Paolino had lost no time in getting Padre Pio into his monastery and in letting the people of San Giovanni Rotondo know that they could now hope for extraordinary happenings. "The preparation was long; the insinuation was light-handed, subtle and insistent . . . And there came, after a while, the stigmata—and what propaganda there was then!"

The archpriest Don Prencipe had tried in vain to contain the excitement of the inhabitants of San Giovanni, then of the Gargano Peninsula, then of the whole of Puglia. Padre Pio's fame rapidly occupied the collective imagination. As Monsignor Rossi reported, to most of the populace "Padre Pio was a saint who performed miracles, and there was no possible discussion about that. There were those who, with pitiful ignorance, declared he was Jesus Christ himself."[51] "Souls were becoming excited to the point of delirium," said the archpriest Prencipe; he had personally witnessed "5,000–6,000 people exclaiming that there had been a miracle and clustering around the person who had received grace."

In the pitiless judgment of Monsignor Rossi, "not even one of Pio's miracles was real." It was untrue that a "young man afflicted with a hunchback" had been "at least partly made straight." It was untrue that the court chancellor of San Giovanni Rotondo, a man with a limp, had walked away with his foot made well. It was untrue that a deaf-mute child, brought before Padre Pio, had regained her speech. It was untrue that a poor retarded man, "of Lilliputian stature" not to mention one-eyed, hunchbacked, and crippled, had been made whole. ("I saw him myself, a sad case, pitiful," said the bishop.) It was pure fantasy too, the story that the San Giovanni parish church bell had suddenly splintered into pieces, after a wrong was done by the archpriest to Padre Pio's confreres. "Such foolish things! And the poor were screaming about miracles!"[52]

Following an ancient inquisitorial tradition, the apostolic visitor from the Holy Office spent part of his time in San Giovanni confiscating and reading letters.[53] He read through most of the correspondence between Padre Pio and his spiritual director, Father Benedetto of San Marco in Lamis; a selection of the letters that the Capuchin with the stigmata had exchanged with his "spiritual daughters"; and some of the missives that Christian souls had sent to Padre Pio from the length and breadth of Italy to ask for a blessing or to give thanks for one. The archives of the Holy Office have preserved several dozen of this last type. To judge by the dates on them—between May and June of 1921—they represent some of the letters that Monsignor Rossi picked up, as it were, from the top of the pile: those that had just landed on Padre Pio's desk during the visit of the Holy Office envoy. At the height of the Roman Inquisition letters were scrutinized to unmask doctrinal heresies, moral failings, and deviant behavior. But there was nothing of that sort in the correspondence of Padre Pio reviewed by Bishop Rossi: nothing more than requests for intercession, offerings of money, expressions of gratitude. Nevertheless, the historian can't but be happy to have the chance to look at those letters. They offer a way to measure the horizons of expectation inside which Padre Pio's reputation grew, and a way to connect to the distant voices of his early followers—the first contingent of the gigantic army of hope that would turn to Padre Pio in the half century to come.

Among those who asked for his aid was a little girl named Eugenia Carnevale of Brescia, who sent the "Most Reverend Father" the sum of ten lire from her change purse to celebrate a mass "so that I can belong wholly to Jesus" and not be susceptible to Satan ("I constantly allow myself to be tempted by the devil"). Father Luigi of Imola, a Capuchin brother from a monastery near Ravenna, wrote to ask Padre Pio to pray that his hearing would return, emphasizing that he was adhering to his vow of obedience: "My Father Guardian gave me the task of writing this letter, and for that reason I also have firm hopes the Lord will grant me this blessing, for I have been obedient to my Guardian." A student from Florence, Miss Errigo, was counting on Padre Pio's help in obtaining high marks on the exam for her diploma. Checchina Massara, the "distressed mother" of a large family from the southern town of Monteleone Calabro, wrote to Padre Pio with various requests for mercy: first, a husband for her oldest daughter, now twenty-three and still unmarried (despite a petition to "our dear Blessed Virgin of Pompeii," who had not been able to help); then prayers for the other four daughters and two sons, "especially for the older of the two, Biagio, age 13, who must now do his gymnasium exams"; and finally, a blessing for her "dear husband," whose health was poor but who remained the family's only breadwinner, "and this is the main thing for which we must pray."[54]

There was nothing very special about these letters of request; they were ordinary documents of everyday faith, reflections of an almost pedestrian Christianity. But the letters of thanks for blessings received were another thing entirely. They were tiny but all-important stones in an edifice being built not only by the enterprising Capuchin brothers but, spontaneously, by ordinary people: the edifice of Padre Pio's reputation, the invisible cathedral of his living sainthood. And the primary laborers on that building site—a construction project stretching across all of Italy—were women.

In Tolentino, Anna Romagnoli had been able to throw away her plaster corset, for the prayers that Padre Pio had sent to heaven on her behalf had cured her spine completely. In Florence, Zaira Bacci worshipped "Sainted Padre Pio" after her husband Ricciotti, whose bronchial disease had been diagnosed as incurable, returned to health. In Cremona, Maria Bergonzi was able to talk once again with her son Francesco, for Padre Pio's intercession had given him back his voice after six months of dumb silence. In Catanzaro, Vittoria Lamanna had been miraculously cured of an "attack of paralysis" and had recovered the faith she had lost after her son was killed during the terrible retreat at Caporetto. In Capua, Anna Lopez's mother and aunts had long despaired about the little girl, born almost blind in 1917—"those poor eyes, reflecting nothing but rottenness"; but then the women had written to the "prodigious friar," and "after a few days, the child opened her eyes, fully healed, and displayed two genuine stars."[55]

To sift through these twentieth-century documents is to be drawn inescapably back to certain medieval stories, like the famous tale of the miracle worker of Corbeny who healed scrofula, so magisterially reconstructed by Marc Bloch.[56] Despite the fourteen centuries that separate the life of St. Marcouf from that of Padre Pio, the collective mentality surrounding the two figures is perhaps not so very different. In twentieth-century Italy as in medieval France, the conviction that a miracle had been performed depended on the belief that there *were* such things as miracles. The rest came almost by itself. The devotion of the believers meant that any cures must be due to the intercession of the saint. The cured and their families became witnesses to a success story, while those cases where illness persisted were attributed to other causes and then repressed from memory. Even in the twentieth century, a reputation for miracle working could spread far and wide without there being either any outright deception or any miraculous cures. Unlike Father Gemelli, the followers of Padre Pio felt no need to make a miracle correspond to medical science; they didn't dream of setting up a *bureau des constatations* like that at Lourdes to vouch that cures were miraculous even by doctors' standards.[57] Like the medieval believers at St. Marcouf, they didn't want to know, they wanted to believe.

Those believers who sent letters to San Giovanni sometimes reminded Padre Pio that they had written to him before, and even complained, with all the tact due to a holy man, that they had never received a reply. Such correspondents obviously imagined they had a personal relationship with the "prodigious friar," even as the expansion of his cult soon made it impossible for him to cope with all the correspondence. In his report to the Holy Office, Monsignor Rossi explained that although the volume of correspondence had diminished after the first explosion (there had been "up to 700 letters a day" in 1919, while in 1921 the friar was receiving "60–70 a day"), it was still impossible for Padre Pio to read such a pile of letters ("there must be 20,000"). Accordingly, his fellow friars went through the mail, passing him only those letters that were the most personal or most unusual. As for replies, the friars would answer those letters in which the writers had enclosed an offering of money or a postage stamp for return mail. It was not true that the replies were merely preprinted form letters that the friars stuffed into envelopes. "The only things already printed are the images," explained Monsignor Rossi: holy cards with pictures of the Virgin or of Padre Pio, on which the friars would write in longhand, "P. Pio prays and blesses."[58]

Bishop Rossi also reviewed a sample of the letters that the Capuchin with the stigmata had received from Father Benedetto of San Marco in Lamis, his spiritual director. Rossi studied those letters with some care and devoted an appendix of his final report to them. He was critical of Father Benedetto, whom he thought too "doleful" and too "intrusive," but he did not see him as the Mephistophelian manipulator whom Father Gemelli had accused of planting the stigmata on Padre Pio.[59]

Bishop Rossi's evenhanded account also helped to dispel some other negative legends about the monastery of Santa Maria delle Grazie. For example, it was said that when Padre Pio celebrated mass it was likely to go on and on—for two or even three hours. Yes, said Monsignor Rossi, the friar did perhaps officiate with "too much devotion . . . measured watch in hand," he spent five minutes on the *Memento* of the living, four or five minutes on the *Memento* of the dead, and two minutes to consecrate the wine! But despite a few drawn-out passages, his overall performance was fine. Yes, he did commit some "small liturgical errors." He didn't bow his head at the name of the Holy Father during the collection. He didn't open and close his hands properly during the *Oremus*. He didn't bow down perfectly at the altar during the *Munda* and the *Te igitur* ("perhaps because of pain in his side"). He wasn't "perfectly precise" in carrying out the Communion ceremony. But Monsignor Rossi thought that these departures from the rules could be explained by Padre Pio's somewhat sketchy ecclesiastical training and by the well-known sloppiness of the Capuchins. There was no need to think they pointed to some kind of sacred folly in which a priest tried to make his Last Supper last forever.[60]

Bishop Rossi was also indulgent when it came to Padre Pio's relations with his "spiritual daughters," even though the mingling of friars and pious women was a problem Church authorities had spent centuries trying to contain. *Béguines, beghards, bizzoche, pinzochere*—these lay sisters were known by many names around Europe. Women who were not ordained but were pious enough to want to live inside a cloister, they often aroused suspicion because they were liminal figures—neither quite lay nor clerical, neither active members of society nor withdrawn and contemplative.[61] The authorities, of course, also worried that these women might stir up dormant emotions in the friars, who were bound to sacred celibacy but tempted every day to use their priestly status for carnal satisfaction. If the priest was particularly charismatic, the problem was even more serious, because then the women might be tempted to sublimate carnal passion in the Passion of Christ—imagining themselves as the sacred Host and dreaming of being devoured. The priest, meanwhile, might seek out their presence as a self-imposed torment, seeing the ordeal of the flesh as the highest measure of his virtue.[62]

For decades, the suspicion that Padre Pio had sexual ties with the lay sisters in the monastery would gnaw at his critics like woodworm in the pulpit. But in 1921, Monsignor Rossi viewed the matter with great serenity, more as a minister of souls than an inquisitor of bodies. Yes, it was true that sometimes in the guest quarters, relations between Padre Pio and the devout women went beyond bounds: there were "women who touched the friar on his sickbed 'to get hold of his sainthood'!" and other acts of "foolish minds and small heads." And it was also true, Rossi wrote, that Padre Pio addressed his spiritual daughters with the intimate *tu*. But the bishop, speaking as a man of the North, said of that practice: "Let us not make too much of it, for we are in the deep South here." On the question of touching, Rossi was likewise quite sanguine. It was one thing to admit that the sexes were not rigorously kept apart in the Gargano monastery, quite another to suggest that the comings and goings of the lay sisters threatened the chastity of Padre Pio. "On this most important point of Christian, religious and priestly virtue, P. Pio is unassailable," Monsignor Rossi wrote to the congregation of the Holy Office.[63] As we shall soon see, however, they did not quite share that opinion.

The Patience of a Saint

In the Church's arithmetic the accounts always add up, at least when it comes to sainthood. When the Vatican hierarchy is quick to respond to the vox populi and treats a living "saint" as if he were already dead and canonized, then the Church can take credit for being sensitive to demands coming from below, for being in tune with the great community of the faithful. But if instead (as happens more often) the hierarchy is cautious and diffident about rumors of a saint in the making, the Church still has an infallible argument in its favor. When it obstructs the "saint's" claim to sainthood by making his path more difficult, the Church can then take credit for having offered the candidate a chance to demonstrate his or her "heroic virtues" of humility and obedience—in other words, the proverbial patience of a saint.

Protected by such impeccable logic, the members of the congregation of the Holy Office have not been afraid to use a heavy hand when a saint in the making first gains a public following. They have often reached for the yellowed decrees of Pope Urban VIII, the seventeenth-century rules governing beatification, to chase away the crowds around a would-be saint.[64] That is precisely what happened in 1922, when the Holy Office decided that the investigatory phase of the Padre Pio inquiry was finished. With the documentation before them, the alternatives before the tribunal of the faith were clear: either follow the suggestion of Father Drehmanns, who had proposed a sort of religious embargo on the figure of the Capuchin friar, or pursue the approach of Bishop Rossi, whose report had recommended no repressive measures. The Holy Office opted for a hard line.

In June, 1922, Cardinal Merry Del Val, the secretary of the Holy Office, sent precise instructions to the heads of the Capuchin order to severely limit the priestly functions and appearances of Padre Pio. "His person must not be the object of any attention or curiosity," the cardinal ordered. "He must not display the so-called stigmata, nor speak of them or allow them to be kissed." And there was more. The Capuchin friar was henceforth to celebrate only the early morning mass and only in the chapel where lay visitors were barred entry. He was to break off all relations, "including correspondence," with Father Benedetto of San

Marco in Lamis. He had to make clear "both to his brothers and to outsiders," expressing himself "both in words and in deeds," his "firm wish to be left in peace to await his own sanctification."[65]

And the greatest peace Padre Pio could find, the cardinal suggested, would come the day his order decided to remove him from San Giovanni Rotondo, from the Gargano, and from Puglia, and packed him off to some Capuchin monastery in northern Italy. There was to be no hesitation: "The Most Eminent Fathers would like to see such a transfer take place right away."[66]

5. A CHANGE OF CLIMATE

Triumph of the Heart

The Catholic University of the Sacred Heart was inaugurated on December 7, 1921. A photo taken at the ceremony shows the founder, Agostino Gemelli, at the center, looking younger than his forty-three years, a priest of serious mien, well aware of his responsibilities as founder and rector. Around him, the first students of the Cattolica crane their necks so their faces will be in the picture. Unlike Gemelli, the students are carefree, jovial, maybe even a tiny bit rowdy, but they too clearly feel the solemnity of the occasion. Sixty years after Italy was united and fifty years after the Papal States were defeated and swallowed up by the new nation, Italian Catholics could for the first time imagine a future in which they were not just guests in the Kingdom of Italy but might aspire to join its elite.

The new university was called "Sacred Heart" in honor of a particular form of devotion to the sacred heart of Jesus that was popular in Italy in the years after the Great War, and which Gemelli had propagated among the troops.[1] The Cattolica was just one part of Gemelli's vast and ambitious plan, which also encompassed cultural projects like the review *Vita e Pensiero* and new programs within Azione Cattolica,[2] the lay movement promoting Catholic values. Gemelli's ideas went far beyond the notions of Don Luigi Sturzo and his Popular Party.[3] In the early 1920s, men like Gemelli did not feel the need for a political party—not even a new, mass political party; they wanted a vigorous "return to Christ." In an Italy that had been utterly changed by the Great War,

they intended to realize that "return" by creating a completely new nation, a new community of the baptized.[4]

Gemelli's aim as rector of the Sacred Heart was explicit: to prepare the citizen as his country expected, the Christian as the Church wanted him.[5] In attendance at the mass for the opening of the Cattolica was Achille Ratti, the archbishop of Milan. After the death of Benedict XV in 1922, Ratti would become Pope Pius XI, and Gemelli would become, in Gramsci's term, an *organic intellectual* within the Church: the man generating the ideas that prepared the ground for Pius's Catholic *reconquista*.[6] The Catholic program would find common ground with the Fascists, insofar as Mussolini himself believed that an accord with the Church of Rome was necessary to build consensus for the regime; but it was also destined to clash with Fascist goals, for the pope's hegemonic ambitions were in competition with Il Duce's. The ancient alliance between throne and altar, constructed on the wreckage of the Great War, threatened to devolve into a bitter battle for supremacy.

Without getting ahead of ourselves here, let us note that in the winter of 1921–22, it looked like the Church might prevail, in a stirring resurgence after the terrible defeat of the Papal States in 1870. A sign of the changing climate was the series of conferences held by the philosopher Giovanni Gentile in 1920, published under the title *Religious Treatises*. In those addresses, Gentile argued that Italy needed religion more than culture and that the state required faith before it had secular rule.[7] Was it any surprise that Monsignor Francesco Olgiati, Gemelli's right-hand man in Milan, hailed the opening of the Catholic University as "the dawn of a new era"? The "red rag" of the Socialists would soon disappear from Italian squares, Olgiati believed, and so would those "idiotic" Fascist war chants. "The Heart that has loved men so much is triumphant over everyone and everything."[8]

The Church intended to vigorously contest anticlericalism, and the laity would be enrolled in the battle. Father Gemelli was perhaps the most sensitive—and certainly the most hardworking—interpreter of such a campaign.[9] Pius XI's Church encouraged lay participation, expanding the social activities of Azione Cattolica and demonstrating, via an intense program of beatifications and canonizations, that lay Catholics could be sainted. Of course, sainthood could bring its own complications. The prelates who met in Pisa in 1922 to consider the beatification of the lay Catholic Gemma Galgani, she of the stigmata, were cautious about those "wounds of Christ," which they feared could incite forms of popular religiosity too closely tied to exterior signs.[10] The persistent vitality of ancient habits and longtime religious practices posed a challenge to Pius XI's ability to regularize devotion around Italy. Especially in the south of Italy, the confraternities tended to be more influential than the lay association Azione Cattolica, and the cult of the saints often prevailed over the teaching of catechism.[11]

Padre Pio's case was merely the tip of this southern iceberg, but it was particularly bothersome to the Church, to judge by the rigorous inquiry carried out by Monsignor Rossi on behalf of the Holy Office and by the actions of Monsignor Angelo Roncalli (the future Pope John XXIII) in the fall of 1922. After long service as a priest in his native Bergamo, Roncalli had arrived in the Vatican the year before to serve as the chief for Italy of the Propaganda Fide, the church office concerned with spreading the faith. In mid-November 1922, Roncalli thus found himself traversing Puglia as the national coordinator for the missionary movement. But unlike many other men of the Church, who in those years had ventured up the Gargano hills to reach San

Giovanni Rotondo and meet the famous Padre Pio, Roncalli pointedly chose to stay away from the Capuchin friar.[12]

Just three weeks earlier, Padre Pio's illustrious follower, the Fascist MP Giuseppe Caradonna, had led his "Pugliese cavalry" in the March on Rome.[13] It's unlikely, however, that there was any political motive behind Monsignor Roncalli's avoidance of Padre Pio; Roncalli, if not actually a Fascist, was himself a man of order, all "fatherland, family and religion."[14] Roncalli's decision was based, instead, on a distaste for Padre Pio's type of spirituality, and it foreshadowed a confrontation that would take place almost four decades later: the dramatic events of 1960 when John XXIII, reacting to a scandal about Padre Pio's confession practices, ordered the most draconian measures to contain the Capuchin friar's cult.[15] In 1923, when Roncalli's work for the missions took him back to Foggia and also up to the Gargano Peninsula, he had a second opportunity to arrange a meeting with Padre Pio, but once again his compass did not send him toward the friar with the stigmata—in fact, he explicitly refused an offer to visit.[16]

Roncalli's chilliness might have in part been a result of his close friendship with the Dutch priest Joseph Drehmanns, cemented during

1921 when the two took part in a demanding trip around northern Europe on church business.[17] Drehmanns, besides being the trusted assistant to the prefect of the Propaganda Fide cardinal Van Rossum, was also an adviser to the Holy Office, and he had been, as we saw, one of the Vatican's toughest critics of the Padre Pio cult. Roncalli's ties to his Dutch colleague, to judge by their correspondence, were particularly warm—unusually so for that generally reserved Italian;[18] so it is plausible that Drehmanns might have confided to him at least some of the inquisitorial findings on Padre Pio.[19] Thus, without ever having met the holy man of San Giovanni Rotondo, the future Pope John XXIII may have formed a negative opinion of the friar and the people around him.

In any case, the notion of sainthood that Roncalli had begun to develop after his seminary days[20] had nothing whatsoever in common with the notion held by Padre Pio's followers. Both as a scholar of the Counter-Reformation and as a simple priest, Roncalli had been sensitive to what we might call "local sanctitude"—the necessary relationship between a special Christian and the community to which he or she belonged. But as the years went by, Roncalli began to pay more attention to something like global sanctitude, the "vast horizons" of Catholicism[21] rather than the narrow, sometimes fraudulent kinds of devotion and miracle cults—the "fanaticism" of the Padre Pio worshippers, as he would call it.[22] Roncalli had also stayed in touch with Gemelli after the war, and he shared with his fellow Lombardy priest a desire to get the faithful more directly involved in Catholic liturgical practice and to move them away from folk beliefs.

Beginning in 1923, the going would get tough for the friar with the stigmata. The historian might almost be tempted to refer to some nineteenth-century verse from Heinrich Heine's *Romanzero*, about religious jousting in medieval Spain: "Those who tilt here serve not ladies / Are no gallant paladins / In this combat all the knights are / Rabbis grave and Capuchins."[23] Except that there were few rabbis in 1920s Puglia. This battle would be fought between Capuchins and Capuchins, refereed by Fascists.

A Complicated Transfer

The measures that the Holy Office had ordered in 1922 had not worked to contain popular devotion to Padre Pio, and the Vatican viewed the situation with increasing uneasiness, for it threatened to encourage similar cults of miracle workers and stigmatics. On Good Friday, 1923, the twenty-eight-year-old Elena Aiello, a nun at the convent of the Sisters of the Most Precious Blood in Cosenza, Calabria, began to bleed so copiously from her hands, her feet, and her sides that she provoked surprise among the local doctors, excitement among Calabrian Catholics, and the interest of the national press.[24] In the following weeks, as the awed pilgrims began to head to Cosenza as well as San Giovanni Rotondo, the Vatican decided it had enough mysticism on its hands, and launched a counterattack by releasing the results of its 1922 investigation of Padre Pio's presumed miracles and stigmata. "Non constare de eorumdem factorum supernaturalitate," said the declaration published on May 31, 1923: there was no proof of any supernatural involvement. Both the friars of the San Giovanni monastery and the worshippers of Padre Pio were invited to take note.[25]

When the echo of the Holy Office pronouncement reached the Gargano mountains a few days later, to many there it sounded like the first step toward what the Capuchin hierarchy had already hinted at the year before: Padre Pio's transfer to someplace far from San Giovanni Rotondo, someplace even more remote and hidden—perhaps in Italy, perhaps somewhere else in the world. And so on June 25, just about all those whose livelihood and raison d'être depended on Padre Pio's daily presence in San Giovanni met in the Piazza dei Martiri: his Capuchin confreres, the lay sisters, the poor of San Giovanni, and the faithful from all around. With them, true to the pact sealed during the *biennio rosso*, were the veterans and the war disabled, as well as many landowners, professionals, and members of the middle classes. At the front of the crowd was Francesco Morcaldi, a lawyer, former leader in the Popular Party, and president of the veterans, who had been elected mayor two months previously at the head of a huge clerico-fascist alliance. Morcaldi liked to boast of his close ties with MP Caradonna, whose conspicuous presence in the March on Rome had earned him the job of undersecretary at the Ministry of Posts.[26]

Thanks to a faithful correspondent in San Giovanni Rotondo, readers of *Il Mattino* in Naples received a detailed description of that meeting on June 25. "With a brief show of fireworks, almost the entire population was called to order in Piazza dei Martiri, all the associations with their flags and the local band." There were at least five thousand people present out of a town of twelve thousand inhabitants, even though the town was "already empty for the harvest and the threshing." Morcaldi didn't mince his words: the day that anyone came to take away Padre Pio, the mayor would remove his tricolor sash of office and carry out his duty to the hilt as a private citizen. "The members of the crowd, in the grip of powerful feelings, were unable to do anything but wave their hats and handkerchiefs—they had such lumps in their throats they couldn't even speak," the paper reported. Morcaldi then led the crowd to Santa Maria delle Grazie and ordered the father guardian, Brother Ignazio of Jelsi, to revoke all restrictions on Padre Pio. Faced with the angry mayor and a hostile crowd, the guardian could do little but obey. Just then the friar with the stigmata appeared at the monastery door, "waxy-faced, his eyes lowered, swollen with tears." The faithful uttered a "formidable yell," "placards were waved," and "bells were rung." And Padre Pio, before the crowd, raised his hand in benediction.[27]

"United yesterday, the Fascists declared, by leading the demonstration, that they were in full solidarity with the people"—so *Il Mattino* spelled out the moral of the story the paper had drawn from the events in San Giovanni Rotondo.[28] That unity was notable because the Fascists of Puglia had not always shown a united front in the previous months. After the March on Rome, the two National Fascist Party leaders from Puglia, Giuseppe Caradonna and Achille Starace, had turned rivals. Furthermore, tensions had emerged everywhere in Italy between the movement's center and its periphery, dividing the moderates of the party in Rome from the radicals on the local level: the followers of Mussolini, who had become a man of government, from those who looked back nostalgically to the early days of fascism, when it was an insurgent movement.[29] Inside the province of Foggia, how-

ever, Caradonna's power appeared unquestionable—all the more reason to offer an edifying display of "total unity" around the "little friar," "our Padre Pio of Pietrelcina."[30]

A photograph published in the Roman paper *Il Messaggero* illustrates that moment better than any words.[31] It shows a group of men standing together in front of the friary gate at Santa Maria delle Grazie. Farthest to the right is the monastery's father guardian, Ignazio of Jelsi. Next to him is the local president of the Association of Disabled Veterans, Michele Mondelli. In the center stands the Levantine little figure of Francesco Morcaldi ("Don Ciccio" to his friends, "Ciccillo" to Padre Pio), a man who would spend the half century to come riding the waves of regime change—serving as the mayor of San Giovanni from 1923 to 1927; the *podestà*, as the Fascists called the mayor, from 1927 to 1929; the Christian Democrat mayor from 1954 to 1958; and from 1963 to 1965 a director of the Farm Board, provincial commissioner for public works, first president of the Tourist Board, and holder of dozens of other public offices. Next to Morcaldi stands Padre Pio, his eyes lowered, his hands, in their gloves, joined; and next to him is Ezio Maria Gray, a Fascist MP from Piedmont passing through Puglia, who had wanted to meet the Capuchin with the stigmata.

It was a striking show of solidarity, but group portraits do not actually solve problems. Thanks to the demonstration of June 25, the mayor and the faithful had gotten the father guardian to suspend restrictions on Padre Pio, but it was clear that the real solution had to come not from San Giovanni Rotondo but from Rome. And so, in early July, Morcaldi led a delegation from San Giovanni to the capital. This group included the notary Giovanni Giuliani, the local secretary of the Popular Party, Luigi Massa, and Vincenzo d'Errico, commander of the militia.[32] The little delegation got a benevolent reception from the Vatican secretary of state, Cardinal Pietro Gasparri; but Cardinal Donato Sbarretti, prefect of the Congregation of the Council, which oversaw the discipline of the clergy, kept his distance.[33] In truth, it made little sense to think that a touch of homespun lobbying would be enough to overturn an official pronouncement of the Holy Office. Morcaldi and company returned to San Giovanni with the comfort of a few words of solidarity, but also with the anxious concern that the Vatican could order Padre Pio to be transferred at any moment.

After the official publication of the Holy Office opinion on Padre Pio's miracles, the Italian press treated Padre Pio with some caution. "The Vatican Refutes the Supposed Miracles of Padre Pio of San Giovanni Rotondo," headlined *La Gazzetta di Puglia*, following up the next week with an article spelling out why the Church was right to be careful when it came to claims of holiness, even when dealing with the "well-known" Padre Pio, whose fame had "spread all over Italy."[34] On July 21, the *Corriere della Sera* reported "Demonstrations in Favor of a So-Called Saint," pointing out that the pilgrims to San Giovanni came not just from nearby towns but from faraway places, and that among them were "even men of science, high prelates, writers and journalists." "The presence of Padre Pio is a real opportunity for the town," the paper continued: each visitor leaves his or her handful of coins, which the holy friar plans to convert into "hundreds of thousands of lire in public works, aid to the poor, assistance for war orphans, trousseaus for young women."[35] The cult's spiritual fortunes, the article implied, were closely linked to its financial benefits for the people of the Gargano.

The patina of time can be misleading, in this case about Padre Pio's real notoriety in 1920s Italy. Had a poll been taken in 1923, it would have surely established that only a tiny percentage of Italians had then heard of Padre Pio. Nevertheless, the dispute about how to handle the "Saint" was real. As the debates swirled around him in that summer of 1923, Padre Pio reacted with a combination of seraphic modesty and obedient resignation—and with the display of innocence of one who, having frequented the lives of the saints, knows that every Life has a chapter on "persecutions" at the hands of skeptics. When the mayor of San Giovanni, Morcaldi, back from the Vatican, informed Padre Pio that he was likely to be transferred in a matter of days, the Capuchin sent him a letter so full of heavenly charity that half a century later it would be incised on one wall of his crypt. He was willing to undergo any kind of mortification, Padre Pio wrote to the mayor, to prevent "doleful events" that might bloody San Giovanni. If he must be transferred, so be it; it was the will of God and his superiors. Anyway, to leave would not mean to forget. "I will always remember this generous people in my poor prayers," the friar said, expressing the wish that his bones come to rest "in a quiet corner of this land."[36]

Even as the Capuchin was writing his letter to the mayor, the order to transfer him had already been signed by the Capuchin minister general, Father Giuseppe Antonio of San Giovanni in Persiceto. It was addressed to Father Guardian Ignazio of Jelsi and copied to Father Cherubino of Castelnuovo, minister provincial of Ancona, the city on the Adriatic far to the north of San Giovanni Rotondo that Rome had chosen as Padre Pio's new home. Writing to the Capuchin minister in Ancona, the head of the order advised him it would be best to move Padre Pio "to a remote friary" to which "the curious" would find it difficult to make their way, where "false and exaggerated rumors" would be unlikely to arise, and where the "letters addressed to P. Pio" would no longer receive any replies.[37] In fact, the minister provincial of Ancona had already decided upon the monastery of Cingoli and had informed Father Guardian Pietro to that effect. "Ancona is no place for saints," Father Cherubino wrote with some sarcasm, announcing the imminent arrival of the "precious gift."[38]

The Royal Mail delivered quite a few letters about Padre Pio's destination in August of 1923. One of the most ardent was sent from Tortona to a prelate in Rome. Don Luigi Orione, founder of the charity Humble Works of Divine Providence, had been contacted by friends of

Padre Pio in the hopes he could persuade the Vatican to stop the friar's transfer. But just as Don Orione was about to act on this request, the Lord appeared to him—at the altar where he was celebrating the morning mass—and reminded him that all priests owe obedience to the Church unto death. And so, Don Orione wrote, he agreed that Padre Pio must depart San Giovanni, out of respect and devotion to the Holy Office. How could such earthly misadventures in any way modify the friar's destiny in the afterlife? "Padre Pio must be Jesus on the Cross in full, and enjoying the love of Jesus and the Holy Church, be crucified in the joy of charity" was Don Orione's judgment—the justice of Solomon or the justice of Pilate, as you like.[39]

Near the end of the month, a more surprising letter arrived on the desk of General Emilio De Bono, one of the "quadrumvirs" of the March on Rome, whom Mussolini had named national chief of police. The letter came from the Capuchin minister general, Father Giuseppe Antonio, and it was about Padre Pio. Father Antonio explained that the little friar of San Giovanni was supposed to be sent to a monastery in the Marche region, but that the move had not taken place because there had been threats of "serious and worrying reprisals" from some citizens of the Gargano town. The delay was unacceptable; the transfer must be carried out, and the ultradevout had to be made to stop stirring up trouble and preventing the authorities from maintaining public order. The Capuchin minister general was counting on De Bono to make sure the transfer took place without any serious consequences. "From this moment P. Pio of Pietrelcina is at the disposition of Your Excellency's direct and indirect orders," he wrote, "while I the undersigned will guarantee maximum docility on the part of the above-mentioned father and his confreres at San Giovanni Rotondo."[40] In effect, the Capuchins were handing the chief of police the job of deporting Padre Pio.

The order's concerns about possible reprisals derived from a show of force that the little friar's Praetorian guard had made on August 15, the Feast of the Assumption (as it happened, the third anniversary of that fateful day when Padre Pio blessed the Arditi flags, sealing his tie with the Fascio d'Ordine). Padre Pio had celebrated the morning mass, and all was quiet until sunset. In the evening, however, eight Fascists appeared at the friary with clubs in hand and let it be known that any attempt to remove Padre Pio would be met with violence.[41] Although he was usually very laconic in his letters about anything beyond the spiritual realm, this time Padre Pio himself decided to warn the order's vicar provincial, Father Luigi of Avellino. In the event he was forced to move, he said, the "inflamed populace" would inevitably take revenge on the local priests, whom his followers considered the villains in his ecclesiastical persecution. His own life, he added, could be in danger: two years previously, when a rumor spread that Padre Pio was leaving the Gargano by his own choice, a man from San Marco in Lamis had come up to the friar in "the public church" and pointed a pistol at him, shouting, "Better dead among us than alive for others!"[42]

Why, Padre Pio asked Father Luigi, had no one taken the responsibility of acknowledging this grave danger? He alone, "the principal actor of this drama, if in a passive role," had had the courage to speak! He alone was honest enough to acknowledge that if he were deported, no public security measures would be able to prevent the worst.

> It is clear to me and to anyone else who knows this town that not even a prolonged state of siege would prevent terrible, bloody reprisals. You know better than I what the religious passions of a populace can be. And this populace, so ardent and full of still primitive instincts—who wants to pretend that their threats are hollow?[43]

In those same days, Padre Pio gave a handwritten note to one of his "spiritual daughters," Angela Serritelli. It spelled out what he considered his last will and testament. Should the inhabitants of San Giovanni Rotondo prefer to kill him rather than see him sent away, his last wishes were that the civil and judicial authorities should commute the sentences of his assassins. "I don't want a hair touched on my behalf. . . . no matter whose. I have always loved everyone, I have always pardoned, and I do not wish to descend to my grave without having pardoned whoever wants to end my days."[44]

The hagiographic tradition has it that just when there seemed to be no alternative to Padre Pio's transfer, the arrival of the police in San Giovanni produced yet another miracle. According to this legend, the

Public Security functionary sent to San Giovanni Rotondo to carry out the transfer, Deputy Inspector Carmelo Camilleri, was so taken with Padre Pio that he returned to Rome without lifting a finger. He told General De Bono that the only proper course was to allow the living saint to remain where he was.[45] Police documents, however, tell a less edifying story. Camilleri, who was stationed not far from San Giovanni, was already becoming known for his tough, "no-holds-barred" fight against those who opposed Mussolini's regime, and had "won the approval" of local Fascist leaders, among them "His Excellency Giuseppe Caradonna." His specialties included confiscating red flags, arresting anyone who made offensive remarks about Mussolini, closing down clandestine union organizations, and more. "He has often made mass arrests of persons leading subversive parties," a carabinieri commander reported, "helping to block, at least in part, their anti-national activities."[46] It seems that Deputy Inspector Camilleri was a public servant well connected with Fascist circles on the Puglia plain—and therefore, we can assume, unwilling to break the unwritten pact linking the friars of Santa Maria delle Grazie with the local *squadristi*.

It is not clear why the police should have been expected to carry out the request of the Capuchin order to transfer Padre Pio, when the main threat to public order derived not from the little friar's presence in San Giovanni but from the threat of his removal. Back in 1919 the prefect of Foggia had already established that the forces of order were not to be called upon to arbitrate things like miracles and stigmata, and his successor as prefect had an easy time explaining to the Interior Ministry the advantages of maintaining the status quo. If the Capuchins really wanted to transfer Padre Pio, drastic security measures were in order; but it would be best, all things considered, to leave matters as they were. Among that "exasperated" populace, the prefect noted, were fanatics who spoke "of actually doing away with Padre Pio so as to keep at least his body in San Giovanni."[47]

The authorities at the Ministry decided on an immediate "suspension of the transfer,"[48] leaving the Capuchin order with nothing but its own resources to discourage the Padre Pio cult. Rather than insist on a forced relocation, the Capuchin hierarchy in the Vatican decided to institute a scorched-earth policy around the friar. They would try to isolate him, if not from the people of Gargano, then at least from the rest of Italy's faithful. On April 6, 1924, the procurator general of the order, Father Melchiorre of Benisa, sent a toughly worded memorandum to the guardians of all Capuchin monasteries. It was now forbidden to pass on any information about Padre Pio "either verbally or in written form," and it was forbidden to circulate his "images or sayings." "Anything that can in any way call attention to Padre Pio" was outlawed. It was also forbidden to advise anyone to make a pilgrimage to the friar with the stigmata or send "notes or letters" along with anyone traveling to San Giovanni Rotondo.[49]

"Let us behave as if we have never heard of" Padre Pio, the procurator general concluded his message to the guardians.[50] Three months later, the Holy Office was just as stern. A Monitum—a solemn admonition—issued on July 24 reiterated what the tribunal of the faith had ordered the previous year, adding a further note that urged believers to cut off all relationships, and cease correspondence, with Padre Pio.[51] Thus the Vatican hierarchy renewed its efforts to realize what Father Drehmanns had hoped for, the extinction of Padre Pio's memory on earth.

Rosaries and Daggers

In that summer of 1924, most Italians had other things on their minds than the misadventures of a Capuchin friar with stigmata. On June 10, less than two weeks after delivering a passionate speech in the Chamber of Deputies denouncing Mussolini and charging the Fascists with electoral fraud, the Socialist MP Giacomo Matteotti disappeared. Suspicion soon fell on Amerigo Dumini, a member of Mussolini's secret police, and his gang of *squadristi*. For seventy terrible days, until Matteotti's body was found—he had been stabbed with a carpenter's file and buried in a shallow grave just outside Rome—the trauma of his disappearance stunned the nation. It was a genuine psychodrama that struck the collective imagination not only for its political implications[52] but for its religious dimensions. From the start, the anti-Fascist leaders cast the MP's disappearance in mystical terms: unlike the "mere" martyrs of the Risorgimento,[53] Matteotti was a genuine Christ figure. Even before his body was recovered, the Socialist leader Filippo

Turati linked Matteotti's "sacrifice" with the resurrection of Jesus.[54] Such rhetoric reflected a vast current of feeling that found its expression in an entire liturgical apparatus built around the missing MP: lighted candles, celestial revelations, photos hidden inside prayer books, and "remains of the Cross" laid on the street where Matteotti was kidnapped.[55]

For the next twenty years Fascists and anti-Fascists would wage a posthumous battle over Matteotti: one side scribbling the mark of the cross, the other wiping it out; each side with their own "holy cards," depicting Matteotti or Mussolini; both battling over whether mourners should be allowed to visit the dead man's tomb in the town of Fratta Polesine.[56] A few months after his disappearance, an anthology of Matteotti's writings was published under the title *Holy Relics*.[57] Two years later, after a rigged murder trial allowed Dumini and the other killers to go free, a major in the Fascist Party's Militia for State Security actually sold at auction the blade Matteotti's murderers had left in his chest.[58] It was a relic, like the "holy truncheon" of the *squadristi* song celebrating their favorite weapon.[59] But even before the Matteotti murder, fascism was already proclaiming that the *squadre* were saintly, and also, to a certain extent, that saints needed *squadre*. Perhaps the most eloquent expression of that nexus was pronounced by a man who had befriended and protected Amerigo Dumini: Kurt Suckert, the official of the Fascio in Tuscany who was soon to become known as the writer Curzio Malaparte.[60]

In a 1923 afterword to a reprint of his *Revolt of the Damned Saints*, Malaparte offered an impressive "Portrait of Italian Affairs"[61] that provides insight into the evolution of clerico-fascism. Right from the terrible defeat at Caporetto in October 1917, said Malaparte, the soldiers had felt the need for a spiritual and military guide, both saint and strongman—an "imposter" and "miracle-worker" who could "heal the sick, prophesy, perform . . . charlatanry of all kinds," and also lead peasant-soldiers against the urban bastions of humanism and liberalism, of democracy and modernity. They yearned for "some kind of saint, a dirty, bearded friar with bare shins . . . with trinkets, medals, snake-skins, necklaces of bones, glass rosaries, stigmata, scars, deep, luminous eyes." Ever since Caporetto, the soldiers had prayed for "a terrible 'Italian Christ'" who would avenge "the real Italy, the Italy of the people and the countryside, ancient, Catholic and anti-modern," punishing those "petty Italians" drunk with egalitarianism and cowardice, with sleep and connections, with "unnatural coitus" and "fat buttocks on the face."[62]

Malaparte did not need to add that the "ever-so-Christian populace of the Carso" had found such a guide in Benito Mussolini. He did, however, make a point of showing how the March on Rome had represented the political and moral revenge of the damned saints of Caporetto—the soldiers now transformed into peasants in revolt, woodsmen, mowers, shepherds, grape and olive pressers, "red with grape must, red with the earth's blood." They marched with flowers in their guns, flying the standards of their guilds, waving their spoilers' clubs, their foot soldiers' helmets, their Arditi fezzes, their black kerchiefs, their war amulets, carrying images of the Virgin atop their poles, wooden statues of their small-town saints, "hermit saints, healer saints, pacific saints, war-like saints, avenger saints." St. Martin on horseback, St. George with his spear, St. Lucy with her eyes on a plate, St. Rocco with his unguents for the plague, St. Anthony among the pigs, St. Christopher at the ford, St. Joseph with his carpenter's plane,

St. Agnes of the seven swords—in Malaparte's improbable portrait these were the household gods of the black legions that had marched on Rome in 1922. A mystic and ferocious people, with rosaries around their wrists and pitchforks on their shoulders; cross and dagger, mercy and violence, justice and death.[63]

Malaparte's vision was so manifestly distorted that a historian would be ill-advised to try to apply it to the little Gargano stage on which the knights and the Capuchins of San Giovanni Rotondo were arrayed. Still, this was not just literary posturing.[64] Malaparte was clever enough to recognize right away what other Fascists would finally be resigned to only much later (despite all the Catholic masses celebrated in various Italian cities on the first anniversary of the March on Rome):[65] the fact that the Fascist revolution had rapidly become a clerico-fascist revolution, and it was precisely its clerical component that gave it an epochal quality, a historical role. The soldiers-turned-*squadristi* had acted on behalf of Jesus and the Church. What's more, they had done so not merely when they came down from their Apennine villages behind oxcarts and "squeaking wagons," not merely when they entered the "moribund cities" pushing statues of saints, little boxes full of amulets, and "great triumphant Crucifixes" before them—but also when they unsheathed their daggers and plunged them into the flesh of their enemies.

Giovanni Gentile, Mussolini's first minister of public instruction, also recognized something like what Malaparte saw in the new historical era that culminated with the March on Rome. Despite his political and ethical differences from Malaparte, Gentile shared with him a fundamental belief that "really-existing Catholicism" was the ideal religion for Italians.[66] Accordingly, when Gentile reformed the schools, he introduced classes in Catholic doctrine and required a crucifix to be hung in every classroom. He also emphasized the teaching of "regional culture," which meant local folklore, and which opened the way to a new flowering of sainthood in school texts.[67] Quarantined for more than half a century, the so-called Italian saints became the new heroes of a clerico-fascist creed to be spread among the juvenile populace.[68]

In 1926, the seven hundredth anniversary of his death, St. Francis of Assisi would become the central figure of this movement, celebrated in the catchy D'Annunzian formula as "the most Italian of saints and the most saintly of Italians."[69] With Father Gemelli leading the way and the whole of Umbria mobilized in a whirl of propaganda and tourism, with Il Duce himself playing on the idea that St. Francis—the Poverello of Assisi, the "poor one," the "mendicant-saint"—was his precursor,[70] the Franciscan year marked the greatest overlap between Italy of the cross and Italy of the fasces until the 1929 Lateran Treaty. More than a million and a half visitors went to Assisi between 1925 and 1927, journeying from every corner of Italy.[71] St. Francis was in fashion, to a degree that distressed lay Franciscan elitists like Giovanni Papini and Domenico Giuliotti, who were disgusted to see the La Verna countryside profaned "by the stink of gasoline and oratoria," to hear the belching and the mewing of the phony pilgrims, as well as "the loud nocturnal monkish concerts on the precipice where Francis received the stigmata."[72]

The Franciscan order had begun to prepare for the solemn occasion in 1924, the year marking the seven hundredth anniversary of St. Francis's stigmata. Father Vittorino Facchinetti, professor of medieval history at the Cattolica and a rising star in political Franciscanism,[73] published a thick volume about the founder's five wounds, refuting any somatic or psychological explanation in favor of an exquisitely supernatural one.[74] Not to be outdone, Father Gemelli devoted an entire issue of *Vita e Pensiero* to the miracle of La Verna, when St. Francis received the stigmata on the mountainside. The onetime positivist now recalled a promise he had made nearly twenty years before, when Paul Sabatier had asked him to write a study on the wounds of St. Francis. Gemelli's contribution to the occasion was titled *St. Francis's Stigmata Judged Scientifically,*[75] and it showed that he clearly had not forgotten his 1920 meeting with Padre Pio.

An Empty Miracle

The text that Father Gemelli published in 1924 was extraordinary in many ways. It spoke the jargon of modern science fluently but obeyed a logic that was anything but scientific. In recognizing the marvelous historical reality of St. Francis's stigmata, Gemelli also built a case for why it was impossible that any other saint could ever have stigmata. In other words, he transformed the *alter Christus* of the thirteenth century into a superhuman bulwark to hold back any pretenders in the twentieth.

The paper began with a small white lie, for Gemelli insisted he had "always felt repugnance" about investigating St. Francis from a scientific point of view and had only done so at the "insistence of friends."[76] As we know, however, in the period after his conversion, few intellectual challenges had seemed so worthy of his consideration as the wounds of St. Francis; as a doctor-seminarian he had intended to study them to learn the truth, the "whole truth"—without any theological, philosophical, hermeneutic, or mystical compunctions.[77] After this little prologue, Gemelli began by praising recent studies in the phenomenology of mysticism. The turn-of-the-century mind-set had been superseded, he proclaimed; Lombroso-style medical materialism was dead and buried, and neurologists, psychologists, and psychiatrists no longer fell back on the all-purpose diagnosis of hysteria. "The equation of saint and madman, neurosis and beatitude, insanity and mysticism no longer finds any serious defenders," wrote Gemelli by way of introduction to his paper.[78]

Neurosis stood on one side, beatitude on the other; that was the new consensus reached by the international scientific community, said Gemelli. Anyone who still insisted on studying mysticism as a symptom of mental illness was starting out on the wrong foot. The leading authorities had agreed to render unto Caesar what was Caesar's, to God what was God's. On one side were the outward signs of false mysticism: gangrenous sores of the epidermis of the hands, feet, and chest that were caused by hysteria and its corollary, self-mutilation. Not by chance, virtually all the bearers of these bogus stigmata were women: "I do not wish to say for all, but for many, too many, the diagnosis of hysteria is well-founded." On the other side were the interior manifestations of exceptional spiritual grace—the personal austerity, the consuming love for Christ of such genuine mystics as St. John of the Cross, St. Bernardino of Siena, St. Philip Neri, St. Alphonsus Liguori. And not by chance, none of these saints had anything unusual inscribed on their bodies, no divine brands "apart from the heights achieved in the exercise of virtue and love of God."[79]

In short, Father Gemelli denied there was anything supernatural about the skin lesions vulgarly described as stigmata.

> These are nothing but a phenomenon of "psittacism," which is to say that the ill person procures the lesions artificially, although it is difficult to observe and demonstrate that. The proof lies in the fact that the wounds are incised more or less deeply, but never below the subcutaneous connective layer. Often, the phenomenon is periodic, in the sense that at certain times the wounds grow deeper and bleed. Many presumed cases of stigmatization are nothing more than common hysteria, among which psittacism manifests itself as an imitation of the wounds of Christ.[80]

And what of the five wounds of St. Francis of Assisi? The most famous Franciscan in Italy was hardly going to use the occasion of the seven hundredth anniversary of the day the saint received the stigmata to declare his skepticism about that miracle. On the contrary; Gemelli was not content merely to assert that Francis's wounds were those of a genuine Christ figure, that God had pressed "the last seal" (in Dante's famous words) on his body, and that a good Christian must believe, no questions asked, proof or no proof, science or no science.[81] Instead, the rector of the Cattolica pointed to a passage from Thomas of Celano that Sabatier had cited in his *Life of St. Francis*, in which it was said that the saint's stigmata had been not wounds but fleshy growths, not indentations in the skin but nails made of flesh. "If only for this reason," wrote Gemelli, "St. Francis of Assisi must be considered the only genuine stigmatic." The false stigmata of the hysterics "are always excavations, devastation, sores," while in the case of St. Francis there was "the creation of new cells, that is, a proliferative process."[82]

God had not taken away, he had *added* something to the special body of St. Francis. This miraculous neoplasmic process was responsible for the one and only case of genuine stigmata in the history of Christianity. All the rest, anything that involved the subtraction of cells and the death of tissues—open wounds, bloody sores, necroses of the skin—was the result of secret manipulations that any hysteric could undertake all by himself, using darning needles, chemical tinctures, and whatever else was needed to create stigmata à la Grand Guignol. Such wounds pointed only to the same "puerile quality seen in other exterior manifestations of hysteria."[83] Whether these manifestations assumed the form of stigmata or of a crown of thorns, of ecstasy or levitation, they belonged to the sphere of madness, not of miracles.

Here Gemelli cited his own experience in the Padre Pio affair—without mentioning the friar's name, which, he said, he must necessarily conceal because high Vatican officials had required his discretion. In Pio's case, said Gemelli, he had been able to "ascertain with certainty" a diagnosis of hysteria, "to which many of these strange simulations of holiness can be traced." Gemelli then melded his account of Padre Pio and his stigmata into a larger discussion of other fanatics of sainthood that he had had occasion to observe: a woman with a crown of thorns stuck on her head, another with an image of the Sacred Heart on her breast, and yet another who, at the moment she swallowed the Sacred Host, simulated drops of blood that emanated from the consecrated wafer.[84]

The only thing that really interested Father Gemelli about figures like Padre Pio was the almost wondrous contrast between appearance and reality—the baroque grandeur of the Christo-mimesis next to the would-be saints' flat, narrow horizons. "In these cases of hysterical stigmata, so outwardly rich and exuberant, you find a desperate spiritual poverty. You could say that God has performed an empty miracle, to reveal and make known a grace and a holiness that do not exist."[85]

The Value of a Soul

The scientific authorities cited by Gemelli had perhaps agreed to render unto Caesar what was Caesar's, to God what was God's; but when it came to the Fascist regime and the Catholic Church, the distinctions were not quite as scrupulously maintained. In 1925, four years before the Lateran Treaty, the two powers were already carefully studying where their interests might coincide. The need for order and discipline, for authority and hierarchy; the critique of secular culture and modernity; the suspicion of liberalism and democracy; the use of ritual as a method of moral cohesion and persuasion; a vision of society and the sacred as fused and all-encompassing—such were some of the elements of an ideological common denominator between Mussolini's rule and the Church of Pius XI.[86] There was also an actual piece of legislation to seal the tacit clerico-fascist accord: a law that excused the clergy from military service and that brought the civil calendar in line with religious holidays (among other things, giving less importance to the Italian civil holiday the Vatican most despised, the September 20 anniversary of the defeat of the Papal States).[87] The measure also outlawed Freemasonry and introduced the religious feast of Christus Rex, henceforth an emblem of the Catholic *reconquista* of Italian society.[88]

The year 1925 opened with Mussolini's famous speech in Parliament on January 3, in which Il Duce claimed moral and political responsibility for the Matteotti killing.[89] Even as Mussolini was intimidating his opponents into silence, St. Peter's Square rang out with the voice of a certain Monsignor Carlo Salotti, who—heedless of the regime's acknowledged violence—spoke with pride about the Catholic-Fascist cause.[90] The Vatican asked for railway fare reductions for pilgrims coming to Rome for the Jubilee Year, and the Italian government

obliged. A bill on economic measures in favor of the clergy made sure that both the bishops and regular orders got substantial increases in income.[91] In Milan, the city government revived an ancient custom in which the town porters offered holy oil to St. Aquilino, one tiny example of the widespread Fascist resurrection of forgotten folklore that, in a country like Italy, often meant reviving cults of the saints.[92]

But none of this did anything to resolve the problem of Padre Pio. In fact, in the spring of 1925 the question of his transfer to the Marche region again became an active issue. The new vicar provincial of Foggia, Father Bernardo of Alpicella, imposed on Padre Pio a strict code of behavior: he was not allowed to approach women in the sacristy, could not associate with the faithful outside the confessional, was ordered not to let anyone kiss his hands.[93] Meanwhile Father Giuseppe Antonio, the head of the Capuchin order, went knocking on the door of the Fascist government once again. Father Giuseppe Antonio asked General Francesco Crispo Moncada, the national chief of police, to forcibly transfer the friar with the stigmata to Ancona "with the maximum haste and secrecy."[94] What happened next, to all intents and purposes, was a replay of the events of 1924. The prefect of Foggia warned the chief of police it would be unwise to do anything hasty. If the police really intended to carry it out, the transfer must come as a surprise, and once the friar was deported at least 150 carabinieri would be needed to patrol San Giovanni Rotondo for several months, for the townspeople had not forgotten "either recent or long-ago bloodshed."[95] Faced with such a scenario, Crispo Moncada decided to ask the prefect to cautiously maintain the status quo.[96]

But if the police were cautious, Padre Pio's followers were anything but. During 1925, they not only deployed their *squadre* but also engaged in espionage. A group of influential Capuchins who were unhappy about the order's treatment of the friar enrolled Monsignor Cornelio Cuccarollo, the bishop of a town in the Puglia-Campania hills, in a scheme to collect sensitive information about Monsignor Pasquale Gagliardi, archbishop of Manfredonia, whose archdiocese included San Giovanni Rotondo.[97] It was the start of a war inside the Church that would go on for the next forty years—a war of documents, both legitimate and counterfeit; memoirs, both public and secret; and books, both published and confiscated, that would push the Holy Office to ever more exhausting efforts to verify sources and evidence.[98] It was a genuine ecclesiastical feud not only over the question of where Padre Pio should live, but also over the spiritual and economic costs and benefits of his fame as a holy man.

The forces in the field resembled those deployed around the friar at the start of the 1920s. Padre Pio's supporters included the hard-liners among the Capuchins of Santa Maria delle Grazie as well as his faithful Gargano followers, some high-ranking personages in the Catholic institutional and pastoral hierarchies, and a handful of lay intermediaries (some of whom we will get to know all too well) who acted as a link between the humble followers and the Church. His detractors had their own Gargano inner circle, made up of the longtime clergy of San Giovanni Rotondo and the archdiocese of Manfredonia, along with large sections of the Capuchin order, both its central officials and local authorities. The party of the detractors could also count on apparently impartial ecclesiastical figures who were in fact directly involved in the Padre Pio affair, if only for reasons of competition between religious orders. The Franciscan Friars Minor, for example, were notoriously wary of the Capuchins, who had split off from the Franciscans in a 1528 scission, so it was no surprise that even four centuries later Gemelli the Franciscan regarded the Capuchins with a reproachful eye.[99]

In 1925 Don Orione, the founder of the Humble Works of Divine Providence, who had previously bowed to the Church's decision to relocate Padre Pio, now began to lobby in Vatican circles[100] in favor of a medical report filed by a Roman doctor named Giorgio Festa. Dr. Festa, who had seen Padre Pio in 1919 and 1920, was enchanted by the perfume emanating from his bloody hands and remained convinced that the stigmata had a supernatural etiology.[101] In the spring of 1925, he submitted a report on the Capuchin's stigmata to the Holy Office. More than seventy typewritten pages long, this extended manifesto was his attempt to counter Father Gemelli's brief but pointed 1920 evaluation of the friar.

Festa had never seen Gemelli's report, however, because the Holy Office had refused to release it. Instead of attacking it directly, therefore, Festa focused his efforts on trying to demolish Gemelli's published paper of 1924. How could a reasonable person maintain that the only true stigmata of Christian history were those of St. Francis, Festa demanded, merely because they manifested themselves as proliferative—while all other cases, including Padre Pio's, were symptoms of hysteria because they manifested themselves as dying tissues? Gemelli, argued Festa, had presented no concrete arguments, either histological or psychological; he asked to be believed on faith, "ipse dixit." At best, his thesis deserved "intense pity" for the contrast between its scientific weakness and the intellectual arrogance with which he expressed himself.[102]

The prestigious Italian Jesuit journal *Civiltà cattolica* weighed in on the same side. In a review of Father Gemelli's essay on St. Francis's stigmata, the Jesuit publication concluded that it was "neither exact nor prudent" to say that the man from Assisi was the only true stigmatic in all of Christian history.[103] Nevertheless, the Holy Office continued to hold Father Gemelli the most reliable expert on stigmata, and he was asked to reply officially and in writing to Dr. Festa's comments. Gemelli took almost a year to do so, but when he did, in April 1926, the document he produced was devastating.[104]

Telling the tale from the beginning, Gemelli recounted how six years previously, playing "the game of the convinced and converted doctor," he had gained the trust of the Capuchins of San Giovanni Rotondo and of Padre Pio, who had agreed to show him his wounds. Father Benedetto of San Marco in Lamis had even offered him some souvenir photos of the stigmatic friar as well as handkerchiefs soaked with his blood, Gemelli said. But it would have required something quite different to convince Gemelli those wounds had a supernatural nature.

> Anyone with experience in forensic medicine, and above all in the infinite variety of sores and wounds that self-destructive soldiers presented during the war, can have no doubt that these were wounds of erosion caused by the use of a caustic substance. The base of the sore and its shape are in every way similar to the sores observed in soldiers who procured them with chemical means. The color of the base, the shape of the margins, their thickness, etc., all suggest this.

Gemelli had also employed his psychological skills during the visit to San Giovanni. He had asked Padre Pio "to express himself on holy matters," and found—it was "a very painful surprise"—that the little friar was utterly unable to do so.

> In Padre Pio we see the well-known characteristics of a notable degree of mental deficiency with a consequent narrowing of the field of knowledge. He is the ideal partner with whom former Minister Provincial Father Benedetto is able to create an incubus-succubus pair . . . He is a good priest: calm, quiet, meek, more because of the mental deficiency than out of virtue. A poor soul able to repeat a few stereotypical religious phrases, a poor, sick man who has learned his lesson from his master Father Benedetto.

When this psychological profile was combined with the evidence that the Capuchin's stigmata were erosive rather that proliferative, the clinical picture was complete. Padre Pio was "a psychopath" whose self-destructive compulsion would disappear only when he was removed from the "suggestive atmosphere" of San Giovanni, an atmosphere of which he was both "cause and effect." Removed to a secret place and put under the care of a competent physician, the little friar would at least have the chance to be cured of the sores on his skin, if not of his irremediable poverty of spirit. Otherwise he would continue to cause spiritual and pastoral damage, for his proselytizing could only alienate the souls of the faithful from God. Faced with the "contagiousness" of such phenomena, Gemelli insisted, the Holy Office had to impose absolute isolation on "poor sick souls like Padre Pio." Dangerous to themselves and others, they were therefore "subjects to remove from society."

Father Gemelli's clinical judgment was not mere personal prejudice, and he was not the only one to discuss Pio's stigmata as symptoms of a disease. The official publication of Italian psychologists, *Rivista di psicologia*, featured an article in 1926 in which the renowned scientist Vincenzo Bianchi presented Padre Pio's wounds as an extreme limit of what suggestion and autosuggestion combined could produce in the most serious cases.[105] Nevertheless, another affair that Father Gemelli was involved in during this same period suggests with what sovereign nonchalance he exploited his scientific reputation, handing out marks of infamy and labels of madness left and right. In January 1926, the Vatican asked Gemelli to visit Don Ernesto Buonaiuti, a prominent anti-Fascist and an illustrious scholar of the history of Christianity. The Church considered heretical Buonaiuti's view that Christianity was a creed that responded to the forces of history rather than a set of timeless truths, and they wanted Gemelli to deliver him an ultimatum. If Buonaiuti did not give up his university teaching once and for all and cease publishing his unorthodox books, the Holy Office would impose on him the harshest measures that canon law foresaw.[106]

When he went to meet Buonaiuti, Gemelli came with that zeal for investigation that was so much part of his character, not to mention the prestige that derived from being the founder and rector of Italy's Catholic University. But Gemelli also brought with him, as Buonaiuti wrote to a friend, an unconcealed suspicion that Buonaiuti was either "a dissembler or a sick man" and "a paranoic."[107] As a result, Buonaiuti simply hardened his position, expressing resolve and even pride in his modernist approach to the history of Christianity and to the proper forms of Catholic ministry.[108] Gemelli's visit thus hastened the Holy Office's decision to excommunicate Buonaiuti, making him a pariah of the Church and condemning him to moral isolation and economic ruin. The diagnosis that Gemelli issued for Don Ernesto was very much like the one that he applied to Padre Pio: Buonaiuti needed treatment "not from the priesthood, but from professionals who assist unhappy psychic deviants."[109]

The Franciscan liked to project an image of himself as a man who combined the honesty of a priest with the authority of a scientist; and as it happened, Father Gemelli had many opportunities in those years to unmask imposters. He judged Padre Pio of San Giovanni Rotondo to be a phony mystic, both self-destructive and mentally deficient. He diagnosed Don Ernesto of Rome as either an astute simulator or a wretched madman. He even had an opinion about the famous Amnesiac of Collegno—the mysterious case of patient number 44,170 in the Collegno psychiatric hospital near Turin, a case that captivated all of Italy in 1927. A widow from Verona thought she had recognized the man as her husband, Giulio Canella, who had disappeared during World War I. The police and magistrates had identified him as a swindler by the name of Mario Bruneri. Without hesitating for a minute, Gemelli accepted the challenge of determining the truth. Twenty years before, he had known the real Canella, a scholar of philosophy and pedagogy, and the two of them had founded a review, the *Rivista di filosofia neoscolastica*. When the Turin prosecutor asked Gemelli to visit the hospital for the insane at Collegno to see if he recognized the man, the Franciscan took the opportunity to submit the amnesiac to a tough philosophical and theological interrogation. He concluded the man could not be the learned and very religious Canella, all but providing the magistrate with the proof to convict the swindler Bruneri.[110]

For years, as long as the mystery of Collegno continued to fill up the pages of Italy's major newspapers, Gemelli was held to be the standard-bearer of the "Brunerians" against the "Canellians"; and the latter—the ones who believed the amnesiac was really Canella—would denigrate Father Gemelli and his phony certainties in terms very similar to those used by Padre Pio's devotees.[111] What a "pitiful impression" he made, this doctor without any discretion, this friar without mercy, "dispensing sentences after a half-hour of professorial inquisition." "Whether you like it or not, this vehement, arrogant man will step forward, his habit only just covering his army shin-guards," wrote one Cannelian. "He sets himself up as a judge, who comes, who sees . . . and who sentences with the speed of a new Caesar, who believes in himself because of his rank, it's all so simple, it's all so easy, it's all so speedy and . . . it's all so legitimate, everything else can be tossed aside—respectable families and witnesses, doctors and psychiatrists, as if they were so many rubber toys!"[112]

Chiseled in Christ

Father Gemelli's reply to the accusations Dr. Festa had raised with the Holy Office about Gemelli's evaluation of Padre Pio bore the date of April 6, 1926. The following day, Violet Gibson, a fifty-year-old Irish aristocrat who genuinely was mentally unbalanced, took a shot with a revolver at Benito Mussolini, grazing him on the nose.[113] It was the first in a series of attempts on Il Duce's life that would culminate with an attack in Bologna on October 23 and lead to the so-called Special Laws for the Defense of the State, the formal beginning of the dictatorship.[114] Those failed assassination attempts did much to cement the political alliance between the Fascist regime and the Catholic Church. On October 4, delivering a sermon in the Assisi Cathedral, Cardinal Merry Del Val, legate of Pius XI to the celebrations for the seventh Franciscan centenary, asserted that Mussolini was "visibly protected by God." During the following weeks, the vaults of Italian churches rang with the sounds of the *Te Deum* in thanks for the preservation of Il Duce's life. On Christmas Eve the pope himself explained the failed attacks as the "near visible intervention" of Providence.[115]

Nineteen twenty-six was also the year in which Mussolini's ex-mistress Margherita Sarfatti laid the first stone in the Duce cult with her epoch-making book, *Dux*.[116] Although Sarfatti argued that any "fetishism" about Il Duce's body was foolishness, she nevertheless approved of such fetishistic behavior when it came to the uneducated: the women of Abruzzo ("widows and mothers of the war dead mostly") who had wanted to touch Mussolini on his visits to their towns "as they do, in that ancient land, with fetishes and relics";[117] the women of Sicily who had greeted Il Duce with their "arms raised stiff in invocation," believing him to be a messenger from their dear loved ones who had died at the front.[118] Mussolini himself, in his preface to *Dux*, spoke of how he had been marked as a man for the many, with "a stigmata that . . . one carries from birth," born to lead as others are born intelligent or mentally deficient.[119]

Those figurative stigmata marking him as a public man may have been congenital, but on his path to power he had also acquired other ones as well. On the Carso during the Great War, a trench mortar had exploded, and forty-two pieces of shrapnel stuck in the flesh of Corporal Mussolini like "the arrows of a St. Sebastian."[120] After the war, Mussolini used those wounds to build an image of himself as a political leader ready to fight in the trenches alongside the humblest of men, to embody the suffering of Italians right up to annihilation, and then rise again to redeem the nation and lead it along paths of glory.[121] Duly reproduced in *Dux* was the photograph of Corporal Mussolini laid on

a primitive stretcher, his head bound in gauze, his limbs immobile, more dead than alive.[122] Another photograph, taken a few months later, showed the wounded soldier among the convalescent veterans in Milan, leaning on a pair of crutches, unsteady on his feet, but destined by Providence to get well.[123]

Even more reverent than Mussolini's ex-mistress was the man who stood as the very symbol of the war disabled, Carlo Delcroix. It was he who found the strong words needed to describe the pact Mussolini had made with the severely war disabled. Delcroix, who had lost both his eyes and his hands in the Dolomites, and who believed that those wounds had granted him both a moral compass and happiness, portrayed Mussolini as a reincarnation of Christ and his recovery as a kind of salvation.[124] After he was wounded, the future Duce had been carried for first aid to the church in the little Friuli town of Doberdò—the same church D'Annunzio wrote about in *Prayer for Doberdò*, where the poet imagined St. Francis kneeling before an altar piled with the helmets and the boots of those who had died in battle. Then, and only then, studying his hands made red by the blood-red land of the Carso, Mussolini felt he had received "the last investiture," the stigmata of his own Passion. As Delcroix described the moment: "The man of our times had to see his own blood and feel the claws of the vulture dig in, he had to be bitten and slashed in order to become more worthy, to become invincible."[125]

By 1926, Fascist Italy's Christ figure was more Benito Mussolini than it was Padre Pio of Pietrelcina or the Socialist deputy Giacomo Matteotti. Prayers that mimicked the Creed were recited to him, and so were praises borrowed from the medieval liturgy of *Christus vincit*.[126] Il Duce was considered better than anyone at performing miracles, including the miracle of healing. How many children—according to regime propaganda—got well after a photograph of Mussolini was laid under their pillow; how many of the deaf and dumb recovered their speech in order to swear loyalty to the founder of the empire; how many pregnant women tacked a portrait of Il Duce on the wall so as to transmit his virtues to the creature in their wombs![127] And then there were his even more amazing feats, like the time Mussolini stopped the lava from flowing down the side of Etna.[128] Such beliefs betray an enduring Italian taste for excess, for circus prodigies, for coups de théâtre—but also the growing ideological connection between fascism and Catholicism, with its ancient culture of the wondrous and the supernatural, of miracles, resurrection, and the Last Judgment.[129]

With the Lateran Treaty and Concordat now not far away, the rhetoricians of the regime would begin to talk about "the vortex of the faithful" around Il Duce as the unequivocal evidence of a deep "Italian religiosity."[130] Fascism was paradoxically all the more modern, they said, because it had revitalized the millenarian cult of the saints. Catholicism, meanwhile, was the most successful prescription ever for a hierarchically governed society.[131] And both—the nation and the Church—were now "chiseled in Christ":[132] that strange Christ with no beard and no hair, the Redeemer of Predappio, Mussolini.

6. LIVES OF THE SAINT

The report that Agostino Gemelli sent to the Holy Office in 1926—perhaps the most negative document ever written about Padre Pio of Pietrelcina—contained one very interesting note. After describing the Capuchin friar as something of a simpleton who was completely under the sway of his superior, Gemelli drew the attention of the Vatican tribunal to another figure in Padre Pio's circle: "a certain Emanuele, that's all I can remember of his name." A few months earlier this Emanuele had come to see Gemelli, presenting himself as a schoolteacher. He told Gemelli that Vatican officials were making a serious mistake in challenging Padre Pio's miraculous powers, and that, should the Holy Office forcibly transfer the friar to another district, his followers would fight back "with force, including armed force."[1]

That warning, in Gemelli's opinion, showed just how dangerous the cult around Padre Pio was becoming. "A sort of family, a congregation of souls (both men and women) taught and led by Padre Pio has grown up in San Giovanni Rotondo," Gemelli wrote, and various members of this clan had approached him to complain that he was hostile to the holy friar. Gemelli urged the Holy Office to investigate this Emanuele in particular, who seemed to be a man of dubious moral conduct. As Gemelli saw it, he was "the ringleader" of that little group of people clustered around Padre Pio.[2]

Although Gemelli did not remember the ambiguous character's surname, his appraisal was astonishingly perceptive, even more so than he could have known. Over the decades to come, Padre Pio's tale would be decisively shaped by this one man, whose full name was Emanuele

Brunatto. He would be Peter to the Gargano Christ: the first and most important apostle, the founder of the cult. Though most of the hagiographies of the Capuchin friar have carefully avoided mentioning this impresario of sainthood, the story of Padre Pio cannot be told without telling that of Brunatto. In 2003, after Padre Pio was canonized, one very devout Catholic journalist did dedicate a pamphlet called *The Man Who Saved Padre Pio* to Brunatto's life and adventures,[3] but like the other hagiographers he did not do the work of a historian—that is, researching the circumstances, weighing the evidence, and interpreting the events.

Until now, therefore, a side of Brunatto's life has remained hidden, a side that, as we will see, throws an entirely new and somewhat sinister light on Padre Pio's history and reveals a hidden side of this grassroots religious cult. The Emanuele who aroused Gemelli's suspicions during his brief visit in 1926 was a man gifted with unusual intellectual abilities, if not with spiritual substance; a con man of great talent, infinite imagination, and world-class enterprise. After Brunatto arrived on the scene, Padre Pio's horizons would expand far beyond the walls of his Capuchin friary and the Vatican palaces where Church dignitaries debated whether he was a holy man. Soon, they would reach Paris, Brussels, Berlin, and even more distant lands.

Emanuele Brunatto, to sum up his life in the bluntest of terms, was a chronic liar, a ruthless extortionist, and an incorrigible double-dealer. At the same time, he was capable of coordinating a vast political, financial, and espionage network that put Padre Pio's devout followers in direct contact with the top of the Fascist hierarchy and with the leaders of the Vatican administration. It was he who, working behind the scenes, persuaded the Holy Office in 1933 to relax the restrictions it had imposed on Padre Pio's priestly role. And it was due to Brunatto that the project that would crown Padre Pio with sainthood—the building of a great modern hospital in the heart of the archaic Gargano Peninsula—first took off in 1941. Without Brunatto's hard work, the Padre Pio cult might never have overcome the obstacles in its way and blossomed into its astonishing postwar prosperity.

Brunatto was also the author of one of the earliest biographies of Padre Pio, which he wrote under the pseudonym of Giuseppe De Rossi.

Published in 1926, the biography was aimed at getting Fascist opinion-makers to spread the word about Padre Pio. Increasingly, the wounds of Christ were becoming political stigmata, sanctifying the clerico-fascist regime.

The Padre Pio Party

Brunatto's work was not quite the first book written about Padre Pio. The earliest biographies of the Capuchin friar were published in 1921, in a Spain bedecked with sweating crucifixes, by Brother Peregrino da Matarò.[4] The first to come out in Italy was written by Giuseppe Cavaciocchi, a journalist for the Roman newspaper *Il Messaggero*, and was published in 1924. Both Cavaciocchi's and Brunatto's biographies had the same title, *Padre Pio of Pietrelcina*, and both of them were placed on the Vatican's Index of forbidden books.[5] There was nothing very significant about that censorship, though; the authors had simply neglected to get ecclesiastical approval before writing. A more interesting point in common is that these first two Italian biographies of Padre Pio, each of them illustrated with photographs, were issued by the same publisher: Giorgio Berlutti.[6]

And so, before looking into Cavaciocchi and Brunatto's books (which hindsight shows were the original sources of Padre Pio's claims to sainthood), we would do well to examine the figure of the publisher. Little known to historians,[7] Berlutti deserves some attention, because he belongs among those who took part in what has been called "the intellectuals' March on Rome"[8]—that is, those figures in the world of ideas who early on threw their support to Mussolini. The appearance of the two Padre Pio biographies on Berlutti's list in quick succession is unlikely to have been sheer coincidence. Rather, it points to a deliberate strategy, a conscious decision to promote the figure of Padre Pio among the Fascist intelligentsia.

Born to a humble family, Berlutti studied at the Catholic seminary of Tuscania, near Viterbo, and then opened a paper goods shop in the town. Around the end of World War I, as he was turning thirty, he moved to Rome and opened a print shop in Piazza Navona. "In those days," a police report from 1931 says, "they called it the 'Loanshark

Press' because he would loan authors small sums of money, forcing them to sign notes at high interest rates."[9] Politically, Berlutti started out by approaching the Socialist Party, but when he was rebuffed he turned to the nascent Fascist movement, "proposing himself as a publisher to writers connected with the movement when other printers, concerned about reprisals, were reluctant to publish party propaganda."[10] A member of the Italian Fascist Party as early as 1921, Berlutti was shrewd enough to back a winning horse in the Fascist intellectual Giuseppe Bottai, then an editor on Mussolini's newspaper. Bottai agreed to edit a series on politics called "Arguments of the Day"—really little more than a summary of the sentiments of the Fascist paramilitaries and war veterans—for Berlutti's press, and Berlutti soon found himself well placed to take advantage of Mussolini's rise to power. He even managed to get the contract to publish Mussolini's *Program of Government*,[11] with commentary by Bottai, after the March on Rome in 1922.

Such connections explain how a tiny press was able, from 1923 on, to boast so many of the leading cultural and political figures of the new regime among its authors. Besides becoming, in effect, Mussolini's unofficial publisher,[12] Berlutti brought out works ranging from Futurist provocation to hypernationalist memoirs, from anti-Liberal tracts to Fascist propaganda.[13] His titles went all the way from pious to nihilist—from books like *Franciscan Lyrics* by Father Luigi Zambarelli, a celebration of St. Francis prepared for the seven hundredth anniversary of the appearance of his stigmata, to the likes of Stefano Maria Cutelli's *Lions That Laugh*, a Nietzschean ode to the Blackshirts by a Roman lawyer who would go on to be the leading theoretician of racial superiority.[14]

In short, even before Padre Pio appeared on his list, Giorgio Berlutti had already experimented with the heady amalgam of clerico-fascism. And it wasn't just in the books he published that Berlutti embraced the growing overlap between the Catholic and Fascist faiths. His name crops up everywhere in the Fascist cultural effort—led by the philosopher and minister of education Giovanni Gentile—to meld sacred rite with profane ritual and use folklore as the instrument to educate the masses. Under the aegis of the Fascist national association for organized recreation, Berlutti worked to persuade intellectuals to celebrate popular traditions, beginning with festivals for local patron saints.[15]

He was also co-opted by the Ministry of Public Instruction to help reform the system of public libraries,[16] and served for several years as the editor of the periodical *Bibliografia fascista*, which aimed to enroll intellectual support for the regime.[17]

In 1926, the year he published Brunatto's biography of Padre Pio, Berlutti's luck was running high. He got the call to found the Libreria del Littorio (The Lictor Library), the Fascist Party's semiofficial publisher, which opened under the motto—supposedly of Mussolini's coinage—"book and rifle, the Fascist model."[18] Ideas and action, the culture of the schoolroom and that of the shooting range: the regime wanted to encourage both,[19] and they knew of no one better than Giorgio Berlutti to guarantee the new publisher's fidelity to Il Duce. Brunatto's biographical efforts thus found more than just a congenial publisher. They found the broadcast tower of the National Fascist Party—which, as of 1926, would be the *only* party on Italy's political horizon.

The Friar of Christ and the Papal Antichrist

As we have seen, Brunatto's book was not Berlutti's first encounter with Padre Pio of Pietrelcina. In 1924, he had published the biography by Giuseppe Cavaciocchi, commissioning the book from a series of articles that the journalist had done on the Capuchin friar for *Il Messaggero*. The book would be a "stunning success," predicted Cavaciocchi and Berlutti, because the whole world considered Padre Pio to be "of exceptional importance."[20]

Cavaciocchi was not new to the journalistic scene. He had started working in Florence at the turn of the twentieth century, had moved north to Cuneo, in Piemonte, and then to Livorno before landing in the capital in the momentous year of 1922, when Mussolini came to power. Back in 1897, he had enrolled as a gung-ho twenty-five-year-old volunteer in the Legione Cipriani, a regiment of Garibaldini and Socialists who went off to fight with the Greeks against the Turks.[21] But by the mid-1920s, the onetime Freemason Cavaciocchi had become a diehard Fascist, who would soon move from his perch at *Il Messaggero* to Mussolini's press office, part of the "consensus factory" that Il Duce established when he seized power.[22] By the 1930s Cavaciocchi would be one of the main promoters of the cult of *mussolinismo*[23]—the worship of Il Duce even at the expense of Fascist principles—and in addition to his pioneering tome *Padre Pio of Pietrelcina*, could boast the authorship of one of the more slavish tributes to Il Duce, *Mussolini: A Critical Synthesis*.[24]

Where the biographer seeks to sharply delineate a personality, the hagiographer needs to show that a particular life conforms to the universal requirements for sainthood.[25] The subject's childhood and adolescence thus take on a special importance, for in a saint's life the end reiterates the beginning in a repeated revelation of the same facts.[26] Equally important to hagiography is the inclusion of a certain amount of boilerplate—because every saint recalls the virtues of an earlier saint, and all recall those of Jesus Christ. True to this formula, Cavaciocchi begins his tale of Padre Pio in the town of Pietrelcina, in rural Campania, where the future saint had showed himself to be a special child. According to Cavaciocchi, the early life of young Forgione was marked by a powerful mystical drive. He showed no interest in girls, nor did puberty bring on any emotional upheaval. Instead, he fought terrible battles with the devil inside the "four rustic rooms" of the family house, days and nights of hand-to-hand combat with evil spirits that "hurled him from the bed to the balcony, tossed books in his face, slapped him, and attacked him ever more fiercely the more he resisted their

temptations." Once he defeated these diabolical adversaries, the rest was easy. There were the first hints of the stigmata in his seminary cell and in the barracks where he lived as a priest during the First World War; the five bold wounds that appeared on September 20, 1918, the agonizing wonders of an out-of-the-ordinary body; and the popular excitement, from the copious offerings of money for good works to the armed Fascists who came to guard the friary and prevent his deportation.[27]

Having outlined this story, Cavaciocchi related his own visit to the Capuchin friar's Gargano monastery, seeking, at this point, not information but confirmation—not *facts* but *proof* of the superhuman nature of Padre Pio. He had arrived in San Giovanni Rotondo on a chill, damp afternoon, following a "spasmodically bumpy" ride in the mail van along the "wild and solitary" road that ran from the Tavoliere plain to the Gargano mountains. He had been met by the mayor, the energetic local Fascist Party chief, and, in the absence of a hotel, had been lodged with a customs guard named Calogero Vinciguerra—a fine fellow "with two big gold stripes on his hat," a hardworking wife, and "four young and very attractive daughters" who were "naturally" lay sisters, "like all the other 1,300 women of San Giovanni Rotondo." Just as receptive and pleasant was Padre Pio's secretary Angela Serritelli, an elementary school teacher who also served as generalessa of the army of the lay sisters, and who promised assistance to Cavaciocchi during his visit. In short, the public relations network of San Giovanni Rotondo sprang to life to receive this journalist who had come down from Rome to learn about Padre Pio.[28]

The Capuchin friar's local promoters would not regret their hospitality. Thanks to Cavaciocchi, Padre Pio's body—until then the province of medical investigations with their dry scientific language—would now belong to the glorious realm of literature and art. Readers of this first Italian book about Padre Pio would discover "the regularity and fullness of his noble, handsome face," whose "perlaceous pallor" was emphasized by the "dark reflections" of his hair, mustache, and beard that would have been "dear to Titian's brush." Those readers could dwell on Padre Pio as he conducted the mass, his every gesture charged with a transcendental meaning intensified by the all-too-human pain of the stigmata. They could admire the moral fiber of a man capable of

remaining seated in the confessional from 4 a.m. until 11 a.m.—five hundred of the faithful confessed and absolved—and then, after mass, of standing for another hour and a half while he distributed a mountain of communion wafers.[29]

Cavaciocchi spared no excess in his portrait of Padre Pio: "This was the St. Francis I saw in my youth in Guercino's celebrated painting at the art museum of Cesena and which the dynamic Lombard artist Angelo Landi recently painted in a lunette for the chapel at Gabriele D'Annunzio's Vittoriale residence." The friar was a "renowned miracle-worker," he said, as was demonstrated by the case of Lello Pegna, a "young Israelite" from Florence, who had gone blind following a mysterious illness. Hoping to regain his sight, Pegna had first gone to Rome to study Catholicism, but when no miracle cure was forthcoming had made his way down to the Gargano mountains. There, he met Padre Pio and was baptized by him. "Three months later the eyes of the newborn Christian again saw the light." Such prodigious feats meant that Padre Pio's holy nature was known far and wide. And yet, though his fame was spreading fast, he remained approachable to all—even to the crowds of children who whirled around him, tugging on his cassock to get a *santino,* a holy card, and running off, triumphant.[30]

Padre Pio gave out nothing more than those little holy cards, Cavaciocchi explained. The pilgrims who came to San Giovanni Rotondo, however, keen to get their hands on something he had touched, were ready to break the seventh commandment and steal all kinds of sacred vestments—his zucchetto, purificator, or hand towel—and take them home to worship like relics. And where was home? If the guestbook at Calogero Vinciguerra's house was any indication, the majority of the pilgrims came from Tuscany, followed by Liguria, Lazio, and Lombardy, with a few from the southern regions of Puglia, Sicily, or Sardinia. The Padre Pio cult thus by no means confirmed the cliché of overheated southern religiosity; it was a national phenomenon. Indeed, it was an international one: according to Cavaciocchi, when he inspected it in 1924 the guestbook contained the signatures of many believers from abroad, from Spaniards to French and Belgians, Argentinians and Brazilians, Chileans and the Irish, Germans and Russians.[31]

Such an influx of pilgrims obviously put a strain on the lodgings of San Giovanni Rotondo, yet the town council nevertheless voted against building a hotel. They were concerned about "commercializing" the cult of Padre Pio, Cavaciocchi said, and wanted to make sure that no one thought they were "mass-producing" Pio's reputation as a saint. For the same reasons, the superior of Santa Maria delle Grazie decided that although he had "three splendid photographs" of the Capuchin monk's stigmata, he would not let them be reproduced. All in all, there was a strange, rarefied atmosphere in San Giovanni Rotondo, almost as if the presence of the stigmatic friar had created a state of permanent grace. "The mindset of the people became more elevated, more pure; the taverns emptied out; cursing disappeared; petty and political crimes faded away." In the year of Our Lord 1924, the little microcosm of San Giovanni Rotondo pointed to a better world to come, a nation and a planet dedicated to the spirit of a new Gospel.[32]

Saints perform miracles, and the best miracle, if not a faith healing, is a conversion. From what Cavaciocchi has to say, Padre Pio had no rivals in this department. The edifying tale of a neophyte that the *Messaggero* journalist met during his stay in San Giovanni served as one example. The convert, who called himself Emanuele Pederzani, was "a young man I felt I had seen somewhere, but could not remember where." Until the previous year this Pederzani had been an ordinary unbeliever, devoted to living the good life. Although he'd fought bravely in the war as a captain in the Alpine troops, said Cavaciocchi, he had never bothered to look after his soul, focusing exclusively on pleasures of the flesh. After this young libertine had climbed up to San Giovanni Rotondo and met Padre Pio, however, "he converted. He divested himself of his elegant clothes, burned his novels, began to fast, and for nine months now, every morning, no matter what the weather, has gone up that hill to serve mass and take communion."[33]

This "Emanuele" was the same one who, two years later, would pay a visit to Father Gemelli (calling himself a schoolteacher, although, as it turns out, he had no teaching degree of any kind) and threaten hell-fire and brimstone in defense of Padre Pio. With a phony surname—one of the many we'll come to know him by—this was Brunatto. Cavaciocchi thought that he had seen him somewhere, and perhaps he had: if we can believe a Fascist spy who had infiltrated the world of journalism and mentioned both in a subsequent report, the two met in 1922–23 in Rome, where Brunatto was working at *La Tribuna* while Cavaciocchi was at *Il Mondo*.[34] Their contact must have been fleeting, for Cavaciocchi didn't recognize the Roman journalist in the aging altar boy who assisted Padre Pio with the mass. If only Cavaciocchi had known what the Fascist police would dig up on Pederzani-Brunatto just a few years later, his tale about this miraculous conversion would have been even more dramatic than the one about a well-dressed, novel-reading bon vivant won over by God.

According to *The Man Who Saved Padre Pio*, Brunatto, born in Turin in 1892, had worked as a salesman of ladies' magazines, a stock boy, a bookkeeper, and a broker before being called up in the army, where he fought an uneventful First World War as a quartermaster sergeant in military logistics—uneventful, that is, except for some run-ins with a military tribunal for black-market trading in rations.[35] After the war he worked as a salesman of chemical products and in 1920 was convicted in absentia to a one-year sentence for bankruptcy. That sentence, as Fascist military intelligence records show, was swiftly followed by new convictions for fraud and forgery.[36] Brunatto was thus a fugitive from justice when he arrived in Rome and managed to get accredited as a journalist at *La Tribuna*—before heading off to Puglia to be dazzled by Padre Pio and write his landmark biography of the Capuchin priest.

There's nothing in the archives to show exactly when Brunatto met his publisher, Giorgio Berlutti, nor how he later came to be bankruptcy auditor for Berlutti's Libreria del Littorio press. There are no documents that tell us how a small-time crook from the provinces,[37] with no trace of Fascist credentials before the March on Rome, could become a figure of such regard in the regime that during a court appearance in 1930 he was defended by no less an attorney than Arturo Rocca, brother of the powerful minister of justice, Alfredo Rocca.[38] We can, however, thanks to the meticulous Vatican archives, be sure of the date on which the Holy Office formally placed Brunatto's pseudonymous *Padre Pio of Pietrelcina* on the Index of forbidden books: it was April 23, 1926.[39]

Among the hundreds of hagiographic accounts dedicated to the life of Padre Pio, Brunatto's is by far the most significant. It contains more details, reveals more about political connections, and has shaped Padre Pio's reputation more than any other life. It was, in short, the model for all the hagiographies of Francesco Forgione to come, the material on which for decades new accounts were based. This is not really surprising, considering the apostle Emanuele's notable talent for promoting the Capuchin friar, beginning with the clever idea of telling some of his story as if in the words—real or imagined—of the saint himself. Framed like a long interview, Brunatto's book allowed readers the thrill of hearing something like the voice of the new Messiah in person.

Not that everything in Brunatto's book was original. Some parts of his mystical itinerary seem to be lifted from Cavaciocchi's version. Like Cavaciocchi, he begins with stories of Padre Pio's childhood and youth, marked by the signs of a marvelous fate to come: young Forgione's battles with the devil, which left him weak and bloodied; the young seminarian's capacity to mortify the flesh by eating nothing but the morning communion wafer for weeks on end; the Dantesque account of Padre Pio's stigmatization, when the Lord inscribed his "great seal" on the friar's body. He recited, too, similar proofs of his miraculous nature: the mysterious scent of violets; the miraculous healings and conversions;

the bilocation, or ability to be in two places at once, common to saints. And Brunatto's *Padre Pio* also tells—albeit in greater detail than Cavaciocchi—of the trials and tribulations the friar underwent in medical examinations and counterexaminations, with Dr. Romanelli from Barletta and Dr. Festa from Rome in the role of the good doctors and Dr. Gemelli of Milan playing the bad one.[40]

Brunatto's description of Padre Pio's astounding humanity also borrows somewhat from previous accounts, but he added one original ingredient that would endure as part of the lore about the friar's personality. Padre Pio, said Brunatto, was a man who liked to jest and joke. He was virtually a comic actor: "His talk is spiced with humorous anecdotes that come from who knows where and never seem to end." What a devil of a saint he was, able to perform miracles like Jesus and deliver one-liners like a stand-up comedian! A down-home Redeemer, Padre Pio, who by playing down himself played up his amazing gifts. On summer days, Brunatto said, he liked to toss *bocce* with the other friars in the courtyard, yelling if he missed a shot and cheering if he won. How amazing it was "to watch him pick up those wooden balls soiled with dirt in hands covered by fingerless gloves, under which the Wounds of Christ are bleeding." Better than any of the friar's hagiographers before him or after, Brunatto managed to capture how naturally Padre Pio expressed the supernatural. "He's perched between two lives, smiling, conversing with the beings of two worlds."[41]

Another new ingredient in Brunatto's biography—politely censored in post–World War II versions of the story—was the way he promoted the Padre Pio cult as a sterling example of clerico-fascism. It wasn't just a love of strong language that led the former con man to describe the local support for the Capuchin friar in terms that evoked Blackshirt brawls ("there's a strong desire for a thrashing in the air," "feels like time for a beating," and so forth). He wanted to link the religion to the politics, the cult of Padre Pio to the cult of Il Duce. Accordingly, "among the first" champions of Padre Pio we find "His Excellency Caradonna," as Padre Pio supposedly put it, "the likeable, heroic First Fascist of Puglia, who devotes all his generous and impetuous energy to the rebirth of his region." Brunatto wanted to demonstrate, complete with direct quotations, how much Padre Pio admired Il Duce.

"He's toiling for posterity," he has the Capuchin friar saying of the Fascist leader. "We pray to God because his life is in danger and the Lord would not want him to go missing just now!" And all this long before any cardinal or pope had thrown his weight behind Mussolini.[42]

But the real force of Brunatto's biography lay in something else: the book's tone of open, militant provocation, its bold challenge both to local ecclesiastical officials and to the Church hierarchy, including, indirectly, Pope Pius XI. Since the moment when the Capuchin friar began to be an annoyance to Church officials, no one had so boldly denounced the authorities as Brunatto did behind the *nom de plume* Giuseppe De Rossi. No one had dared to say that the plan to transfer Padre Pio amounted to a "systematic repression," an "infernal plot" to "obstruct his mission." No one had used such strong language—based on strong evidence that obviously came from an inside source—to condemn the Vatican persecution of the Capuchin friar of San Giovanni Rotondo.[43]

We've heard this part of the story before, as detailed in the papers of the Holy Office. Still, it's worthwhile hearing it again, this time laced with vitriol, as Padre Pio's most gifted and implacable evangelist describes the events from the friar's perspective. "A clandestine itinerary is being prepared in great secret, a nighttime escape by car to some place of perpetual isolation, far away, in some mountain friary, perhaps abroad, where no one will ever find him again." "There are some officials who would presume to put Padre Pio in a clinic and subject him to a psychiatric evaluation." "He isn't allowed to write. Not one line, not even a signature, not even to the people of his hometown. Those holy words full of grace and divine love must no longer be written, they must no longer comfort the doubters, support the weak, heal the sick." "The atmosphere has turned to ice around him; his brothers seem to be made of stone when faced with his agony." "Alone. No one to perceive the passion of his bleeding heart. All around him buzz poor witless friars, tossing the rags dripping with the blood from his side into the sewers."[44]

Ultimately, Brunatto's biography depicts Padre Pio as a tacit but stern opponent of nefarious papal power, with Pius XI as the Antichrist occupying St. Peter's. The Padre Pio cult is prophetic, apocalyptic—and how could it have been any different, suggests Brunatto, considering how much the friar had been isolated and tormented by the

Church? "This ever so humane man, who lives the same life as his believers, who disturbs us, who makes the chill corridors of his cloister ring with apostolic cries is . . . misunderstood," writes Brunatto, likening him to a modern-day Savonarola. He is wounded, but not broken.

> In fact his prayers, especially in recent months, his ever so quiet and contained prayers—during which his face takes on a mysterious grace—his prayers which stretch on for hours in silence, nearly always close with a precise, fervid, anguished, repeated invocation: "Freedom! Freedom! Freedom!" Sometimes even when he is on the altar, we hear the words "Freedom! Freedom!" burst out, imploring, insistent, startling.[45]

According to Brunatto, Padre Pio saw the Church as incapable of rightly preaching the word of Christ, and had told his closest followers, both lay and clerical: "I do think, yes, that a punishment awaits us priests, a grave punishment."[46] This was "a terrible warning," Brunatto said of those words he attributed to Padre Pio—words that had echoed through the halls of the San Giovanni Rotondo monastery, as "solemn as an oracle."[47]

Let Him Be

Confronted with such all-but-open hostility, Vatican authorities did more than just place Brunatto's *Padre Pio* on the Index Librorum Prohibitorum. Reviving a custom that went back to the late sixteenth and early seventeenth century—that is, to the golden age of the Roman Inquisition—the Vatican command imposed a form of censorship even more effective than simply prohibiting Catholics to read the book: they withdrew as many copies as possible from the market. Even Don Orione, who in the war inside the Church stood in Padre Pio's camp, was drawn into the action, which was to be a costly measure for his Humble Works of Divine Providence.[48]

In the days of the Counter-Reformation, the Index and the Holy Office often launched such a book battle with great energy, for it represented a crucial moment in the wider war of memory that always raged around an aspiring saint. The degree to which hagiographies circulated, spreading word of miraculous deeds among the people, would determine whether a saint triumphed—advancing toward an eventual elevation to holiness—or was defeated and his memory gradually obliterated.[49] In twentieth-century Italy, of course, a hagiographic text did not have quite the same weight that it had three or four centuries earlier, when the Inquisition authorities boasted of "destroying" the worship of many saints, "all of them minor and lacking the approval of Rome," and when reading or not reading a book could mean the difference for a Christian between salvation or eternal damnation.[50] Nevertheless, when the first hagiographies of Padre Pio were published, the Church of Pius XI decided to employ real censorship—hunting down the books, confiscating them, and destroying them.[51]

In the spring of 1926, Giorgio Berlutti's presses were still printing Brunatto's *Padre Pio of Pietrelcina* when the pope's emissaries knocked on the door, ready to acquire all the copies and send them to be pulped. To judge by how hard it is to find the book in Italian libraries today, the Vatican worked with impressive efficiency. Brunatto's *Padre Pio* became a bibliophile's rarity, on a par with the hardest to find heretical texts of the sixteenth century; and although this volume did become the key hagiographic account of the life of Padre Pio, it was only because Brunatto tenaciously wrote and rewrote the book, finding ways to circulate it more or less clandestinely. Padre Pio's ranks of followers, meanwhile, sought out the work as if it were a gospel all the more sacred because it was forbidden.

But it would be a mistake to think that Brunatto's hagiographic account remained so powerful only because its suppression met with resistance from below—from local officials and the faithful of San Giovanni Rotondo, for example. The Church was unable to close the book on Padre Pio and silence word of his holiness because the detractors of the stigmatic friar also met resistance from on high, from ecclesiastical figures near the top of the Vatican hierarchy. In June 1925, Brunatto— presenting himself as Emanuele De Felice, administrator of the United Electric Companies of San Giovanni Rotondo and San Marco in Lamis—was able to get an audience with Cardinal Pietro Gasparri, the Vatican secretary of state. Gasparri then helped him send a long memo to the Holy Office describing the mystery of Padre Pio's "sparkling" stigmata, San Giovanni Rotondo's miraculous transformation from "Communist city" to Christian Mecca, and Brunatto's own metamorphosis from hardened sinner ("violent, a bully, capable of the worst actions") to tireless zealot.[52] Cardinal Sbarretti, prefect of the Congregation of the Council, also seems to have looked favorably on Padre Pio's cause.[53] Whatever the Vatican command might rule, there was evidently a lobby inside the Vatican in favor of the friar with the stigmata, ready to use every means to blunt the actions of the Holy Office against him and his apostles.

In the twentieth century as in the sixteenth and seventeenth, sainthood was a complex game, played out according to jurisdictional logic as well as spiritual judgments, involving both hardheaded factional conflicts and ecclesiastical balances of power at the highest level.[54] The case of Padre Pio was no different. Both in the highest ministries of Rome and in the modest churches of the Gargano, it became a boxing match of moves and countermoves, feints and counterfeints, legitimate punches and below-the-belt hits. In 1927, for example, Sbarretti's Congregation of the Council, in agreement with Cardinal Gasparri, decided to send a Roman prelate, Monsignor Felice Bevilacqua, to San Giovanni Rotondo to investigate charges of corruption among the local clergy. As Bevilacqua's lay coinvestigator, the council named one "Highly Illustrious Professore Emanuele De Felice," resident at Via del Babuino 197, Rome—in short, Emanuele Brunatto.[55] Thanks to this appointment, the supreme fraudster was given a chance to compile a thick dossier of scandal based on the deeds and misdeeds of the priests of San Giovanni and the archbishop of Manfredonia, which he would use in his blackmailing activities for years and even decades to come.

But while the Congregation of the Council was apparently so favorable to Padre Pio that they were willing to enroll his leading promoter, the Congregation of the Consistory, which supervised the dioceses, took a different line. Cardinal Gaetano De Lai, the secretary of the consistory, advised the Holy Office that the "low-life comedy of Padre Pio" was soon to end, for "the Lord seems to be preparing the liquidation of this poor priest, without any fuss and without our intervention."[56] And far from Rome, between the Tavoliere plain and the

Gargano mountains, there were other Church dignitaries no more benevolent than De Lai toward the friar with the stigmata. Monsignor Gagliardi, the archbishop of Manfredonia, wrote repeatedly to the Holy Office to denounce the "merchandizing" friars of Santa Maria delle Grazie and the "opportunistic" Padre Pio.[57] (Given such antipathy, it is perhaps not surprising that Monsignor Gagliardi was among those targeted for investigation by Bevilacqua and Brunatto.) Monsignor Fortunato Farina, the bishop of Foggia, was less involved in the clash, and he thought Padre Pio guilty of no more than "being overly artless"; still, his opinion of the religious atmosphere in San Giovanni, as he conveyed it to the Holy Office, was not favorable. None of the miracle healings had actually been proven, nor had Padre Pio's prophecies been shown to be supernatural, nor his ability to read the minds of the faithful or any of the other miracles attributed to the friar. What was striking instead was how this popular cult had been transformed into a well-oiled machine to collect offerings. Monsignor Farina had seen with his own eyes the circulars "printed up in the Spanish language" by the Capuchins of San Giovanni in order to take advantage of the religious market in Spain and Latin America.[58]

All this, said the bishop of Foggia, was tainting the already polluted atmosphere of San Giovanni Rotondo. "I believe it would be best," concluded Monsignor Farina in his message to the Holy Office, "if P. Pio could be transferred to another friary where he could live far from public notice. He would be purified, he would become more saintly, if he is already a saint; and if not, a pernicious fraud to which the faithful are prey would be eliminated." Once again we see the time-honored repressive logic the Church employed with presumed living saints: if this fellow is an imposter, let us use Providence as an instrument to unmask him; if he's a saint, let us use Providence as an instrument to make him merit sainthood by enduring the most arduous trials.

Politics further complicated the religious conflict over Padre Pio. As the Fascist regime was getting ready to sign the Lateran Treaty, finally compensating the Church for the 1870 defeat of the Papal States, the Fascists were tempted to weigh in on various internal Catholic feuds—institutional, personal, canonical, liturgical, and diplomatic.[59] We can see a hint of that temptation in Mussolini's new willingness to

become personally involved in religious initiatives. For many years he had declined all such requests, but beginning with the Franciscan Year of 1926 and the Capuchin fourth centenary in 1928, Il Duce agreed to be part of various patrons' committees.[60] Ecclesiastical dignitaries, for their part, fought among themselves to embellish their activities with some connection to Mussolini. On the eve of the Concordat, the official magazine of the Capuchin order was brandishing Il Duce's patronage of their centenary as if it were a weapon against their longtime rivals, the Franciscan Friars Minor.[61] At the same time, the Franciscan Vittorino Facchinetti was so much in the dictator's graces that he was invited to Villa Torlonia to be tutor to Mussolini's children.[62]

Even after his death, Mussolini would enjoy special treatment on account of his patronage of the Franciscans and the Capuchins. After his body was stolen from its grave by some neo-Fascists on Easter 1946, a peculiar joint venture between Milanese Franciscans and Capuchins from Cerro Maggiore would hide Il Duce's corpse away for more than a decade, until his remains were finally put to rest in a crypt in his hometown Predappio cemetery.[63] Meanwhile in the here-and-now,

Padre Pio also gained advantages from the religious inclinations of the Fascists. After a miraculous assist from the little friar cured him of a serious illness in 1927,[64] the ever-more-intense devotion of the local Fascist boss Giuseppe Caradonna would be a counterweight to the hostility toward the Gargano mystic on the part of religious authorities.[65] Perhaps because of this, as well as the indestructible solidarity of the San Giovanni community, the regime was more and more inclined to treat the little friar as a local notable rather than as a threat to public order.

Sent by the minister of the interior to San Giovanni Rotondo in April 1929 to monitor the Padre Pio cult and the "rebellious instincts of that rough population," Inspector General Pietro D'Orazi filed a reassuring report with Rome. It was true, he wrote, that in the past the cult had set in motion "the powerful engines of fanaticism and commercialization." But following seven years of good Fascist administration and thanks to "the discipline that has penetrated the masses"—"the perfect organization of the National Fascist Party" and "preventive policing as spelled out in the most recent law on Public Security"—the situation had normalized. There was no longer a soul in the Gargano who questioned the simple virtues of Padre Pio, "a friar of limited learning but great practicality, a humble, modest man." In any case, the cult was showing signs of weariness and seemed to be declining. "The clamor around the friar's person has died down and his following has become insignificant at present," Inspector D'Orazi reported. Accordingly, he suggested, proposals of a forced transfer should be postponed sine die.[66]

"Nobody throngs to the monastery today," the prefect of Foggia confirmed to ministry officials in Rome. To remove the friar with the stigmata would thus be "highly impolitic," said the prefect, "all the more so because, I repeat, he no longer gives rise to any popular movement or following." The worst thing to do would be to stir up trouble: the mere rumor, recently heard in town, that a transfer was imminent had upset the entire populace. "It would be best to ignore the presence of P. Pio in San Giovanni, to leave him alone in his friary, where anyway he does only good, modestly, judiciously, and with much good sense," the prefect concluded, echoing D'Orazi's views exactly.[67]

The prefect's report, preserved in the State Archives, has been annotated in the margin by the national chief of police. Under a stamp that reads "After Consultation with His Excellency the Head of the Government" is a handwritten comment noting the will of Il Duce: "Fine, leave him undisturbed."[68]

The Road to San Giovanni

It was not entirely true that Padre Pio had become insignificant. Certainly, his cult was somewhat subdued, a decade after its first explosion. The repressive measures the Vatican had put in place—the limitations on the friar's priestly activities, the control of his correspondence, the prohibition of pilgrimages, the hagiographies placed on the Index and destroyed—had had their effect. There was a shift, too, in the climate of imminent epiphanies and millenarian hopes that had been so characteristic of the postwar period. The need for the sacred was less urgent, the demand for intercession less dramatic. Paradoxically, the new links between the Fascist regime and the Catholic Church, sealed by the Lateran Treaty of 1929, meant that there was less public interest in Padre Pio, for in the age of the Concordat the figures of Pope and Duce towered over a little provincial Capuchin. Nevertheless, if one looks for them, the traces of a continuing curiosity about Padre Pio are not hard to find.

In some cases, that curiosity was so indiscreet as to be profane, even sacrilegious. In the summer of 1925, for instance, "in the hottest hour of the afternoon," a squadron of automobiles pulled up in front of the monastery. "Armed with canes, binoculars and road maps, their clothing in disarray, green and yellow sunglasses tilted up on the visors of their hats, beards white with dust, foreheads lined with sweat, eyes bewildered in the strong light," the unlikely pilgrims asked a lay brother to let them in to see Padre Pio. Heading the clamorous group was Antonio Baldini, plump bookworm, former journalist with *La Voce* of Florence and *La Ronda* in Rome, and commentator for *Corriere della Sera*, who would write up his account of that irreverent excursion to San Giovanni for the Milanese daily.[69]

In the darkness of the monastery chapel, Baldini and his fellow journalists made out the figure of Padre Pio seated in one of the choir stalls. "Was he praying? Was he sleeping? Was he conversing with the angels?" The Capuchin friar had turned a "dim yellow face" on the visitors, studying them with questioning eyes "under the squarish fore-head of a conscript." Then, in a weak voice, he had asked them why they had come in. Shamelessly, the group announced they were interested in his stigmata. "Be a good man and let us see just a little," they said to him. "Oh no, I can't," Padre Pio had replied in his "little voice without timbre, the voice of a talking cricket," like Pinocchio's conscience. The friar had begun to fidget on his choir stall, looking at the visitors and at the door behind them, perhaps because he wanted to send them away, or perhaps out of fear that the father guardian might find him talking to outsiders. Finally the intruders left the chapel and entered the monastery, where a number of the friar's "wee brothers" were standing at the gate.

The journalists asked Padre Pio's confreres if he was still performing miracle cures.

> It was wonderful to behold how all those framed by that doorway wanted to have their say, friars with long, pointed beards, friars with round, full beards, friars with bellies and ropes tied around them that irresistibly made one think of certain Doré illustrations. But except for one enthusiastic simpleton who, for the greater glory of the order, would have happily led us to believe there were continuous miracles at San Giovanni, all the other wee friars did their best to make us understand, with reticent voices and evasive looks, with conscience-stricken faces and hands held high, in bland phrases served up without oil or vinegar, in so many expressions of "I don't know" and "I don't think so," so many "I wasn't here" and "I came later," that everyone in the monastery took the side of the Holy Office against the poor man on his knees in the chapel.

Padre Pio brought to mind the story from Manzoni's *The Betrothed* of the good, earnest priest Fra Cristoforo confronted with foolish and opportunistic Fra Galdino.

> We quickly understood that here there was a confederacy of
> Fra Galdinos against Fra Cristoforo, as in all the monasteries

of this world, and just because of that little bit of publicity that a Fra Cristoforo can't help but make for himself just by being Fra Cristoforo. No man, it has been said, is a hero to his own valet. Just imagine if a friar is inclined to see a saint in the man in the next cell.

Various travelers less impertinent than Baldini and company also took the road to San Giovanni, other souls more susceptible to sainthood. The writer Riccardo Bacchelli, for example, offered a sympathetic sketch of Padre Pio in a 1929 article for *La Stampa*. Arriving unannounced at Santa Maria delle Grazie, Bacchelli had found the friar in the midst of a prosaic but rather intimate operation, the shaving of his tonsure. The shaving apparatus was not working well, and Padre Pio's hair was being torn out, which he endured with patience. The conversation that followed, though informal, seemed especially meaningful to Bacchelli. Padre Pio, he wrote, "spoke of fine things with illiterate words." "He did not mention the stigmata or any miracles, almost as if he had forgotten about them. And this, in my humble opinion, when I thought about it again, inclined me both to marvel and respect." In the end, the deeply Catholic Bacchelli came down from the Gargano mountains with the distinct impression that he had met a future saint.[70]

Going on a pilgrimage to San Giovanni Rotondo and meeting with Padre Pio had not yet become a journalistic cliché or literary set piece, as it would a couple of decades later.[71] Still, in the 1930s, when the Holy Office was still dead set against recognizing Padre Pio, intellectuals were already devoting memorable pages to the friar with the stigmata. The Trieste-born Alberto Spaini—a leading scholar of German literature, a translator, and a noted theater critic—went down to San Giovanni Rotondo as a correspondent for the cultural page of the Bologna daily *Il Resto del Carlino*, and in May 1931 produced the best piece of journalism ever written on the Capuchin friar.[72]

Spaini approached the Pugliese town where Padre Pio lived with the sensibility of a man from the Slovenian borderlands.[73] He understood the Gargano mountains even before visiting them because he had been raised on the harsh mountains of the Carso.[74] When it came to describe for the Bolognese "the spectacle that Padre Pio has looked upon for fifteen years," Spaini didn't want for words, because that spectacle reminded him vividly of his youth. There was the familiar way the mountains fell off rapidly toward the plain, the white line of the beach in the mist on the horizon, and on the other side the snow "rosy and unreal at sunset." Above all, in the Gargano as in the Carso, there was the magical vitality of stone: "the bedrock, where it emerges, is covered with aromatic bushes, here and there crowned by a few pines or cypresses." In Padre Pio's land, Spaini did not see the worn-out stereotype of bare, lean, formless nature, but instead the "rather florid appearance" of "olive groves and wheat fields." The white spot made by the monastery of Santa Maria delle Grazie looked "very cheerful" to him in the midst of the green garden surrounding it.[75]

The inhabitants, "monumental and savage," were different, however. In Spaini's description, there is nothing florid about their faces; too many show the pallor of malaria or the reddened eyelids of trachoma. All the young people have moved away to seek their fortunes, and the town's main street and the alleys running off it are full of women "with red stockings and noisy little clogs, sheathed in long, severe shawls." There are swarms of children and "huge, somber men, nearly all elderly,"

who are "extraordinarily decorative" in their black cloaks with leather collars and who pace around in groups of four or five "with the suspicious air of conspirators." The women and the old men come and go on the road that leads to the friary, the women mincing along in little flocks "clackety clack on their clogs," the men leaning on knotty sticks, hiding their "fiery eyes" behind the "insolent folds" of their hat brims.

Only a discerning theatergoer could depict Padre Pio's world the way that Spaini, then the leading Italian critic of German theater, did.[76] It took an eye trained on stage sets to note the difference between the naked little church of Santa Maria delle Grazie, its walls slaked with quicklime, and the triumph of stuccowork and marble of the other Gargano churches, "still weighed down with superstitious Spanish feudalism." It took an expert eye to ferret out the detail in a photograph pinned to the wall in the monastery—a photograph of a 1928 fresco in which St. Francis was "the exact portrait of Padre Pio" and where, among the faithful on their knees, one "looked very much like Mussolini."[77]

And it took Spaini's eye as a theater critic to appreciate the finesse of Padre Pio's *performance*: to see how differently the Capuchin friar behaved depending on whether he had before him the humble people of Puglia or "frivolous tourists" like himself. In the latter case, Padre Pio did little to conceal his lack of interest, his indifference for the souls of those worldly travelers. But with genuine, unworldly believers, the friar was adept at modifying his gaze, his voice, and his gestures to meet the most personal needs of each, to respond to their most secret expectations. This, Spaini wrote, was the real miracle: "like a mirror he alters his face and the soul that speaks through his eyes, like a mirror that replies differently to every soul that steps up to inquire." The five stigmata and the healing of the incurably ill were nothing compared to the "great vital force of freedom and consolation" that flowed out around Padre Pio. It was this force that had drawn men and women to come from afar, and had even persuaded some of them to stay and build a group of little houses right underneath the friary garden wall—so they could spend the rest of their lives near this man of consolation.[78]

It was a singular place, the Gargano, a fertile territory for the most varied of experiments in religious rebirth.[79] While Alberto Spaini was

visiting San Giovanni Rotondo, Donato Manduzio, a disabled veteran in the nearby town of San Nicandro who had a reputation as a healer and a wise man, told of a vision that had come to him the previous summer. A mysterious personage had appeared to him in a dream and gave him an unlit lantern. The next day, an acquaintance had handed Manduzio a Bible—the first one that he had ever seen. Struck by the stories of Adam and Isaac and Jacob, Manduzio decided that his dream was a sign for him to rekindle the light of the Old Testament. He began preaching among the farmers, field hands, and women of the town, and soon enough several dozen of them had become ardent followers of Judaism.[80]

A self-taught peasant the prophet of the Pentateuch? The rabbinical authorities in Rome regarded the Jewish convert with much the same suspicion with which the Vatican officials approached Padre Pio. It was not until 1946, when Manduzio was on his deathbed, that the Great Rabbi of Rome agreed to a collective circumcision of the Jews of San Nicandro, who soon left for Israel to find their promised land.

A Failed Publisher

At the moment when the Concordat between Italy and the Vatican was signed, the top two enemies of the Vatican censors seem to have been

Gabriele D'Annunzio and Padre Pio. Reviewing the changes to the Index between 1925 and 1929, the leading Fascist review, *Gerarchia*,[81] reported that the most conspicuous new entry was the complete works of D'Annunzio; the hotheaded, swashbuckling writer's conversion to Franciscanism, loudly broadcast from his home at the Vittoriale, had obviously failed to convince the congregation of the Index. The other significant new entry, wrote *Gerarchia*, were "two books on the little Franciscan friar Padre Pio of Pietrelcina."[82]

As we know, these were the two hagiographies, written by Cavaciocchi and Brunatto, that Giorgio Berlutti had published in 1924 and 1926. Brunatto's book had been, in a way, a commercial success for Berlutti, because the Vatican censors had bought up the entire print run; nevertheless, within a few years Berlutti was in financial trouble. The ambitions of the onetime paper goods salesman from Tuscania proved greater than his means when he took on the financially demanding, politically tricky Libreria del Littorio to publish Fascist texts. The publishing house had Mussolini's imprimatur—he was listed on the Libreria del Littorio's letterhead as "distinguished patron"—but the high rent for showy offices, the salaries for as many as 150 employees, the purchase of excess supplies that included "more than thirty typewriters," and the personal expenses necessary for Berlutti's new role as the party's preferred publisher all added up to a flood of red ink.[83] Moreover, the depression of 1930 had brought a noticeable decline in consensus for the regime, and publishing political propaganda for the National Fascist Party was not necessarily a good way to make money.[84] By February 1931, the Libreria del Littorio had over a million and a half unsold volumes in its warehouses.[85]

The unwanted merchandise included stacks of an ultra-Fascist book for very young readers written by Berlutti himself, a moralizing work that paid homage to both Mussolini, "an outsize man sent by Providence to save Italy and make it great," and St. Francis, who had demonstrated how we could live "in peace and happiness on earth by practicing the commandments of Jesus."[86] Such genteel rhetoric disgusted onetime radical Fascists like Carlo Emilio Gadda, who ridiculed what he called the "rot-worship" and "religious carnivalism" of an Italy that had forgotten the glory of battle.[87] Berlutti pleaded with high-ranking

Fascists to provide more subsidies for the Libreria del Littorio (which police informers disparaged as merely an attempt to fill his own pockets),[88] but even their conspicuous assistance was unable to stop the publishing house from plunging swiftly toward bankruptcy.

The business misfortunes of Berlutti—who had bet not once but twice on the commercial appeal of Padre Pio—suggest how low the friar's stock stood at the start of the 1930s. The Capuchin's metamorphosis into a darling of the Fascists had not been enough to counterbalance the measures taken by the Holy Office against him and his followers. A pastoral visit by Monsignor Alessandro Macchi, pro tempore head of the archdiocese of Manfredonia after Monsignor Gagliardi resigned, added to the official pressure. In a report made in January 1930, Macchi painted the usual dark picture of the atmosphere at Santa Maria delle Grazie. There was the intolerable presence of the *bizzoche*, the pious women buzzing around Padre Pio with medicines, clothes, and perfumes. There was Padre Pio's disturbing reply when asked about the possibility he might be transferred: "I will go, but I decline all responsibility," he had said with a shrug of his shoulders. There was the reprobate Brunatto, who had already left San Giovanni but remained a favorite of the Capuchin friar, and who continued "to skim off large sums, especially from America, behind the back of the self-styled saint."[89] All in all, there were enough negative elements that Pope Pius XI himself advised the Holy Office to proceed without delay in transferring Padre Pio from his Gargano monastery.[90]

A dozen years after the stigmata first appeared on the Capuchin friar's body his cult looked ready to burn out, the way so many such devotional flames in the Italian south had sputtered out in previous centuries under the suffocating repression of the Inquisition. But there was something that Padre Pio's enemies had not taken into account: Brunatto's unquenchable determination, his formidable dedication to Padre Pio, and his entrepreneurial genius—a genius that would border on the criminal.

7. RASPUTIN REBORN

Judgment Day

"Bologna leads all other Italian cities in devotion to Padre Pio," wrote Alberto Spaini in his 1931 article in *Il Resto del Carlino*.[1] Were his words merely a flourish of journalistic hyperbole, to catch the attention of his readers and flatter them a little? No, it seems they weren't. All the evidence indicates that by the 1930s, Bologna—in the center-north of Italy, far from the Gargano Peninsula—really was the capital of the Padre Pio cult. The first to complain about it was the archbishop of Bologna himself, Cardinal Nasalli Rocca, in his correspondence with the Holy Office. Despite warnings that had been several times published in the diocesan bulletin, he wrote, there continued to be "much propaganda about visiting Padre Pio."[2]

Among the reasons for this surprising connection was the fact that Francesco Morcaldi, the ex-*podestà* of San Giovanni Rotondo, had studied at Bologna University and had many friends in the city. Morcaldi published several ardent tributes to the friar in *Il Resto del Carlino*,[3] and a number of articles drawn from Giuseppe Cavaciocchi's 1924 book *Padre Pio of Pietrelcina* had also appeared in the Bologna daily.[4] Further pieces about the friar had appeared under a pseudonym concealing the ubiquitous Emanuele Brunatto.[5] Riccardo Bacchelli, the pilgrim to San Giovanni whose emotional account we've already read in *La Stampa*, was himself from Bologna; and so was Alberto Del Fante, an obscure printer with a past as a Freemason, who in 1931–32 published two richly detailed hagiographies of Padre Pio—both immediately put on the Index by the Vatican.[6]

As converts go, Del Fante was quite a striking specimen. At the start of the 1920s, when he was a director of the National Association of Veterans, he had been a leading light inside *Italia laica*, early fascism's most hard-line anticlerical voice—a magazine whose motto was Voltaire's *écraser l'infame*. There, ardent Fascists could read corrosive comments on Giovanni Papini and his mystical best seller *Life of Christ*, presented as an example of "decadence of body and mind."[7] And there, under Del Fante's byline, the national and local press was ridiculed for trumpeting the life and miracles of "a second-rate friar" by the name of Padre Pio, "who has the amazing ability to emit the fragrance of lilies, turn wooden legs into legs of flesh, make the blind see, heal the incurable, make imbeciles intelligent, bring forth hair on the heads of the bald, give loose ladies back their virginity, make drunkards drink water, change wolves into lambs, and whatever else you can think of."[8]

But in the fall of 1930, a miracle cure turned Del Fante himself from an extreme skeptic into an apostle of the man with the stigmata. His nephew, Enrico, had been declared by doctors in Bologna to be incurably ill. When Enrico was brought back to health by the intercession of Padre Pio, Del Fante immediately announced that a miracle had taken place and that he was converting.[9] He then wrote two hagiographies— rich with miracle healings and conversions as well as mysterious perfumes, apparitions, bilocations, pardons, and prophecies—which began to attract the following of many Bolognese believers. Meanwhile, Morcaldi and Padre Pio's local supporters in San Giovanni were doing everything they could to keep the tension high by spreading rumors that Padre Pio would be forcibly transferred. In the spring of 1931, Morcaldi and some twenty other inhabitants of the town were reported by the police to judicial authorities for having forced open the gate of the monastery at night so they could mount a guard around the friar with the stigmata.[10]

The spring of 1931, in fact, marked the high point of Vatican persecution of Padre Pio. Inspired by various factors—including the press campaign in favor of the friar in *Il Resto del Carlino*; blackmail by

Brunatto, who was threatening to publish his dossiers on ecclesiastical misdeeds;[11] and the revival of devotion in San Giovanni Rotondo—the Vatican command launched a new attack on the Padre Pio cult. In March, Santa Maria delle Grazie was removed from the control of the minister provincial in Foggia and placed in the hands of the Capuchin order's central command.[12] In April, Pius XI asked the Holy Office to mobilize Cardinal Eugenio Pacelli, the new secretary of state, and the nuncio to the Italian government, to find out the government's opinion— "especially that of Mussolini"—about "the popular agitation in favor of Padre Pio."[13] In May, Monsignor Macchi, interim head of the diocese of Manfredonia, advised the Holy Office to wipe out the persistent cult ("the postman assures me that P. Pio continually receives money in the mail") by adopting draconian measures. He suggested that Padre Pio should be forbidden to take confession from women, to write letters, or to enter the monastery visiting room, and that his fellow friars be kept away from him.[14]

Judgment Day came on May 13, 1931. At the suggestion of the Holy Office, Pius XI ordered that Padre Pio be relieved of almost all his faculties as priest. In practice, he was no longer to have any powers of the divine. He would still be allowed to say mass but solely in the monastery's internal chapel, where only other friars could enter, not in the main church, which was open to lay visitors.[15] He could not hear confession, not even the confessions of his fellow friars. He could not teach seminary students. He could not take on the spiritual guidance of his followers. By the end of May these decisions were passed down the hierarchy from the pope to the secretary of the Holy Office, to the minister general of the Capuchin order, to the minister provincial in Foggia, and from there to the man in question, while the Vatican daily *L'Osservatore Romano* informed the rest of the ecclesiastical community.[16] For the next two years, until the summer of 1933, Padre Pio would live as a virtual prisoner in his friary.

The local protest came immediately, too massive and too quick to have just been stirred up by a handful of fanatics. Veterans from San Giovanni Rotondo sent telegrams to the headquarters of the Capuchin order in Rome,[17] and these were followed by petitions overflowing with names. In many ways, it was an astonishing spectacle. In 1931 Italy, where the Fascist regime had certainly not trained people to raise their voices, thousands of men and women stood up against the Vatican, putting their half-illiterate signatures on a plea to bring back Padre Pio. There were some 2,300 signers from San Giovanni, another 2,000 from San Marco in Lamis, and almost the same number from Pietrelcina. The signatories from San Giovanni included the mayor, the chief judge, and the local secretary of the Fascist Party, plus several elementary school teachers: Angela Serritelli ("secretary of the women's Fascio"), Nina Campanile, Elvira Serritelli, Maria Pompilio, and Filomena Campanile, all of them faithful followers of Padre Pio.[18]

A few months later, Padre Pio's followers tried the political tack. The leaders of the San Giovanni war veterans appealed to the Holy Office, emphasizing that Padre Pio had been decisive in establishing clerico-fascist rule in San Giovanni. The veterans, "gathered round the *tricolore*," recalled how their flag had been "blessed" by the little friar at the height of the *biennio rosso*, "while out in the square Satanic Bolshevik mayhem held sway." Now, eleven years later, the good people of San Giovanni wanted nothing but peace, and the only one who could give them that was "the humble follower of St. Francis."[19] Such appeals, however, did not seem to move the Vatican. As soon as the first wave of protests in favor of Padre Pio had appeared, Pius XI ordered the clergy "to take no account . . . this being undue interference with ecclesiastical authority."[20] Nor did the telegrams and letters from those who wrote to the Holy Office privately from across the country have any effect at all. This time, the Church of Rome was determined to separate Padre Pio from his followers.[21]

In the Iron Circle

The fury of the Vatican against this "good Capuchin who lives in a small town in Puglia surrounded by great popular veneration" astonished one Roman priest who had himself been the target of some papal thunder, albeit for quite different reasons. "It is hard to understand," wrote Don Ernesto Buonaiuti—the professor of Christian history excommunicated for his modernist views and one of the few in Italy to refuse to sign the Fascist loyalty oath[22]—why the Holy Office "has begun to be hostile to him and persecute him with all the means at its disposal . . . How strange and peevish is this ecclesiastical world of ours!"[23] In truth, however, there was very little that was strange or surprising about the treatment of Padre Pio. It wasn't strange that the Holy Office was so hostile to the Gargano friar during a period in which Pius XI's centralizing, authoritarian approach was colliding head-on with the laity's wish for a less institutional, more communitarian Church.[24] Nor was it strange that Buonaiuti—who had long seen value in bringing mysticism to the community of believers—felt sympathy for Padre Pio and his cult.[25]

But as the war around Padre Pio continued to rage, changes in the Vatican hierarchy were making room for a new approach to the Gargano cult. The death of Cardinal Merry Del Val meant that Cardinal Donato Sbarretti—who, as the head of the Congregation for the Council, had been sympathetic to Padre Pio—now became secretary of state. Cardinal De Lai ceased to be the head of the consistory and was replaced by Cardinal Raffaele Carlo Rossi, the Discalced Carmelite who had filed an indulgent report on Padre Pio with the Holy Office in 1921 and whom the followers of the friar considered a convert to their cause.[26] At the local level, meanwhile, the friar's most obstinate detractor, Archbishop of Manfredonia Pasquale Gagliardi, was no longer in office. His place had eventually been taken, following Monsignor Macchi's interim service, by Monsignor Andrea Cesarano, who arrived after a decade's service with the Vatican delegation in Istanbul and who was completely without prejudices regarding all the factions battling in Puglia.[27]

These new nominations did not immediately alter Padre Pio's destiny, especially since the Vatican had a lingering suspicion of popular religiosity—so much so that Monsignor Giovanni Battista Montini, an influential aide of the secretary of state and later Pope Paul VI, considered even the miracles of Lourdes suspect.[28] But gradually, different signals started coming from Rome. Gemma Galgani, the would-be nun with the stigmata whose writings had moved the young Padre Pio to plagiarism, was finally beatified in 1933.[29] True, when Pius XI signed the beatification decree, he did not mention her stigmata, a hint of how cautious the Church remained about miracles and the supernatural.[30] Still, when Gemma was officially placed on the list of the beatified, the followers of Padre Pio had reason to think that conditions might be changing for him too.

In the meantime, the Capuchin friar's promoters continued what efforts they could. In Rome, Dr. Giorgio Festa published a huge tome, *Between the Mysteries of Science and the Light of Faith*, in which he described each of Padre Pio's five stigmata millimeter by millimeter, devoting hundreds of pages to detailing a Christo-mimesis that he believed had no parallels in Christian history except, perhaps, for St. Francis.[31] Before publication, he showed the typescript to Cardinal Pietro Gasparri, the secretary of state. Gasparri's comment on the matter of the stigmata was surprisingly frank, given the usually guarded language of such exchanges: "I quite agree; I cannot believe in a painful fraud that goes on for 14 years!"[32]

In Bologna, the convert Alberto Del Fante was busy putting together a little band of family and friends who all had in various ways experienced Padre Pio's miraculous powers. They included men and women, the wealthy and the humble, some of whom we'll meet again later in the story: the seamstress Carolina Giovannini, the surveyor Ubaldo Cuppini, Del Fante's brother-in-law Antonio Tonelli, and Federico

Abresch, a photographer of German origins who had his studio right in the center of town. The way Del Fante's hagiographies were merchandized is perhaps revealing of the mentality of this little lobby: promotional postcards for them bore slogans like "Padre Pio, the Most Talked-About Man of the Day" and "Is Padre Pio a Saint? Read the Book to Find Out."[33] In the face of such brashly commercial efforts, it is perhaps not surprising that the Vatican daily *L'Osservatore Romano* published a poisonous little item to say that a copy of Del Fante's *True History: Padre Pio of Pietrelcina, the First Priest with Stigmata* had been "sent to the Holy Father" but was "promptly returned to the sender."[34]

Emanuele Brunatto, for his part, was upping the stakes, letting it be known he was about to publish a tell-all book about Padre Pio's enemies. The book was to be called *Letter to the Church*, and Brunatto threatened to include not merely the information that he (as Professor De Felice) had collected on the misdeeds of the Gargano clergy, but also explosive revelations on the sex lives of high Vatican dignitaries.[35] The news of imminent publication set off a thriller-style chase: Brunatto had hidden the documentation and the proofs of the book away in Germany for safekeeping, while his sometime friend the politician Francesco Morcaldi of San Giovanni Rotondo offered to steal them and pass them on to ecclesiastical officials if they would free Padre Pio from his virtual prison conditions. Morcaldi did manage to get the page proofs of *Letter to the Church* to the papal nuncio in Munich, who in turn sent them to Rome by diplomatic pouch. But when it came to the documents on which Brunatto had based his book, Morcaldi was out-foxed. He obtained what seemed to be the right papers, and passed them on, in the dark interior of a Roman church, to messengers who had been dispatched by Cardinal Rossi; but he would later learn that Brunatto had taken care to hide the real originals of those documents, and so the Vatican had only received copies.[36]

As these machinations went on, Brunatto left Italy for Paris and threatened to publish his book directly in French as *Les Antéchrists dans l'Église du Christ*. This time, Padre Pio himself took up pen and ink to try to dissuade him.

> I do not wish to obtain my liberation or rehabilitation with repulsive acts that would make the lowest of delinquents blush . . . I absolutely cannot permit you to defend me or try to free me by throwing dirt—and what dirt—in the face of those whom you and I and all of us have a sacrosanct duty to respect. Your defense of me is a real dishonor, and I do not wish, I repeat, to obtain my liberation and regain the faculties that have been taken away from me by such means. The ill-fated publication of this book will not only provoke all the evil of which you are the cause, it will also certainly make it harder for all those whom you want to defend.[37]

Then, all of a sudden, things changed. Even as Brunatto continued to threaten publication, Vatican authorities decided—unilaterally, it could almost be said—to loosen their grip on Padre Pio. On July 13, 1933, the Holy Office informed the Capuchin order that some of the restrictions on the friar had been lifted. The gesture was presented as an act of grace granted to him for the special Holy Year of 1933, commemorating the 1900th anniversary of Christ's death.[38] In fact, the change of heart was due to the influence of Archbishop Cesarano of Manfredonia, who had quickly decided upon taking up his new office that Padre Pio was a pastoral resource for the diocese rather than a problem.[39] Beginning in the summer of 1933, the Capuchin was once again allowed to say mass in the friary church, open to both the clergy and lay persons. Ten months later, his liberation continuing, he was permitted to hear confession both from lay sinners and his fellow friars. Although some of the prohibitions that had been imposed in 1923 remained in place—he was still forbidden any physical contact with the lay sisters, for example—the worst of his persecution was over. Padre Pio was no longer a prisoner.

And so the highborn and the influential, both lay and clerical, were soon to be found once again taking the road to San Giovanni, mingling with all the anonymous pilgrims. The roster of names—enough to make a hagiographer proud—included the blue-blooded aviator General Francesco De Pinedo; the arctic explorer and engineer Umberto Nobile; Prince Mario Colonna; the well-connected Countess Virginia Silj, sister of Cardinal Augusto Silj and sister-in-law of Cardinal Gasparri; and the renowned educationalist Maria Montessori. But in many ways the most interesting visitor of all was Don Giuseppe De Luca,[40] perhaps the most cultivated and restless mind in the Church of Pius XI. A sophisticated scholar of the history of Christian spirituality, De Luca decided one day to climb the winding road to San Giovanni, knocked on the door of the Capuchin monastery, met Padre Pio, and was dazzled.

The letter in which De Luca wrote to his friend Papini about his visit to the Gargano is an astounding, captivating account of the divine made manifest.

> Padre Pio, dear Papini, is a sickly, ignorant Capuchin, very much the crude southerner. And yet (bear in mind that besides making confession to him, I also dined with him and we spent a great deal of time together), and yet—God is with him, that fearful God that we glimpse in revery and which he has in his soul, unbearably hot, and in his flesh, which trembles constantly, wounded, sometimes more, sometimes less, moaning atrociously, as if battered by ever more powerful gales. I truly

saw the *holy* there, holiness not of action but of passion, the holiness that God expresses. Although he is a man of very meager intelligence, he offered me two or three words that I have never found on the lips of other men, and not even (and this is harder to admit) in the books of the Church . . . There is nothing of ordinary spirituality about him, nor is there anything extraordinarily miraculous, stunning, or showy; there is merely *intelligentia spiritualis*, a free gift from God. And there is a passion, even a human passion, for God, dear Papini, that is so beautiful, so ravishingly sweet that I can't tell you. The love of woman and the love of ideas are nothing by comparison, they are things that do not go beyond a certain point, whether near or far. While the love of God, how, I do not know, burns, and the more it burns the more it finds to burn. I have the absolutely certain sensation that God and man have met in this person.[41]

De Luca's comments are all the more interesting because in that same letter to Papini, he revealed deep reservations about Padre Pio's entourage. "The local priests," he wrote, "are involved in dirty dealings." Furthermore, De Luca endorsed the disciplinary measures that were keeping the friar under house arrest. "The Holy Office did not condemn him," he told Papini; "they merely placed him inside an iron circle, which is not a bad thing, in these vulgar times, for it protects him from American-style publicity and rivalry among miracle-working sanctuaries."[42]

Some thirty years after that 1934 visit to San Giovanni, De Luca, writing in *L'Osservatore Romano*, would publicly denounce the promise of miracles emanating from places like Santa Maria delle Grazie and would even go so far as to suggest Padre Pio himself was guilty of fraudulent behavior. But that would be the opinion of a priest who had meanwhile risen to the upper levels of the Vatican and become an insider with Pope John XXIII.[43] In the 1930s, in a prosaic Fascist Italy that he felt badly needed the spiritual poetry of the Church, the erudite De Luca could easily be tempted to see in the rough Capuchin the incarnation, the "fountains of mercy" that he was seeking in the Christian tradition.[44]

As he wrote in a Florentine Catholic review shortly before his visit to San Giovanni: "Four hundred years from now, the saints who lived between 1850 and 1930, saints we're not even aware of, will be the true and glorious witnesses to this Christian time."[45] The concrete mercy practiced by a humble friar in remote Puglia, De Luca believed, could be assimilated into his blue-blooded Tuscan Catholicism: both valued a Church that was pure because it was down to earth, rich because it was simple, generous because it was poor.

A Dangerous Saint

The restoration of priestly powers to Padre Pio did not put an end to all the tensions surrounding him. In July 1933, the Department of Public Security in Rome opened a file on the Capuchin friar, and the documents it collected show the extent of the controversies that continued to swirl.

Among the informers that the Department of Public Security relied on was the journalist Cesare Mansueti, whose contacts at high levels inside the Capuchin order had led him to view Padre Pio as a second Savonarola.[46] If Mansueti is to be believed, the order's "hatred" for the "famous Capuchin" derived from his apocalyptic preaching. The friar with the stigmata was also said to be "sharply critical of Vatican luxury" and ready to prophesy a grim future for the pope. "According to Padre Pio," Mansueti said, "the Pope will pay a price for his attachment to worldly things, for the opulence he displays as an Earthly Power. He will have to return to the spirit of Christ and be no more than His representative on earth, but with humility, without arms and armies, embassies, special trains, etc." The man on the throne of St. Peter, to meet the requirements spelled out in the Gospels, would have to live in just two rooms, remain far from politics, and be open to all. "An aristocratic Pope, far from the crowds, whom no one may approach, is not the Pope of Christ, and the treasures he possesses, he should not possess; he should distribute them to the poor." Such were the sentiments, Mansueti reported, that were being spread in the mountains of the Gargano. It was no surprise, then, that the Holy Office forbade Padre Pio to act as a priest, that it confiscated his mail and prevented anyone from taking his picture. "The Vatican fears the power of Padre Pio of Pietrelcina," Mansueti went on. "He is a very dangerous saint."[47]

Padre Pio as the proud spokesman for a primitive Church against the Antichrist who had usurped the papal throne? The depiction sounds similar to Brunatto's 1926 *Padre Pio of Pietrelcina*, but it doesn't correspond to what was reported about Padre Pio by other sources.[48] Perhaps these stories Mansueti said he had heard inside the Capuchin order were no more than the fabrications of a spy who was handsomely paid regardless of whether what he said was true or not. On the other hand, perhaps Mansueti's reports contained a kernel of truth, a hint of the Church's reasons for suppressing the Padre Pio cult. It's interesting, in light of Mansueti's intelligence, that between producing articles about Padre Pio, the Bologna convert Alberto Del Fante wrote extensively about Girolamo Savonarola and Christian prophecy.[49]

Another anti-Pio document in the files of the Department of Public Security was a letter that had been sent to the Holy Office in September 1931 by "a group of five children of the Church."[50] While Mansueti's reports had portrayed Padre Pio as a fiery critic of papal power, this anonymous denunciation reduced the divine mystery of the *alter Christus* to the level of a simple fraud, a country swindle, which the cunning of a few and the credulousness of many had turned into "the lowest and most convincing trick of the century." According to the letter writers, the plan had originally been hatched by Adelchi Fabroncini, an elementary school teacher and local correspondent for several southern newspapers. In the midst of the Great War, Fabroncini had convinced Father Paolino of Casacalenda, the father guardian of Santa Maria delle Grazie, to become the "manager" of a popular cult. The plot was simple: take a friar with "obscure ambitions," spill a few drops of a certain vegetable extract on his hands and feet, and keep the "stigmata" open by brushing on tincture of iodine. After that, you merely had to persuade a court clerk ("a close friend of Fabroncini") to appear in public first limping, then healthy, and get a fake "disabled veteran" to pretend to be miraculously well. Once a popular cult was born, "everything afterwards would be taken on faith with oriental fanaticism."

Shortly after the cult was established, the five anonymous citizens wrote, came the "devil" of the story: Emanuele Brunatto, who was able to take a country swindle and turn it into a national imbroglio. The writers seemed to have a good sense of his background: "This fellow appeared in San Giovanni Rotondo in 1923 to hide out from the police by whom he was wanted because he had been sentenced to four years in prison for fraud and other crimes." Having gained the confidence of Fabroncini and the friars, they said, Brunatto had cleverly woven together hagiographic accounts and blackmail to create a lucrative Italy-wide business soliciting donations ("we're talking about millions of lire") built on the credulity of true-believing simpletons. "Many chickens have already lost all their feathers, but they're still happy about this harmless if painful divestiture because it's on behalf of their beloved Padre Pio."

But not even the Mephistophelean Brunatto could have succeeded at this game had he not had been able to count on Padre Pio's help. The friar was anything but a puppet manipulated by an unscrupulous carnival barker, the anonymous five maintained. He was "the head of a band of real delinquents," exploiting a popular devotion so intense that it encompassed numerous pious women ready to satisfy his sexual appetites. In the eyes of the letter writers, Padre Pio was a "brand-new Rasputin." Like the phony monk and phony healer who had held Orthodox Russia under his sway at the time of the czar, so Padre Pio was keeping Catholic Italy under his sway at the time of Il Duce, exciting "passion, love and interests at the expense of the religion of Christ."

Padre Pio's Locomotives

In February 1931, inside a train compartment on one of their many pilgrimages to San Giovanni Rotondo, Alberto Del Fante and his devout friends Antonio Tonelli and Federico Abresch were passing around *The Miraculous Manifestations of the Limpias Crucifix*, a pamphlet written by the Capuchin father Giannantonio of Romallo. Many of Padre Pio's Italian followers were convinced that Spain's most celebrated sweating crucifix was the marvelous, complementary proof of the superhuman made visible. Spanish Catholics, for their part, had long been dedicated to the little Capuchin friar; as early as 1920, letters signed by Padre Pio and leaves from the rose garden at Santa Maria delle Grazie had been circulated in Spain as miraculous healing devices.[51]

The two miracles—the sweating Christ on the cross and the living Christ in the Gargano—were especially tightly linked in the minds of the most fired-up Catholics because, as Father Giannantonio revealed, the king of Spain himself had sent Padre Pio "a magnificent photograph" of the Limpias cross.[52] Father Giannantonio's pamphlet had been published with Vatican approval, which Del Fante and his friends found annoying: if the Church had allowed this publication even before it officially recognized the miracle of Limpias, why should the followers of Padre Pio be barred from spreading the good news about what was happening in Puglia? On the train to Foggia, the Bolognese pilgrims read and reread the pamphlet all night long until they were "dazed."[53] That little episode of railway piety shows how genuine (or perhaps ingenuous) was Del Fante and company's enthusiasm for Padre Pio, an enthusiasm that many thought bordered on fanaticism. A year later, as the "Bolognesi" continued to insist against all Church interdictions that Padre Pio was a second Christ, the ex-*podestà* Francesco Morcaldi and the schoolteacher Angela Serritelli (who were in fact the leading local promoters of sainthood for Padre Pio) went to Caradonna's wife, a Franciscan lay sister, hoping that her powerful husband could help block the plans of the "desperadoes" from Bologna.[54] Padre Pio himself spoke to Archbishop Cesarano of the "false enthusiasm" of "false prophets, who, however, say they are my followers."[55] In other words, he made a point of keeping his distance from Del Fante and his friends just as he had taken care to distance himself from Brunatto and his plots worthy of a "common criminal."[56]

As the hagiographers have interpreted it, Padre Pio's conduct showed how much respect he had for the rules of the Church and demonstrated his unwavering humility and obedience. But anyone who digs into the archives (something no hagiographer has done) will discover a very different reality. First, despite his protestations, Padre Pio actively maintained direct ties with the "Bolognesi." Second, there was a close, if complicated, relationship between the "Bolognesi" and Padre Pio's principal apostle, Emanuele Brunatto, now living in Paris. And to close

the triangle, Brunatto and Padre Pio were carrying on an uninterrupted dialogue with Morcaldi's intense mediation. What were they
discussing? Not merely the publication of forbidden books on the friar's miracles or the dissemination of holy cards with his signature, but
the creation of a profiteering devotional association to raise money for
Padre Pio.

These events—which I reconstruct here for the first time—belong
to a distinctly modern narrative, one that clashes sharply with various
hagiographic legends. The tale centers on a Roman shareholding company, the Anonima Brevetti Zarlatti, which was acquired in a takeover
and milked for funds to be "donated" to the little friar with the stigmata. It is a story full of surprises, because the Zarlatti company's
industrial scope—selling patents for diesel locomotives—could not
have been farther from any sacred matters. It is a sad story, because
business immediately took a bad turn and it was Padre Pio's followers
who were to pay. It is a sensitive story, because the friar at the center of
the efforts had theoretically taken a vow of poverty. And, finally, it is a
grotesque story, because Padre Pio, though he occasionally seemed to
be in charge, was himself being manipulated by the real mastermind,
the chameleon-like double-dealer Emanuele Brunatto.

The Anonima Brevetti Zarlatti company held several patents for
diesel locomotives. The company hoped to demonstrate the superiority
of its technology to the products of such giants as Fiat and Breda, which
were working on similar projects, and sell its patents to the Italian Rail
System. But when the technicians of Italian Rail carried out their trials
on the Zarlatti prototype, the results were so dismal that the locomotive was simply parked along the Rome-Ostia line and left to rust. In
1931, however, at the prompting of Count Vincenzo Baiocchi, an early
Zarlatti shareholder whose wife had been miraculously cured by Padre
Pio, the company was acquired by new investors. Francesco Morcaldi,
Cesare Festa (brother of the doctor Giorgio), and the Bologna photographer Federico Abresch joined the board of directors. Ubaldo Cuppini, one of Del Fante's associates and the largest shareholder, was
named the new chairman. Del Fante's brother-in-law Antonio Tonelli
also bought a large packet of shares. The new vice chairman was the

Roman lawyer Antonio Angelini Rota, and the managing director—the CEO—was, a police spy reported, "a certain Prof. Brunatto."[57]

Fresh from his failure to stop the Libreria del Littorio from going under, Padre Pio's number one apostle thus settled down in Paris as the boss of the Anonima Brevetti Zarlatti, with the professed intention of selling patents for diesel locomotives on the European market. In the years that followed, he would write dozens of letters on the stationery of sumptuous hotels in Paris, Brussels, and Berlin to his friend "Ciccillo" Morcaldi—letters that spoke both the language of business and the language of faith. They were letters about the negotiations supposedly under way to sell Zarlatti patents to some of the biggest railway companies on the continent—the Société Franco-Belge de Matériel de Chemin de Fer, Krupp, the Compagnie Fives-Lille—but that concluded with such messages as this Christmas sign-off of December 24, 1931: "take all of my heart, so grateful and filled with desire for Jesus, into the sacred wounds of Our Father and say to him many tender things and kiss his habit for me."[58] Fascist secret police in Paris sent word to Rome about the ostentatious lifestyle of the so-called Professor Brunatto, noting that he had "powerful friendships in the political sphere," but also registering the strong suspicion that Brunatto was "an adventurer and a snake-oil salesman."[59]

The tentacles of the regime's police reached deep inside the Brunatto band that had taken over at Zarlatti. For years, informers in both Paris and Rome—some reliable, some not—watched the company's efforts to become something more than a small business on the verge of bankruptcy. In Bologna, meanwhile, the prefecture was systematically reading and preserving all of Brunatto's correspondence with Cuppini, Tonelli, and Giovannini, thus providing the historian with some excellent documentation. For almost ten years, the "Bolognesi" were financing Brunatto as much as their means would allow, with monthly or near-monthly investments, using various expedients to get around the laws prohibiting the export of capital. From 1934 onward, there was growing doubt about how reliable and how honest Brunatto was, yet right up to the end of the decade the shareholders were counting on that diesel locomotive as the secret weapon that would flood Padre Pio with cash. Once the Capuchin friar and his cult became rich, the Church would no longer be able to treat Pio as an imposter, they reasoned. Instead, his miraculous powers would finally earn the respect they deserved.

The archives reveal the unfailing devotion with which Padre Pio's followers trusted not only in his stigmata but in his locomotives. They record, for example, the case of Carolina Giovannini, forty years old, a seamstress-embroiderer by training but too ailing to work. Giovannini lived "in virtual poverty" in attic rooms in central Bologna with a small pension from the Institution of Pious Works for the Disgraced, a charity for the deserving poor. Malicious rumors that she was the mistress of Emanuele Brunatto were unfounded, reported the prefecture. "Such a possibility can be excluded first because Brunatto has never visited Bologna, and also because Giovannini's physical health is far from good. She is all but deformed and suffers from many ailments."[60] However, it was true that a small band of the faithful clustered around her, counting on her to put in a good word with Padre Pio on her frequent trips to the Gargano. According to intelligence reports, they often found that they were offered a deal: she would intercede for them with the friar if they would invest in Zarlatti locomotives. "She owns no property herself but her residence is well frequented by persons of all social classes, but especially the poor, who come to ask for advice, assistance and contacts," the agent wrote.[61] "In this way, there are people in Bologna who pledge their wages to buy Anonima Brevetti Zarlatti shares," said one anonymous letter filed with the prefecture.[62]

The correspondence intercepted by the police makes it clear that Brunatto worked hard for years to convince the "Bolognesi," the Roman shareholders in Zarlatti, and the people of San Giovanni (including Padre Pio) that he was sacrificing himself in every way on behalf of this industrial-religious cause. "I'm being crushed by debts. I've sold my watch and suits, I've pawned my overcoat. I'm exhausted, afraid," wrote Brunatto to Morcaldi in June 1935.[63] But whenever the sums coming in from Italy began to decline, the profiteer changed his tune. Menacing letters, implicit and explicit threats of blackmail, the creation of parallel companies to exploit the Zarlatti patents for his own gain: Brunatto was capable of all this and more to persuade his partners to send him more money. When a woman named Maria Pyle—an American heiress who had been Maria Montessori's friend and coworker[64] before settling down in San Giovanni to pray with Padre Pio—declared that she had been defrauded, Brunatto responded with indignation. Pyle engaged a lawyer to recover the investments she had made in Zarlatti shares, money that seemed to have disappeared; but Brunatto, safely far away in Paris, found some way to wiggle out of this bind too.

The fact that Brunatto was soon hawking locomotive patents on his own behalf as well as in his capacity as managing director of Zarlatti added further complexity to the financial dealings. At one point, he announced that he would generously concede to the Zarlatti shareholders "10 francs per horse power of every engine of every locomotive sold" under his own name in countries where Zarlatti had not yet entered the market. In return for this munificent willingness to accommodate, he would need a onetime payment of two hundred thousand lire, plus 5 percent of future Zarlatti profits.[65]

Carolina Giovannini traveled to Paris several times to hear Brunatto reassure her about the company's future. On other occasions, Tonelli and Abresch went to Rome to get the lawyer Angelini Rota to try to pressure Brunatto to show some concrete results. But Brunatto never failed to find a way to get out of a jam, promising brilliant results that were always just about to arrive. "The Russian orders are being actively negotiated. The People's Commissar and the directors of the Soviet rail system think our method is the most interesting. If this news is correct, the USSR will immediately order thirty locomotives," Brunatto wrote in a letter to Morcaldi in which he also declared himself on the brink of suicide. A few months later, writing from Berlin, he told Zarlatti chairman Ubaldo Cuppini that the German railways were extremely interested in the company's patents, and urged him to deposit money in an account belonging to Brunatto's brother-in-law in the Italian city of La Spezia.[66]

Brunatto also tried to get Anonima Brevetti Zarlatti involved in a new industrial adventure: the making of charcoal from the two hundred thousand tons of railroad ties dismantled annually in Italy, using a secret new process revealed to him by some "engineers from the East."[67] As for Francesco Morcaldi down in San Giovanni Rotondo, Brunatto sent frequent promises of "a suitable and steady job" in Rome or Paris.[68] One could go on forever quoting from the documentation of this interminable joke, but we'll content ourselves here with two last vignettes: Tonelli begging Brunatto to send him "a bolt or some other such small souvenir" from the Zarlatti prototype locomotive so that he could hold a memory of this sacred business enterprise, while urging Brunatto in the same letter to " be industrious, for so God wants it, to bring Jesus to the many souls longing for light from our dearest Padre Pio";[69] and the ex-seamstress Giovannini, back from an expedition to Paris, writing to Brunatto to promise that "next week I'm going to buy the wool and I hope to make you a nice, new sweater, ever so warm and light."[70] In terms of sheer charisma, it seems that Emanuele Brunatto was no less gifted than the Capuchin friar of San Giovanni Rotondo.

And what was Padre Pio's role in the Anonima Brevetti Zarlatti affair? Anyone tempted to think he was uninvolved only needs to decipher the handwritten note of 1931 in which the friar with the stigmata took care to record that "the 550 shares of the Serritelli sisters break down as follows: 250 to Antonietta, 50 to Angela, 50 to Elvira, 100 to Marietta, 100 to Margherita."[71] Other sources also document Padre Pio's direct involvement in the Zarlatti business. "Padre Pio is strongly insistent, so lose no time," one of Morcaldi's friends from San Giovanni wrote in March 1931 about the friar's keen desire to see them buy up the

Zarlatti shares.[72] In the following two years, the near-prison conditions in which the friar was confined probably kept him from following the business too closely. But as of 1934, letters exchanged by Brunatto and Carolina Giovannini begin to mention their "mutual counselor," whose desires in the matter are held to be decisive.[73]

Obviously, the faithful who had invested in Zarlatti shares were not keen to publicize the association of their company with a friar committed to a vow of poverty, but they didn't manage to erase every trace of him. Padre Pio had encouraged the deal from the beginning in hopes of bringing money to his remote Gargano convent, and he continued to believe in diesel locomotives despite all of Brunatto's dicey dealings. In September 1937, the friar asked Morcaldi to send a letter to Paris in which, "with hands joined" in prayer, he would entreat Brunatto "not to create any problems about selling the rights" to one of the company's patents "so it can be traded in the United States." With determination worthy of a higher cause, Padre Pio sought to convince his acquisitive disciple Morcaldi that profits were just around the corner. "My son, do not make these humble people despair, for they are not in a condition to make even small sacrifices. Anyway, three percent is not to be despised," he said, referring to the modest return expected from the U.S. deal.

"Please take care of this, Ciccillo, and don't waste time or miss the propitious occasion."[74]

But Brunatto, back in Paris, had in the meantime found himself a game considerably bigger than the Zarlatti scam.

For the Greater Good of the Fascist Fatherland

In the years that Emanuele Brunatto was the top executive of a shareholding company dear to Padre Pio, he was also a spy for the Fascist regime. Probably right from his arrival in Paris in 1931, and certainly from 1935 onward, the front offered by Zarlatti—the offices on Boulevard Haussmann, the travels as managing director, the negotiations over locomotive patents—allowed Brunatto to mask his main activity: infiltrating those sectors of the French political arena that were neither on the right nor on the left.[75] At a time when the Third Republic was torn by political-financial scandals and by doubts about what diplomatic and military approach to take with the new totalitarian powers, Brunatto found a role for himself as an agent provocateur inside the Parti Radical—the oldest, most divided, and most corrupt party in France.[76]

In those years, Mussolini's spies in Paris were so numerous that they spent most of their time spying on one another. The best information about Brunatto's doings thus made its way to Rome thanks to the zeal of Pitigrilli, the novelist of sex and sin who had gotten to know his fellow Turin native in the early 1920s, when both of them were making the rounds of the newspapers in Rome. Coming across his old colleague in the Italian literary-political demi-monde in Paris, Pitigrilli jumped at the chance to sell whatever information he learned about him.[77] Another source reporting on Brunatto in the French capital was Vincenzo Bellavia, a spy for the mysteriously titled agency OVRA, Mussolini's secret police.[78] And then there was the journalist Italo Sulliotti, editor of the Paris edition of La Nuova Italia, the party organ of the Italian Fasci abroad, whom Brunatto considered a trusted friend.[79]

The Paris gossip about a man like Brunatto could reach the most fanciful extremes. In December 1935, Bellavia suggested one day that Brunatto had "a direct relationship with Il Duce" and the next that he was working "on behalf of Giustizia e Libertà," a leading anti-Fascist group.[80] Six months later, the same informer aired his suspicions that the "misfit" Brunatto was connected to the anti-Fascist exile Carlo Rosselli.[81] By October 1936, Bellavia had finally decided that Brunatto was no anti-Fascist conspirator, and noted instead his "reputation as an insider to secret things nearly everywhere that political intrigues are forged in Paris." This reputation was enhanced by rumors that Brunatto had a special relationship with Italian chief of police Arturo Bocchini—a relationship that supposedly went back to an inquiry Brunatto had carried out "on behalf of the Church and in favor of a holy friar at a place called Pietraccina, I think, a town near Avellino."[82]

In his role as a spy for OVRA, just as in his job with Zarlatti, the Brunatto that emerges from the archives is a consummate self-aggrandizer. This doesn't mean that he never had an impact on major events, the kind that appear in history books. Brunatto played a notable role, for example, in the French political crisis of the fall and winter of 1935, after Mussolini's troops invaded Haile Selassie's Ethiopia. On October 9, the general assembly of the League of Nations in Geneva decided to punish Italy with economic sanctions, and in the weeks that followed French prime minister Pierre Laval was called to task for what his opponents in Paris saw as a markedly pro-Italian foreign policy—scandalously pro-Fascist, his accusers said. Under pressure, the Laval government seemed about to fall, and the prime minister needed the support of the Radicals in the Assemblée Nationale to pass a confidence vote. At the end of a December 28 session that was among the most dramatic in Third Republic parliamentary history, ninety-three Radical deputies voted against the government—but fifty-nine Radicals voted for Laval, and he was able to remain in office with a twenty-vote majority.[83]

It was to be a short-lived triumph for Laval, who would soon step down, not to return until seven years later as prime minister of the Vichy government. But for Mussolini, the French parliamentary vote of December 28, 1935, was a real victory, an act that would weaken the sanctionist front against him. And it was the trickster of Boulevard Haussmann who could claim credit for that victory, obtained at the height of the Ethiopian offensive. "If the prime minister did not fall," the informer Sulliotti told authorities in Rome on January 2, 1936, "it was due *exclusively* to the personal and spontaneous initiative of one Italian working on his own, Engineer Brunatto." Maneuvering over "a territory fertilized by the broadest and most shameless corruption," Brunatto was able to take advantage of his connections to bribe the Radical vice president Léon Archimbaud. "In return for the money, Archimbaud, although he personally voted against [Laval], agreed to shift some thirty Radical votes . . . to give Laval the narrow majority that kept his government alive."[84]

Brunatto got the cash needed to buy the Radical votes—some 120,000 francs, it seems—from the Italian embassy in Paris.[85] It was a large sum, but money well spent in the eyes of the Fascist government if it helped the antisanctionist cause. Still, Brunatto complained to Sulliotti that Italian embassy officials hadn't treated him with sufficient respect after he successfully completed the deal.[86] The two spies had such a close relationship at the time that Brunatto used his colleague to ferry cash whenever he decided to squeeze more money out of the Anonima Zarlatti shareholders. In January 1936, for example, Brunatto told Ubaldo Cuppini, the chairman of Zarlatti, that unless he got more money he would leave the company and pocket all the proceeds that they were about to receive for the sale of patents in the Soviet Union. ("I have informed San Giovanni of this *final* step!" thundered Brunatto.) Cuppini was instructed to show up at the Hotel Flora on Via Veneto in Rome and give "Commendatore Sulliotti" the sum of one hundred thousand lire in a sealed envelope, making sure not to say anything.[87]

The Italian embassy officials were not the only ones who treated Brunatto highhandedly. In conversation with Pitigrilli, he complained that the French notables of the Third Republic whom he was obliged to meet in the course of handing out bribes were arrogant: "With these Frenchmen it's not enough to grease the wheels. You have to deliver the money with a gloved hand and thank them for having accepted it."[88] For his own part, Brunatto did not hold them in high regard, not at all: he was convinced that the entire Third Republic was for sale, and that foreigners merely had to step in and exploit the situation. In the fall of 1936, when the government headed by Léon Blum—the *Front Populaire* government that had won parliamentary elections in the spring—

showed the first signs of faltering, Brunatto thought about repeating the operation he had done with Laval, but this time to send the government down rather than to save it. The idea was to "set deputy Archimbaud and his friends in motion" (as one OVRA informer euphemistically put it) so the Radical Party ministers in the Blum government would resign and make the government fall. At that point, the path would be clear for a return to power of the old guard, who would guarantee French neutrality in international affairs vis à vis Mussolini's Italy.[89]

Unlike Brunatto's previous plan, this one never came to fruition. Nor did anything come of the plots he was hatching during the spring of 1937 on a rather different political and diplomatic front: the Vatican. The Church of Rome was agitated because Pius XI's health was growing steadily worse, and a new conclave seemed imminent.[90] Looking ahead toward that "sorrowful event to come," Brunatto had sent chief of police Bocchini a package containing the new galleys of his old black book on the Church, *Les Antéchrists dans l'Eglise du Christ*.[91] He also managed to get him the following message.

> Your Excellency is aware that I possess a voluminous archive on intrigues involving cardinals, groups, cliques of prelates more or less influential in the Church. To prevent a bad Pope from being elected is to render a service to one's country, but it is also to render a service to the Church, of which I am a child. In the event, I am prepared to put myself at Your Excellency's disposition and provide all the material that you consider useful.[92]

In another letter, Padre Pio's number one apostle "strongly" urged Bocchini to evaluate how his "industriousness" and his "intelligence" as an Italian in France could be "put to use" in light of the coming conclave, "for the greater good of the Fascist Fatherland."[93]

Brunatto as an undercover pope-maker, Bocchini's secret agent in a dirty game of trying to elect a pontiff favored by the Mussolini regime? Such was the scenario that he tried to lay before the police chief, pretending he was replying to a request that had come from Bocchini via Sulliotti.[94] The archives suggest, though, that the would-be pope-maker was not considered very credible by the police. Writing to Sulliotti, who had meanwhile moved to Budapest as chief of the Italian Fasci in Hungary, Bocchini gave him a dressing-down: "I know nothing of this, for although I spoke with you of Brunatto, as we did of many other Italians resident in Paris, I would never have dreamed of giving you any such instructions."[95] Sulliotti, in turn, informed Bocchini that he had had nothing to do with the matter, that the whole Vatican scenario had emerged out of Brunatto's galloping imagination. And yet, "despite everything," Sulliotti still thought that Brunatto was a "good fellow." "During the long months in Paris I watched him work like a crazy man for our cause, and—I'd like to think—disinterestedly, and making personal sacrifices."[96]

Sulliotti's words fell on deaf ears. In the spring of 1937, Bocchini repeatedly advised the most important emissaries of the regime in Paris to have nothing to do with Emanuele Brunatto. "A person absolutely not to be trusted and to keep at a distance, being an undependable element;"[97] "a huckster who offers no guarantee of seriousness and honesty."[98] Such was the verdict on the fixer who had finally gone too far.

Bread and Wine

Apart from the locomotives, the several years following Padre Pio's "liberation" marked a relatively happy season in the friar's life and a return to normality. In 1935, the recently named minister general of the Capuchin Order, Father Vigilio of Valstagna, made a visit to San Giovanni Rotondo, signaling newfound agreement inside the order about the position of the Capuchin with the stigmata and reviving his worship.[99] Two months later, on August 10, Padre Pio was able to celebrate the twenty-fifth anniversary of his ordination. A great crowd gathered for it in the monastery church, and Monsignor Cesarano himself, the archbishop of Manfredonia who had tilted the scales decisively in Padre Pio's favor, made an appearance.[100] The atmosphere around the friar had improved so much that his onetime spiritual director Father Benedetto of San Marco in Lamis was allowed to publish—albeit discreetly—an anthology of their correspondence.[101] Far away in Paris,

Emanuele Brunatto was not wrong in perceiving that "good news" was coming out of San Giovanni Rotondo.[102]

The historian, meanwhile, would be wrong to judge Brunatto as no more than a phony apostle. The fact that we have unveiled his second and third lives does not imply that Brunatto's allegiance to the Capuchin was all merely a show, falsehood, and duplicity. In fact, he continued to be a genuine devotee of Padre Pio, and for several decades to come he would live in hopes of seeing the *alter Christus* triumph over the Pharisees of the Vatican. Even the discovery that Brunatto was a scheming Fascist through and through—moving from the Roman offices of the Libreria del Littorio to the lobby of the Palais-Bourbon in Paris with money from the Italian embassy in his pocket, corrupting the deputies of the Third Republic, and promoting Mussolini's diplomatic interests—even this was fully consistent with his devotion to Padre Pio. After all, religious life in San Giovanni had taken a turn toward clerico-fascism as far back as the early 1920s, and the friar with the stigmata never did anything that would earn him a reputation as an adversary of the regime.

Perhaps the best way to understand Brunatto is not by sifting through the archives but by looking at the literature of the period—at the best seller *Bread and Wine*, for example, a novel by the anti-Fascist emigrant Ignazio Silone that was published in German in 1936 and in Italian a year later.[103] Silone's book, like Fogazzaro's 1905 *The Saint*, focused on what sainthood meant in the twentieth century. Even more than that: between the title, with its Eucharistic flavor, and the decision to make the protagonist a man of thirty-three years old, Silone's book was a bold and heartfelt effort to portray a modern Christ figure. The novel was hardly meant to be a reflection on Padre Pio or Emanuele Brunatto, yet the tale, set on the eve of the war in Ethiopia, was made up of the same ingredients as their real-life story: religious faith and political faith, Christo-mimesis and miracles, betrayal and regret, stigmata and spies, prophecy and police.

The protagonist of *Bread and Wine* is Pietro Spina, a revolutionary who hides from the police in the mountains of Abruzzo disguised as a priest. The local villagers see him as a living saint. Telling the stories of his miracles, they ask each other, rather terrified, if he is Christ in person.

It wouldn't be the first time Jesus disguised himself and came down to earth to see how the poor live, says the girl from Fossa. And then she adds, in a tiny voice: Have you noticed whether his hands and feet are pierced? That is the the surest way to know if it is Him. He can disguise himself all he wants, but if it is really Him, he won't be able to hide the stigmata left by the nails with which he was crucified.[104]

The village innkeeper is uncertain what to do, and wonders if it would not be advisable to call the carabinieri. ("On the door of the inn there hangs a sign giving 'Rules for Hoteliers,' but the arrival of Jesus is not on the list.") Suddenly, an ex-revolutionary named Luigi Murica appears on the scene. Murica had sold himself to the Fascist regime and participated in their dirty plots, but he has also suffered over it. Finally confessing his misdeeds to the priest, he hopes for absolution and rebirth.[105]

Silone certainly put something of himself in that tormented figure of the police informer,[106] although his own role as an informer on his onetime Communist comrades would only be revealed many years later. But we are also free to see something of Emanuele Brunatto in Murica. Perhaps he, too, hoped one day to return from the boulevards of Paris to the Gargano mountains—to confess all his sins to Padre Pio, be absolved, and then reborn.

8. THE SORROWS OF THIS WORLD

Swastikas

A month after Germany's invasion of Poland started World War II, some of Padre Pio's most enthusiastic followers realized one of their long-standing dreams. Along the road connecting the center of town with the Capuchin monastery, they were able to build a Via Crucis, fourteen markers of stone and marble each depicting a scene from the Passion. A commemorative plaque paid tribute to a pious lady from Bologna who had dreamed up this work and raised the money for it among her fellow believers: Carolina Giovannini, the penniless but enterprising seamstress we met before as one of the dupes of Emanuele Brunatto's confidence tricks.[1] The ceremonial unveiling took place on October 4, 1939, with Monsignor Cesarano, archbishop of Manfredonia, presiding, and it was covered in detail by the Bologna paper *Il Resto del Carlino*. Padre Pio himself had departed from his usual cloistered way of life, the paper reported, coming out "among the people" for several hours, "laboriously protected by the carabinieri" who held back an adoring crowd. The *Carlino* didn't fail to note that the inauguration of the Via Crucis fell on the feast of St. Francis of Assisi. As guns echoed across Europe, what could be finer than celebrating Padre Pio on the same day that St. Francis was being honored as one of Italy's patron saints? The new pope, Eugenio Pacelli—Pius XII as of March 1939—had just that summer declared St. Francis and St. Catherine of Siena patron saints of Italy. As for Padre Pio, by deciding to immerse himself in the crowd, he was following in the footsteps of the Poverello:

like him "whose face is marked by all the world's suffering," Pio was accepting a role as protector of the nation.[2]

Italy entered the war on June 10, 1940, and as Mussolini's armies met with defeat on fronts from Africa to Russia, Padre Pio's followers began to direct more and more prayers toward the Gargano. Until 1939, an average of about nine thousand letters addressed to Padre Pio arrived at Santa Maria delle Grazie each year. In 1940, the number rose to twelve thousand; in 1942, it stood at fifteen thousand, and by 1945, the letters numbered more than twenty thousand a year.[3] Evidently—as had happened at the end of the Great War, when the horror of the trenches was followed by the terror of the Spanish flu epidemic—the overwhelming anxiety and despair drew many believers to put their hopes in the friar with the stigmata.

After June 1940, several of the friar's followers hastened to make it known that their hearts beat only for Mussolini and the Axis. In Bologna there was Alberto Del Fante, the onetime Freemason-turned-hagiographer and leader of a small lobby of Padre Pio zealots. Paris had just fallen under Hitler's blitzkrieg and Italian soldiers had just thrust their knives into France's dying Third Republic when Del Fante decided to publish his own contribution to the situation: a political pamphlet titled *If Only They Had Believed Us*. That is: if only France had accepted Germany and Italy's proposal to ally with them, rather than tie itself hand and foot to Britain and its servants in the League of Nations! Now the French were going to pay a huge price for their foolish decision, and the British had better resign themselves to a similar destiny. "Within days the Swastika will be flying over the Tower of London," Del Fante predicted, "and a new Europe, founded on the principle of justice, will emerge." Il Duce and the Führer, Del Fante wrote happily, would indeed offer Europe an olive branch—but an olive branch stuck on the points of 150 million bayonets.[4]

In occupied Paris, another of Padre Pio's apostles, Brunatto, also greeted the *pax hitleriana* with enthusiasm. He did so in the new guise of playwright, with a Franciscan-themed drama called *Frère Soleil* presented under the revealing pseudonym of Emanuele De Pio. In October 1941, Brunatto was able to mount the play at no less a space than the Vieux-Colombier, the distinguished Rive Gauche stage that would feature Jean-Paul Sartre's *No Exit* a few years later.[5] In his preface to the printed text of *Frère Soleil*—published for the play's fiftieth performance and thus proof of some success with his audience—Brunatto-De Pio explained that St. Francis of Assisi offered a model to occupied France, showing that only good works could redeem fallen men and nations. In Brunatto's play, St. Francis keeps his stigmata hidden, revealing them only when the time comes to win over the symbolic sinner, the Wolf, to the cause of true Christianity.[6]

Brunatto's support for Hitler's New Order had begun long before the blitzkrieg and the fall of France. Between 1937 and 1938, although he was no longer considered reliable by his OVRA bosses, the putative Zarlatti engineer still did his part for the cause of international fascism. Italian informers in Paris continued to forward to Rome the numerous tips he passed on to them, particularly his reports about the clandestine military backing lent by the French Communists to the Republicans in Spain.[7] And the resourceful Brunatto also joined the board of a journal sponsored by the Permanent International Committee of Veterans and by its president, the *mutilato* Carlo Delcroix. *Parliamentary and Diplomatic Report: A Monthly Review of World Political Activity*, as the publication was somewhat pompously called, made such a strong case for appeasement that it resembled a pro-Nazi pamphlet.[8] Brunatto, writing in the journal under the pseudonym "P. Lepieux," published reports from Germany brimming with admiration for Hitler's autobahns and for the marvelous leisure-time organization Kraft durch Freude. He also found time for articles that were less directly political, such as a panegyric to the Catholic Church's regular orders (the "orders of the Rule" governed by precepts such as poverty and obedience): these were, in his words, "the real aristocracy of the Church."[9]

Even after the outbreak of war made travel difficult, two of Padre Pio's most faithful followers, Francesco Morcaldi and Cesare Festa, found their way to Paris to put pressure on Brunatto regarding the Zarlatti dealings, still hoping that the locomotive business would finally take off.[10] But now that the German Panzers had taken control of the French capital and the Third Republic had given way to the Vichy government, Brunatto had other matters on his mind. He had not entirely forgotten the Padre Pio cult; indeed, as we shall soon see, the first apostle was still quite devoted to the Christ of the Gargano. He had simply moved on to new pastures. Under German Occupation, Brunatto had become a first-rate collaborationist, happily at the service of the Wehrmacht and the SS.

Hotel Majestic

Nazi-occupied Paris was not an easy place for theater lovers, who had to contend with unheated halls, falling bombs, electric power that came and went, and a subway that stopped running at 11 p.m. And so Brunatto's satisfaction at seeing his Franciscan drama remain on stage for the entire autumn of 1941 in spite of all the obstacles is thoroughly understandable. It is likewise little surprise that when the text of *Frère Soleil* was published the following spring, Brunatto proudly sent a gift copy to Rome to the attention of Il Duce Benito Mussolini.[11]

If he had not forgotten St. Francis of Assisi—tales of whose life from the fourteenth-century anthology *Little Flowers of St. Francis* were quoted word for word in many scenes of his play[12]—even less did Brunatto forget Padre Pio during the Occupation. In June 1941, shortly before making a name for himself as a playwright in Nazi Paris, the con man from Turin had quite dramatically demonstrated his unshakable faith in the Capuchin with the stigmata. Through the Banque Italo-Française de Crédit, Brunatto deposited a conspicuous sum in an account of the Credito Italiano di Firenze registered under the name of the Committee for the Construction of the Hospital of San Giovanni Rotondo: some 3.5 million francs, at a time when the average French monthly salary stood at about one thousand francs. In Brunatto's rather generic description, the deposit represented "money belonging to Italians residing in France."[13] This money was the financial base on which the followers of Padre Pio in San Giovanni Rotondo would build, outside the Capuchin monastery, the hospital that would become known as the Casa Sollievo della Sofferenza, the House for the Relief of Suffering.

"It has never been clear from where such a sum in francs, so large for those times, could have come, whether from Brunatto's all-but-empty pockets, or from the royalties of the Zarlatti patents," wrote the enviably nonchalant author of that little hagiography of Brunatto, *The Man Who Saved Padre Pio*, sixty years later.[14] But where the hagiographer can merely marvel, the historian must seek to provide answers. Where *did* the money come from that financed the laying of the first stone for Padre Pio's hospital? Certainly not, as we know, from those tattered patents for diesel-powered locomotives that "Engineer" Brunatto had tried in vain to sell to railway companies across half of Europe. Nor did it bubble forth from the extemporaneous generosity of some mysterious Italians living in France. A look into the archives produces a different answer. The money that founded the Casa Sollievo della Sofferenza did come from Brunatto's pockets—but those pockets were bulging full, not empty. During the year that followed the fall of France, those pockets filled up with millions and millions of francs that Brunatto earned trafficking on the Parisian black market.

The con man from Turin had always had a soft spot for the black market. A quarter of a century previously, when he was fighting in World War I as a quartermaster for the Royal Army Commissariat, Brunatto had ended up on trial for speculating on the sale of army rations.[15] Now here he was, at it again in France in the summer of 1940. Losing no time after the arrival of the Germans in Paris, Brunatto used the same office on Boulevard Haussmann where he had pretended to represent Zarlatti as the headquarters of a provisions service for the German troops stationed in the capital. His trading company Itala was one of the many *bureaux d'achats* that proliferated in Occupied Paris, attracted partly by the surprising disorganization of the German army provisioners and partly by the mountains of cash handed out daily to the Germans by the Banque de France under the draconian rules of the armistice.[16]

According to a report by the antifraud department of the Paris police prefecture, by October 1940 Brunatto already had at his disposal "vast warehouses" full of all kinds of merchandise. Tinned meat, canned tuna, soap, sugar, coffee, condensed milk, wines, and spirits; there seemed to be no victual or commodity that was beyond the reach of Padre Pio's apostle, nor any item for which he would not break the price rules. Alerted by German military officials, in January 1941 the antifraud department looked into the speculative profits Brunatto was making. It found, for example, that he had bought a shipload (240,000 pieces) of Monsavon soap bars at 1.5 francs apiece and turned around and sold them for 3 francs each, then at 4 francs. "In that operation alone M. Brunatto earned 480,000 francs profit," the antifraud officials reported. The following month, they estimated that Brunatto's profits ranged between 19 and 45 percent.

In August 1941, the German military tribunal of Greater Paris informed the state prosecutor of the Seine Tribunal that the Germans had brought a case against Brunatto for charging illegally high prices. In those same weeks, at the joint initiative of German and French officials, the Itala warehouses were shut down and the merchandise in them was confiscated.[17] The German military tribunal quickly found Brunatto guilty of profiteering, condemning him to three months in prison and a penalty of 600,000 francs.[18] Our playwright, all set to celebrate the Franciscan merits of the *pax hitleriana* on the Vieux-Colombier stage, suddenly looked like he might have to pay a high price for his rations trafficking. But he was reprieved. Who knows? Perhaps it was his very reputation as a man of the theater that led German officials to decide to pardon him, sparing him the indignity of a prison sentence.[19]

The black market was a paradise for collaborationists.[20] Whether they were dealing with the millions of French families under rationing or supplying the German Occupation forces, doing business on the black market demanded—beyond a network of connections with agricultural and industrial producers—some kind of rapport with the Militärbefehlshaber, the German military command. Many of the black market collaborationists were not particularly ideological. They didn't care much about Hitler's merits or Philippe Pétain's Vichy government propaganda; they were only interested in economic exchange and reciprocal favors. The owners of trading companies had much to offer the soldiers and officers of the Wehrmacht, for whom being stationed in Paris was something of a gift of destiny—a sort of holiday compared to being on the Eastern Front. In Paris, they could enjoy meat, cheeses, and the best wines in the world. And for their part, the Germans had much to offer to the big and small bosses of the black market: money, privileges, and various kinds of social access.

The traffickers were often men on the rise, propelled upward by the extraordinary circumstances of the Occupation. Some of them were little captains of industry from the outskirts of Paris: with the right introduction, enterprising wholesalers, vineyard owners, and cattle growers from the provinces could get rich in the capital (and then perhaps have a chance to take over the goods confiscated from the Jews during "Aryanization"). Other traffickers were old workhorses getting a second chance, men of the 1930s for whom the Nazification of French society meant something like a rebirth: businessmen who had gone bankrupt in the Great Depression, middlemen of various degrees of misfortune, self-declared economic victims of the Front Populaire. In the French version of Hitler's New Order, they saw not only the chance to participate in a massive redistribution of wealth but also a way to take unexpected retaliation for their bad fortune.[21]

Emanuele Brunatto was this second type of profiteer. The locomotive salesman who had lived for a decade in Paris on the backs of Padre Pio's followers, and who had had only mixed success as a spy for the Fascist regime, was reborn in the Occupation as a little king of the black market. The topography of his life remained much the same, centered in the patrician quarters of the Rive Droite between the Opéra and the Arc de Triomphe. But these places had acquired a different aspect and significance after June 1940. Street signs had begun to appear in German, and at every corner there were red and black markers pointing the way to the Kommandantur, to the Militärbefehlshaber, and the other nerve centers of Nazi power. Many economic collaborationists went back and forth across the Seine to do business at the Hotel Lutetia with the Abwehr, the German service for espionage and counterespionage.[22] And on the Rive Droite, Brunatto was often to be found at the Majestic, the hotel that housed both the German military command and the offices for propaganda and censorship. "Brunatto Emanuele, business representative accredited at the Hotel Majestic," reads the name on the criminal file opened on the Italian profiteer in 1944 after the Liberation of Paris. Under "nature of infraction," the file says "Traffic with the enemy."[23]

His 1941 conviction for profiteering had not been enough to scare Brunatto away from the golden world of buying and selling, perilous as it was. After he was forced to close his company Itala, he had opened a new *bureau d'achats,* giving it the very erudite name of a devoutly Christian king: "Comptoir François Ier." He now specialized in supplying jam and chocolate to the Germans. According to calculations done after the Liberation by the Committee to Confiscate Illegal Profits, Comptoir François Ier sold more than seven thousand tons of jam—worth 93.6 million francs—to the German forces between 1941 and 1943. Sales of chocolate were valued at 42 million francs. At a commission of 3 percent on jam and 5 percent on chocolate, Brunatto's profits thus totaled 4.9 million francs. He also produced and sold a tea substitute under contract to the Feldpost. His net profit on ersatz-tea sales of 2,559,377 francs was an astonishing 1,324,532 francs, plus a commission of 907,634 francs. (Again, this is at a time when the average French monthly wage was around 1,000 francs.) Not surprisingly, given these numbers, the man from the Hotel Majestic enjoyed an upswing in his style of living. He rented a couple of buildings on Avenue de Wagram and bought himself a villa in Isle-Adam, the Paris suburb dear to Honoré de Balzac.[24]

But Brunatto's rich earnings after 1941 were nothing compared to the stratospheric gains he had realized in the eight or nine months after the fall of France, before the Itala company was shut down. The committee on illegal profits estimated that between October 1940 and May 1941, Brunatto had supplied the German Occupation forces with 738,000 bottles of wine: Champagne Malherbe, Champagne Berthelot, Champagne Leclerc, Champagne Clicquot, Graves supérieur, Châteauneuf-du-Pape, a 1934 Sauternes, and other marvelous nectars from his Faubourg Saint-Honoré warehouse,[25] on which he earned a commission of 5 francs per bottle. He had also sold 1,705,500 bottles of cognac and other spirits, with a commission of 8 francs per bottle. His gross profit just from the alcohol sales was thus 17,334,000 francs![26] These numbers, particularly for the first year of Occupation, stand up alongside those of the leading French black market traders of the period—such legendary war profiteers as the Moldavian immigrant Joseph Joanovici and the Russian Michel Szkolnikov.[27] And they are numbers that belong at the heart of Padre Pio's story. The Casa Sollievo della Sofferenza, that worthy hospital founded by the little friar with the stigmata, would float on the profits of all the alcohol with which Brunatto saturated the Wehrmacht's Parisian banquets. By June 1941, when he deposited those 3.5 million francs in a Florence bank account in the name of the Committee for the Construction of the Hospital of San Giovanni Rotondo, Padre Pio's top apostle had already earned five times that much pouring out wine and champagne to toast the Third Reich.

Yet it would not be fair to think that Brunatto's only concerns in Occupied Paris were trafficking and profiteering. As we've come to expect by now, in the early 1940s he was leading several lives at once. If the accounts of the committee on illegal profits are right, for example, he spent (or rather squandered) several million francs from his black-market earnings to finance the Bureau of Cinematographic Studies for Animated Cartoons, which he set up in his offices on Avenue de Wagram.[28] The tireless Brunatto, it seems, was on the lookout for a new and revolutionary animation technique that would allow him to capitalize on the success of animated cinema in Vichy France.[29] And such entrepreneurial efforts were not the only beneficiaries of the fortune that Brunatto had made in jam and alcohol. After the war, a onetime employee of Itala named Lucien Monnier recalled that even under German Occupation, Brunatto continued to do good works. "He was mystical," Monnier explained. Perhaps that was why Brunatto gave generously to several Parisian parishes, thus ensuring that the poor would be fed.[30]

The ways of the Lord are infinite, or so they say. Brunatto may have been a fat-cat profiteer, but over the course of three years (from February 1941 to February 1944), he spent at least 1.3 million francs funding Boisson Chaude, a service that distributed free meals every day at the rail stations Gare Saint-Lazare and Gare de Lyon. In a period photo, we can clearly pick out Emanuele Brunatto—his handsome salt-and-pepper hair, his distinguished bearing, his elegant dark overcoat—at the inauguration ceremony for one of the Boisson Chaude kitchens. He's standing there with the prefect of Paris, Charles Magny, and a group of other men and women from various walks of life, all of them caught up in the solemnity of the moment: the evil of the world war redeemed by the good of Christian charity. We have no way of knowing whether Brunatto

was conscious of the direct connection between the hunger of the many and the plenty enjoyed by lords of the black market. The expression on his face gives us not a clue.

Did Brunatto's place "among the princes of the dirtiest part of the French black market" make him one of the "most sordid figures in all of Italian life," as a high Fascist official told Mussolini in 1944?[31] Or was he merely a generous dispenser of Catholic charity? Or both?

The Flying Capuchin

"I hear that on the 8th of April the famous Padre Pio of Pietrelcina, the Franciscan with the stigmata who lived in San Giovanni Rotondo, died," wrote Giovanni Papini in his diary on May 9, 1944. He regretted that he had not made a pilgrimage to the Gargano in time to see the friar. ("I would have gone if the war had not intervened.") "I also hear," Papini wrote, "that on the verge of death he announced that the war was near its end—that it would come just one month after his passing."[32] It was, obviously, a false report, like many of the rumors that circulated in an Italy lacerated by the world war and by internal strife.

False reports, too, interest historians, however, because they bear witness to anxieties, hopes, fears, and profound shifts in collective sensibilities. Here, the erroneous news that reached the author of the *Life of Christ* at his mountain retreat outside Arezzo points to a muddled association between Padre Pio's reputation for prophecy, his status as a Christ figure and martyr, and popular hopes for peace. As for Papini, in that period the ultra-Fascist, ultraracist writer was ever more taken up by his Christian identity. In July 1944, at the La Verna sanctuary devoted to St. Francis, he joined the third order of the Franciscan Friars Minor as a lay brother.[33]

With Italy in ruins, one did not have to be a Franciscan to reflect on the timeliness of the Poverello's teachings, on the ways that the Church could comfort souls and protect bodies, on the enduring symbolic value of the most ancient Christian rituals. The diary of another influential Florentine intellectual—Piero Calamandrei, an exemplary anti-Fascist—shows how the moral landscape of even the most secular Italians was scattered at this time with religious signposts. Evacuated to the village of Colcello in southern Umbria after Italy surrendered to the Allies on September 8, 1943, Calamandrei discovered nearby "a cave in the woods where they say St. Francis slept," and was impressed by the shrine with its "crude painting" of the saint in prayer. Attached to the corners of the painting were ID-sized photographs of young men from Colcello who had been called up in the war, "all these young men wearing the uniforms of the *bersaglieri* or the air force . . . stuck there by their families with a prayer for their safety." In May 1944, Calamandrei traveled to the local Capuchin monastery, a place half-empty in peacetime but which was now a center for refugees, full of nuns, friars, teachers with orphan children, and "other solitary souls." Each received a bed to sleep on and a bowl for meals. There was music to pray by, but behind it there was always the sinister sound of the bombs falling, the ever-present undertone of war.

> Throughout our walk, we were accompanied by the buzzing
> of airplanes and far-away explosions in all directions. On our
> way back to the monastery, walking along the edge of the
> woods that surround it, you could hear, deep in the ilex wood,

a canticle sung by male voices, perhaps the Canticle of Mary for the month devoted to the Virgin that is now beginning. There were many of them and they sang nicely, perhaps in honor of the novice friars. They were praying for peace. At the end, we heard this: "O Holy Virgin ... *Boom!* ... pray for me." The bomb exploding was like a punctuation mark—like an answer.[34]

For civilians even more than for soldiers, death came from the heavens during World War II—the same heavens, perversely, to which men turned to ask God for protection.[35] Southern Italy was affected as much as the rest of the country; after September 8, 1943, the bombing of strategic targets in Naples, Salerno, and Bari increased.[36] Among the humble (and not only the humble), rumors and omens about the bombings mixed together with dreams and nightmares, truth and hearsay;[37] and out of all this grew a new element in the vox populi about Padre Pio. The word soon was that he not only possessed the gift of levitation— a gift attributed to another Capuchin of the seventeenth century, St. Joseph of Copertino, also venerated in Puglia[38]—but also had a special ability to fly, and could intercept enemy bombers and thus protect the civilian population.

Back in 1942, Calamandrei had noted in his diary the (false) report that Pope Pius XII was about to leave St. Peter's and move to the church of St. John Lateran in order to prevent Rome from being bombed. "They call him the anti-aircraft Pope," Calamandrei wrote; he liked to record popular wisecracks that captured the national mood.[39] But on July 19, 1943, American bombers had wreaked havoc on the humble neighborhoods of San Lorenzo, the Prenestino, and the Tiburtino.[40] The people of Rome thus learned at their expense that the aura of the Eternal City was not enough to protect them, nor could a visit from the Holy Father spare them from further harm. After the bombing of July 19, he had gone out into the ruined streets to offer the consolation of his charismatic presence, but Rome was struck by another devastating bombing attack on August 13.

Down in Puglia, meanwhile, Padre Pio would turn out to be—at least in the minds of those who believed in his gifts—far more of a savior. In the summer of 1943, Allied bombers began to attack both

Foggia and Bari on the plain, destroying, among other things, the Capuchin monastery of Sant'Anna, and forcing the order's provincial administration to move to San Giovanni Rotondo; but bombs never fell on the Gargano Peninsula, which convinced many good Christians that Padre Pio was protecting them. After the Liberation, statements made by several British pilots did the rest, lending Padre Pio the aura of a living antiaircraft system. For decades after 1944, there were ex-pilots of the RAF ready to swear that a bearded friar with his arms open wide had appeared in front of their gun sights, darts of flame leaping from his fiery eyes, and persuaded them to return to their bases without dropping their murderous munitions on the Gargano.[41] (A comic book artist would later capture the moment of confrontation: "I forbid you to drop any bombs on San Giovanni and the region!" "I'll be damned! A flying monk!"[42])

The rumors of Padre Pio's celestial exploits soon traveled beyond Puglia, spreading across the peninsula to Naples and the slopes of Vesuvius. Along the way, they picked up little adjustments, refinements, and modifications. To the historian's ear, the most intriguing of

these new versions involved Padre Pio's ability to protect not only helpless civilians but the bomber pilots themselves, up in the sky. (In this,
too, the Capuchin followed the lead of Joseph of Copertino, patron
saint of aviators.) A vivid example of this story comes up in Norman
Lewis's shrewd memoir *Naples '44*, his account of life as a British officer
stationed in Naples with the Field Security Service of the U.S. Fifth
Army. Far too attentive an observer to miss the multitudinous and
many-colored local manifestations of popular religiosity, Lewis recalls
hearing about "miracles galore" in those days. There was a Neapolitan
Lady of Lourdes, for example, to whom the Virgin had revealed herself
repeatedly at Campi Flegrei. And from not far away, along the road
from Naples to Benevento, came another, no less amazing, report.

> At Pomigliano we have a flying monk who also demonstrates
> the stigmata. The monk claims that on an occasion last year
> when an aerial dog-fight was in progress, he soared up to the
> sky to catch in his arms the pilot of a stricken Italian plane and
> bring him safely to earth. Most of the Neapolitans I know—
> some of them educated men—are convinced of the truth of
> this story.[43]

Such reports of a flying friar—whose hands with their bloody wounds
were more powerful against enemy incursions than any weapon—
clearly emerged from a deep mythopoeic wellspring that went beyond
even the cult of Padre Pio, and points to a crucial dynamic in modern
Italian history. The events of World War II had deprived the Italian
"diarchy" (Mussolini and King Victor Emmanuel III)[44] of its moral
and political authority and given that authority to new protectors and
new masters. It's impossible to overstate the role assumed by the Catholic Church during the war—as Mussolini's star was plunging and
the royal family's image fading[45]—in helping Italians in many ways,
both spiritual and material. With the state too weak to look after its
citizens, the Church of Pius XII took on much of the job.

The assumption of that epochal responsibility lent Pius XII an
almost transcendent aura, and the Church's capacity to be present in
moments of need helped to reconcile Italians with the Vatican and

make the memories of papal defeat in 1870 disappear forever.[46] What clerico-fascism had initiated, though with some ambiguity and tension, the Second World War brought to completion: the pope came back to the center of Italian public life as a sovereign. After fifty years as the city of the king and twenty years as the city of Il Duce, Rome was once again the city of the pope,[47] and the Church became once again what it had been for centuries: the strongest, if not the only, glue holding a weak, messy, and divided country together. The new cults of the Virgin that sprang up from one end of the peninsula to the other[48] marked a powerful revival of the sacred, and the flying friar of the Gargano reflected the same urge.

By April 25, 1945, when all of Italy was liberated from German Occupation, it was easy enough to say anything and everything about Padre Pio's gifts. Already in June, Alberto Del Fante—perhaps forgetting his own tiny role as an Axis propagandist?—was proclaiming that the friar's intercession had kept the notorious Hermann Göring Division from deploying in San Giovanni Rotondo. Del Fante also noted the differences between the Germans and the Anglo-Saxons who had met with Padre Pio. Under German Occupation, he wrote, "very few soldiers of the swastika" had "bent their knees before the Cross of Christ," while "the Allied soldiers, even the Protestants, go to Padre Pio and there have even been some conversions." And what an edifying spectacle there had been at San Giovanni Rotondo the previous Christmas! Hundreds of soldiers "of all races and all nationalities" had attended Christmas Day mass, and Padre Pio ("the living Host") had personally given out the sacred communion wafers.[49]

Free Italy offered free rein for the most extravagant reports on the friar's prodigious doings, but a particular specialty soon began to emerge in the hagiographic reports: besides his airborne role as a flying friar, Padre Pio now frequently appeared as a deus ex machina who, in one way or another, was able to save Fascists from the clutches of bloodthirsty partisans. According to one story, a schoolteacher in central Italy, accused of having collaborated with the Germans in transporting munitions, was seized in her home and taken out to be shot. On her way to execution, holding a picture of Padre Pio that she had grabbed on the way out of the house, she prepared herself to die.

Suddenly a loud "Stop!" was heard, pronounced in the unmistakable voice of the friar with the stigmata, and the firing squad commander called a halt. So the teacher was able to return home safe and sound.[50]

Padre Pio's intercession was also credited with saving the onetime *ras* of Foggia, Giuseppe Caradonna, who had joined Mussolini's Social Republic after Italy's 1943 armistice with the Allies. He was arrested by self-appointed partisan police on April 29, 1945, the same day that Mussolini and Clara Petacci were strung up by their heels in Milan's Piazzale Loreto. Condemned to death on the spot, Caradonna was dragged off to face a firing squad; but suddenly the figure of Padre Pio leaped in, shielding Caradonna from the riflemen, and all their guns misfired. Caradonna, a skilled attorney, was then able to take advantage of the general bewilderment to argue that, as a hero of the Great War, he should be spared, and the partisans finally decided simply to send him to Milan's San Vittore prison.[51]

A Friar and Two Brothers

On May 16, 1947, on some eight acres of land next to the Capuchin friary of San Giovanni Rotondo, workers began to level and terrace the ground to build the Casa Sollievo della Sofferenza. In the months and years that followed, more than 3.5 million cubic feet of rock would be removed so that—out of nothing, there in the remote mountains of the Gargano where it had always been an effort just to keep a basic doctor's office running—a genuine cathedral of medicine could be built. It would be a model facility, five stories high and more than three hundred feet wide, inspired by the latest in medical knowledge and fitted with the most advanced medical equipment. When the hospital opened, nine years after ground was broken, the *New York Times* magazine wrote that the medical complex of San Giovanni was "among the most attractive and modern in the world."[52]

Today, more than half a century after the Casa Sollievo della Sofferenza admitted its first patients, it has become a cliché to say that creating this hospital was the one genuine and indisputable miracle performed by the Capuchin with the stigmata. But hoping to sidestep cliché, and lacking the canonical prerequisites for transcendental interpretation,[53] the historian must treat this miracle in the very same way as the other miracles attributed to Padre Pio, posing questions to the sources from our vantage point in the here and now. What did the project mean in Padre Pio's mind? What were the circumstances that permitted it to develop? What impact did the Casa Sollievo have on devotion to Padre Pio?

The first thing to note about the project is that in 1947, when construction began, the idea of building a hospital at San Giovanni Rotondo was already a quarter of a century old. As early as 1922, Padre Pio had expressed the desire to take advantage of all the religious enthusiasm around him by using the money from his most generous donors to build a small hospital. In March that year, he explained to Giuseppe Orlando, a friend and fellow priest from Pietrelcina, that "as for the hospital, things are going well: we're now about to do the bidding on contracts for the second round of works and this summer I hope that all will be finished."[54] In fact, he had to wait until January 1925 before the place opened its doors—with two wards, fourteen beds, and a plaque giving Padre Pio full credit for the construction.[55] In 1938, this hospital, which had been built in one wing of a former convent for Poor Clare sisters, was damaged by an earthquake and could no longer be used. This meant that San Giovanni was once again without decent medical facilities, but one thing was now clear: Padre Pio did not intend to relieve the suffering around him only by means of miracles, with his own famous healing powers. He was also going to rely on the work of others, on the benefits of their scientific knowledge and their excellent hospital facilities.

From the time that the Casa Sollievo building site began to dominate the landscape of San Giovanni, making visible the profits Brunatto had earned on the black market in Nazi Paris, Padre Pio's other followers also rushed to contribute their pennies to the expensive works, and his hagiographers—quite numerous by the late 1940s—rushed to find words to tell of this marvelous charity. Each day, they wrote, countless sums both large and small found their way to San Giovanni, thanks to the great and the humble, the rich and the poor, the famous and the nameless: "the plain five dollars of the American laborer, the twenty-five dollars of the kitchen maids at the Waldorf Astoria Hotel in New York, the thirty pesetas of a follower in Cartagena, the ten Swiss francs of a believer from Lugano, the hundred lire bill of an Italian widow." For a couple of weeks after they arrived, the envelopes the faithful had entrusted to Padre Pio would lie scattered around his cell; then the friar would collect the money, twist the offerings together into a handkerchief, and pass the handkerchief to the two managers of the building site. The managers would then convert the money into "cement, diesel, iron bars, marble real and artificial, crockery, boilers, linens, elevators," everything they needed to build a hospital "so impressive that from Foggia—and we are some thirty kilometers as the crow flies from Foggia—it can be seen and admired like a genuine monument."[56] Brick by brick, the building grew, watched over by the Capuchin friars and lay brothers.

It was thus in real time, while the building site was still crawling with surveyors and workers, that the hagiographers perfected their message that the hospital was Padre Pio's most amazing miracle. And it was also in those days, between the end of the 1940s and the beginning of the 1950s, that the hagiographers identified a female figure to worship alongside Padre Pio for bringing this miracle forth. First in the bulletin reporting on the hospital's progress, then in various pieces of devotional propaganda, we learn that the most important financial contribution to the Casa Sollievo had come from the English journalist

Barbara Ward—no mere scribbler but the foreign editor of the *Economist*, the most distinguished politico-economic weekly in the world.[57] A fervent Catholic,[58] Ward had visited San Giovanni in the fall of 1947 and was enchanted by Padre Pio. Ward's fiancé Robert Jackson was then working as deputy chief of the United Nations Relief and Rehabilitation Administration (UNRRA), the UN agency for postwar aid and reconstruction;[59] and thanks to Ward's involvement, the UNRRA directed 250 million lire to the construction efforts, enabling Padre Pio to finish the work that Brunatto's contribution had enabled him to start.

There did seem to be something providential about this quarter-billion-lire windfall, an impression heightened by the fact that, in the hagiographic version, commander Jackson abandoned his Protestant roots right on the eve of his marriage to Miss Ward and converted to Catholicism.[60] But like everything else in this story, the UNRRA funding must be examined with a dry eye, an eye trained on facts rather than miracles, on bottom lines rather than wedding dresses. The UNRRA funding was only about half the size of Brunatto's 1941 donation; still, it was quite a large sum for its time, the equivalent of more

than $4 million today. How was this money maneuvered through complex institutional byways, from the UN's New York headquarters to San Giovanni Rotondo, to benefit Padre Pio's hospital at the expense of other health emergencies? The Casa Sollievo, however miraculous, was born in particular social, political, and diplomatic circumstances. The priority given to health care in reconstruction Italy, the relationship between leaders of the Christian Democratic Party and the Vatican, and the workings of international aid before the Marshall Plan came into effect were all decisive.

In the years just after the war, the inhabitants of the Gargano Peninsula were not the only Italians in need of medical care. Although UNRRA judged the situation in Italy to be less desperate than that in other war-torn countries, general hygiene and public health were still very poor.[61] There were worrying outbreaks of typhus and smallpox, endemic in the ports of Naples and Taranto and latent in vast parts of the south. The threat of malaria had returned after the retreating Wehrmacht sabotaged the drainage systems on the plains that the Fascist regime had built in the 1930s.[62] Medicines were scarce, particularly in the south. And well-equipped hospitals were scarce everywhere, as a result both of Anglo-American bombing and the raids made by the

German occupiers, who had systematically requisitioned ambulances, mattresses, beds, sheets, surgical instruments, and X-ray equipment.

In principle, decisions about priorities were up to the high commissioner for hygiene and public health, who answered directly to the prime minister's office. There was also an Italian delegation to liaise with UNRRA on aid matters, likewise reporting to the prime minister—a sort of ministry without portfolio created by the first Alcide De Gasperi government in 1945. In practice, the Catholic De Gasperi, who was inclined to favor the Church's interests in the aid field, limited the powers of the high commissioner.[63] The delegation to UNRRA thus played a decisive role in allocating funding for Italian health and hygiene.

Among the first to understand how important UNRRA would be was Lodovico Montini, a Christian Democratic leader who had already worked with international organizations after World War I. Lodovico also happened to be the brother of Giovanni Battista Montini, the Vatican deputy secretary of state who would later become Pope Paul VI. In December 1945, just as De Gasperi was about to be sworn in as prime minister, Lodovico Montini called De Gasperi's attention to the crucial role that UNRRA was destined to play in postwar reconstruction, warned him of trouble if representatives of parties other than the Christian Democrats held top positions on the delegation to the UNRRA mission to Italy, and implicitly put himself forward to be chairman of that delegation.[64] De Gasperi immediately agreed, and soon Montini became the prime minister's key liaison with UNRRA—as well as, through his brother, with the Vatican secretariat of state.

The picture that emerges from the UN archives for 1946–47 is thus rather bizarre: the principal representative of the Italian government liaising with UNRRA was Lodovico Montini, while the principal representative of the Vatican for UNRRA purposes was Giovanni Battista Montini.[65] Spurgeon Keeny, an energetic American serving as the chief of the UNRRA mission to Italy, made every effort to separate Italian needs from Vatican needs (though his attitude toward dignitaries from the Holy See bordered on veneration);[66] still, he often found that a meeting would consist of himself and the two Montini brothers. Robert Jackson, meanwhile, who as deputy director general of UNRRA was Keeny's boss, would often meet with either one of the two brothers without distinction.[67]

Under the overall criteria for aid established by the UNRRA mission to Italy, a project like Padre Pio's hospital had little hope of obtaining funding. The agency's guidelines called for structural interventions, not for financing of individual local efforts. In March 1947, Keeny sent a memo to New York stating that the Italian mission would spend its money on three objectives: the resumption of the fight against malaria, a fifteen-year TB campaign, and a campaign against trachoma. There were some funds to rebuild and modernize hospitals, but, faced with a shrinking budget, Keeny insisted that choices about where to spend the money must depend on a "careful selection."[68]

For his part, Lodovico Montini insisted that all funding decisions should be made exclusively between UNRRA and his delegation, and urged that the various ministers of the De Gasperi government—all of whom had their own priorities—be kept out of the process. This would save time, he argued, and also prevent the UNRRA funds from becoming "a bone of contention in the political arena."[69] It was Montini's euphemistic way to justify keeping all the decision-making power in his own hands, which allowed him to use his job to promote the Church's causes.[70] Under Montini, the delegation to UNRRA was openly a Catholic aid project—so much so that the delegation's newsletter was subtitled "A Supplement to *Il Seminatore*, Organ of the Pious Foundation Vittorino di Camillo."[71]

A 1947 letter written to Keeny by the other Montini, the Vatican deputy secretary of state, offers a specific example of the kinds of expenditures that the Church was hoping to fund with the international community's postwar munificence. Good Italian priests, Giovanni Battista Montini explained, were busy "in the struggle to provide for the daily needs of the body," and they urgently needed new vestments: tunics and habits, as well as underwear, socks, and shoes for more than 120,000 priests, monks, and nuns. "I do not think I need lay stress on the personal concern of the Holy Father in this matter," Montini added for extra emphasis.[72] Somewhat embarrassed, Keeny replied that as an organization with a secular mission, UNRRA "could only approve a plan whereby members of the clergy and religious orders would be included as Italian citizens." Accordingly, Keeny wrote to Giovanni Battista Montini, he would send this request for approval to the Italian government—that is, to . . . Lodovico Montini.[73]

As this little episode suggests, there was a great deal of confusion (and commingling) of interests between the two Montini brothers, although formally they represented two different states. And there's every reason to think that both Lodovico and Giovanni Battista Montini were being courted during this period by the Padre Pio lobby, with its influential members in the capital. The attorney Antonio Angelini Rota, for example, whom we've already met as vice chairman of Anonima Brevetti Zarlatti, was described in 1946 as a sort of De Gasperi government trustee with the UNRRA mission to Italy.[74] Others in Padre Pio's circle had started cultivating their connections even earlier. The Holy Office archives reveal that Antonio Tonelli from Bologna, Alberto Del Fante's brother-in-law, was corresponding directly with Giovanni Battista Montini as of 1941.[75] Nor did Tonelli's efforts stop at the level of the Vatican deputy secretary of state: Tonelli wrote directly to Pope Pius XII himself[76] and made sure that the Holy Father was sent a "crucifix blessed by Padre Pio."[77]

The American Friend

The first few months of 1948 marked a further politicization of international aid. As Italian parliamentary elections, pitting the Christian Democrats against the Communists, loomed on April 18, the Cold War was growing very heated indeed. The De Gasperi government was presenting itself (not wrongly) as the American advance guard—a bulwark against the popular front of Communists and Socialists who, De Gasperi warned, were conniving with the Soviets.[78] Many saw the Italian election of 1948 as a crucial political showdown, and in their eagerness to affect the outcome figures such as U.S. secretary of state George Marshall and U.K. foreign secretary Ernest Bevin were all—as Barbara Ward put it in the *Economist*—tossing Italy some morsels from the plate of international policy. The Italian election, Ward went on, was both "a warning and a portent." On April 18 Italy would either show the world the amazing power of international aid—or the West would be served a warning that not everything could be bought with money.[79]

As of late 1947, the UN mission to Italy had been replaced by the explicitly American agency Aid from the USA (AUSA), and the Italian delegation to UNRRA had been refashioned as the Amministrazione Aiuti Internazionali (AAI). Little had changed in this reshuffling, though: like its predecessor, AAI was run by Lodovico Montini.[80] His decision making remained as autonomous as ever, and the criteria by which he selected projects to support were still quite murky.

On March 11, 1948, Montini's AAI sent a list with numerous public health funding requests to AUSA. At the top of the list was the following item: "Number 1. Project name: Casa Sollievo della Sofferenza, San Giovanni Rotondo (Foggia). Amount requested [by the project]: 252,261,920 lire. Funding proposed [by AAI]: 100,000,000 lire. Scope of project: Creation of a hospital to be named after Fiorello La Guardia."[81] Those few lines, brief but significant, testify to some very clever string-pulling by the Padre Pio lobby.

How did the name of the Little Flower, the just-deceased former mayor of New York City, get attached to a hospital in the Gargano? Most likely, that was Robert Jackson's contribution to Padre Pio's cause.

Between 1946 and 1947, Fiorello La Guardia had been director general of UNRRA—that is, Jackson's immediate superior. He had brought to the job a contagious energy, inexhaustible vitality, and red-blooded impatience that impressed all those who dealt with him.[82] After La Guardia died in the fall of 1947, Jackson might have recalled that it was from the city of Foggia that Fiorello's father, Achille, a musician, had emigrated to the United States. And Jackson must have known that the U.S. Congress would not hesitate to approve funding for a hospital dedicated to the popular former mayor and former Republican congressman from New York.[83]

There is nothing in the American archives to confirm the hagiographic legend dispensed by Del Fante, who wrote that La Guardia himself "took up a collection among Italians in the U.S., who donated, via AUSA, some 250 million lire." There is likewise no support for Del Fante's claim that La Guardia, "being of Italian origin, wanted his ancestral lands to be furnished with a great hospital, but, above all, to make himself a mouthpiece for the desires of the Most Reverend Padre Pio."[84] The only thing that La Guardia—who was raised Episcopalian—seems to have had in common with Padre Pio of Pietrelcina is wartime service in the vast skies over the Gargano. While the friar was famous for having ascended there during World War II to prevent the Allied bombers from dropping their loads, La Guardia had frequented that same wild blue yonder during World War I when he was a U.S. Army instructor training pilots out of the Foggia airport.[85]

Nevertheless, the American archives do offer some insights into why the La Guardia–Padre Pio link might make sense in terms of propaganda. In the eyes of Italians, and especially southerners, the Second World War had given both men enormous visibility. While the Capuchin from San Giovanni was adored for his antiaircraft powers, the ex-mayor of New York was worshipped—courtesy of a program aired every Sunday, in Italian, on NBC shortwave radio—as the living incarnation of miraculous, invincible America.[86] Between 1943 and 1945, more than a thousand Italians, most of them from the south, wrote letters to the Little Flower, addressing him as a kind of secular saint, asking for aid or for a blessing. Old companions in arms from the Great War, women who had been seduced and abandoned by Yankee soldiers, clerks in the civil service whose wages wouldn't carry them through to the end of the month, mothers of sons in war and mothers of newborns, anxious about their children's fates—a vast, troubled humanity wrote to La Guardia, begging him for help. And the Little Flower found time to reply to his devotees, or at least to forward their letters to the UNRRA offices.[87] In the collective imagination of a certain part of postwar southern Italy, La Guardia was indeed the ideal personage to help realize Padre Pio's dream hospital.

Just a few days before the Italian elections, the prime minister's office released the following communiqué.

> The Italian government has approved the allocation of 250 million lire from the UNRRA Lire Fund to build a large hospital in San Giovanni Rotondo in the Foggia province. The hospital will be dedicated to the memory of the former Director General of UNRRA Fiorello La Guardia, whose family comes from that area, and it represents new tangible proof of the valuable aid UNRRA has given to Italian reconstruction and to assisting those who most suffered the war's tragic consequences.[88]

As we can see, there was no mention of Padre Pio, nor of the Casa Sollievo della Sofferenza. There was, however, a significant departure from the request that had been sent by AAI to AUSA a few weeks earlier. Rather than limit the funding to 100 million lire, the De Gasperi government had decided to go all out, allocating 250 million of the 252 million lire that had been requested by San Giovanni Rotondo. Against all official guidelines for aid allocation, the Padre Pio lobby had succeeded in persuading Lodovico Montini of the great value of their project. Other lobbyists were less fortunate: the entire Red Cross organization, for example, got only 130 million lire.[89] And the disproportion is even more evident when we look at the funding for other hospitals: while the so-called Ospedale Fiorello La Guardia got 250 million lire from the UNRRA fund, all the other hospitals in the whole peninsula combined got a mere four times that much in reconstruction funds, just one billion lire.[90] In the battle for American aid to health care, Padre Pio was the big winner.

Despite obliging press releases, the decision-making process by which the De Gasperi government allocated money to the Gargano hospital was profoundly opaque. And after the electoral triumph of the Christian Democrats in April 1948, that secrecy led to a comedy of errors. That summer, the New York friends of La Guardia were planning a tour of various European countries to take part in ceremonies for aid projects dedicated to the Little Flower's memory. Down in San Giovanni, Padre Pio's followers would need to organize a public event to dedicate the hospital under construction to La Guardia, an event that obviously had to involve the relevant representatives of the newborn Republic of Italy. Yet no one—not the Italian embassy in Washington, the prefecture in Foggia, the Ministry of the Interior, the Foreign Ministry's Office of Ceremony, or even Giulio Andreotti, the prime minister's undersecretary—seemed to know anything at all regarding the construction project.[91] Even the director general of AAI was unable to answer questions about the enterprise for which his agency had helped to secure a quarter billion lire.[92] Padre Pio's hospital, it seemed, had been delivered by a stork.

It would be up to an English-speaking journalist even better known then than Barbara Ward to draw out the moral of the story. Freda Kirchwey, legendary director of the progressive magazine the *Nation*, was traveling with the friends of La Guardia, and from the moment the delegation got to Rome the hardheaded liberal journalist understood that "in Italy the Vatican directly or indirectly ran the whole show." That became even clearer to her in the days that followed, when the friends of La Guardia climbed up the switchback roads to the San Giovanni building site to deliver their secular benediction. Along the way, the procession of cars was greeted by ranks of farmhands shouting "Viva l'America!" and "Viva La Guardia!" But when they arrived in San Giovanni and sat down on the stage perched over the hospital's foundations, the delegation immediately understood who was the real star of the event. It was not the dear departed mayor of New York, nor the prefect of Foggia stiffly dressed in his dark suit, nor the archbishop of

Manfredonia complete with stole and miter. No, wrote Kirchwey, "the hero of the afternoon was Padre Pio, an amiable, bearded monk whose fame has spread, so his followers assured us, up and down the length of Italy."[93]

Like someone taking a speed course in cultural anthropology, Freda Kirchwey observed the spectacle of the Capuchin friar posing for photographers, the crowd of country women battling to kiss his gloved hands, the riot police charged with holding back the adoring crowd. A militant Christian Democrat from Foggia came forward to escort the American journalist into Padre Pio's presence, offering her the privilege of a private meeting with him.[94] "All gazes, affection and ceremony were directed toward Padre Pio," the friar's onetime spiritual director, Father Agostino of San Marco in Lamis, wrote in his diary.[95] Finally, it was Padre Pio himself who blessed the plaque crediting UNRRA with financing the hospital and officially naming it for Fiorello La Guardia. The following year, La Guardia's name would fleetingly appear on the facade of the building as it went up. But it would disappear as the work continued, to be replaced by the words that still adorn the hospital today: *Casa Sollievo della Sofferenza*.

An Immense Benefit

In that year of God's grace 1948, Padre Pio offered to return the De Gasperi government's favor. Just before the April 18 elections, the friar "sent word to the head of the government" to let him know how closely he was following the political battle.[96] The diary of Father Agostino of San Marco in Lamis says little about how Padre Pio communicated his thoughts about the epic political showdown to De Gasperi, just that Padre Pio had promised to exercise a "potent" influence on the vote that would "decide the fate of Italy and the world." The friar with the stigmata, Father Agostino wrote, was promoting the "victory of the party of order" both "with his prayers addressed to the Lord" and "with his words addressed to men."[97]

We do not know what Alcide De Gasperi felt in his heart of hearts about Padre Pio, for the Christian Democrat always kept his personal religious sentiments very private. But we do know something about the efforts by the Padre Pio lobby to gain the support of top government officials. They surface, for example, in a 1946 letter that Angelo Roncalli, the apostolic nuncio to Paris (and the future Pope John XXIII), wrote to De Gasperi. Although Roncalli rarely corresponded with the prime minister, he had recently met De Gasperi in person while attending the Paris peace conference and had come away with an "excellent impression."[98] Sending him renewed best wishes for success in the negotiations, Roncalli wrote to

> offer your Holiness the opportunity to meet Dottor Emmanuele Brunato [*sic*], a distinguished Italian . . . who conducts economic and social studies here in France and directs an organization called L'Entreprise Coopérative. Your correspondent knows and appreciates this man of certain Catholic faith and distinct religious piety, and believes that a meeting of spirit and ideas could be exceptionally fruitful for Italy's present and future interests.[99]

To what extent Brunatto corresponded to Roncalli's description—whether and how much he merited being called a distinguished Italian and a pious Catholic—is not really the historian's job to judge. We can, however, note the repeated contacts between the papal nuncio and the promoter of Padre Pio. Roncalli's diaries are thick with names, reflecting the numerous audiences he hosted in Paris—so many that it would be foolish to try to draw any conclusions from them. The list of appointments for 1946 shows that meetings between the future John XXIII and the author of *Frère Soleil* were not an infrequent occurrence. "Long audience with De Pio on aid and other matters," wrote the nuncio on August 29, 1946.[100] Four days later: "De Pio this evening, I wrote an introduction for him to De Gasperi."[101] "Sig. De Pio" appears once more in Roncalli's diary on November 15, and "Sig. De Pio (Brugnet)" turns up yet again on December 11.[102]

At a time when collaborationists were being pursued and punished in France,[103] Brunatto had every interest in hiding behind various pseudonyms, for he was wanted by the police for "covert dealings with the enemy." A fugitive from justice after February 1945, he would be condemned to death in absentia by the Paris Military Tribunal in September 1948, though the sentence would be reviewed in 1951 by the Marseilles military court and reduced to five years in prison. (In 1953, Brunatto would receive an amnesty from the Lyons military court, and the sentence would ultimately be annulled altogether by the Court of Cassation.)[104] It must be said that Roncalli probably knew nothing of Signor De Pio's Nazi-Fascist past in 1946, when he was receiving him at the mission to discuss "aid and other matters." It seems unlikely that a diplomat as cautious as Roncalli would have written to De Gasperi about Brunatto in glowing terms had he suspected that the man before him was a hardened fugitive from justice. On the other hand, if the nuncio *had* gotten a whiff of something, that would not necessarily have shocked him either; this was the same Roncalli, after all, who did all he could to keep as many prelates accused of collaborationism as possible off General Charles de Gaulle's black list.[105]

Although his distrust of any visionary or miracle-working Catholicism remained strong, Roncalli the papal nuncio in Paris paid more attention than he had in the past to matters that went beyond the austere precepts of the Lombardy church of his origins. There is no other explanation for why he was so willing to receive "Sig. Brugnato," who, as Roncalli had known right from their very first meetings in the spring of 1945, was a "man who adored Padre Pio."[106] Contrary to what Pope John XXIII would write in 1960—when he said he had never had anything to do with Padre Pio, nor ever discussed him "with anyone at all"[107]—it is clear that Roncalli's connections with Brunatto in Paris made him curious about the Capuchin with the stigmata. Thus, on February 6, 1947, the nuncio sat down to write a letter that was strangely candid compared with the cautious approach more typical of this experienced diplomat. The letter, it must be said, was addressed to a friend: Andrea Cesarano, who before becoming archbishop of Manfredonia had spent many years with Roncalli on missions to the East.[108] Roncalli's letter to Cesarano asked him to "write me something about Padre Pio . . . There are those here who admire and venerate him. I have no preconceptions about him, but I would like to hear what his bishop has to say."[109] Having been exposed to what we can imagine was

an assiduous promotional campaign from Brunatto during his audiences, Roncalli took advantage of his longtime friendship with the archbishop of Manfredonia to learn more about the Capuchin with the stigmata.

In his reply, a month later, Monsignor Cesarano wrote that he had "excellent" knowledge of Padre Pio of Pietrelcina. Before he had arrived to lead the archdiocese of Manfredonia, he told Roncalli, the "popular fanaticism" the friar inspired had brought severe countermeasures on the part of the Holy Office. ("They were necessary," Cesarano noted.) "I saw him for the first time in 1933 and he lived in his friary like a genuine recluse," Cesarano wrote of that time when Padre Pio was forbidden any contact with the outside, even epistolary contact, and forbidden to celebrate mass except in the private chapel. But when the archbishop had decided to go past the iron ring imprisoning the friar and talk to him directly, what an extraordinary impression the man had made on him! "I found him to be calm, serene, playful, fully willing to submit to the orders he had taken."[110]

Andrea Cesarano's Christian faith was too profound for him to

puzzle over the question of the friar's stigmata in a letter to Angelo
Roncalli. Cesarano was not a doctor wanting to work out the etiology
of those wounds; nor was he a scientist wanting to verify whether the
miraculous phenomena attributed to Padre Pio were natural or not.
The archbishop of Manfredonia was a pastor of human souls, concerned about the salvation of his flock, and his flock was the same as
that of Padre Pio. "They say he has the stigmata, and in fact he always
wears gloves. It's not my place to judge his holiness, his miracles, his
prophecies, etc., however, one can't avoid saying that he is a man of
prayer, of profound piety and solid virtue . . . Everyone considers him a
saint, and the spiritual benefit that brings is immense. Obstinate sinners convert, high-ranking personages come away edified and moved,
all leave him comforted and reconciled with the Lord." Even before he
wrote to Roncalli, the archbishop of Manfredonia had made his ideas
about Padre Pio clear to the highest powers in the Church. In 1933 he
had sent Pius XI a report on the basis of which Padre Pio was given
back the powers of his priesthood. And more recently, communicating
with Pius XII, Cesarano had reiterated the "exceptional virtues" of the
friar with the stigmata.[111]

Thirteen years after that 1947 exchange of letters, Cesarano and
Roncalli would once again face the question of whether Padre Pio's
Christian virtues were genuine. The former, still archbishop of Manfredonia, and the latter, now the Holy Father, would have to deal with a
grave crisis regarding the Capuchin friar—and they would arrive at a
far less indulgent judgment than Cesarano had voiced in his letter.[112]
But for now, we must keep our eyes on the year 1948, and on the weeks
leading up to the elections, during which Padre Pio's confreres reported
a large number of miraculous doings. There was the Communist from
San Marco in Lamis who had driven along the road past the monastery
shouting "Down with Padre Pio! He is soon to die!" and was quickly
struck down: "the blasphemer was seized by colic" and returned to San
Marco "in unspeakable pain." Things didn't go much better for the
woman who, on election day, having recognized Padre Pio among a
group of friars on the way to the polls in an automobile, called him a
vulgar name. "Having pronounced the word, the woman . . . slipped
and fell to the ground, breaking her hip. She was carried home and

could not vote." There was, in short, material galore for hagiographers to come.[113]

"Padre Pio was immensely pleased about the victory of the Christian Democrats on April 18," noted the father guardian of Santa Maria delle Grazie after the triumph of Alcide De Gasperi and his party, on the same diary page in which he expressed his pleasure that more and more believers were making their way to San Giovanni Rotondo every day.[114] In those weeks around Easter, the influx of visitors was so great that Father Agostino did not particularly notice, among the thousands and thousands of pilgrims, the distinctive features of a twenty-eight-year-old Polish priest then studying for his doctorate in theology at the Angelicum University in Rome. Unremarked, Karol Wojtyla—one day to be Pope John Paul II—thus made his first visit to Padre Pio.[115]

9. THE WHITE HAND AND THE RED

The ten years after 1948 were Padre Pio's golden age as a living saint. Having obediently submitted to the repressive measures ordered by the Holy Office between 1923 and 1933, having sought the ways of the Lord along the railway lines of Europe with the Zarlatti locomotive, having shouldered the sufferings of Italy and the world during World War II and in the war's aftermath, the friar from Pietrelcina—now in his sixties—was finally enjoying the glory of uncontested devotion, the fame of a sainthood proclaimed far and wide. Now began the "Padre Pio phenomenon," the real mass religious movement.

A look at the evolution of Italian society in the 1950s suggests some reasons why the Gargano cult prospered. Mobility was growing: the improvement of the road network had shrunk the peninsula and the Marshall Plan dollars had enriched it, so that a pilgrimage to the Gargano was something almost everyone could now afford. Words and images were more mobile, too: tales about Padre Pio's miracles, long spread only by word of mouth and through devotional literature, were suddenly everywhere in the kaleidoscopic world of photo magazines. Catholic meeting groups were also growing, filling up space formerly occupied by Fascist associations; the number of Padre Pio's lay followers increased rapidly in an Italy ruled by the Christian Democrats. And then there was the completion of the Casa Sollievo della Sofferenza, which made San Giovanni Rotondo into a place of care and hope not only for Padre Pio's followers but for patients from all over the south of Italy.

The reasons why the Padre Pio cult flourished after the war must also be sought inside the Church—in the Vatican, as well as in the Gargano; with the Holy Father, as well as with the Friars Minor. Significantly, Padre Pio's triumph paralleled that of Pope Pius XII. Beyond the more or less fanciful anecdotes passed down by hagiographers—such as the time the pontiff, looking at a photo of Padre Pio, was supposed to have burst out, "It's obvious he is a saint!"—there were several concrete decisions that Pius XII made about the friar, the most important being to eventually release him from his vow of poverty so that he could take charge of the Casa Sollievo finances. More broadly, the booming devotion to the friar with the stigmata surely owed its energy to a papacy charged with Pius XII's charisma and media skills.[1]

Thus, in the decade between April 1948 and October 1958—between De Gasperi's victory at the polls and the death of Pius XII—circumstances combined to make the Padre Pio cult accessible, visible, and fully legitimate. In Cold War times, the friar with the stigmata could play a role not merely as a generic savior but as a specific political and social actor, confirming once again how malleable and elastic his sainthood was, how wondrously adaptable to changing expectations. Above all, in that decade, being on the side of Padre Pio no longer meant challenging the Church. Veneration for the pope and veneration for the little friar could finally merge, to the greater glory of both.

From Pope Pius to Padre Pio

Pilgrimlike wanderers by profession, the cyclists competing in the 1947 Giro d'Italia took the northern Puglia stage one torrid afternoon in early June. "We were penitents who went from Bari to Foggia to make a vow," wrote the novelist Vasco Pratolini, one of the pack of reporters covering the race. He described for his readers the rough roads of the Tavoliere, where "the asphalt turns to black, sticky mud, the clods of earth are dry as pumice, and the sun digs into the brain and twists the trunks of the olive trees." Despite the midday heat, crowds had turned out in force along the course on the roads from Modugno to Ruvo di Puglia, from Andria to Cerignola. But at the finish line in Foggia, people cared only for the two stars of the race, the famous cyclists Gino

Bartali and Fausto Coppi. They were especially excited about Bartali; his fans pressed in on all sides, held back by gendarmes with muskets. "Two young Franciscan friars hoisted themselves up on my shoulders and those of my colleague so they could see him up close for a moment," wrote Pratolini.[2]

That evening, it was Gino Bartali's turn to behave like a starstruck fan. Although his trainer was furious about it, the champion insisted that he be driven from Foggia to San Giovanni Rotondo to meet Padre Pio and make confession to him.[3] According to hagiographic legend, Bartali, a fervent Catholic, considered himself the spiritual son of the Capuchin friar. Whatever the case, that visit by the cyclist whom Italian Catholics considered their hero—as opposed to his rival Fausto Coppi, who was rumored to be a member of Italy's "other church," the Communist Party[4]—suggests to the historian not only how broadly accepted the Gargano cult had become by postwar times, but also how thoroughly Padre Pio was being transformed into a bona fide celebrity. Bartali was one of Pius XII's favorite sportsmen; he had been received by the pope several times,[5] and he would never have made a pilgrimage to the friar with the stigmata if it had made him look like a dissident within the Church. Padre Pio's fame was now evidently strong enough to make anyone who came in contact with him glow in the reflection, even when the visitor was a star himself.

In the Holy Year of 1950, a different sort of pilgrim on two wheels arrived in San Giovanni.[6] Don Alessandro Lingua, a priest from the far-off Piedmont town of Fossano, had by that time covered "a thousand kilometers of road" on his motorbike. As he would write in *I Saw Padre Pio of Pietrelcina*, a little book published at his own expense, Don Lingua had joined an "unforgettable Jubilee motorcycle rally" along with twenty thousand other bikers from every corner of Italy, arriving in St. Peter's before the pope on June 3. "We came to a halt with our engines hot and quivering, like our muscular hearts before the white, slender, almost transparent figure of the benedictory Vicar of Christ," wrote the motorcycling priest. Afterward, the biker in his tunic set off for the Gargano, having decided that this—"From Pope Pius to Padre Pio"—was the right itinerary for believers. Don Lingua's book was full of spiritual inspiration, if not theological profundities.

The white hand of Pope Pius XII and the reddened one of
Padre Pio are like two divine wings that will make us soar with
the most holy Virgin to the celestial fatherland. The whiteness
and the purity of the first hand are symbols of faith, the red
flame of the second is a symbol of charity, the pilgrims' goal
(and we with them) stands for hope in a better future.[7]

Those apocalyptic times when Padre Pio, pursued by the Holy Office,
seemed a modern Savonarola to his most heated disciples—a proud,
unarmed adversary of the Antichrist ruling the Vatican—were over.
Pio and Pius, "the two prophetic names of love in this sadly bellicose
era,"[8] had joined in a supreme alliance.

If there is any truth to the legends around Padre Pio, yet another
distinguished visitor climbed the Gargano switchbacks in August 1951:
Tazio Nuvolari, a world-class race car driver. Nuvolari, an ardent Catholic who always wore an image of the Sacred Heart on his driver's hel-
met, had crossed Italy not to compete in the epic Mille Miglia road
race[9] but to learn from Padre Pio how long his worn-out body and tired
heart could be expected to keep going. The friar's prediction was
gloomy, but Padre Pio was generous in giving his time to the "Flying
Mantuan": when Nuvolari got home, he told his wife, Carolina, that
they had spent the whole afternoon together. Two years later, just before
Nuvolari died from a stroke, Carolina herself would witness a miraculous bilocation by Padre Pio. There he was, the friar with the stigmata,
in his white surplice and stole over his habit, standing next to the bed
of the dying champion. "He was holding the holy water sprinkler in
his hand and blessing Tazio."[10]

Pilgrims who didn't have Bartali's bicycle, Don Lingua's motorbike,
or Nuvolari's automobile could reach San Giovanni by regular bus service from Foggia. There were three big buses that went "up and down
continually," "making a fortune" for the company that owned them, a
reporter said. The hotels and *pensioni* of Foggia, which had been
enlarged and modernized to meet an explosion of religious-touristic
demand, were also raking it in. "Even in San Giovanni Rotondo" there
was now a hotel (with the predictable name of Villa Pia), whose devout
proprietor, one Madama Goffi, had "become a millionaire in just a few

years."[11] By 1951, according to one of Padre Pio's hagiographers, over one hundred thousand pilgrims a year were coming to San Giovanni. Many of them slept neither in Foggia nor chez Madama Goffi. In winter and in summer alike they would spend the night outdoors, sleeping on the clearing in front of the friary, either because they had not found a bed in a hotel or because that way they could rise early and enter the gates in time to get a seat for Padre Pio's morning mass.[12]

Among the pilgrims coming and going in those years, a few were met with something like reproach from Padre Pio for having traveled all the way to San Giovanni. Near the city of Rovereto in the years around 1950, then near Stresa between 1953 and 1956, there lived a magnificent poet who had been called by the Lord—and by the death-in-life experience of the Great War[13]—to join the priesthood; and while it is doubtful that Padre Pio, who was not much of a reader, knew the poetry of Don Clemente Rebora, he must have heard of Rebora's apostolic talents as a loving spiritual director and a tireless preacher and confessor. "Why do you come to me? Don't you in Rovereto have Father Rebora who is a saint?" Padre Pio would say to the pilgrims coming down from that area.[14] And when, one morning in 1956, three visitors from Vercelli appeared in San Giovanni Rotondo, he had the same reaction. "Don't come to me, you people from up there: go to Stresa to Father Rebora."[15]

Back north, the three good Christians from Vercelli did indeed knock on the door of the seminary where Don Clemente, now terminally ill, was writing some of his finest verse.[16] When the three told him what the friar of San Giovanni had said, Don Clemente is supposed to have wept with astonishment and disbelief. "I've become the Stresa branch of Padre Pio," he said.[17]

Photographs of Christ

A hundred meters from Santa Maria delle Grazie, along the road toward the center of town, stood a building with a sign that read ABRESCH. This was the Puglia headquarters of Federico Abresch, the photographer from Bologna who had been part of Alberto Del Fante's circle and the Anonima Brevetti Zarlatti adventure. While the locomotive business had failed to enrich him and his fellow believers, the same was not true of his photography business. To the contrary, this ex-Lutheran and former theosophist—a convert to Catholicism after Padre Pio miraculously helped him and his wife conceive baby Pio[18]—found the business of reproducing and selling pictures of the holy friar extremely profitable. From the early 1930s to the early 1950s, Abresch had a virtual monopoly on what today we would call Padre Pio's image. When the hagiographies of the friar with the stigmata had photographs—and they nearly always had photographs[19]—these came exclusively from Abresch's archive. Nor was his business limited to photographs; as a promotional postcard of the 1940s explained, it also included publications on Padre Pio's life, "religious objects, and various small souvenirs."[20]

The motorcycling Don Lingua, when he came down to San Giovanni in the Holy Year of 1950, was actually troubled by all those pictures in Abresch's window. "It bothered me, in my easy-going simplicity, so much ostentation and promotion," Don Lingua wrote in his *I Saw Padre Pio*. But when Don Lingua met the friar in flesh and blood, his unease about the photographs dissolved. Afterward, the pictures that had disturbed him came to seem powerful and mysterious. "Morning, evening, in the daytime hours, I study that masculine face and a thousand supernatural thoughts flood my heart with arcane sentiments . . . There is no doubt that Christ lives in this friar, that he speaks in Him and for Him."[21] After all, reasoned Don Lingua in a semiological vein, Padre Pio should not be deprived of his destiny as an icon, in this age in which "everyone and everything is by now photographed. . . . It's the illness of our times, in a way; we're so distracted that something tangible is needed to collect our thoughts. In the midst of so many shameless images, do we not want people to lay their eyes on one who does not tempt, but redeems and exalts?"[22]

A few years later, deploying far more precise hermeneutical instruments (and less orthodox ideological intent) than Don Lingua, Roland Barthes would write his "Iconography of the Abbé Pierre." In this study of the ex-Capuchin priest who shook French bourgeois consciences by using sophisticated tactics like magazine interviews and media events to fight for the most extreme outcasts, Barthes would pay particular attention to the abbé's "beautiful head," which had all the elements essential to a figure of myth. Among the signs of the Abbé Pierre's vocation were his Franciscan haircut, studied in its absence of self-consciousness, and especially his Capuchin beard. It was the beard that identified the Abbé Pierre as—or rather presented him as—a primitive religious man, more impolitic than politically aware, Christ-like rather than power-hungry. In *Mythologies*, Barthes comments on "the eager consumption of these signs on the part of the public," a public made up of the readers of popular magazines and newsreels, "reassured by the spectacle of a physique and a calling" and more and more comfortable with the marketing of holiness.[23]

It would make no sense to apply Barthes's analysis wholesale to Padre Pio's tonsure, his beard, and his legend.[24] Nevertheless, Barthes's semiological questions are precisely those that the Gargano cult had always raised, and even more so beginning in the 1950s—questions about an icon's phenomenology, about a living saint's fame and the devout consumers of that celebrity. And in the case of Padre Pio, the icon bore the most impressive, the most powerful, the most semantically charged signs in all of Christianity: the stigmata. What's more, the friar's reputation as a living saint was backed up not just by generic spiritual assistance but by a unique, unbeatable capacity to perform miracles. It was that marriage between stigmata and miracles that explained Padre Pio's huge popularity in postwar Italian photojournalism. Indeed, historians of photography have recently suggested that Padre Pio was the leading motif in postwar Italy's iconographic imagination, rivaled only by the beauty queen Miss Italia.[25]

Had the friar with the stigmata met Roland Barthes, the semiotician would have had little trouble picking out the cult favorites in Padre Pio's iconography: the photos snapped as he was celebrating communion with his hands ungloved as the liturgy dictates, raising the wine chalice, blessing the bread, kneeling, every gesture of the sacred ceremony displaying the suffering and martyrdom of the Lord in him. As Barthes put it in his acute analysis of the redemptive power of images: "photography has something to do with resurrection."[26] Or, in the words of another Frenchman, the Dominican friar Marcel Dubois: photography is a way of prolonging the incarnation.[27] The Holy Year of 1950 coincided with the first international conference on the Holy Shroud of Turin, the ancient winding-sheet that—courtesy of photographs—had so struck the imagination of believers as to become one of Christianity's most venerated relics.[28] Similarly, the photos of Padre Pio, his wounds and his passion, met a widespread cultural demand for images of the *corpus Christi*—a demand that had been answered in a homemade way by the photos and the *santini*, the little holy cards, made by Federico Abresch, and later by the glossy portraits of the big magazine photographers.

In the early days of the cult, in 1919, Padre Pio's superiors had forbidden him any contact with photographers and journalists, but word soon got around that the prohibition wasn't necessary because the Capuchin himself shunned any kind of publicity and disliked being photographed.[29] In the decades to follow, the story was that Padre Pio had the miraculous gift of being able to prevent his image from taking shape on the photographic plate, should a picture be taken without his consent. Giovanni Santucci, a Franciscan lay brother, could testify to that. As a pilgrim to San Giovanni Rotondo in the early 1930s, when Padre Pio was still deprived of most of his powers by the Holy Office, Santucci had been authorized by the father guardian to visit the friar's cell. While the "Saint" wasn't looking, Santucci had snapped five or six "of those ever-so-forbidden photographs." But as he was leaving, Padre Pio had said to him, in cheerful reproach: "Remember, if you don't put purpose into it, the photograph will not come out." Indeed, when Santucci took his negatives back to a studio in Benevento, the photographer was unable to find anything recognizable on the plates.[30] "Photographers with perfect cameras would sneak in hoping to surprise him, and every shot came out blank. The same cameras could take pictures of other people and of the landscape, but never Padre Pio," a Sicilian biographer, Don Giuseppe Tomaselli, would write years later.[31]

The Gargano Christ as a reluctant star—this was the legend about Padre Pio in the early 1950s, even though he was by then omnipresent in the media. Perhaps it was that very omnipresence that led some of the faithful to complain that Padre Pio had been turned into a magazine celebrity. The magazine stories "strive for the sensational, and sensation is often achieved at the expense of truth," warned the journalist Carlo Trabucco, who served as a sort of padrepiologist for the Christian Democratic paper *Il Popolo*.[32] But such complaints did nothing to stop the flow of photographers and writers eager to offer their own take on the friar.

In April 1950, a particularly eminent journalist arrived in San Giovanni Rotondo: Orio Vergani, a special correspondent for the *Corriere della Sera*. The two-part article he would write on Padre Pio oozes with that mixture of human empathy and moral frivolity, effortless style and facile judgments that had made him a prince of the newsroom during Mussolini's rule. Vergani had been the great troubadour of Il Duce's charisma,[33] the one who coined the deathless phrase "oceanic rallies" to describe Mussolini's crowds. The piece he wrote in San Giovanni Rotondo is worth examining not only because Vergani was a big name at a major newspaper but because it so perfectly represents what was turned out in those years about Padre Pio and his followers. Vergani misses no ingredient of the hagiographic recipe, though he serves it up in its most sophisticated version. There is the parallel between the dry, burned landscape of San Giovanni and the Palestine of Mt. Carmel. There is the link between the poor of San Giovanni and all the *misérables* of Italian literature, from Ignazio Silone's hardworking Abruzzo peasants to Carlo Levi's destitute Lucanians. There is the comparison between Padre Pio's adopted home and the native town of Bernadette Soubirous, the mystic of Lourdes. There is even a prophecy: "One day, perhaps, the little town of San Giovanni Rotondo will be as famous as Lourdes."[34]

Vergani's portrait of the "Saint" also follows the conventions. Like many of his colleagues, the journalist from Milan had initially intended to interview and photograph the friar; but after he arrived in San Giovanni, he changed his mind. "One can't *interview* a man who has borne the signs of the stigmata on his hands and feet for thirty-two years," he said. Vergani instead contented himself with observing Padre Pio for an entire day, while the friar tirelessly performed what was his sole activity apart from the morning mass: hearing private confessions for ten to twelve hours straight, women in the morning and early afternoon, men in the evening. "My eyes—and they have seen much—could not get enough of the sight," Vergani wrote. "It was so mysterious, that . . . simple image of the peasant-friar, seated, as he has been every day for thirty-two years, on the rustic throne of his confessional, listening—one time to the right, then to the left, the two slow files of

penitents advancing in turn—to the history of the sins of this world." Padre Pio enchanted Vergani with his rough candor, with that "manner of a sheep-farmer and a shepherd of souls at the same time" with which he maintained order in the two ranks of candidates for absolution.[35]

For the most part Vergani contributed no more than an extra sprinkle of writing talent to the familiar clichés. But there were times when his prose took off, and his real newsman's sharp powers of observation bequeathed some gems to posterity. One such moment comes in his description of the little church of Santa Maria delle Grazie, a description all the more evocative today following the addition of a larger church built in the late 1950s and the immense one designed by the architect Renzo Piano that was inaugurated in 2004. When Vergani saw the place in 1950, that little church was exactly the same—not a decoration changed, not a single new painting added—as it had been in September 1918 when Padre Pio received the stigmata. "Without one piece of marble or bronze or gilt," it was "still extremely humble." Carved out of a space in the monastery, the church did not have a real facade. It was only a bit larger than a chapel, and the only interior ornaments were several geometric patterns on the walls that the painters seemed to have copied from a nineteenth-century manual of decoration.[36]

But what made Padre Pio's little church extraordinary, said Vergani, was that all of it, from the entrance to the nave, from the altar to the doors, was "covered in penciled script." Church officials did not allow votive offerings to be brought to San Giovanni Rotondo, nor silver hearts for the altar or marble plaques, but who could prevent the faithful from writing down their requests for Padre Pio's intercession? While waiting for confession—perhaps fearing that their contact with the friar through the confessional screen might be too brief—many took out a pencil and confided their requests for help to the walls. "And so," Vergani wrote, "the church is entirely covered in extremely tiny handwritten missives, in infinite appeals, in numberless entreaties, in public confessions of suffering, all of them signed, many with addresses, as if Padre Pio might reply." If people believed that those five wounds had been bleeding for decades, why might they not imagine that the friar would read, one by one, all the confessions and pleas on the wall?

"Every few months the friars come down to the church at night with a bucket of whitewash and erase everything, but no one doubts that in the meantime Padre Pio's prayers have interceded for all."[37]

Miracles on the Eve of the *Miracolo*

Miracles were everywhere in mid-twentieth-century Italy—even on movie sets. In 1948, Roberto Rossellini, with Federico Fellini as his writer, had cast Anna Magnani in *The Miracle*, in which a madwoman gets pregnant by a vagabond who pretends to be St. Joseph, father of Jesus.[38] The following year, Cesare Zavattini wrote *Miracle in Milan* for Vittorio De Sica, sending the poorest of the poor to fly on broomsticks through the skies of a better, fairer world. At the same time, according to an article published in the Catholic newspaper *Avvenire* in November 1950, the renowned Italian comic actor Antonio De Curtis—celebrated under his stage name, Totò—was working on a film to be called *The Miracle*. The story was about a priest and his sacristan who fake a miracle in their church to attract believers. But after the intervention of the actor Carlo Campanini, an ultradevout follower of Padre Pio, De Curtis changed his mind. "Totò as a priest, you can well imagine where that would have ended up. Well, that film is not to be. And as soon as [Totò] has fulfilled his contract with the production company, he will head right off to see Padre Pio."[39]

Meanwhile, if the newspapers and popular magazines of the 1950s are to be believed, the Capuchin with the stigmata never stopped performing miracles for a minute. That pervasive *miracolismo* (a term whose first appearance linguists date to 1950–51)[40] offers fascinating clues for the historian. As the medievalists have shown us, the notions a society develops about its miracles tell us many things about how individuals relate to the sacred and about a community's horizon of expectations.[41] In the case of Padre Pio, the media's logorrhea about his miracles was part of a more general phenomenon. On the eve of that great transformation that would be known to Italians as the *miracolo economico*—their "economic miracle," when Italy ceased being an agricultural nation and became an industrial one[42]—publicizing Padre Pio's miracles was a way of clutching on to a world that was disappearing.

As Vergani put it, that was the world of the "peasant-friar" sitting on "the rustic throne of his confessional," the world of the farmer women kneeling before him, "young lasses with flowered kerchiefs to cover their hair, old ladies wearing their black shawls."[43] At the same time, the portraits of Padre Pio in the photo magazines also pointed to the future, with a postmodern logic in which the sacred and the spectacular are tightly bound together.[44] In 1966, the publisher Longanesi put out a book titled *Padre Pio* in a series called "Famous People," a series that had begun with Sophia Loren and proceeded through Maria José, the last queen of Italy.[45]

Padre Pio's miracles spoke the language of both the sensational and the intimate, the evident and the occult, public and private. The media coverage only hinted at the extent of popular religiosity—a religiosity made up, as it had been under fascism, of miracles announced by word of mouth, of tenacious networks of letter writers, of organized devotional entrepreneurship. *New Truths*, a book by Alberto Del Fante published in Bologna in 1951, was divided into two parts: the first contained all the articles that provincial newspapers had devoted to Padre Pio's miracle healings during the 1940s; the second presented a selection of the letters that the *miracolati* had sent to Del Fante about their cures.[46] "A humble, devout, secret little Italy lives in constant contact with Padre Pio," wrote Roberto De Monticelli in 1955.[47] A reporter for *Epoca*, De Monticelli was well placed to interpret the world of Padre Pio zealots, for he made it his business to plumb the hidden depths of a country in transformation—the murky, ambiguous, nostalgic corners of an Italy where people still took pride in the conquests of Empire, still grew sentimental about the royal family they had sent packing in 1946, still pitied Il Duce's much-traveled body.[48]

De Monticelli was among the first to notice how prayer groups were fanning the booming Gargano cult. Such groups were often headed by a person who claimed to be in contact with Padre Pio, hearing his voice and receiving his counsel on various matters, "both in direct apparitions—and they cite places and dates—or through the presence of a perfume." The perfume might be of roses, of violets, of oriental tobacco; the smell of carbolic acid, meanwhile, pointed to negative advice, choices to avoid.[49] De Monticelli also wrote about how Padre

Pio's miracles could set off chain reactions, as had happened in the case of Paolo M., a Milanese boy whom doctors had declared a hopeless case after a terrible fall from a window. The boy had lain unconscious for three days in a Policlinico hospital room, his mother unable even to pray. But the bed next to Paolo was occupied by a newborn from La Spezia with a brain tumor, and the newborn's mother had given Paolo's mother a photograph of Padre Pio and told her to put it under her son's pillow. That night, the room filled up with the fragrance of roses, and Paolo, restless, had put his hand under the pillow and taken hold of the photograph. At dawn he woke up, recognized his mother, and calmly asked her, "Where are we?"[50]

Pasquale R., a young greengrocer from Lecco pictured in *Epoca* smiling behind his fruit stand, also owed his health to what might be called a contact miracle. Confined to a wheelchair for thirteen years because of a bone disease, having undergone two unsuccessful operations, Pasquale was cured when one of Padre Pio's spiritual sons, Paolo C., waved a crucifix over his legs. Paolo C., in turn, had himself become a *miracolato* when he went to the Gargano following a tonsillitis that had spread to his eyes and blinded him. He had asked Padre Pio for "at least one eye" and was restored to health.[51]

None of the friar's followers had forgotten the miraculous cure he had performed in 1947, when he gave eyesight to "the blind girl of Ribera," a seven-year-old Sicilian named Anna Di Giorgi who had been born without pupils in her eyes.[52] Padre Pio seemed less eager to help, however, when the famous sculptor Francesco Messina—who had converted because of the friar's intervention[53]—called on him to ask his intercession for the equally famous writer Papini, reduced in his last years to almost complete blindness. "I know nothing of Giovanni Papini," said the Capuchin brusquely. "He's the one who wrote the *Life of Christ*," Messina explained. "Many write of these things" was Padre Pio's evasive reply. Still, he did agree to gaze intensely at a photograph of Papini, who got back some of his eyesight within a week.[54]

To read the Italian press of the 1950s is to imagine all of Italy wrapped in a mist of heavenly powers that begins in the Gargano and spreads out, multiplying the supernatural gifts of Padre Pio. There was the case of Commendatore Enrico De Bernardi, a musical instrument maker from Genova, who in 1950 discovered his own ability to heal by the laying on of hands. That very spring, De Bernardi decided to visit San Giovanni Rotondo, to ask the holy friar for an explanation and some advice. Padre Pio told him that his healing powers had a divine origin, and asked him to attune those powers to God's will.[55] From then on, for more than twenty years, the ailing flocked to De Bernardi's villa on the Riviera to benefit from the mysterious balm of his hands. The blind, the lame, the heart patients—some five thousand people came to him each year, and many went away feeling well again.[56] De Bernardi's first encounter with Padre Pio was followed by many more, and it was directly from the friar's hands that the commendatore received, in 1953, the habit of a Franciscan lay brother. He was admitted into the order with the name of Fra Pio Luca.[57]

Besides the miracle healings, Padre Pio specialized in miracle conversions. Such conversions were especially in demand in 1950s Italy; the elections of April 1948 had kept the Communist wolf at bay, but they had not eradicated the menace. Italy was right up against the Iron Curtain, and the strength of the Italian Communist Party made many feel like the country was under direct threat from the hydra-headed Soviet Union. Accordingly, every golden book about the miracles of Padre Pio contained a chapter on the conversion of Communists. All these tales are much the same, variations on the evangelical theme of the lost sheep. The converted man might be one Costante Rosatelli, a surveyor and professional militant from Velletri, "organizer of improvised political rallies and road blocks," who one fine day looking out his window saw a friar staring at him: that friar was Padre Pio, who called him to San Giovanni and persuaded him to change his life.[58] Or he might be the textiles merchant Giovanni Bardazzi, a hotheaded Communist from Prato in Tuscany, who when called by Padre Pio became the most docile of followers, always going back and forth from Tuscany to the Gargano. "Each time he would bring an old party comrade," and when they got back home, "two out of three . . . would tear up their party cards."[59] In yet other stories, the convert might be Italia Betti, known as the Pasionaria of Emilia, a teacher from Bologna who had dropped everything and everyone— her students at the Liceo Galvani, the party federation, the local headquarters of the Union of Italian Women—to abjure her faith in communism before the Capuchin with the stigmata. In order to be able to breathe the air of Padre Pio, Betti had now settled in San Giovanni Rotondo, "she who once traversed her region on a motorbike to bring the word of Lenin."[60]

In their hunger to engulf the other side, the hagiographers even went so far as to claim Giuseppe Di Vittorio, the very embodiment of Puglia communism and the Italian workers' movement, as a potential Padre Pio disciple. In fact, Di Vittorio was a sort of secular equivalent of Padre Pio, a living saint of the revolution; photographic portraits of him, like those of the friar, had been wildly popular as far back as the 1920s.[61] After Di Vittorio's death in 1957, rumors began to circulate that the union leader had planned to visit Padre Pio but had held back "for reasons of party decorum and in order not to run the risk of being converted."[62] In any case, the hagiographers wrote, when Di Vittorio died, the Capuchin with the stigmata said a prayer for him too. Because Padre Pio prayed for everyone, always.[63]

The Saint of Police Informers

"To write about Padre Pio you need another Padre Pio," insisted the most modest of the friar's hagiographers.[64] Nevertheless, that onerous job was performed time and again in the years after 1948, when the number of books about the life and works of the *alter Christus* exploded. Were there perhaps too many for the Vatican's taste, despite the conciliatory approach that it had by now adopted toward the Gargano cult? Whatever the case, in 1952 the Holy Office placed eight such hagiographies on the Index, diligently listing them in alphabetical order according to the surnames of the authors. Apollonio, Donato, *Encounters With P. Pio* (Foggia: Cappetta, 1951). Argentieri, Domenico, *The Prodigious Story of P. Pio* (Milan: Tarantola, 1951). Camilleri, Carmelo, *Padre Pio of Pietrelcina* (Città di Castello: Società Tipografica Leonardo da Vinci, 1952). Delfino Sessa, Piera, *P. Pio of Pietrelcina* (Genova: Demos, 1950). Greco Fiorentini, Guido, *P. Pio, Marvelous Being* (Santa Maria Capua Vetere: A. Beato, 1949). Lotti, Franco, *Padre Pio of Pietrelcina* (San Giovanni Rotondo: Anresch, 1951). Pedriali, Gian Carlo, *I Saw Padre*

Pio (Foggia: Cappetta, 1948). Trabucco, Carlo, *The World of P. Pio* (Rome: Giacomaniello, 1952).

The Holy Office decree was quickly reported by the Vatican paper *L'Osservatore Romano*,[65] which also provided some clarification. The eight books about Padre Pio had been banned in conformity with articles 1383 and 1399 of the code of canon law, which stipulated that the Church must review and approve "books and pamphlets that tell of new apparitions, revelations, visions, prophecies, miracles, etc." Because none of the authors had obeyed these rules, the Holy Office was obliged to censor them. The list of forbidden books was to be seen as no more than "an example" that applied to the "very numerous" similar publications. The Vatican newspaper made it clear that the prohibition did not imply any critical judgment of Padre Pio on the part of the Holy Office, and noted that "Padre Pio himself has said several times that there are things written and said about him that are wonderful, but not true"—hinting that perhaps the Vatican hierarchy had a similar opinion on the matter.[66]

The eight censored books all offered roughly the same content, recounting the hagiographic stereotypes one by one. The most interesting of the group, by virtue of its authorship, was the volume written by Carmelo Camilleri—the former police inspector who had been sent to San Giovanni Rotondo in August 1923 to study plans to transfer the friar with the stigmata, and who had advised his superiors not to proceed with the move.[67] Thirty years after that celebrated "miracle," Camilleri wrote up his own version of the events. According to this account, he had arrived at the monastery at the orders of the national chief of police himself, General Emilio De Bono, and the "prodigious friar" had immediately recognized him although they had never met before. Thanks to his sixth sense as an investigator, Inspector Camilleri had then determined, based on "irrefutable documentary proof," that the miracles attributed to Padre Pio were an "inexplicable but incontrovertible fact." Back in Rome, he had informed the chief of police of this, adding that any attempt to deport Padre Pio would lead to "certain bloodshed." That report had led General De Bono, "who had a very high opinion of religion and who deep in his soul was a convinced, devout, and practicing believer," to meet with the ecclesiastical authorities and persuade them to revoke the transfer order.[68]

It is an edifying retelling, but what really interests the historian about Camilleri's book is that it points to a surprisingly common type among Padre Pio's hagiographers: the police informer. It turns out that more than one of those who sang the friar's praises during the De Gasperi years had worked with political intelligence under the Fascists. Emanuele Brunatto, as we have seen, indulged in espionage alongside his many other activities in France, and after the fall of fascism the Padre Pio cult became a safe refuge for the troubled consciences of other such former spies.

The Sicilian-born Camilleri had a checkered history. Arrested as a deserter in 1917 and amnestied after the war, he had worked as a journalist before getting hired as an assistant police inspector. Among his claims to fame were the arrests in Turin of the editor Antonio Gramsci and the staff of *L'Ordine Nuovo*, the Communist paper, in 1921; his participation in the March on Rome in October 1922; and his tough repression of "Pugliese subversion" on the Tavoliere plain and the Gargano mountains in 1923–24.[69] His brief career in the police came to an end in 1928 in Milan, where he was involved in somewhat murky investigations into a terroristic attack that took place at the Milan Fair.[70] Sentenced to five years in *confino* (internal exile) for organizing his own spy network parallel to OVRA, Camilleri was pardoned by Mussolini in 1932 thanks to the help of the Jesuit Pietro Tacchi Venturi. Following some not very illustrious years, during which he sold spittoons and then gas masks, Padre Pio's future hagiographer was arrested for fraud in 1937. Once again sentenced to *confino*, he spent two years in the Tremiti Islands penal colony before once again Father Tacchi Venturi interceded with Il Duce, winning him a second pardon.[71]

Camilleri was not exactly a man of model ethics, nor one particularly to be trusted. From his confinement in the Tremiti Islands, Camilleri wrote letters to Mussolini dripping with regime fealty, boasting of how all the other prisoners in confinement detested him—especially the Communists from Turin, who had not forgotten his role in the investigations of *L'Ordine Nuovo*.[72] After the Liberation, however, Camilleri would boast instead of his pedigree as a diligent anti-Fascist. To hear him tell it, after the massacre at the Milan Fair in 1928 he had courageously tried to deflect the investigators' attention away from the putative Communist terrorists, although unfortunately he had been unable to prevent the main suspect—Romolo Tranquilli, brother of Ignazio Silone—from being sentenced to prison, where he died a few years later.[73]

During the 1950s, Camilleri loved to recall his glory days of policing the crowds and serving on the vice squad.[74] Yet underneath the aura of pride were traces of remorse and guilt, feelings that give a special charge to the Padre Pio worship of many Mussolini regime functionaries who survived into the democratic era. "Padre Pio speaks to penitents in the name of God, he scrutinizes them thoroughly, perceives their failings and their moral weaknesses, sounds them out with his deep, sure gaze, brings their guilt to light and arouses their remorse," Camilleri writes in his life of Padre Pio, and follows up with a long quotation from Manzoni on the doctrine of penitence.[75] Perhaps it was remorse, too, that spurred devotion to Padre Pio on the part of the Fascist informer par excellence, Pitigrilli—the man who ratted on the Turin leadership of Giustizia e Libertà and had them arrested.[76] In 1948, after his past as a spy was revealed, Pitigrilli fled to Argentina, but just a year later this master of libertine best sellers like *Cocaine* was turning out *Pitigrilli Talks About Pitigrilli*, a book ripe with pious Catholic sentiments that culminates in a pilgrimage to San Giovanni Rotondo to hear mass celebrated by the living Christ.[77]

A pilgrimage to San Giovanni—a sort of genre unto itself in the religious literature of those years—also provided the plot of the 1951 pamphlet *Padre Pio of Pietrelcina, First Knight of Righteousness* by Antonio Di Legge and Vincenzo Epifano. They told of taking a "wild ride" from their hotel in Bari to the Gargano mountains, inebriated with "a sense of being on wings of grace," and then of the "wordless consolation" they derived from watching Padre Pio celebrate communion.[78] Their book had much in common with the other devout lives of Padre Pio, though it was somewhat more emphatic, boldly asserting that "Padre Pio is He who perpetuates Christ in these hard, sad years: he is another Christ."[79] The two men asked Padre Pio's spiritual protection for the girls' orphanage they had founded in Caserta, and showed off their respective bona fides: Di Legge presented himself as the marquis of Piperno, bearer of the Lateranese Gold Cross, founder and director of the St. Rita of Cascia Combined Charities, while Epifano was the general secretary of the same charity. They omitted to mention, though, that Antonio Di Legge was yet another man in the Camilleri and Pitigrilli mold, a sterling example of a Fascist police informer turned Padre Pio zealot.

The self-styled marquis had been born into a modest family in 1902 in Piperno, a town south of Rome. "Gifted with intelligence, a clever tongue, and an ingratiating manner," as the Lazio carabinieri command wrote of him in 1928, he had been able to get a job while quite young in the Piperno city government, meanwhile serving as reporter for *Avanti!* and local secretary of the Socialist League.[80] Eventually Di Legge became one of the leaders of the Communist Party in Rome, but "the Matteotti business"—as he would euphemistically describe the murder in a later letter to Il Duce—left him "nauseated." Observing the "cruel, obscene, deceitful campaign conducted by the opposition against the Regime and Your Excellency," this militant of the Third International became a secret Fascist political informer. In the summer of 1924, while all of Italy was caught up in the drama of Matteotti's disappearance, Di Legge settled down in Riano Flaminio, sending in daily reports on the Communists from the very place where Matteotti's body would be discovered.[81]

The Communist Party leaders quickly unmasked the traitor, exposing him to the scorn of his comrades and rendering him useless to the Fascist police. Di Legge was left to roam around Italy in search of pickup jobs and expedients: counterfeiter in Velletri, waiter in Ostia, building site foreman near Savona, delivery boy in Trieste, unemployed in Rome. In 1927, Padre Pio's future hagiographer tried to get back into the information business by selling some false reports on the clandestine Communist Party, but he was caught by the Rome police department and sentenced to thirty-six months of *confino*. After his release, Di Legge reinvented himself as a scholar and a historian,[82] but he never lost his old love of being an informer. In 1937, he wrote to the Rome police commissioner proposing to once again take on the role of spy. It is a letter of priceless candor, in which every twist and turn of his past was put to use.

Will gladly carry out activities in the field of confidential information, but as a regular employee under the directorate of Public Security. Can produce from the following environments (opportunities to confirm information in all cases): ex-Communists; Communists; ex-Socialists; Socialists; ex-political-confinees; Italian and foreign journalists; commercial, bank, and private informers not authorized by police; foreign diplomatic representatives dealing with the Royal Army; economic and political milieux, including Trieste, Genova, and Savona; recruiters of clandestine forces; comments from foreign press (absolute priority); counterfeiters of checks; possible attempts to reorganize, etc.[83]

In July 1940, the Rome police commissioner informed the national Department of Public Security that Di Legge had been "struck off the list of subversives for having given certain proof of repentance," which in police lingo meant that he had regained his informer's stripes, most likely with Fascist espionage inside the Vatican.[84] After the armistice in September 1943, Di Legge worked with the Black Brigades in Rome, energetically hunting down partisans.[85]

It would be wrong to pretend that such a figure exemplified the followers of Padre Pio, the great majority of whom never had anything to do with either the Italian Communist Party or the Fascist secret police. Still, we cannot but notice how many spies of the Fascist regime gravitated toward the Gargano cult after the war. Religious propaganda offered the regime's men-with-a-past—men like Camilleri, Pitigrilli, and Di Legge, to say nothing of Brunatto—a welcome spiritual home. They no longer had to put their faith in the inevitably profane gospel of politics, nor in a redeemer as fatally flawed as Il Duce; the gospel from the Gargano was a sacred language, and the friar with the stigmata offered an amazing shortcut between the human and the superhuman. "The twentieth century," said Pitigrilli, "is the century of Padre Pio."[86]

The Faith Healer's Hospital

For the Italian writer Guido Piovene, who spent several years in the 1950s traveling up and down the Italian peninsula reporting for a radio program, a stop in San Giovanni Rotondo was practically obligatory. Upon reaching the Gargano, Piovene devoted some hours to Monte Sant'Angelo, a few kilometers from San Giovanni, with its sanctuary—famous in the Middle Ages—where Christian tradition had it that Archangel Michael had appeared. Then, crossing the invisible barrier of "magical effervescence" that surrounded Padre Pio "and even hid him," Piovene arrived in the little town where the friar lived. Miracles were in the air as soon as he entered the lobby of the hotel. An American diplomat told Piovene how a mysterious friar had appeared before him twenty-five years before in the United States and persuaded him to convert from Judaism. Only recently, while flipping through "a photo magazine," he had identified that friar, and he had now come all the way to Puglia to thank him.[87]

The following morning, Piovene walked up to the Capuchin friary to be present when Padre Pio said mass. In the clearing in front, the troops of believers who had come from all over Italy were lit up by the first rays of dawn. They had gathered to be near "the only man alive in this country who is known as a saint." Piovene, who was celebrated for his *Letters of a Novice*, an epistolary novel in the voice of a young nun, had no trouble finding words to describe the scene: the pandemonium of lay sisters crowding around the locked door to the church, the way they erupted into the space once the door was opened and frenetically occupied the territory between the first row of seats, the altar, and the narrow passage through which Padre Pio came out of the sacristy. "As soon as he appears they attack him, touch him, try to get his attention, compete with each other to show their zeal, making him stumble, sometimes trampling on his feet with their stigmata sores." As for the gifts of the living Christ, Piovene, well known as a journalist for his accounts of Il Duce's miraculous powers, was not short of words there either.[88] During the mass Padre Pio was ecstatic, Piovene said, carried away, but somewhat laboriously, "with a sort of see-sawing between elation and fatigue." His hands were bare, and in the center of his palms lay the "great reddish stain" of the stigmata. He looked sorrowful and pained during the rite, especially when he knelt, as the liturgy demanded, on his right knee. But besides reliving Christ's sacrifice, Padre Pio carried on a dialogue with Him. "His mass is, at the same time, both tragic and intimate," wrote Piovene.[89]

Piovene visited San Giovanni just as the Casa Sollievo della Sofferenza was about to be inaugurated. Unlike Orio Vergani, who had reported on the world of Padre Pio when the hospital was still just a construction site, Piovene could thus see the enormous impact of the Casa Sollievo on its Gargano surroundings. He could see the impressive contrast between the model hospital and the Capuchin friary just a few steps away, "the poorest and most dilapidated" that Piovene had ever visited. From what he could make out from the hallway, the cells were identical to the bedrooms of the poorest peasants of the south; and the interior seemed to be terribly damp, if the friars' crooked gait was any indication. And yet Padre Pio daily received there "many millions" of lire, offerings that had been enough to finance the marble halls of the Casa Sollievo and other expensive works. The "little friary" shrank to nothing before the hospital, the civic buildings, and the hotels under construction along the road into town. "We are seeing a whole city rise around the reputation of a man," wrote Piovene in his *Voyage in Italy*,[90] and he couldn't have described any better how San Giovanni Rotondo had been transformed from a dirt-poor farm town into the capital of the modern Gargano.

When Padre Pio inaugurated the Casa Sollievo della Sofferenza in May 1956, with some twenty thousand of the faithful in attendance, the press saluted the event with a torrent of excited prose. "Where thirty years ago there were but rocks and bushes, today the pure white mass of a fairytale hospital rises," gushed one newspaper. "On the rough slopes, a white monument to charity," headlined another. "The greatest miracle of Padre Pio, the Saint of San Giovanni Rotondo," said a third.[91] It would be hard to say that such comments were over the top; as the photographs accompanying these articles attested, the hospital did indeed look like a cathedral rising out of a blasted heath. We know,

of course, that the miracle of the Casa Sollievo was not due entirely to the Capuchin's supernatural powers. The hospital had benefited not only from the donations of Padre Pio's followers but also from profits picked up by Emanuele Brunatto on the Paris black market, and from funds cleverly diverted from United Nations accounts by the Vatican–Christian Democrat joint venture. Whatever the source, though, from 1956 onward the inhabitants not only of San Giovanni Rotondo but of the Gargano, of Puglia, and of the entire south had an excellent new hospital at their disposal: one hundred beds; four operating rooms; a delivery room; a room to set broken limbs in plaster; six rooms to dress wounds; separate wards for internal medicine, surgery, urology, orthopedics, obstetrics and gynecology, and pediatrics; radiological, cardiological, and anesthesia services; and outpatient clinics for all these and other specialties.

Apart from its impact on the health of the population, the Casa Sollievo della Sofferenza was a first in Italian (and European) religious life because its founder was, after all, a miracle healer. Traditionally, the healer-saint had established his credentials in *opposition* to the knowledge of medical doctors, who were seen as arrogant, expensive, and useless.[92] Since the nineteenth century, the effort to bridge the gap between scientific explanations and miracle cures had come entirely from the medical side—as with the *bureau des constatations* at Lourdes, for example, where miracle cures were examined using modern symptomological and statistical techniques.[93] With the Casa Sollievo, however, Padre Pio headed in the other direction, not from science toward miracles but from miracles toward science.

Leading the friar in that direction, perhaps, was his membership in the Capuchin order, the only mendicant order whose rules permit its members to practice medicine and pharmaceutics.[94] Padre Pio never fully went over to the side of Hippocrates; his openness to medical science didn't prevent him, for instance, from joining most of his fellow Catholics in considering pain a path to grace. (As we can see from his correspondence,[95] the friar was convinced that nothing ennobled man more than suffering, for suffering favored communion with Jesus.)[96] Nevertheless, the outcome was remarkable: a little country friar, whom all considered ignorant, and whose reputation as a saint rested on his renown as a faith healer, was the one to bring an army of doctors to the Gargano. He even achieved in his own lifetime what his toughest adversary would only realize after death. The Casa Sollievo della Sofferenza opened its doors five years before the Faculty of Medicine of the Università Cattolica del Sacro Cuore, the medical school and hospital in Rome that would be named after Agostino Gemelli, and through which Gemelli had hoped to establish Catholic hegemony over Italian medicine and science.[97]

Father Gemelli died, at the age of eighty, in 1958, ten years before Padre Pio. He died having known, in the twilight of his life, the satisfaction of having been a real visionary: by the end of the Second World War the Cattolica in Milan had become an outstanding university, the forge of a national elite.[98] His successes did not soften his attitude toward Padre Pio; as an old man, the Franciscan was every bit as suspicious and pugnacious in fighting the friar with the stigmata as he had been when younger. Rector Gemelli wrote several times to the Holy

Office in the 1940s and thereafter, calling the attention of the tribunal of the faith to the friar's unjustified claims of sainthood.[99] But by the 1950s Father Gemelli was rowing against the current in trying to stop the tide of Gargano devotion,[100] and his battle was clearly lost once the hulking Casa Sollievo began to cast its welcome shadow over the harsh San Giovanni countryside.

With the hospital Padre Pio was once again obliged to take up a role he had assumed during the troubled times of the Anonima Brevetti Zarlatti, that of allocating share packages. This time he was on more solid financial ground, but there was also more risk involved. Was he a manager, or was he an owner? At first, to get around the vow of poverty imposed by the rules of the Capuchin order, Padre Pio had thought of separating the Società Casa Sollievo, which ran the hospital, from a corporation that would be the hospital's legal owner. The Società Casa Sollievo could then be organized as a congregation of the Franciscan Third Order, with Padre Pio as its director. The Church hierarchy had no complaints about such a plan, but it created fierce tensions inside the little world of San Giovanni.[101] And so, in the spring of 1957, Padre Pio appealed directly to Pope Pius XII, asking to be allowed to issue in his own name "nearly all the shares" of the Società Casa Sollievo—shares that he would in turn deposit in the Istituto delle Opere di Religione, the Vatican financial institution, which in those years was becoming a genuine central bank.[102] The pope said yes immediately, effectively releasing the friar from his vow of poverty.[103] That September, a special meeting of the Società Casa Sollievo handed Padre Pio 199,999 out of the 200,000 shares in the hospital, retaining only one symbolic share. Besides being the director of the Casa Sollievo della Sofferenza, Padre Pio thus became its owner.

All in all, 1958 was thus a relatively good year for the friar of Pietrelcina. He did have to contend, of course, with the usual infirmities a man over seventy might expect—that and the five harrowing wounds. There was also some "suffering," according to Father Agostino of San Marco in Lamis, caused by having to supervise the Casa Sollievo as well the building of the "Big Church" that was going up "alongside the little one." And the end of the year was indelibly marked by the news

that came from Castel Gandolfo early in the morning of October 9. Padre Pio's "whole soul was in pain for the death of Pope Pius XII," Father Agostino recorded in his diary. "But then the Lord let him see Pius in the glory of Paradise."[104]

10. A STRAW IDOL

La Dolce Vita

Pius XII's death was a cruel one, if only for the way his body came hurtling into media history when the pope's physician, Riccardo Galeazzi Lisi, sold photos of his last hours to a magazine. As the world learned to its dismay, in the end, a pontiff's body is just like any other body.[1]

It was not easy to accept the death of Jesus's representative on earth. Twice, in 1954 and in 1958, the Swiss doctor Paul Niehans, an expert on aging and "rejuvenation," had used his secret "cell therapy" on Pius,[2] in a modern-day version of the special treatments that a medieval pope would receive from his *archiatrus*.[3] Those two visits to the Vatican earned Dr. Niehans a nomination to the Pontifical Academy of Sciences, but the pope himself got no benefit whatsoever.[4] Instead, there came Galeazzi Lisi's deathbed betrayal—retribution, in a way, for all the efforts Pius XII had made to control the media in his lifetime, during which he had cultivated a carefully contrived image of his own grace.[5] "This is the way a pope dies in the age of the photomagazine and mass media," the weekly *Il Mondo* summarized the events, referring both to the photo scandal and to Pius's huge, grandiose funeral.[6]

Within the ecclesiastical community, the merchandising of the papal body was seen as a symptom of the Church's more general malaise in the aftermath of Pius XII's highly ritualized and hierarchical papacy. Historians are still debating to what extent the election of Angelo Roncalli, then the patriarch of Venice, as Pope John XXIII was

a conscious response by the conclave to that malaise. In any case, soon after Pope John took office he adopted provisions to prevent such a scandal from recurring. He made a rule that no photographs could be taken of the papal corpse until the body had been dressed in episcopal garb. He also ordered that the funeral ceremony be conducted according to a more sober liturgy than in the past, and did away with the special contraption that allowed the pope's body to disappear with a theatrical flourish into the crypt of St. Peter's. Stripping the papal burial rite of those dramatic touches and what he saw as pointless high sacrality, John XXIII sought to make sure the death of future popes was not "tabloidized."[7]

But by the late 1950s, faith and the media, the sacred and the spectacular had become so tightly bound as to defy a pope's best intentions. John XXIII could exclude as many photographers as he wished from the rooms of a deceased pope, but the *paparazzi* (another neologism from those years, derived from the name of the photographer in Fellini's film *La Dolce Vita*) still had their lenses trained on the living. In San Giovanni Rotondo the flash bulbs were popping nearly every day as Padre Pio celebrated the Eucharist with bare hands, the stigmata highly visible. Roncalli himself was under the lights from dawn until dusk, besieged by photographers and the subject of constant chatter about his heroic works and wondrous holiness.

The highest form of scoop the press could aspire to were revelations that involved *both* "good Pope John" and the Capuchin with the stigmata. In 1959, for example, *La Settimana Incom Illustrata*,[8] one of the biggest photo magazines of the time, published an "exclusive" cover story with the title "Padre Pio predicted Roncalli would become Pope," complete with a photo of the aging little Capuchin (a tiny picture next to a giant one of the stunning young actress Claudia Cardinale). To his boilerplate account of Padre Pio's life and miracles, the magazine's special correspondent in San Giovanni Rotondo added a "never before published" tale that demonstrated "the Capuchin's extraordinary divinatory powers." According to the article, the future John XXIII had traveled to the Gargano in 1956 to meet Padre Pio, who had predicted his election as pope. This visit had remained a secret until after the death of Pius XII, when, "right before the doors of the Conclave were opened" to announce the new pontiff, the just-elected Roncalli confided to several cardinals he had been moved by that "unique prophecy." That evening, "one of the new pope's first telegrams went to Padre Pio."[9] The story, indeed, had never been published before, for good reason: it was completely invented.

The *Settimana Incom* scoop came out just as another miracle marked Padre Pio's existence: another miracle cure, although this time the friar was the patient, not the healer. During the summer of 1959, the Capuchin with the stigmata had been so ill that doctors had despaired of saving him. Bronchopneumonia, pleurisy, lung cancer—the diagnoses varied, but the death sentence pronounced by the doctors summoned to San Giovanni was always the same.[10] Between May and July Padre Pio was too sick to say the mass or even to attend it, and it was only by means of a loudspeaker installed in his cell that he was able to follow the service in the monastery church. Then, on August 5, came the miracle. In those days a small wooden statue was traveling, mostly by helicopter, around Italy: a likeness of the Virgin carved to commemorate Mary's 1917 appearance to three shepherd children in the skies over Fatima, in Portugal. When the statue reached San Giovanni, a "human tide quivering with excitement" met the "Celestial Pilgrim" on the clearing in front of Santa Maria delle Grazie.[11] All were possessed by the same idea: that Our Lady of Fatima could save Padre Pio.

The miracle happened right on schedule. Father Agostino of San Marco in Lamis recorded the moment.

Just as the helicopter with the sacred statue of the Virgin prepared to depart from the friary, Padre Pio spoke to the heavenly Mother, his heart burning with love: "My sweetest Little Mother, ever since you came to Italy I have been suffering from the torpor of illness, and now you are leaving and you say nothing?" . . . In that moment Padre Pio felt a kind of mysterious force in his body, and he said to his brothers, "I am well again!"[12]

Who knows whether this wondrous news from the Gargano reached Federico Fellini, who was just then preparing the opening scenes of his masterpiece *La Dolce Vita*, with their image of a statue of Christ hauled by a helicopter through the skies of Rome. In any case, Our Lady of Fatima's intercession for Padre Pio underlines the parallel between the expansion of the Gargano cult into a mass phenomenon and the explosion of sightings of the Virgin in postwar Italy. Both the stigmatic Capuchin and the Marian apparitions spoke to the same religious sensibility, charismatic and visionary.[13]

Right from the start of his mystical career, Padre Pio himself had seen the Virgin appear many times, and he had been amazed to discover that the same was not true of Father Agostino. "You don't see the Madonna?" he had asked him with great curiosity on the eve of the Great War.[14] Padre Pio's Marian conviction stayed with him, glowing like a flame in 1948 Italy[15]—the golden age of flying and weeping Virgins, great weapons in the Church's arsenal for its battle against communism.[16] As for the small, mostly female army of the faithful who were lucky enough to catch sight of the Madonna in Cold War Italy,[17] they often reported being in contact with Padre Pio and sometimes said that he was responsible for the sighting.[18] In glitzy magazines and in humble parish newsletters, in memorable sermons and in cheap hagiographies, Padre Pio's miracles fused with Marian apparitions until they became a single story, a gospel of literal presence and symbolic protection.[19]

Sweetmeats and Tape Recordings

The three shepherd children who saw the "Virgin of the Rosary" appear in a field near Fatima in Portugal in 1917 had reported three secret revelations from the Virgin. Lucia dos Santos, the only one of the children to survive to adulthood, had revealed two of these—a vision of hell and the prediction that an atheist Russia would cause World War II—in 1941, but she had sealed up the third one in an envelope with instructions that the secret not be revealed before 1960. In August 1959, just when the statue of Our Lady of Fatima was bringing Padre Pio back to life, a member of the Holy Office passed along that envelope to John XXIII, but the pope decided not to publicize its contents.[20] His successors, Paul VI and John Paul I, would also remain silent about that most mysterious prophecy in modern Catholicism (a prophecy that had, however, been miraculously revealed to Padre Pio, according to the vox populi).[21] The "third secret" would not be disclosed until 2000, when it would be interpreted as a reference to Ali Agca, the Turkish hitman who shot and nearly killed Pope John Paul II in 1981. The Virgin, many believed, had intervened to sway the assassin's hand.

For the most heated devotees of the Virgin, Pope John XXIII's decision not to divulge the "third secret" of Fatima in 1960 was a mistake.[22] But that choice reflected Roncalli's dislike of all devotional excess, of any kind of piety that was visible and expressive rather than considered and private.[23] "I truly do not think I am made for ecstasy," the patriarch of Venice had confessed to himself in 1958. Two years later, just months before the conclave that would declare him pope, he had deplored "the cheap altars where male and female saints are worshipped," where "the *ignorant devotion* of the faithful is stirred up to exploit their faith and their money."[24] In 1960, Albino Luciani, the bishop of Vittorio Veneto (who for just thirty-three days in 1978 would be John Paul I) expressed similar sentiments in the bulletin of his diocese. Besides warning Catholics about the dangers of "unconscious Marxism and conscious secularism," Monsignor Luciani urged his flock to avoid "muddled and obscure kinds of worship," "those that reveal exaggerated crazes for the supernatural and the unusual." The sole example Monsignor Luciani offered was the cult of Padre Pio.

> The faithful need solid bread (the mass, catechism, the Holy Sacraments) to nourish them, not chocolates, pastries, and sweetmeats that fill them up and dupe them. Among such indigestible sweetmeats, the Bishop notes, are pilgrimages to P. Pio on organized bus tours. Although himself a holy man, P. Pio has some followers whose behavior borders on the ridiculous, on superstition. Priests are forbidden to participate in or lead "pilgrimages" to S. Giovanni Rotondo. As for "prayer groups," the Bishop has not, when asked, permitted them to be formed. Should there be such a group in some parish, it may continue but with reserve, but it would be better if it were allowed to wither away, and let no new ones be created.[25]

Some of Padre Pio's followers saw Monsignor Luciani's hostility as a product of infighting within the Capuchin order, caused by certain bishops coveting the money that the faithful sent to the Gargano.[26] But many in the Church, including the minister general of the Capuchin Order himself, Father Clement of Milwaukee,[27] were beginning to regret the consequences of the freedom that the Gargano cult had enjoyed under Pius XII.

The most serious issues in San Giovanni Rotondo involved confession. Confession had long been a problem for the Church; as far back as the sixteenth century, Cardinal Charles Borromeo had promoted the confessional booth because it permitted a minister of God to listen to confessions without seeing or touching the penitents, and thus without the risk of inflaming his sexual desires. The enforced distance was meant to help men of the cloth overcome the temptation of *sollicitatio ad turpia*—leading the witness, you might say; that is, deliberately drawing the penitent into graphic sexual discussion, "that great abomination ... by which" the priest "satisfies his unbridled and bestial appetites."[28] But even this clever piece of furniture had its difficulties; while the sins revealed to the priest were supposed to be rigorously kept secret, the gesture of kneeling before him to tell those sins and obtain absolution was supposed to be thoroughly public. In an attempt to offer both absolute privacy and full visibility, some parish priests had introduced dividing screens designed to let the penitent be seen but not heard, while others asked the faithful to stand away from the confessional while waiting their turn. But neither of these strategies quite worked with Padre Pio. His fiery temperament often led him to make emphatic gestures when he opened and closed the confessional grate, and to raise his voice when he granted or denied absolution, so that what was meant to be secret became public knowledge. This was not quite the patient peasant-friar who sat and listened to the history of the world's sins, as Orio Vergani had described him. Rather, Padre Pio the confessor tended to break most of the sacramental rules.

The overwhelming number of penitents eager to confess to Padre Pio posed additional problems. In the early 1950s, the swarm of Christian souls around Padre Pio's confessional had led the Capuchins of San Giovanni Rotondo to introduce a booking system, so that only those with a numbered ticket could now hope to kneel before the friar with the stigmata.[29] Even such measures, however, were not enough to cope with the enormous armies of believers signing up for confession. What's worse, the reservation system had been placed in the hands of lay sisters who were longtime members of the friar's inner circle, and

they took advantage of their privileged position to do more or less whatever they wanted. Soon, they were changing the numbered tickets, manipulating lists of penitents, and dictating to Padre Pio exactly when he should occupy his post in the confessional.

These rather unorthodox practices, when added to the envy that much of the church felt regarding the offerings going to the Gargano and John XXIII's distaste for too-charismatic celebrations of Christianity, combined to produce a highly volatile situation. At seventy-three, Padre Pio found himself at the center of another great drama, no less significant than the persecutions by the Holy Office three decades earlier. The affair would reach its climax with the revelation that some of the friar's adversaries had conspired to place recording devices in his cell—and possibly even in his confessional—in order to spy on the intimate life of the living Christ.[30] From what we know, the Holy Office did not instigate the taping, but it is clear that the pope himself was also growing increasingly anxious at this time about the propriety of Padre Pio's relations with his devotees.

The private diaries of John XXIII offer a special insight, from the pinnacle of the Holy Roman Church, of the steady accumulation of his concern. In a "Misc. Note" of January 1960, he commented on the circle of women around Padre Pio, noting down the names of "three *ultra-faithful*: Cleonice Morcaldi, Tina Bellone, and Olga Ieci." "At times there appears a *countess*, somewhat vaguely defined," continued the note, which seemed to raise somewhat trivial questions for a pope involved in preparing Vatican Council II. "Is *Countess* a real title or merely a nickname?"[31] To some extent, Pope John's scrutiny of every feature of the female presences around Padre Pio ("and Cleonice is also called *queen*") can be explained by his well-documented and profound disgust at the mere idea of physical contact with women.[32] But it was also clearly connected to the very real intermixing of clergy and lay folk at Santa Maria delle Grazie. On April 30, the pope noted he had had a significant exchange "a propos of P. Pio" with Father Clement of Milwaukee, the Capuchin minister general. And on May 28, he recorded a "quite warm and candid visit" from the bishop of Padova, Monsignor Bortignon, the Church's leading critic of the friar with the stigmata.[33]

Less than a month later, on June 25, the situation exploded. In the spring of 1960, Monsignor Pietro Parente, the assessor of the Holy Office, had taken possession of the tape reels from the monastery. Finding that those tapes suggested sexual misbehavior on Padre Pio's part, the assessor had no choice but to hand them over to the Holy Father. John XXIII was so struck by what Monsignor Parente told him that he did not even record his state of mind in his diary (which, although private, was also semiofficial), but on four sheets of paper that have never before been published.

> Extremely serious information about P.P. and S. Giov. Rotondo from Msgr. Parente this morning. [Parente's] face and heart ravaged. Thanks to the Lord's grace I feel calm and almost indifferent, as when dealing with a troubling religious mania that is, however, nearing a providential resolution. I am sorry about P.P., who does have a soul to save, and for whom I pray intensely. The events—that is, the discovery by means of tapes, *si vera sunt quae referentur* [if what they imply is true], of his intimate and improper relations with the women who make up the impenetrable praetorian guard around his person—point to

a terrible calamity of souls, a calamity diabolically prepared to discredit the Holy Church in the world, and here in Italy especially. In the serenity of my spirit, I humbly persist in thinking that the Lord *faciat cum tentazione provandum* [is doing this as a test of faith], and that out of this immense deception will come lessons for the clarity and the well-being of the many.[34]

John XXIII apparently never listened to the tapes himself.[35] Although he observed the formality of caution, he showed no doubts about what the Holy Office assessor told him. His notes display no suspicion that reports about the immoral behavior of an ailing seventy-three-year-old friar may be false, nor that those reports might derive (as Padre Pio's friends would later argue) from the extravagant attachment of one of his spiritual daughters, who went so far as to boast that she had had carnal relations with the friar. As Pope John saw it, the sexual exuberance of the *alter Christus* merely confirmed the "calamity of souls" that he had diagnosed decades previously, when he had twice crossed Puglia as the head of missions for the Propaganda Fide but decided not to travel to San Giovanni Rotondo. In his note of June 25, 1960, the pope thus expressed both his sorrow about discovering Padre Pio's shame and the personal pride of one who has not been touched by it. "The reason for my spiritual tranquility, and it is a priceless privilege and grace, is that I feel personally pure of this contamination that for forty years has corroded hundreds of thousands of souls made foolish and deranged to an unheard-of degree," he recorded.[36]

On June 26, John XXIII wrote on the fourth page of his private notes: "Today I called my Secretary of State, Card. Tardini, up here to agree upon how we shall proceed, in silence, with justice, and great charity."[37] Between the lines of pious jargon, the message is clear: the pope was about to order a new apostolic visit to San Giovanni to subdue the "contamination" in the Gargano.

With His Feet on the Ground

The job of apostolic visitor to the Gargano fell to Monsignor Carlo Maccari, secretary general of the Rome diocese.[38] Of Umbrian origins,

Maccari was then just under fifty years old and reputed to be of strong character and solid piety. (In his later career, he would be bishop of Mondovì, then archbishop of Osimo and Ancona—not to mention the target, for some thirty years, of Padre Pio's followers, who accused him of being a terrible hypocrite who came to persecute in the guise of pacifying.)[39] On July 19, Maccari met with the secretary of the Holy Office, Cardinal Alfredo Ottaviani, and the assessor Monsignor Parente; that afternoon he was received by the pope, who advised him to handle the "fearful prospect" of his visit to San Giovanni according to the rule of *omnia videre, in charitate corrigere* (observe all, correct with love).[40] Maccari's task risked being all the more sensitive because the fiftieth anniversary of Padre Pio's ordination was approaching on August 10 that year. Indeed, Maccari's reception on the part of the clergy and lay population of San Giovanni was anything but enthusiastic, and their welcome did not improve during the two months that he remained in San Giovanni.[41]

Much like Monsignor Rossi, the Discalced Carmelite who had carried out the apostolic visit of 1921, Monsignor Maccari met with Padre Pio repeatedly: nine times in all, with the friar sworn anew each time to truth and secrecy. But in his diary of those days, the apostolic visitor noted that those meetings soon became "a real torment" both "for him and for me." In theory, the Vatican envoy and the friar agreed on everything: on the need to make the legal status of the Casa Sollievo more precise; on the need to regulate access to Padre Pio's confessional, so that it would not be determined by the whims of a few zealous female followers; on the fact that photographers and journalists should be kept away to avoid too much media exposure. In practice, however, there was a barrier of reciprocal mistrust between Monsignor Maccari and Padre Pio. "It's clear by now that he does not believe in me and hides the truth; how can I believe him when he says he is sincere and trustworthy?" wrote Maccari after a month of "enervating pursuit of the truth" about Padre Pio.[42]

The friar with the stigmata, for example, did not conceal from the apostolic visitor his suspicion that the Vatican wanted to get hold of that fount of cash offerings that came to San Giovanni, and his belief that the hard line against him derived from the greed of large sectors of the Church. And he conceded little to Monsignor Maccari, who tried in vain to persuade him that there was a common need to impose some order and dignity on the devotional practices at Santa Maria delle Grazie. What about the fanatical scenes by the lay sisters in church and in the reception room? Padre Pio "asked me repeatedly, he almost begged me, not to forbid the post-confession kiss, at least," wrote Maccari. And what about the pilgrims who insisted on seeing the friar up close, even when they hadn't managed to get a numbered ticket for confession? It was natural that the Eucharist was seen by some as "a sort of 'show,' " the friar retorted. The press that celebrated his miracles—the newspapers, magazines, the pious books? "He told me rather fiercely, 'I've never even seen the newspapers and the photographs, what can I do? And as for the pamphlets, that's the bishops' problem—they are the ones who approve them.' " Padre Pio was obstinately stonewalling his visitor. "Reticence, narrowness of mind, lies—these are the weapons he uses to evade my questions . . . Overall impression: pitiful!" Maccari confided to his diary.[43]

Despite these private opinions, Monsignor Maccari's report to the Holy Office was studiously impartial. He was indulgent about the friar's spotty religious education and his casual grasp of theology, which he blamed on his southern origins and his ill health as a seminarist. He skated lightly over the friar's stay in "the hospital for the self-injured" during the Great War. Describing a day in the life of Padre Pio, with mass at the altar and hours in the confessional, Maccari admitted that it was heavy going for a man of his age, though far from miraculous. He found no fault with the friar's daily celebration of the mass. And his overall judgment about Padre Pio's role as a confessor was positive, although he did have some criticisms about form (there was no curtain on the confessional to conceal Padre Pio from public view, and the lay sisters had too much power in dictating time and place). "Many, many people speak with admiration and emotion of the peace and joy found in making confession with Padre Pio," Maccari wrote to the Holy Office. These included not just the lay sisters and the humble women of the town, but also women of the middle class and upper bourgeoisie, as well as bishops and priests, professionals and businessmen. At the same time, the apostolic visitor noted that Padre Pio was far from an ascetic, far from being so absorbed in his heavenly dialogue as to have no concern for earthly vanities. "Innumerable threads, visible or not, keep him in close contact with the outside world," Maccari wrote. "The Capuchin lives in the world of today . . . and he has his feet on the ground." In fact, Padre Pio's life revealed entirely too much "contamination between the sacred and the all too human."[44]

Monsignor Maccari's report looked closely at the routines of Santa Maria delle Grazie, routines both ordinary and unusual. In particular, he provided portraits of three women whom he saw as the virtual bosses of local devotion: Cleonice Morcaldi at the top, and Tina Bellone and Caterina Telfner just below her in authority. (There was no mention of Olga Ieci, who had featured in John XXIII's diary.) Morcaldi, a retired teacher, was "intelligent and extremely cunning," Maccari wrote. Although not very imposing ("slightly shorter than average height, wearied by her years and various infirmities, with a grimace to her mouth derived from paralysis"), Morcaldi had a simple, clear manner of speaking and was able to discuss spiritual matters almost as if she were an abbess. She exercised direct control over the cash that moved back and forth between the friary and the Casa Sollievo hospital, and she did not shrink from the admiration of those who thought that she herself was gifted with special powers. According to charges made by Elvira Serritelli—who denounced herself to Maccari as having been Padre Pio's mistress from 1922 to 1930—Morcaldi had taken her place after 1930 and was still enjoying the carnal favors of the living Christ in 1960.[45]

Tina Bellone was the youngest of the three. Unmarried, well-off, she had moved into a house next to the monastery in order to be near the church, to which she was drawn "with a hysteric's unconscious violence." As the apostolic visitor saw her, she was "the classic unbalanced type." Countess Telfner had a more picturesque story to tell; a woman in her forties, she owed her title to an aristocrat from Perugia who had seduced her while she was his maid and then agreed to marry her. The couple later moved to San Giovanni Rotondo, where the count was in charge of the real estate company connected to the Casa Sollievo. Monsignor Maccari had met the countess three times, coming away with a "pitiful" impression. Fresh-faced and graceful, Caterina Telfner, along with Tina Bellone and Cleonice Morcaldi, would leap at Padre Pio after every mass, kissing him "on the chest, on his arms," and "caressing him, squeezing him." The friar didn't resist; indeed, he was so obliging that a San Giovanni carabinieri officer was moved to tell Maccari that "if it weren't him, and he weren't old, I'd say he was in love!" Father Pellegrino of Sant'Elia a Pianisi, one of the friars questioned by Maccari, had a subtler interpretation. He thought the effusions on display were not sexual but pointed instead to Padre Pio's "twisted sense of self," for the three women had convinced him that he was owed as much veneration as Jesus Christ.[46]

Monsignor Maccari suspended judgment about whether Padre Pio had carnal relations with his favorites, leaving the impression he thought Elvira Serritelli's self-accusation was untrue yet not ruling out the possibility that the friar had yielded to Cleonice Morcaldi's temptations. Instead, the apostolic visitor focused on trying to make the Holy Office understand just how extensive the Padre Pio phenomenon was. The "fanaticism" went far beyond little San Giovanni, he wrote, radiating out to wherever the Capuchin's spiritual daughters resided, and fermenting "idolatry and perhaps even heresy." Spread by the printed pamphlets the pilgrims carried, the holy cards with photos of the "first stigmatic priest," the large-type headlines of the photo magazines, even by records that reproduced "the true voice of Padre Pio of Pietrelcina," propaganda for the Gargano cult had reached the proportions of an "industry" advertising a product—miracles—by means of "religious conceptions that oscillate between superstition and magic." Meanwhile, prayer groups, continuing their accusations against the Vatican hierarchy and even the pope himself, were afire with accusations that the Lord had charged Padre Pio with a mysterious, astonishing mission, said Monsignor Maccari.[47]

And what about Padre Pio himself in all of this? "Here we have another disturbing side to this religious figure," reported Maccari. Although the friar made a pretense of indifference to the ideas and passions bubbling all around him, in fact he was by no means obviously opposed to this "mastodontic . . . machine" of propaganda. A firm gesture on his part would have cooled the zeal of his followers, but the Capuchin was careful never to make it. There was something uncompromisingly ambiguous about him, something that could not quite be pinpointed in his deeds, his words, or his silences. How could one be sure that Padre Pio himself was not the primary material force behind the "vast and dangerous organization" of his devotees? Perhaps, Maccari thought, he himself headed up the "gigantic network that in good faith or not-so-good faith creates the psychological grounds so that 'extraordinary' (hard to demonstrate) events may occur, so that there are 'conversions' (which thanks be to God, take place around every good priest), and reports of 'sainthood,' etc. etc."[48]

We could go on citing from Monsignor Maccari's report to the Holy Office, for the apostolic visitor's words, from the twilight of Padre Pio's existence in San Giovanni Rotondo, are very much like those the historian himself might choose as he nears the end of his exploration of the *alter Christus*'s earthly endeavors. They are words that explain the explicable but also refuse to explain, that surrender to the ineffable. Entire libraries of history will never be able to account for that *something* that makes certain individuals more charismatic than others, be they Martin Luther or Giuseppe Garibaldi, Adolf Hitler or Padre Pio. As Maccari put it:

> How is it that a man who has no exceptional natural qualities and who is anything but free of shadows and defects has been able to build a popularity that has few equals in the religious history of our times? How does one explain the irresistible fascination exerted by this man of the faith with a weary air about him, with rough manners and a disagreeable voice? How do we adequately account for the growing fanaticism around his person, the blind faith of the humble and the great in his powers, considered almost superhuman?[49]

The quest for an explanation tormented Monsignor Maccari all the more because his doubts as a man of intellect were compounded by his doubts as a man of faith. If Padre Pio did not live the life of holiness that his many followers attributed to him, how was it that "God's loving providence" could allow "so much deception"? And why did He choose "such a deficient instrument" to carry out "such vast and lengthy good works"? That the friar's works were significant went without saying; for decades Padre Pio had been a formidable "instrument of mercy, pardon, and peace" in Italy and in the world. But why had the Lord given such a great responsibility to such a small and petty person?[50]

The apostolic visitor ended his report to the Holy Office with a list of practical measures—the umpteenth attempt by the Church to solve the Padre Pio problem. He recommended that the friars of Santa Maria delle Grazie be gradually replaced, and that when a new father guardian was nominated he should come from outside the province. He urged a new legal statute be drawn up for the Casa Sollievo to separate more clearly the spiritual "healing" carried out by the Capuchins from the medical role of the doctors. He proposed a tighter rein when it came to granting the diocese's imprimatur on pious books about Padre Pio. He suggested that the friar's morning mass take place a few hours later, to disrupt the daily schedule of the *bizzoche*. And, finally, he proposed that the faithful be allowed to make confession to Padre Pio no more than once a month.[51] By the end of 1960, the Holy Office had decided to apply all of these recommendations, concluding from Maccari's report that the friar's reputation as a holy man was questionable. "The visit confirmed certain painful doubts about Padre Pio's spirit and conduct, especially in terms of his obedience to the monastic rules, his ascetic behavior, and his reserve in relations with women."[52]

At the end of his last meeting with Padre Pio on September 19, Monsignor Maccari had had an idea about how the friar might redeem the negative impressions of him from Rome.

> Before I left him, as I was accompanying him to the refectory, I said: "Why not write a filial letter to the Holy Father, to renew your vows of absolute obedience and your devout love?" And he replied: "I don't know how to write . . . my hand shakes . . ." And when I insisted, he added: "Please, monsignor, do not insist . . . Otherwise you will make me upset and I will not be able to do anything . . . Me, write to the Pope . . . I'm not capable."[53]

For his part, the pope never dreamed of writing to Padre Pio. The previous year, after the "scoop" in *Settimana Incom*, John XXIII had asked his secretary to inform Monsignor Cesarano, the archbishop of Manfredonia, that the magazine's announcement—"Padre Pio Predicted Roncalli Would Become Pope"—was "totally invented." "I never had any relations with him, nor did I ever see him or write to him, nor did it ever cross my mind to send him blessings, nor did anyone ask me directly or indirectly anything about this, neither before nor after the Conclave, nor at any other time," he wrote.[54] (His memory betrayed him in that list of denials, for he had forgotten his contacts in Paris with Emanuele Brunatto.) The scandal of the tapes had then further reinforced John's suspicions of the friar with the stigmata. And when he met with Monsignor Maccari to hear about the apostolic visit as it neared its end, the pope recorded his private view of matters in San Giovanni Rotondo: "Unfortunately down there, P.P. has shown himself to be a straw idol"—an *idolo di stoppa*, in the Italian expression.[55]

Stoppa (oakum, made of jute fibers) has served the Church for centuries as a symbol of the transitory nature of human life, being burned symbolically during the papal investiture to the chant of *sic transit gloria mundi*.[56] The metaphor that John XXIII thought appropriate for Padre Pio was a pitiless one.

A Pseudo-Christ

Even as the Holy Office was pondering Monsignor Maccari's report, the archbishop of Manfredonia wrote to the pope's secretary, Monsignor Loris Capovilla, to congratulate the pontiff on his "holy inspiration" in sending the apostolic visitor to San Giovanni Rotondo. Monsignor Cesarano said he thought that Maccari had been eminently wise in carrying out his mission, and that the results were already visible, despite the protests of the "usual swindlers, exploiters, and speculators who prey on poor, foolish believers." At last, those from outside San Giovanni could take their places at Padre Pio's confessional without having to submit to the capricious rule of the lay sisters. There were no more brawls inside the church, and the once rambunctious worship was beginning to look like proper devotion. However, warned the archbishop, the lobby of the fanatics had not been entirely laid to rest. Down there in San Giovanni, they were playing on the old legend that Rome was persecuting Padre Pio, "with the same old refrain: 'They're taking P. Pio away!'" And these fanatics were also busy elsewhere: Monsignor Cesarano referred to "a real criminal association that is still howling, no longer openly, but insidiously, sowing dissension and spreading falsehoods."[57]

Now, if that criminal association were to have a boss, we know he would have answered—apart from any aliases—to the name Emanuele Brunatto. And sure enough, that irrepressible con man showed up once again in the Padre Pio story soon after Monsignor Maccari's visit. He did so with a letter from Paris to the office of the Vatican secretary of state—a five-page letter into which he poured all his faith in Padre Pio's sainthood, all his determination to promote the friar's good works, and his ideas about how to accomplish that. He began by recalling the large contribution he had made in 1941 to get Padre Pio's hospital off the ground. That first donation and all his later contributions were "sacred, inalienable, reparatory offerings placed under the exclusive judgment of Padre Pio." Brunatto was incensed because he had heard rumors of a Vatican plan to take the management of the Casa Sollievo della Sofferenza out of the hands of the friar's trustees. He denounced this idea as a legal and moral monster dreamed up by Maccari, "that moron who pretends to speak in the name of the Most Holy Father." The secretary of state was not to let this expropriation happen! Otherwise, Brunatto had in hand "the galleys of a book" based on certain "unique and irrefutable documentation" about the Church that might displease the Holy See.[58]

Brunatto's archive of clerical misdeeds was apparently bottomless. For decades he had been brandishing book galleys as if they were explosives, and the conclusion of his letter (to which, for once, he signed his real name) was wholly in character: "I threaten no one, but I am ready—and all my friends are ready—to blow up this diabolical cabal that has gone on for a third of a century, if Padre Pio's liberty is touched or if even the smallest modification of the structure of his works is made."[59] This remained a constant theme for Brunatto from that point on, as he wandered from one European metropolis to another—Paris,

Rome, London, Geneva—perpetually warning that he was about to unleash a new scandal relating to the Vatican's hard line against Padre Pio of Pietrelcina, and each time finding the Vatican ready to take up secret negotiations with him.[60] In the end, Padre Pio's top apostle did not have a chance to make good on his bluster. He would die in Rome one morning in February 1965, in circumstances that Padre Pio's hagiographers judged to be mysterious, suggesting that he had been poisoned.[61]

Aside from Brunatto's extortionist maneuvers, Padre Pio's followers mainly turned to the press to try to minimize the consequences of Monsignor Maccari's visit. Thanks to the pro-Pio bias both among Catholics and in the media, it wasn't difficult to broadcast the message that the friar was being persecuted by rogue elements within the Vatican. "Padre Pio Betrayed" was the title of an "investigative report" published in a leading weekly in the fall of 1960, for example. Its author, Libero Montesi, a respected journalist, fell hook, line, and sinker for the version of affairs promulgated by the zealots of San Giovanni, describing Padre Pio as a "prisoner in his monastery" and Monsignor Maccari as the man who "had put the bars up."[62] In the media, the efforts of "good Pope John" to control devotion in San Giovanni were made to look like a harsh restraint on popular religious expression.

Throughout the 1960s, the popular press mounted tireless campaigns on behalf of the friar with the stigmata, castigating his detractors as enemies of the true Church and turning the story into a gripping tale of sainthood and betrayal.[63] Basing themselves mainly on the material that Emanuele Brunatto had been collecting for decades, their articles were soon transformed into books that shaped the new hagiographic line: Padre Pio as a lonely hero battling the mighty Church of John XXIII.[64] The mass media photo magazines of the 1970s and '80s followed a similar template, and by the 1990s and 2000s a new generation of enterprising writers was putting out "definitive biographies" of the "miracle saint." Printed by mainstream publishing houses, these books quickly climbed the national best-seller lists.[65]

It is typical of the hagiographic genre to reiterate other, earlier texts—the *Lives* and *Passions* of a saint written by his or her contemporaries. Later authors often merely rewrite the early versions, so that what is supposed to be history is really no more than memory.[66] We need not be surprised, therefore, if these so-called biographies of Padre Pio add up to no more than a rehashing of the same reports about the living saint and his miracles that had flourished in the Gargano since 1918. What *is* worth looking at is the social and political humus that fed the so-called investigative reporting: the right-wing forces, from papist to monarchist to neo-Fascist, that were busy trying to revive the spiritual heritage of clerico-fascism in the second half of the twentieth century.[67]

The journalists who in those decades devoted themselves most wholeheartedly to the media canonization of Padre Pio were the same men who were cooking up nostalgic feuilletons about the dear departed Mussolini, his poor little mistress Claretta Petacci, and Rachele, his indomitable wife.[68] When he was not flattering the friar with the stigmata, Mino Caudana was wowing the readers of *Il Tempo* with serial tales like *The Blacksmith's Son*, an evangelical account of the life, death, and miracles of Il Duce.[69] Francobaldo Chiocci, an ex-militant in the neo-Fascist party the Italian Social Movement, was a zealous recycler of anecdotal trash that would establish him as both the admiring biographer of Emanuele Brunatto and the author of a saccharine *Lady Rachele*.[70] The friar's most ardent fan in the group was the journalist and neo-Fascist Giorgio Pisanò, who also distinguished himself in the postwar battle to politically rehabilitate the Nazi-backed Republic of Salò.[71] Meanwhile, *Il Secolo d'Italia* was publishing articles about Padre Pio under the byline of Giorgio Berlutti—the printer from Viterbo who had disappeared from view when his Libreria del Littorio went bankrupt in the early 1930s but who resurfaced as an author during World War II, with titles in the vein of *We Believe in Il Duce* alternating with others like *Return to Love in the Footsteps of Jesus*.[72]

The way that Il Duce and Padre Pio coexisted in the reactionary imagination of the 1960s should not really surprise us. Both ideology and the personal itineraries of the principal players were contributing factors: the legacy that Mussolini-era clerico-fascism transmitted to post-Fascist Republican Italy, and the fact that many of those who broke into journalism after the war had been knocking around in neo-Fascist circles. Nevertheless, the vitality of Duce and Saint in the 1960s reflects not only what the right-wing press was ready to supply, but also what Italian society was demanding. In a country giddily suspended between archaism and modernity, two stars of the twentieth century—Il Duce, dead, and the Saint, living—met a powerful need for grace and charisma. Above all, they met a still burning need for miracles.

It would fall to Father Giuseppe De Luca—a former Fascist and the onetime enthusiast of Padre Pio who had written such an admiring letter about him to Papini back in 1934[73]—to produce a stern indictment of the sort of miracles on which the worship of the Capuchin friar rested.[74] In the weekly column that John XXIII asked him to write for *L'Osservatore Romano*,[75] De Luca evoked the remote Basilicata region where he had grown up at the beginning of the century. Recalling the traveling salesmen who came to make their pitches for all kinds of useless goods, De Luca suggested that it was not so different from contemporary Italy, where swarms of "quacks, swindlers, tricksters, witches, spiritualists, and other voodoo peddlers of the same stripe" sold not only foolish gadgets and knickknacks but actual miracles—including miracles of healing, which false Christian piety suggested were the crux of belief.

"False Christs and false prophets will appear," wrote Don De Luca, quoting the Gospel of Matthew.[76] Few readers of *L'Osservatore Romano* would have failed to notice that the leading false Christ whom De Luca referred to was the miracle worker of San Giovanni Rotondo.

The Final Pageant

One measure of Padre Pio's importance in twentieth-century religious history is the way that his fortunes went up and down with each new pope. Between 1918 and 1968, every pontiff tried, directly or indirectly, to put his stamp on Padre Pio. Benedict XV was skeptical about the nascent saint and allowed the Holy Office to pursue him. Pius XI was even more suspicious; under his papacy the Church divested the friar of nearly all his priestly powers. Pius XII, on the other hand, allowed the Gargano cult free rein. John XXIII, however, took a big step backward and devoted much effort to containing the worship of the "Saint."

Paul VI—born Giovanni Battista Montini—was the last pope to rule over Padre Pio's earthly life, and he, too, left his mark. While he had been Vatican deputy secretary of state after World War II, Montini had played an important role in securing UNRRA funding for the Casa Sollievo hospital.[77] Upon being elected pope in June 1963, he lost no time in showing his benevolence toward Padre Pio once again. In February 1964, the Holy Office notified the Capuchin minister provincial in Foggia that the Holy Father wanted Padre Pio to exercise his ministry "in full liberty." A few weeks later, Padre Pio was allowed once again to meet with women who wanted to talk to him. The following year, Cardinal Alfredo Ottaviani, acting for Pope Paul, would instruct the Capuchins to ceremonialize Padre Pio's seventy-seventh birthday with the dispensation that he could behave "as if he were no longer bound by the Capuchin vow of humility."[78] In short, Paul VI did all he could to make the friar's last years untroubled.

Providence took care of the rest. According to several of his followers, during the summer of 1968, the stigmata on Padre Pio's hands began to heal. On September 20 of that year, at a mass to celebrate the fiftieth anniversary of the appearance of those holy wounds, some

sharp-eyed observers, looking at the friar's bare hands, noted that the stigmata had disappeared altogether.[79] Did this mean that Padre Pio's role as a Christ figure had now been played out to the full? Was he soon to die and then be reborn?

Padre Pio breathed his last just three days later, during the night of September 23, 1968. In a report to his superiors, Father Carmelo of San Giovanni in Galdo, the father guardian of Santa Maria delle Grazie, wrote that when he saw the body the wounds "were completely healed and showed no scars." Was this one more gift from the Lord, to spare the friar the holy suffering he had undergone in life? Or did it simply mean that Padre Pio had no more blood left in his body? Father Carmelo did not attempt to answer these questions.[80] Hadn't another Puglia saint, Joseph of Copertino, been found after death without blood in the pericardium, "his very heart dry"?[81]

Often in Christian history, when a saint approached death his suffering miraculously disappeared.[82] Still, the last miracle of Padre Pio's life—the disappearance of the stigmata—created some problems for the Capuchins laying out his body. When it was placed in the bier for the funeral ceremony, there was really no need for half gloves on the

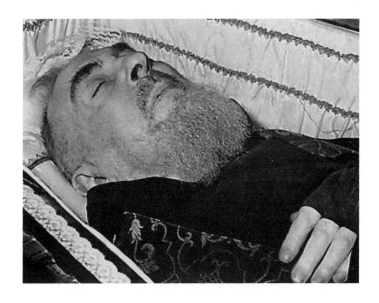

friar's hands or socks on his feet like those that had served for fifty years to hide the bloody mystery of the five wounds. With the wounds now healed, there was nothing left to hide. Padre Pio could now have his hands free—as, after 1918, they had only been during the Eucharist—and he could now, in death, embrace the Capuchin rule that explicitly forbade wearing socks. But his father guardian saw things differently. If Padre Pio's body were laid out with his hands and feet bare, the disappearance of the stigmata might give rise to "false and hasty interpretations" and create "scandal among the humble," he wrote. It was better to leave the impression that the stigmata were still in place, rather than venture an explanation that was "for many reasons impossible to make to the great majority."[83] And so the many thousands of Christians who filed by the bier saw Padre Pio as he had been for the previous half century: with hands and feet covered to conceal the painful, sacred gift.

It seems unlikely that Father Carmelo had read Roland Barthes. And yet, the father guardian's decision to clothe Padre Pio's body with gloves and socks hewed very close to the analysis Barthes made in *Mythologies* when he wrote about the iconography of the Abbé Pierre.[84] Padre Pio's legendary status was also based on the power of an icon, and the stigmata were a significant feature of that icon. For half a century, it had been the friar's job not only to perform miracles but to embody Christ. That had been Padre Pio's brand image in the twentieth-century market of Christian faith, and after his death consumers would have been suspicious if the product were in any way adulterated.

EPILOGUE: MAY 2, 1999

"Let us not try to understand. The destiny of some saints, in life, is among the deepest mysteries of the Church." So Ignazio Silone summed up his *Story of a Humble Christian*, a play about Pope Celestine V that he published in the same year that Padre Pio died.[1] And in fact, the story of the friar with the stigmata demonstrates the paradoxes of sainthood in modern times. When a saint is first recognized, he or she belongs to a particular place and time. How does such an exquisitely local figure become a universal model for the greater church? The journey to sainthood is not a simple one.[2]

Holiness may first be *perceived*—as an image, an odor—long before it is expressed in words.[3] Hagiography serves to remove the figure of the saint from the immediacy of the senses—sight, touch, smell—and transport it to the realm of language; it takes flesh and makes it word. But hagiography depends on official sanction, for the Church forbids saints to be recognized as such before the official process of canonization, and even goes to the trouble of repressing word of any sainthood that has not been officially declared. On the other hand, canon law states that a saint can be recognized as such after his or her death only if he or she had *already* been renowned as holy in life. Thus Christian saints, from the Middle Ages onward, have had to live on the cusp between local and global, between immediate and delayed, as well as on the very slippery divide between the mundane and the otherworldly. Saints are utterly unlike ordinary people, yet they live in the here and now, like everyone else. They are deeply immersed in a transcendent time frame, yet dependent on a profane sequence of events, on earthly time.[4]

As a twentieth-century saint,[5] Padre Pio fully experienced this ancient, complicated balance, but with an additional complication: the means of communication intrinsic to modernity have greatly speeded up the rhythms of hagiography and have vastly enlarged the geographic reach of its message.[6] From the late nineteenth century onward— thanks to the postage stamp and the railroad, photography and lino- type, the automobile and the inter-city bus—the vox populi that builds a reputation for sainthood has found formidable new instruments to spread the word.[7] In turn, the Church has increasingly mistrusted all charismatic and miracle-based devotion, which is always at risk of devolving into what is called superstition. And the progress of ratio- nalism has also made the Church itself more cautious about proclaim- ing sainthood, so as not to expose itself to the criticism of the skeptics.

All these factors (to which we must add the Capuchin friar's unique status as a priest with stigmata) help to explain why Padre Pio of Pietrelcina's story was so troubled, so laborious, so fitful. And they help to account for a final performance: the one offered in St. Peter's Square in Rome on a glorious spring day in 1999.

❖

On Sunday, May 2, 1999, with more than a million of the faithful from all over gathered before him, Pope John Paul II celebrated the beatifica- tion of Padre Pio. Karol Wojtyla himself, by this time, was a man of suffering, visibly ill with the disease that would bring his life to an end. He had visited the friar with the stigmata in the spring of 1948 as a young theology student; he had returned in 1974 as cardinal arch- bishop of Cracow; he had come to San Giovanni Rotondo as pope in 1987 for the centenary of the friar's birth.[8] Now, in beatifying Padre Pio, he was completing his devotion.

Nearly eight hundred years before, when Pope Gregory IX signed the bull that made Francis of Assisi a saint, the pope was careful not to make any mention of Francis's stigmata.[9] John Paul II took an entirely different approach, choosing to emphasize Padre Pio's role as a Christ figure. "Those who went to San Giovanni Rotondo to hear his mass, to ask his advice, or to make confession to him could detect in him the living image of a suffering, risen Christ," explained the pope during

the ceremony of beatification. "Marked by the 'stigmata,'" Padre Pio's body "displayed the intimate link between death and resurrection that composes the mystery of Christ's return."[10] The friar from the Gargano was also worthy of sainthood for other reasons: for the charity that had led him to found the Casa Sollievo della Sofferenza, for the humility that he had shown during the painful trials he underwent on his path to perfection. But what made Padre Pio exceptional in the story of Christianity, made him comparable to no one but St. Francis, was the fact that he had offered an "exact replica of the stigmata of Our Lord." "He was bread broken for men hungry for God the Father's pardon," said John Paul II.[11]

We shouldn't read these words as mere phrase-making, nor can they be dismissed as just garnish for the generous sainthood policy of Pope John Paul II—a willingness to beatify so flexible and inclusive as to be all but indiscriminate.[12] Padre Pio's beatification, quickly followed by his canonization in 2002, was the last act in a long conflict, the last battle in a war inside the Catholic Church that had gone on for sixty years: from September 20, 1918, when Padre Pio was pierced by the stigmata, until October 16, 1978, when Karol Wojtyla was elected pope. As late as May 1976, the prelates of the Congregation for the

Doctrine of the Faith (as the Holy Office was now called) had said no to examining the case for Padre Pio's beatification, on behalf of which Monsignor Wojtyla and nineteen other cardinals had filed an appeal. But after the election of the pope from Cracow, the matter was quickly reopened. Within a few years, first the Congregation for the Doctrine of the Faith and then the Congregation for the Causes of Saints had agreed to allow that case for beatification to go ahead.[13]

From the seventeenth century onward, beatification ceremonies in St. Peter's Square have served a dual purpose. As baroque performance events, they served to stage—and promote—the spectacle of sainthood. As ecclesiastical occasions, they served to demonstrate the good relations between high Church and low, between the clergy and lay believers, between high-ranking Vatican officials and the great community of the baptized.[14] On May 2, 1999, the ceremony for Padre Pio also served those two purposes. It offered a spectacle in which Catholicism still looked fresh, sprightly, and attractive on the eve of the third millennium. And it buried forever the complicated, embattled side of Padre Pio's experience as a living saint. But the May 2 ceremony was also designed with a third purpose in mind. By openly declaring that Padre Pio was the bread of the Supper and the replica of the Crucified

Christ, John Paul II meant to affirm his notion of the Church as incarnation[15]—that is, a Church not as the "people of God," as John XXIII had proposed in Vatican Council II, but as the "mystical body of Christ," as in Pius XII's encyclical by the same name. A Church to see, to smell, to touch, just as for half a century the body of Padre Pio had been seen, smelled, and touched.

❖

Meanwhile, close to the Capuchin friary at San Giovanni Rotondo, a new church devoted to the cult of Padre Pio was nearing completion. Designed by Renzo Piano, one of the world's best-known architects, the building stood as proof of the gigantic leap in scale that the cult had made in fifty years. The tiny old chapel—the one "without marble or bronze," its whitewashed walls covered with pencil script, which Orio Vergani had so memorably described—had given way to a larger church built during the economic boom of the late 1950s, and that one was yielding in turn to a twenty-first-century temple of glass and concrete, big enough to hold eight thousand of the faithful and with room for many thousands more in the plaza outside.[16] Vergani, writing in the *Corriere della Sera* in 1950, could not have been less prescient when he

wrote that Padre Pio's little chapel would remain "ever-so-poor" through the ages. And Piano's monumental edifice could not be less in keeping with the rules of sobriety laid down in the sixteenth century by the Capuchin order's founders: "Make the church . . . small," "spaces should be small and unadorned, both churches and habitations."[17]

Padre Pio's faithful—millions every year—throng to San Giovanni Rotondo, players in the religious drama that is a pilgrimage to a famous sanctuary. The steps they take are predictable, almost prescribed, as if veneration for a mystic were itself an outward form of mysticism.[18] Near Padre Pio's tomb, behind rows of windows like those at a post office, functionaries of the cult take care of the bureaucratic side of saintly intercession: the masses, the novenas, the written requests for grace to lay on the saint's sarcophagus. The "customers" (as Paul VI defined them)[19] are equally divided—according to sociological studies—between men and women, northerners and southerners, city dwellers and country folk.[20] Around Santa Maria delle Grazie and the Casa Sollievo della Sofferenza, the town of San Giovanni has grown into a city of thirty thousand people. There had been 25 hotels in 1978; now they total 150, and there are some 100 restaurants and 150 cafés.[21] From time to time a debate about this flourishing business of sainthood—about the tourist industry, the medical services at the hospital, or the uses to which religious offerings are put—will explode, then die down.

But the devout of the third millennium do not need to go all the way to the Gargano to commune with Padre Pio. They can subscribe to *The Voice of Padre Pio*, a glossy monthly magazine published in six languages, hundreds of thousands of copies of which are printed by the Capuchin provincial administration. They can tune in to the satellite channel Tele Padre Pio and watch as a fixed camera shows off the endless queue of the faithful lining up to see the tomb of the saint. Or they can merely look around them, in the streets and squares, in the cafés and stores, in the workplaces and cemeteries of their cities. In today's Italy, images of Padre Pio are everywhere: the statue in the park, the calendar on the wall, the figure in the Christmas crèche, the sticker on the windshield, the holy cards and framed pictures in the market, the crocheted portrait, the vinyl garden statue, the carving on the tombstone.

The stigmatic friar's virtual existence positively takes flight on the Web, where enthusiasts of postmodern sainthood can satisfy their fetishistic passion for relics, their petty bourgeois fascination with the weird, or their extreme taste for the paranormal.[22] And this proliferation of Web sites reflects a reality that is anything but virtual, a sort of pulp nonfiction that is documented every day in the human interest pages of the newspapers. A young Roman who has been in a coma for ten years, attached to a mechanical ventilator, is saved from dying during a blackout by two guardian angels: "the holy cards of Padre Pio and Pope John that his family once stuck on the machine with tape."[23] An elderly mother from Livorno prays over the dead body of her son, looks after him as if he were still alive, and expires herself next to his putrefying remains, surrounded by dozens of pictures of Padre Pio.[24] A young Roman mother who decides that she would rather die than have a second gangrenous leg amputated keeps a photo of Padre Pio by her side even though she has lost her faith.[25] A family from Foggia—father, mother, and son—die in a gas explosion that destroys their house, but the two daughters are saved thanks to the intervention of Padre Pio, whose portrait hangs on the only wall that did not collapse.[26] The relatives of the carabinieri officers who died in Iraq kneel before the flag-draped coffins, with images of Padre Pio and Mother Teresa set up between the biers.[27]

In Niccolò Ammaniti's recent novel *The Crossroads,* today's ambiguous Italian humanity—the smooth-talking Catholic social worker, the depressed trickster–night watchman, the murderous cripple—all have just two things in common: their squalid lives and their devotion to Padre Pio.[28] Ammaniti was right on the mark when he wrote of the Gargano saint as the idol of the humble, the forsaken. ("God takes it out on the losers," he said.)[29] But Padre Pio does not merely come to the aid of the pariah-Christians, the last who will one day be the first. He also comes to the aid of Italy's powerful—and they want to be sure we know it. Thus Giulio Andreotti, the very symbol of postwar Christian Democrat rule and now a life senator with a penchant for history, declares that "Padre Pio is the most important thing that has happened between 1900 and today."[30] Thus Senator Guiseppe Pisanu, former center-right minister, is among the first to reserve a spot in the queue to visit

 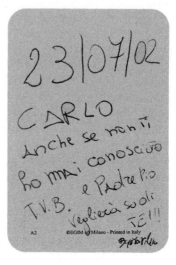

Padre Pio's crypt and file before the TV camera of Tele Padre Pio.[31] Thus the leading centrist politician Francesco Rutelli takes off on a pilgrimage to San Giovanni in order to get inspiration about whom to endorse for the office of president of the republic.[32] And what about Prime Minister Silvio Berlusconi's right-hand man and his favorite journalist, both of whom sport a framed portrait of Berlusconi over their desks with a Padre Pio holy card tucked inside the frame?[33] Or Berlusconi himself, who keeps the friar's holy card in a prominent place in his villa outside Milan, and who managed to sneak a picture of Padre Pio into the glossy book of election propaganda he mailed to millions of Italians?[34]

On Italy's contemporary political stage, private beliefs frequently blend into public matters,[35] and very often Padre Pio is there. He is there even in places that seem to have nothing to do with his story—in Piazza Alimonda in Genoa, for instance, where in July 2001 a young antiglobalization militant named Carlo Giuliani was killed by a carabinieri officer during the Group of Eight summit demonstrations.[36] For several years after Giuliani's death, a kind of lay altar was maintained in the piazza, where sympathizers could meditate, pray, or leave messages of condolence. One of those messages was scrawled on the back of a Padre Pio holy card: just a few words, in the style and language of today's teenagers. "Carlo, even though I never met you, T.V.B. [I love you] and Padre Pio will look out for you!!! by Marilena."[37]

NOTES

Abbreviations

AAI:Amministrazione attività assistenziali italiane e internazionali (Italian and international aid bureau)

ACDF: Archivio per la Congregazione della Dottrina della Fede (Vatican Archive for the Congregation of the Doctrine of the Faith, formerly Holy Office)

ACS: Archivio Centrale dello Stato (State Archives, Rome)

AFSCIRE: Archive of the Foundation for Religious Sciences John XXIII, Bologna

AJM: Archives de la Justice militaire (Military justice archive, Le Blanc, département Indre, France)

ASV: Archivio Segreto Vaticano

CPC: Casellario politico centrale (Political dossier archive)

DAGR: Divisione affari generali e riservati (General/confidential affairs division)

DGPS: Direzione Generale di Pubblica Sicurezza (Chief of police)

DPP: Divisione Polizia Politica (Political intelligence division)

MI: Ministero degli Interni (Interior ministry)

SPD: Segreteria particolare del Duce (Office of Il Duce)

UNA: United Nations Archives, New York

UNRRA: United Nations Relief and Rehabilitation Administration

Prologue: September 20, 1918

1. Pio da Pietrelcina, *Epistolario*, vol. 1, *Corrispondenza con i direttori spirituali (1910–1922)*, Melchiorre da Pobladura and Alessandro da Ripabottoni, eds., fourth edition, Edizioni Padre Pio da Pietrelcina, San Giovanni Rotondo, 2000, p. 1094 (to Father Benedetto of San Marco in Lamis, Oct. 22, 1918).

2. Ibid., pp. 1090 and 1094 (Oct. 17 and Oct. 22, 1918).

3. Survey by A. Bobbio, "I più amati dagli italiani: i santi nella storia," *Famiglia cristiana* 76, no. 45 (Nov. 5, 2006), pp. 66–69.

4. See Pio da Pietrelcina, *Epistolario*, vol. 1, p. 234 (to Father Benedetto of San Marco in Lamis, Sept. 8, 1911) and p. 669 (to Father Agostino of San Marco in Lamis, Oct. 10, 1915).

5. See G. Procacci, *Dalla rassegnazione alla rivolta. Mentalità e comportamenti politici nella Grande Guerra* (Rome: Bulzoni, 1999), pp. 340–64.

6. See A. Becker, *La guerre et la foi. De la mort à la mémoire, 1914–1930* (Paris: Armand Colin, 1994), pp. 17–50.

7. See M. Isenghi, *La Grande Guerra* (Florence: Giunti, 1993), p. 90; and M. D'Amelia, *La mamma* (Bologna: il Mulino, 2005), pp. 195 ff.

8. A. Cortellessa, *Fra le parentesi della storia*, in Cortellessa, ed., *Le notti chiare erano tutte un'alba. Antologia dei poeti italiani nella Prima guerra mondiale* (Milan: Bruno Mondadori, 1998), pp. 148 ff.

9. See S. Owen, *Great War*, in J. L. Houlden, ed., *Jesus in History, Thought and Culture. An encyclopedia*, ABC-Clio, Santa Barbara, 2003, vol. 1, pp. 323–25; M. Franzinelli, ed., *Il volto religioso della guerra. Santini e immaginette per soldati* (Faenza: Editore Faenza, 2003).

10. See A. Gibelli, *L'officina della guerra. La Grande Guerra e le trasformazioni del mondo mentale* (Turin: Bollati Boringhieri, 1991).

11. Cortellessa, *Fra le parentesi della storia*, p. 361.

12. See S. Delaporte, *Les gueules cassées. Les blessées de la face de la Grande Guerre* (Paris: Éditions Noêsis, 1996); B. Bracco, *I caduti e i mutilati della grande guerra a Milano: retorica della morte e uso politico del corpo*, in Bracco, ed., *Combattere a Milano, 1915–1918. Il corpo e la guerra nella capitale del fronte interno* (Milan: Editoriale Il Ponte, 2005), pp. 99–117.

13. Pio da Pietrelcina, *Epistolario*, vol. 1, p. 1097 (to Father Benedetto of San Marco in Lamis, Nov. 13, 1918).

14. N. Moscardelli, *Tatuaggi* (Florence: Libreria della Voce, 1916).

15. E. Tognotti, *La spagnola in Italia. Storia dell'influenza che fece temere la fine del mondo (1918–1919)* (Milan: Angeli, 2002).

16. See F. Morcaldi, *San Giovanni Rotondo nella luce del Francescanesimo* (Parma: Edizioni Mantilli, 1960), p. 173.

17. Father Giovanni Perin, in E. Franzina, *Lettere contadine e diari di parroci di fronte alla prima guerra mondiale*, in M. Isenghi, ed., *Operai e contadini nella Grande Guerra* (Bologna: Cappelli, 1982), p. 138.

18. See A. Prosperi, *L'eresia del Libro Grande. Storia di Giorgio Siculo e della sua setta* (Milan: Feltrinelli, 2000), pp. 234–35.

19. See M. Bloch, *The Royal Touch; Sacred Monarchy and Scrofula in England and France*, J. E. Anderson, trans. (1924; London: Routledge and Kegan Paul, 1973).

20. See É. Fouilloux, *Le due vie della pietà cattolica nel XX secolo*, in G. Alberigo and A. Riccardi, eds., *Chiesa e papato nel mondo contemporaneo* (Rome-Bari: Laterza, 1990), pp. 293 ff.

21. See J.-M. Sallmann, "Sainteté et société," in S. Boesch Gajano, ed., *Santità, culti, agiografia. Temi e prospettive* (Rome: Viella, 1997), pp. 337–39.

22. Methodological considerations are in P. J. Geary, *Furta sacra. Thefts of Relics in the Central Middle Ages* (Princeton: Princeton University Press, 1978), pp. 3 ff.; and in A. Boureau, *L'événement sans fin. Récit et christianisme au Moyen Âge* (Paris: Les Belles Lettres, 1993), pp. 9 ff.

23. See M. de Certeau, *Mystique*, in *Encyclopaedia universalis*, vol. 12, Encyclopaedia universalis, Paris, 1985, pp. 874–76; A. M. Kleinberg, *Prophets in Their Own Country. Living Saints and the Making of Sainthood in the Later Middle Ages* (Chicago: University of Chicago Press, 1992).

24. M. D'Eramo, "Francesco Forgione, la brama di credere," *Il Manifesto*, Aug. 6, 2002.

25. Too many to list here; some titles appear below in notes. For a more serious spiritual portrait, see P. Zovatto, *Padre Pio: il santo più carismatico del secolo*, in Zovatto, ed., *Storia della spiritualità italiana* (Rome: Città Nuova Editrice, 2002), pp. 701–98.

26. Y. Chiron, *Padre Pio. Le stigmatisé* (1989; Paris: Perrin, 2004); C. B. Ruffin, *Padre Pio: The True Story*, Our Sunday Visitor, Huntington, Indiana, 1991; J. Bouflet, *Padre Pio. Des foudres du Saint-Office à la splendeur de la vérité* (Paris: Presses de la Renaissance, 2002).

27. Ch. J. McKevitt, "Suffering and Sanctity. An Anthropological Study of a Saint Cult in a Southern Italian Town," Ph.D. thesis (Department of Anthropology), London School of Economics, 1989; M. I. Macioti, "L'ultimo dei beati: padre Pio da Pietrelcina," *La critica sociologica* 129 (June 1999), pp. 139–50; P. J. Margry, "Merchandising and Sanctity: The Invasive Cult of Padre Pio," *Journal of Modern Italian Studies* 7, no. 1 (2002), pp. 88–115.

28. I. Silone, *Bread and Wine*, Eric Mosbacher, trans. (1955; New York: New American Library, 1986).

29. See S. Boesch Gajano and M. Modica, eds., *Miracoli: dai segni alla storia* (Rome: Viella, 1999); R. Michetti, ed., *Notai, miracoli e culto dei santi: pubblicita e autenticazione del sacro tra XII e XV secolo* (Milan: Giuffrè, 2004).

30. See A. Vauchez's excellent "Les stigmates de saint François et leur détracteurs dans les derniers siècles du Moyen Âge," in *Mélanges d'archéologie et d'histoire* 80 (1968), pp. 595–625. Also C. Bernardi et al., eds., *Il corpo glorioso. Il riscatto dell'uomo nelle teologie e nelle rappresentazioni della resurrezione* (Pisa: Pacini, 2006).

31. W. A. Christian, *Moving Crucifixes in Modern Spain* (Princeton: Princeton University Press, 1992), esp. pp. 51 ff.

32. A. Prosperi, "Storia della pietà, oggi," *Archivio italiano per la storia della pietà* 9 (1996), p. 28.

33. See A. Melloni, "Archivi della chiesa e storia del fascismo," *Il Mulino* 5 (2003), p. 883.

34. Vauchez, "Les stigmates," p. 623.

35. See Stanislao da Campagnola, *L'angelo del sesto sigillo e l' "alter Christus." Genesi e sviluppo di due celebrazioni francescane nei secoli XIII-XIV*, Università degli studi di Perugia, Perugia, 1971; G. Miccoli, *Francesco d'Assisi. Realtà e memoria di un'esperienza cristiana* (Turin: Einaudi, 1991), pp. 56–84.

36. A. Kleinberg, *Histoires de saints. Leur rôle dans la formation de l'Occident* (Paris: Gallimard, 2005).

37. The "change of climate" phrasing was used by Lucien Febvre to describe another time and place. L. Febvre, "Changement de climat. À Amiens, de la Renaissance à la Contre-Réforme," in his *Au cœur religieux du XVIe siècle* (Paris: SEVPEN, 1957), pp. 274–90.

38. The reference is to E. Rossi, *Il manganello e l'aspersorio* (1958), ed. M. Franzinelli (Milan: Kaos edizioni, 2000); R. A. Webster, *The Cross and the*

Fasces: Christian Democracy and Fascism in Italy (Stanford: Stanford University Press, 1960).

39. See C. Ipsen, *Demografia totalitaria. Il problema della popolazione nell'Italia fascista* (Bologna: il Mulino, 1997); A. Treves, *Le nascite e la politica nell'Italia del Novecento* (Milan: Led, 2001).

40. See G. Todeschini, *Ricchezza francescana. Dalla povertà volontaria alla società di mercato* (Bologna: il Mulino, 2004), esp. pp. 186 ff.

41. On the value of the arcane, see G. Pozzi, *Grammatica e retorica dei santi* (Milan: Vita e pensiero, 1997), pp. 39 ff.

42. A. Gramsci, *Letters from Prison*, ed. Frank Rosengarten, trans. Raymond Rosenthal, 2 vols. (New York: Columbia University Press, 1994). On the figure of "Donna Bisodia" in the popular imagination, see E. Sanguineti, *Giornalino, 1973–1975* (Turin: Einaudi, 1976), pp. 185–87. On unlearned interpretations of Latin, G. L. Beccaria, *Sicuterat: il latino di chi non lo sa. Bibbia e liturgia nell'italiano e nei dialetti* (Milan: Garzanti, 1999).

43. On the limits of a too-sharp distinction between institutional religiosity and popular faith, see G. De Rosa, "Religione popolare o religione prescritta?" in De Rosa, *Chiesa e religione popolare nel Mezzogiorno* (Rome-Bari: Laterza, 1978), pp. 3–21; P. Brown, *The Cult of the Saints: Its Rise and Function in Latin Christianity* (Chicago: University of Chicago Press, 1980); W. A. Christian, *Local Religion in Sixteenth Century Spain* (Princeton: Princeton University Press, 1981).

44. F. Sardelli, *I miracoli di Padrepio che avvenettero veramende, potesse stiantare chi non ci crede. Ame* (Livorno: Mario Cardinali editore, 2002 [collection from the monthly *Il Vernacoliere*]), pp. 60 and 70.

45. Ibid., pp. 60 and 70.

46. See M. Ferraris, *Babbo Natale, Gesù adulto. In che cosa crede chi crede?* (Milan: Bompiani, 2006).

47. A. Murray, *Il santo: l'uomo senza classe sociale*, in Murray, *Ragione e società nel Medioevo* (1978; Rome: Editori Riuniti, 2002), pp. 397–415.

1. A Living Christ

1. U. Aubert, "La nostra inchiesta sulla tragica giornata di San Giovanni Rotondo (dal nostro inviato speciale)," *L'Avvenire delle Puglie*, n.d. (evidently Oct. 18, 1920).

2. A. Del Fante, *Dal dubbio alla fede. A Padre Pio di Pietrelcina* (Bologna: Galleri, 1931), p. 10.

3. See pp. 53 ff.

4. The most reliable source is C. B. Ruffin, *Padre Pio: The True Story*, Our Sunday Visitor, Huntington, Indiana, 1991.

5. See M. Rosa, "La Chiesa meridionale nell'età della Controriforma," in *Storia d'Italia*, Annali vol. 9, *La Chiesa e il potere politico dal Medioevo all'età contemporanea*, G. Chittolini and G. Miccoli, eds. (Turin: Einaudi, 1986), pp. 344–45. See also M. Rosa, *Clero cattolico e società europea nell'età moderna* (Rome-Bari: Laterza, 2006), pp. 118–28; R. Rusconi, "Gli Ordini religiosi maschili dalla Controriforma alle soppressioni settecentesche. Cultura,

predicazione, missioni," in M. Rosa, ed., *Clero e società nell'Italia moderna* (Rome-Bari: Laterza, 1991), pp. 207–74; D. Menozzi and R. Rusconi, eds., *Contro la secolarizzazione. La promozione dei culti tra Pio IX e Leone XIII,* monograph issue of *Rivista di storia del cristianesimo* 1 (2005), pp. 3–131.

6. C. C. Martindale, *Life of Saint Camillus* (Whitefish, Mont.: Kessinger, 2008).

7. See P. Stella, "Il clero e la sua cultura nell'Ottocento," in G. De Rosa, ed., *Storia dell'Italia religiosa,* vol. 3, *L'Italia contemporanea* (Rome-Bari: Laterza, 1995), pp. 106 ff.

8. See S. Vacca, *I Cappuccini in Sicilia. Percorsi di ricerca per una lettura storica* (Rome-Caltanissetta: Sciascia editore, 2003).

9. I draw on G. De Rosa, "La pastoralità nella storia sociale e religiosa del Mezzogiorno," in De Rosa, *Chiesa e religione popolare nel Mezzogiorno* (Rome-Bari: Laterza, 1978), pp. 167–86.

10. See P. Borzomati, *Per una storia della pietà nel Mezzogiorno d'Italia tra Ottocento e Novecento,* in *La società religiosa nell'età moderna* (Naples: Guida, 1973), esp. pp. 622 ff.

11. From G. Cracco, *Prospettive sui santuari. Dal secolo delle devozioni al secolo delle religioni,* in Cracco, ed., *Per una storia dei santuari cristiani dell'Italia: approcci regionali* (Bologna: il Mulino, 2002), p. 47.

12. Padre Pio's remarks, dated 1922, from Alessandro of Ripabottoni, *Padre Pio da Pietrelcina. Un Cireneo per tutti,* Centro culturale francescano convento Immacolata, Foggia, 1974, p. 60.

13. On Capuchin identity see P. Prodi, "I nuovi ordini cappuccini e l'identità cappuccina nella Chiesa dell'età moderna," pp. 8–19; and G. Pozzi, "L'identità cappuccina e i suoi simboli," pp. 48–77, in G. Pozzi and P. Prodi, eds., *I Cappuccini in Emilia-Romagna. Storia di una presenza,* Centro editoriale dehoniano, Bologna, 2002.

14. See S. Nigro, *La tabacchiera di don Lisander. Saggio sui "Promessi sposi"* (Turin: Einaudi, 1996), pp. 141–47.

15. On Capuchin pastoral style, see G. Pozzi, *Grammatica e retorica dei santi* (Milan: Vita e pensiero, 1997), pp. 284–98.

16. See P. Stella, "Prassi religiosa, spiritualità e mistica nell'Ottocento," in De Rosa, ed., *Storia dell'Italia religiosa,* vol. 3, pp. 126 ff.

17. The French Jesuit Auguste Poulain was particularly influential in his *Des grâces d'oraison. Traité de théologie mystique* (Paris: Retaux, 1901).

18. Marchesa Vittoria Colonna, writing to Cardinal Gasparo Contarini in 1536, "Apologia dei Cappuccini," in G. G. Merlo, *Nel nome di san Francesco. Storia dei frati Minori e del francescanesimo sino agli inizi del XVI secolo* (Padua: Editrici Francescane, 2003), p. 397. See also G. Miccoli, "Problemi e aspetti della vita religiosa nell'Italia del primo Cinquecento e le origini del cappuccini," in V. Criscuolo, ed., *Ludovico da Fossombrone e l'Ordine dei cappuccini,* Istituto storico dei cappuccini, Rome, 1994, esp. pp. 27 ff.

19. See C. Cargnoni, "L'immagine di san Francesco nella formazione dell'ordine cappuccino," in *L'immagine di Francesco nella storiografia dall'Umanesimo all'Ottocento,* Centro di studi francescani, Assisi, 1983, p. 165.

20. See J. Bouflet, *Padre Pio. Des foudres du Saint-office à la splendeur de la vérité* (Paris: Presses de la Renaissance, 2002), p. 139.

21. A first biographical sketch of Gemma Galgani is in R. Pierri, *La sposa di Gesù Crocifisso* (Milan: Kaos, 2001). A more solid historical approach is in M. Caffiero, "Galgani, Gemma," in *Dizionario biografico degli italiani*, Istituto dell'Enciclopedia italiana, vol. 53, Rome, 1999, pp. 56–59.

22. See A. Prosperi, "Diari femminili e discernimento degli spiriti: le mistiche della prima età moderna in Italia," in Prosperi, *America e Apocalisse e altri saggi*, Istituti editoriali e poligrafici internazionali, Pisa-Rome, 1999, pp. 343–65; A. Malena, *L'eresia dei perfetti. Inquisizione romana ed esperienze mistiche nel Seicento italiano* (Rome: Edizioni di Storia e Letteratura, 2003), esp. pp. 209 ff.; C. Mazzoni, *Saint Hysteria. Neurosis, Mysticism, and Gender in European Culture* (Ithaca: Cornell University Press, 1996); and R. D. E. Burton, *Holy Tears, Holy Blood. Women, Catholicism and the Culture of Suffering in France, 1840–1970* (Ithaca: Cornell University Press, 2004).

23. See R. M. Bell and C. Mazzoni, *The Voices of Gemma Galgani. The Life and Afterlife of a Modern Saint* (Chicago: University of Chicago Press, 2002), p. 173.

24. Germano di San Stanislao, *Biografia di Gemma Galgani, vergine lucchese*, Tipografia pontificia dell'Istituto Pio IX, Rome, 1907. On the book's success, see Pierri, *La sposa*, p. 174.

25. *Lettere ed estasi della serva di Dio Gemma Galgani, raccolte dal p. Germano di San Stanislao passionista*, Tipografia pontificia dell'Istituto Pio IX, Rome, 1909.

26. Pierri, *La sposa*, pp. 174 and 185.

27. Ruffin, *Padre Pio*, pp. 94 ff.

28. G. Esposito and S. Consiglio, *Il divenire inquieto di un desiderio di santità. Padre Pio da Pietrelcina: saggio psicologico*, Edizioni Cantagalli, Siena, 2002, pp. 223 ff.

29. From 1908 to 1919, Father Benedetto of San Marco in Lamis (1872–1942) directed the Capuchin province of Foggia, a role that Father Agostino of San Marco in Lamis (1880–1963) would himself exercise twice (from 1938 to '44 and from 1956 to '59).

30. See Esposito and Consiglio, *Il divenire inquieto*, p. 372 note.

31. Pio da Pietrelcina, *Epistolario*, vol. 1, *Corrispondenza con i direttori spirituali (1910–1922)*, Melchiorre da Pobladura and Alessandro da Ripabottoni, eds., fourth edition, Edizioni Padre Pio da Pietrelcina, San Giovanni Rotondo, 2000, pp. 266–67.

32. See the letter to Signora Imperiali, Sept. 21, in *Lettere ed estasi*, p. 178.

33. G. Mucci, S.I., "Santa Gemma Galgani e san Pio da Pietrelcina. Plagio o identificazione?" *La Civiltà cattolica* 3670 (May 17, 2003), vol. 2, pp. 362–63.

34. Pio da Pietrelcina, *Epistolario*, vol. 1, pp. 278–79.

35. See M. de Certeau, *Mystique*, in *Encyclopaedia universalis*, vol. 12, Encyclopaedia universalis, Paris, 1985, p. 876.

36. See Mucci, *Santa Gemma*, pp. 367–69.

37. See M. Gotor, *Chiesa e santità nell'Italia moderna* (Rome-Bari: Laterza, 2004), pp. 46 ff.

38. I draw on M. Gotor, "'Un paradosso ombreggiato da oscuro enigma': il mito delle origini e Bernardino Ochino nella storiografia cappuccina tra Cinque e Seicento," in M. Firpo, ed., *Nunc alia tempora, alii mores. Storici e storia in età postridentina* (Florence: Olschki, 2005), pp. 211–31.

39. Mattia da Salò, *Historia capuccina*, ed. Melchiorre da Pobladura, Istituto storico dell'ordine dei cappuccini, Rome, 1946, p. 438. (I thank Miguel Gotor for bringing this work to my attention.)

40. See Bouflet, *Padre Pio*, p. 229.

41. da Salò, *Historia capuccina*, p. 439.

42. So, at any rate, thought one of the leading experts on Western mysticism, Elémire Zolla, in an afterword to Pio da Pietrelcina, "Breve trattato sulla notta oscura," *Conoscenza religiosa* 1 (Jan.–Mar. 1970), p. 10. See also P. Borzomati, "La spiritualità di Padre Pio da Pietrelcina. Aspetti e momenti," in F. Atzeni and T. Cabizzosu, eds., *Studi in onore di Ottorino Pietro Alberti* (Cagliari: Edizioni della Torre, 1998), pp. 587–93.

43. Pio da Pietrelcina, *Epistolario*, vol. 1, p. 1093.

44. Ibid., p. 1090 (to Father Benedetto da San Marco in Lamis, Oct. 17, 1918), p. 1121 (to same, Jan. 29, 1919).

45. A. Murray, *Reason and Society in the Middle Ages* (Oxford: Clarendon, 1985); P. J. Geary, "L'humiliation des saints," *Annales. Économies, sociétés, civilizations* 34 (1979), pp. 27–42.

46. See Pio da Pietrelcina, *Epistolario*, vol. 1, p. 1099 (to Padre Pio, Nov. 16, 1918) and p. 1115 (same, Jan. 1919).

47. See Bouflet, *Padre Pio*, pp. 77–78.

48. Pio da Pietrelcina, *Epistolario*, vol. 1, p. 1129 note (letter, Foggia, Mar. 5, 1919).

49. See the excellent discussion by J.-C. Schmitt, *La raison des gestes dans l'Occident médiéval* (Paris: Gallimard, 1990), esp. pp. 62 ff and 335 ff.

50. "Highest gesture," from ibid., p. 316.

51. The nineteenth-century priest Antoine Crozier did briefly bear stigmata, but no special devotion grew up around him; see J. Bouflet, *Les stigmatisés* (Paris: Cerf, 1996), p. 8.

52. C. McKevitt, "'To Suffer and Never to Die': The Concept of Suffering in the Cult of Padre Pio da Pietrelcina," *Journal of Mediterranean Studies* 1, no. 7 (1991), pp. 57–59.

53. Unsigned article, "Il miracolo di un santo. Un soldato guarito istantaneamente a S. Giovanni Rotondo," *Il Giornale d'Italia*, June 1, 1919.

54. A. Gibelli, *Il popolo bambino. Infanzia e nazione dalla Grande Guerra a Salò* (Turin: Einaudi, 2005), pp. 64–66.

55. See esp. M. Serao, *La Madonna e i santi. (Nella fede e nella vita)* (Naples: Trani, 1902). See also G. Ragone, *Un secolo di libri. Storia dell'editoria in Italia dall'Unità al post-moderno* (Turin: Einaudi, 1999), pp. 50–52 and pp. 81–83; and F. Barbagallo, *Il "Mattino" degli Scarfoglio (1892–1928)* (Milan: Guanda, 1979).

56. Unsigned article, "Il miracolo d'un frate cappuccino. Il 'Santo' di S. Giovanni Rotondo," *Il Mattino*, June 4–5, 1919.

57. Pio da Pietrelcina, *Epistolario*, 3, *Corrispondenza con le figlie spirituali (1915–1923)*, Melchiorre da Pobladura and Alessandro da Ripabottoni, eds., Edizioni Padre Pio da Pietrelcina, San Giovanni Rotondo, 2002. Fabroncini was the brother-in-law of Nina Campanile, another teacher.

58. "Il miracolo d'un frate."

59. Ibid.

60. Ibid.

61. Press coverage about Padre Pio's early miracles: Bouflet, *Padre Pio*, pp. 79 ff.

62. Vatican Archive for the Congregation of the Doctrine of the Faith, formerly Holy Office (henceforth ACDF), Santo Offizio, Dev. V. 1919, 1, *Cappuccini*, P. Pio da Pietrelcina, fasc. 1, doc. 1.

63. J.-M. Sallmann makes a convincing case for this in *Chercheurs de trésors et jeteuses de sorts. La quête du surnaturel à Naples au XVIe siècle* (Paris: Aubier, 1986), pp. 89 ff.

64. ACDF, Santo Offizio, Dev. V. 1919, 1, *Cappuccini*, P. Pio da Pietrelcina, fasc. 1, doc. 1.

65. Ibid., doc. 3 (registered letter, Manfredonia, June 28, 1919).

66. Ibid.

67. See chap. 3, pp. 67–87.

68. See Ruffin, *Padre Pio*, pp. 185–86.

69. Report by the prefect Camillo De Fabritiis, Foggia, June 19, 1919 (quoting statement by Ortensio Lecce), in G. Pagnossin, *Il Calvario di Padre Pio*, Tipografia Suman, Padova, 1978, vol. 1, p. 33.

70. Report by prefect to director of public security, Foggia, June 28, 1919 (quoting subprefect of San Severo): ibid., p. 50.

71. Ibid., June 30, 1919, p. 54.

72. F. Chiocci and L. Cirri, *Padre Pio. Storia di una vittima* (Rome: I libri del No, 1967), vol. 3, p. 130.

73. Sample postcards in ACDF, Santo Offizio, Dev. V. 1919, 1, *Cappuccini*, P. Pio da Pietrelcina, fasc. 4, doc. 130.

74. E. Morrica, "L'avventura francescana a S. Giovanni Rotondo. Quel che ne scrive uno scettico," *Il Mattino*, June 30, 1919.

75. E. Morrica, *Deformazione infinitesima delle evolute delle superficie pseudosferiche nella trasformazione complementare e di Baklund*, Tipografia economica B. Giordano, Pisa, 1901.

76. Morrica, "L'avventura francescana."

77. Ibid.

78. Unsigned article, "I miracoli di padre Pio a S. Giovanni Rotondo," *Il Tempo*, June 3, 1919.

79. See "Le Rosier de Saint-François," a. XIX, 1919, pp. 215–16; "L'Écho de Saint François," a. VIII, 1919, pp. 372–73; *Annales franciscaines*, LVIII, (1919), pp. 261–62.

80. This event is masterfully reconstructed in W. A. Christian, *Moving Crucifixes in Modern Spain* (Princeton: Princeton University Press, 1992).

81. See W. A. Christian, *Local Religion in Sixteenth Century Spain* (Princeton: Princeton University Press, 1981).

82. See Christian, *Moving Crucifixes*, p. 91.

83. Ibid., p. 180. I was unable to review these two texts, published in Catalonia by the same house, and titled *Breve noticia biografica del R.do Pio de Pietrelcina*, Imprenta de Fidel Giró, Barcelona, 1921, and *Sucinta relación de la vida del R. P. Pio de Pietra Elcina vulgarmente conocido con el nombre de "Capuccino Santo,"* Imprenta de Fidel Giró, Barcelona, 1921. Details in ACDF, Santo Offizio, Dev. V. 1919, 1, *Cappuccini*, P. Pio da Pietrelcina, fasc. 3, doc. 55 (Jan. 25, 1923).

84. ACDF, Santo Offizio, Dev. V. 1919, 1, *Cappuccini*, P. Pio da Pietrelcina, fasc. 1, doc. 9, all. 1 (letter to Father Pietro of Ischitella, Sept. 14, 1919).

85. Here I draw on P. Camporesi, *La carne impassibile. Salvezza e salute fra Medioevo e Controriforma* (1983; Milan: il Saggiatore, 1991), pp. 99–100.

86. See C. Frugoni, *Vita di un uomo: Francesco d'Assisi* (Turin: Einaudi, 1995), p. 140.

87. See G. Didi-Huberman's thoughtful "Un sang d'images," *Nouvelle revue de psychanalise* 32 (1985), pp. 123–32. For an overview of the anthropological approach, see V. W. Turner, *Bodily Marks*, in *The Encyclopedia of Religion*, di M. Eliade, ed. (New York: Macmillan, 1987), vol. 2, pp. 269–75.

88. ACDF, letter from Monsignor Costa, Sept. 14, 1919.

89. Bouflet, *Padre Pio*, p. 106. On the gift of tears, see P. Nagy, *Le don des larmes au Moyen Âge. Un instrument spirituel en quête d'institution (Ve-XIIIe siècle)* (Paris: Albin Michel, 2000).

90. ACDF, Santo Offizio, Dev. V. 1919, 1, *Cappuccini*, P. Pio da Pietrelcina, fasc. 1., doc. 9, all. 5 (letter from Father Guardian Paolino of Casacalenda to Minister Provincial Pietra of Ischitella, July 31, 1919).

91. Unsigned article, "Il Santo predice la sua propria fine," *Il Mattino*, June 5, 1919.

92. Unsigned article, "Da S. Giovanni Rotondo. I miracoli del Santo," *Il Foglietto di Lucera*, June 4, 1919.

2. Neurosis and Beatitude

1. Gerardo di Flumeri, ed., *Le stigmate di Padre Pio da Pietrelcina. Testimonianze. Relazioni*, Edizioni Padre Pio da Pietrelcina, San Giovanni Rotondo, 1995, p. 151. Dr. Romanelli's report was attached to a letter of May 19, 1919, to the minister provincial Father Pietro of Ischitella.

2. ACDF, Santo Offizio, Dev. V. 1919, 1, *Cappuccini*, P. Pio da Pietrelcina, fasc. 1, doc. 9, all. 4 (letter to Father Pietro of Ischitella, May 19, 1919).

3. See Bouflet, *Padre Pio. Des foudre du Saint-office à la splendeur de la vérité* (Paris: Presses de la Renaissance, 2002), p. 90.

4. See F. M. Snowden, *The Conquest of Malaria. Italy, 1900–1962* (New Haven: Yale University Press, 2006), pp. 38 ff.

5. Bignami's report is found in di Flumeri, *Le stigmate*, pp. 173–79.

6. Ibid, p. 173 note.

7. Cited in R. Allegri, *Padre Pio. Un Santo fra noi* (Milan: Mondadori, 1999), p. 185 (letter from Father Paolino of Casacalenda to Father Pietro of Ischitella, Aug. 8, 1919).

8. ACDF, Santo Offizio, Dev. V. 1919, 1, *Cappuccini*, P. Pio da Pietrelcina, fasc. 1., doc. 9, all. 6 (letter to Father Giuseppe Antonio of Persiceto, Oct. 19, 1919).

9. *Disposizioni della Definizione Provinciale per il Convento di S. Giovanni Rotondo*, ibid., doc. 9, all. 2.

10. *Relazione del P. Provinciale dei Cappuccini di Foggia al P. Generale dell'Ordine, intorno al P. Pio in data 10 ottobre 1919*, ibid., doc. 14, all. 5.

11. Ibid, doc. 9, all. 5 (July 31, 1919).

12. Dated Vatican, Nov. 19, 1919, Cardinal Gasparri's letter is found in Pio da Pietrelcina, *Epistolario*, vol. 1, *Corrispondenza con i direttori spirituali (1910–1922)*, Melchiorre da Pobladura and Alessandro da Ripabottoni, eds., fourth edition, Edizioni Padre Pio da Pietrelcina, San Giovanni Rotondo, 2000, pp. 1201–2 note.

13. On Monsignor Cerretti's visit, on May 28, 1920, see ibid. p. 1201 note.

14. See chap. 4, pp. 88–115.

15. See L. Mangoni, "L'Università cattolica del Sacro Cuore. Una risposta della cultura cattolica alla laicizzazione dell'insegnamento superiore," in *Storia d'Italia, Annali*, vol. 9, *La Chiesa e il potere politico dal Medioevo all'età contemporanea*, G. Chittolini and G. Miccoli, eds. (Turin: Einaudi, 1986), pp. 975–1014.

16. ACDF, Santo Offizio, Dev. V. 1919, 1, *Cappuccini*, P. Pio da Pietrelcina, fasc. 1., doc. 4 (Apr. 19 and July 2, 1920). Gemelli's letter and an appendix sent a few months later are found in Gerardo di Flumeri, *Il beato padre Pio da Pietrelcina*, Edizioni Padre Pio da Pietrelcina, San Giovanni Rotondo, 2001, pp. 421–27.

17. See chap. 1, p. 16.

18. G. Cosmacini, *Gemelli* (Milan: Rizzoli, 1985), p. 95.

19. P. Sabatier, *Life of St. Francis*, L.S. Houghton, trans. (New York: Scribners, 1914). Published in France, 1894, in Italy, 1898.

20. I draw on J. Dalarun, *La malavventura di Francesco d'Assisi. Per un uso storico delle leggende francescane*, Biblioteca francescana, Milan, 1994, pp. 24 ff.

21. See S. Migliore, *Mistica povertà. Riscritture francescane tra '800 e '900*, Edizioni Collegio San Lorenzo da Brindisi, Istituto storico dei cappuccini, Rome, 2001, pp. 38–43.

22. See P. Mazzarello, *Il Nobel dimanticato. La vita e la scienza di Camillo Golgi* (Turin: Bollati Boringhieri, 2006), pp. 419 ff.

23. See Cosmacini, *Gemelli*, pp. 36 ff.

24. Citations, respectively, from *Il Tempo* e *La Lombardia*, in F. Olgiati, *L'Università cattolica del Sacro Cuore* (Milan: Vita e Pensiero, 1955), pp. 8–12.

25. Renato Simoni, "Il fraticello di Rezzato," *Corriere della Sera*, Dec. 4, 1903.

26. See L. Bedeschi, *Modernismo a Milano* (Milan: Pan, 1974), pp. 8 ff; S. G. Franchini, "Nuovi documenti sugli esordi della Società internazionale di studi francescani fondata da Paul Sabatier," *Rivista di storia della Chiesa in Italia*, a. LI, 1, 1997, pp. 35–96.

27. "Carteggio Fogazzaro-Sabatier," E. Passerin d'Entrèves, ed., *Fonti e documenti* (Università di Urbino) 2 (1973), pp. 7 ff.

28. See the important study by P. Marangon, *Il modernismo di Antonio Fogazzaro* (Bologna: il Mulino, 1998), esp. pp. 146 ff.

29. The leading authority remains M. Ranchetti, *Cultura e riforma religiosa nella storia del modernismo* (Turin: Einaudi, 1963), see esp. pp. 128 ff.

30. A. Fogazzaro, *Il santo* (Milan: Baldini and Castoldi, 1905), pp. 211–12.

31. "Corrispondenza Sabatier-Gemelli," *Fonti e documenti* (Università di Urbino) 2 (1793), p. 661 (letter of Dec. 7, 1906).

32. Ibid., p. 659 (letter of Dec. 2, 1906).

33. Ibid., p. 662.

34. See P. Albonetti, "Padre Gemelli et il modernismo," *Fonti e documenti*, pp. 650 ff; Cosmacini, *Gemelli*, pp. 96 ff.

35. E. Preto, ed., *Bibliografia di Padre Agostino Gemelli* (Milan: Vita e Pensiero, 1981).

36. See "Corrispondenza Sabatier-Gemelli," p. 663.

37. See A. Gemelli, "Le stimate di S. Francesco nel giudizio della scienza," *Vita e Pensiero* 10 (1924), fasc. 10, pp. 580–603. See chap. 5, pp. 133 ff.

38. C. Lombroso, *The Man of Genius* (London: Walter Scott, 1891).

39. See D. Frigessi, *Cesare Lombroso* (Turin: Einaudi, 2003), esp. pp. 274–306; P. Mazzarello, *Il genio e l'alienista. La strana visita di Lombroso a Tolstoj* (Turin: Bollati Boringhieri, 2005).

40. A. Gemelli, *Cesare Lombroso. I funerali di un uomo e di una dottrina*, third edition, Libreria editrice fiorentina, Florence, 1911, pp. 138 ff.

41. Ibid., p. 167.

42. A. Gemelli, "Le guarigioni di Lourdes dinnanzi alla scienza," *La Scuola cattolica*, July 1908, pp. 15–32; Gemelli, *La lotta contro Lourdes. Resoconto stenografico della discussione sostenua alla Associazione Sanitaria Milanese (10–11 gennaio 1910) con note e commenti*, Libreria editrice fiorentina, Florence, 1911.

43. See C. Mazzoni, *Saint Hysteria. Neurosis, Mysticism, and Gender in European Culture* (Ithaca: Cornell University Press, 1996).

44. Among the many sources: J. Didi-Huberman, *Invention de l'hystérie. Charcot et l'iconographie photographique de la Salpêtrière* (Paris: Macula, 1982); J. Goldstein, *Console and Classify. The French Psychiatric Profession in the Nineteenth Century* (Cambridge: Cambridge University Press, 1987); N. Edelman, *Les métamorphoses de l'hystérique. Du début du XIXe siècle à la Grande Guerre* (Paris: La Découverte, 2003).

45. A. Gemelli, "Nevrosi e santità. Risultati della psicopatologia nello studio dei fenomeni mistici," *La Scuola cattolica* 40 (1912), pp. 171–85 and pp. 341–55.

46. Ibid., pp. 177–79.

47. Ibid., p. 346.

48. Among the many sources, see esp. S. Kern, *The Culture of Time and Space, 1880–1918* (Cambridge: Harvard University Press, 1983).

49. See G. Papini and G. Prezzolini, *La coltura italiana* (Florence: Lumachi, 1906). A good guide to Papini's thought is M. Isnenghi, *Giovanni Papini* (Florence: La Nuova Italia, 1972).

50. See Y. Chiron, *Padre Pio. Le stigmatisé* (1989; Paris: Perrin, 2004), pp. 60–63.

51. The note is reprinted in Pio da Pietrelcina, *Epistolario*, vol. 1, p. 316 note.

52. See *Epistolario* and his diary: Agostino da San Marco in Lamis, *Diario*, Father Gerardo di Flumeri, ed., Edizioni Padre Pio da Pietrelcina, San Giovanni Rotondo, 1975.

53. G. De Rosa, "I cattolici," in *Il trauma dell'intervento, 1914–1919* (Florence: Vallecchi, 1968), pp. 165–201; L. Bruti Liberati, *Il clero italiano nella grande guerra* (Rome: Editori Riuniti, 1982), pp. 82–83; M. Franzinelli, *Padre Gemelli per la guerra*, La Fiaccola, Ragusa, 1989.

54. According to the hospital chaplain Giovanni De Dominiciis, in R. Morozzo Della Rocca, *La fede e la guerra. Cappellani militari e preti-soldati (1915–1919)* (Rome: Studium, 1980), p. 83.

55. According to the anonymous military chaplain cited in C. Caravaglios, *L'anima religiosa della guerra* (Milan: Mondadori, 1935), p. 80.

56. Unsigned article in a Lecco periodical, "La Comunione dopo la battaglia," *Il Resegone*, Aug. 13–14, 1915.

57. Caravaglios, *L'anima religiosa*, p. 255. (The officer, Lieutenant Angelo Perron of Turin, died at the battle of Ortigara.)

58. From the "highly confidential" letter of Sept. 4, 1915, Archivio Segreto Vaticano (henceforth ASV), Segreteria di Stato, Epoca moderna, Guerra, 1914–18, rubrica 244, fasc. 127, *Padre Gemelli*, 1915–17, doc. 244.G.6.C.

59. See M. Guasco, *La predicazione di Roncalli*, in G. Alberigo, ed., *Papa Giovanni* (Rome-Bari: Laterza, 1987), pp.126 ff. On Roncalli's role as military chaplain, M. Benigni, *Papa Giovanni XXIII chierico e sacerdote a Bergamo, 1892–1921*, Glossa, Milan, 1998, pp. 288–323, offers a faith-based view.

60. Citations, respectively from A. G. Roncalli/Giovanni XXIII, *Lettere ai familiari, 1901–1962*, L. Capovilla, ed. (Rome: Edizioni di Storia e Letteratura, 1968), vol. 1, p. 48 (to his brother Saverio, May 6, 1917); Archive of the Foundation for Religious Sciences John XXIII, Bologna (henceforth AFSCIRE), *Vita militare*, busta 130, *Alle donne bergamasche* (1917); ibid., busta 130, *I nostri giovanissimi territoriali* (1917).

61. See Morozzo Della Rocca, *La fede e la guerra*, p. 84; M. Guasco, *Storia del clero in Italia dall'Ottocento a oggi* (Rome-Bari: Laterza, 1997), pp. 157–58.

62. The war correspondence of Father Agostino of San Marco in Lamis is found in Pio da Pietrelcina, *Epistolario*, vol. 1, pp. 785–1078.

63. G. Boine, *Carteggio*, vol. 2, *Giovanni Boine-Emilio Cecchi (1911–1917)*, M. Marchione and S. E. Scalia, eds. (Rome: Edizioni di Storia e Letteratura, 1972), p. 183 (letter, Boine-Cecchi, Nov. 30, 1915).

64. D. De Napoli, *La Sanità militare in Italia durante la prima guerra mondiale* (Rome: Apes, 1989).

65. The clergy were not exempt from military service until the Fascist era.

66. According to Chaplain Don Guido Astori, in Morozzo Della Rocca, *La fede e la guerra*, p. 137.

67. The now classic work on the subject is A. Gibelli, *L'officina della guerra. La Granda Guerra e le transformazioni del mondo mentale* (Turin: Bollati Boringhieri, 1991). Other essential reading includes B. Bianchi, *La follia e la*

fuga. Nevrosi di guerra, diserzione e disobbedienza nell'esercito italiano (1915–1918) (Rome: Bulzoni, 2001).

68. From the war diary of the Florentine doctor Gino Frontali, *La prima estate di guerra* (Bologna: il Mulino, 1998), p. 71.

69. C. E. Gadda, *Giornale di guerra e di priglonia* (Milan: Garzanti, 1999), p. 134.

70. See Gibelli, *L'officina della guerra*, pp. 10 and 147.

71. See M. Silvestri, *Isonzo, 1917* (Turin: Einaudi, 1965), pp. 85–86.

72. See P. Melograni, *Storia politica della Grande Guerra* (Rome-Bari: Laterza, 1972), pp. 239–43.

73. See M. Isnenghi, *I vinti di Caporetto nella letteratura di guerra* (Padua: Marsilio, 1967), pp. 28 ff.

74. This volume is analyzed by C. Pogliano, "La grande guerra e l'orologio della psiche," *Belfagor* 41, no. 4 (1986), pp. 381–406, esp. pp. 387 ff. See also V. Labita, "Un libro simbolo: *Il nostro soldato* di Agostino Gemelli," *Rivista di storia contemporanea* 3 (1986), pp. 402–29.

75. A. Gemelli, *Il nostro soldato. Saggi di psicologia militare*, preface by Father G. Semeria (Milan: Treves, 1917), pp. 186 ff.

76. A. Palazzeschi, *Due imperi . . . mancati* (1920), M. Biondi, ed. (Milan: Mondadori, 2000), p. 95.

77. Gemelli, *Il nostro soldato*, pp. 129, 174, 218, 325, 332, 336, respectively. On the eugenic implications of Gemelli's diagnosis, see F. Cassata, *Molti, sani e forti. L'eugenetica in Italia* (Turin: Bollati Boringhieri, 2006), pp. 60–61.

78. Pio da Pietrelcina, *Epistolario*, vol. 1, pp. 957–58 (letters to Father Agostino of San Marco in Lamis, Oct. 29 and Nov. 3, 1917).

79. Ibid., p. 942 (letter of Sept. 19, 1917, to Father Benedetto of San Marco in Lamis).

80. Ibid.

81. ASV, Segreteria di Stato, Epoca moderna, Guerra 1914–1918, rubrica 244, fasc. 405, *Sacerdoti militari nella Caserma Sales di Napoli*, 1916, doc. 244.M.6.a.

82. For Rossi's front-line experience and injury, see G. Fiori, *Una storia italiana. Vita di Ernesto Rossi* (Turin: Einaudi, 1997), pp. 28–29.

83. E. Rossi, *Guerra e dopoguerra. Lettere 1915–1930*, G. Armani, ed. (Florence: La Nuova Italia, 1978), pp. 52–53 (letter of Jan. 18, 1917).

84. See ACDF, Santo Offizio, Dev. V. 1919, 1, *Cappuccini*, P. Pio da Pietrelcina, doc. 14, all. 1, pp. 16–17 (*Relazione e proposte del Rev. P. Gemelli O. M.*).

85. See Gemelli, *Il nostro soldato*, pp. 165 ff. See also R. Morozzo Della Rocca, "Il culto dei santi tra i soldati (1915–1918)," in E. Fattorini, ed., *Santi, culti, simboli nell'età della secolarizzazione (1815–1915)* (Turin: Rosenberg and Sellier, 1997), pp. 225–33.

86. See esp. A. Gemelli, "Perché i cattolici italiani debbono avere una loro Università" (1922), in Gemelli, *Idee e battaglie per la coltura cattolica* (Milan: Vita e Pensiero, 1933), pp. 54–60. On Gemelli's project and its relationship with traditional Catholic practice, the best source is G. Miccoli, "Chiesa e

società in Italia fra Ottocento e Novecento: il mito della cristianità" (1980) in Miccoli, *Fra mito della cristianità e secolarizzazione* (Casale Monferrato: Marietti, 1985), pp. 21–92; See also Miccoli, "Padre Agostino Gemelli, Università cattolica e regime fascista," *Studi storici* 45, no. 2, (Apr.–June 2004), pp. 609–24.

87. ACDF, *Relazione e proposte*, pp. 16–17.

88. Ibid., p. 17.

89. See pp. 49–50.

90. ACDF, *Relazione e proposte*, p. 18.

91. Ibid., p. 19.

92. Ibid.

93. See chap. 4, pp. 89 ff.

94. For an analysis of Gemelli's medical approach seventy years after the fact, see L. Cancrini, "Perizia psichiatrica su padre Pio," *MicroMega* 3 (1999), pp. 194–200.

95. R. Striffler, *Guerra di mine nelle Dolomiti: Lagazuoi, Castelletto 1915–1917* (Trento: Panorama, 1997); H. Schneeberger, *La montagna che esplode. Kaiserjäger e alpini sul Castelletto della Tofana* (Udine: Gaspari, 2003).

96. See C. Caravaglios, *I canti delle trincee. Contributo al folklore di guerra* (Rome: Leonardo da Vinci, 1930), p. iii (epigraph). On Delcroix, see A. Vittoria, "Delcroix, Carlo," in *Dizionario biografico degli italiani*, vol. 36, Istituto dell'Enciclopedia italiana, Rome, 1988, pp. 471–77.

97. See M. Mariani, *Povero cristo* (Milan: Sonzogno, 1920).

98. On the importance of the Fiume adventure in the Fascist imagination, see M. A. Ledeen, *D'Annunzio a Fiume* (Rome-Bari: Laterza, 1975); C. Salaris, *Alla festa della rivoluzione. Artisti e libertari con D'Annunzio a Fiume* (Bologna: il Mulino, 2002).

99. C. Malaparte, *Viva Caporetto. Rivolta dei santi maledetti*, M. Biondi, ed. (1921; Florence: Valecchi, 1995). The best guide to this period of Malaparte's work is M. Biondi, "I giorni dell'ira. Apologia di Caporetto," in Biondi, *Scrittori e miti totalitari. Malaparte Pratolini Silone* (Florence: Edizioni Polistampa, 2002), pp. 13 ff.

100. Palazzeschi, *Due imperi . . . mancati*, pp. 169–70.

101. Soffici's remark is in F. T. Marinetti and A. Palazzeschi, *Carteggio*, P. Prestigiacomo, ed. (Milan: Mondadori, 1978), p. 162 (letter of July 1, 1920).

102. Ibid., p. 143.

103. G. Papini and A. Vallecchi, *Carteggio (1914–1941)*, M. Gozzini, ed. (Florence: Vallecchi, 1984), p. 128 (letter of Sept. 15, 1919).

104. Ibid., p. 119 (letter of July 17, 1919).

105. G. Ragone, *Un secolo di libri. Storia dell'editoria in Italia dall'Unità al post-moderno* (Turin: Einaudi, 1999), p. 101 and note, p. 114.

106. D. Giuliotti and G. Papini, *Carteggio*, vol. 1, 1913–1927, N. Vian, ed. (Rome: Edizioni di Storia e Letteratura, 1984), p. 76 (letter to Giuliotti, Sept. 30, 1920).

107. Ibid.

108. See A. M. Fiocchi S.I., "Giovanni Papini e il padre Enrico Rosa S. I. (Su documentazione del nostro Archivio)," *Civiltà cattolica* 3 (1956), pp. 253–57.

109. The best account remains P. Nardi, *Antonio Fogazzaro* (Milan: Mondadori, 1938), pp. 555 ff.

110. M. Ciliberto, "Tra 'societas christiana' e cesarismo: Giovanni Papini," in S. Gentili, ed., *Giovanni Papini* (Milan: Vita e Pensiero, 1983), pp. 83–91; R. Vivarelli, "Osservazioni su uno scritto politico di Giovanni Papini," in M. Herling and G. Reale, eds., *Storia, filosofia, letteratura. Studi in onore di Gennaro Sasso* (Naples: Bibliopolis, 1999), pp. 746–48.

111. Giuliotti and Papini, *Carteggio*, p. 80 (letter to Giuliotti, Oct. 11, 1920).

112. R. Ridolfi, *Vita di Giovanni Papini* (Milan: Mondadori, 1957), p. 205.

113. Giuliotti and Papini, *Carteggio*, p. 99 (May 7, 1921).

114. The friend was Pietro Pancrazi; see C. Di Biase, *Giovanni Papini. L'anima intera*, Edizioni scientifiche italiane, Napoli, 1999, p. 127 note (letter dated Badia Prataglia, Aug. 5, 1921).

115. From a letter by Pancrazi to Papini, Aug. 15, 1921, in Giuliotti and Papini, *Carteggio*, p. 99 note.

116. Di Biase, *Giovanni Papini*, pp. 129 ff. An exception was the critic U. Ojetti, Papini cattolico, in Ojetti, *Cose viste* (1921; Milan: Treves, 1931), pp. 46–51.

117. G. Papini and A. Soffici, *Carteggio*, vol. 4, 1919–1956. *Dal primo al secondo dopoguerra*, Mario Richter, ed. (Rome: Edizioni di Storia e Letteratura, 2002), p. 109 (letter of June 5, 1921).

118. A. Gramsci, *Quaderni del carcere* (Turin: Einaudi, 1975), vol. 2, p. 1033 and vol. 3, p. 2233.

119. See Adolfo Omodeo, *Tradizioni morali e disciplina storica* (Rome-Bari: Laterza, 1929), p. 70.

120. See M. Ranchetti, *Non c'è più religione. Istituzione e verità nel cattolicesimo italiano del Novecento* (Milan: Garzanti, 2003), p. 64.

121. The offer was made in 1922: see Migliore, *Mistica povertà*, p. 153; Fiocchi, "Giovanni Papini," p. 260; for editorship of *Vita e Pensiero*, see Giuliotti and Papini, *Carteggio*, p. 129 (letter, Papini-Giuliotti, June 16, 1922).

122. So Papini, years later, told Don Giuseppe De Luca: G. De Luca and G. Papini, *Carteggio*, vol. 1, 1922–1929, M. Picchi, ed. (Rome: Edizioni di Storia e Letteratura, 1985), p. 71 (letter of Aug. 22, 1925).

123. G. Papini, *Life of Christ*, D. C. Fisher, trans. (New York: Harcourt, Brace, 1923).

124. My reconstruction is based on H. Carr, "Chaplin Explains Chaplin" (1925), in C. Chaplin, *Interviews*, K. J. Hayes, ed. (Jackson: University of Mississippi Press, 2005), pp. 86–87; see also G. Sadoul, *Vita di Charlot* (Turin: Einaudi, 1952), pp. 185–86.

125. See E. Magrì, *Un italiano vero: Pitigrilli* (Milan: Baldini e Castoldi, 1999), p. 61. For the literary context, see S. Castaldi, "'Cocaina' di Pitigrilli: il romanzo erotico si affaccia al Novecento," *UPenn Working Papers in Romance Languages* 3 (1998–99), pp. 17–28.

126. Among the most acute contributors on these themes: R. Gigliucci, "Appunti introduttivi," in Gigliucci, ed., "Espressivismo di destra," *Sincronie. Rivista di letterature, teatro e sistemi di pensiero*, 6, no. 12 (July–Dec. 2002), pp. 71-86; C. Chierichini, "L'espressivismo oscuro di Giovanni Papini," Convention of the American Association for Italian Studies, Genoa, May 25–28, 2006.

127. G. Papini, *Storia di Cristo* (1921), sixth edition (Florence: Vallecchi, 1933), 1, p. xix.

128. Ibid., 2, p. 641.

129. See pp. 182–84.

130. G. Ungaretti, *Lettere a Giovanni Papini, 1915–1948*, M. A. Terzoli, ed. (Milan: Mondadori, 1988), p. 298 (undated letter written between Oct. and Nov. 1920).

131. See E. Costadura, *D'un classicisme à l'autre. France-Italie, 1919–1939* (Saint-Denis: Presses universitaires de Vincennes, 1999), pp. 218 ff.

132. Mussolini himself signed the preface to the second edition of G. Ungaretti, *Il porto sepolto. Poesie*, Stamperia apuana, La Spezia, 1923.

3. Jesus's Shock Troops?

1. The estimate that there were more victims in San Giovanni Rotondo than in any other massacre during the *biennio rosso* is drawn from M. Franzinelli, *Squadristi. Protagonisti e tecniche della violenza fascista, 1919–1922* (Milan: Mondadori, 2003).

2. See Pio da Pietrelcina, *Epistolario*, vol. 1, *Corrispondenza con i direttori spirituali (1910-1922)*, Melchiorre da Pobladura and Alessandro da Ripabottoni, eds., fourth edition, Edizioni Padre Pio da Pietrelcina, San Giovanni Rotondo, 2000, pp. 1174 ff.

3. See F. Morcaldi, *San Giovanni Rotondo nella luce del Francescanesimo* (Parma: Edizioni Mantilli, 1960), p. 198.

4. See M. Fincardi, "I riti della conquista," in *Contributi. Rivista semestrale della biblioteca A. Panizzi di Reggio Emilia*, nos. 21–22, 1987, pp. 97 ff.

5. See G. Sabbatucci, *I combattenti nel primo dopoguerra* (Rome-Bari: Laterza, 1974), pp. 190–241.

6. See F. M. Snowden, *Violence and Great Estates in the South of Italy: Apulia, 1900-1922* (New York: Cambridge University Press, 1986), pp. 168 ff.

7. See S. Colarizi, *Dopoguerra e fascismo in Puglia (1919–1926)* (Rome-Bari: Laterza, 1971), pp. 132 ff.

8. See G. Serafini, *I ribelli della montagna. Amiata 1948: anatomia di una rivolta* (Montepulciano: Edizioni del Grifo, 1981).

9. If we can believe G. A. Chiurco, *Storia della rivoluzione fascista*, vol. 2, (1920; Florence: Vallecchi, 1929), pp. 103–4. Franzinelli, *Squadristi*, p. 294, does not report the deaths of the clerk, the field hand, and the child.

10. See R. Vivarelli, *Storia delle origini del fascismo. L'Italia dalla Grande Guerra alla marcia su Roma* (Bologna: il Mulino, 1991), vol. 2, p. 473.

11. Unsigned article, "Undici morti ed ottanta feriti a San Giovanni Rotondo," *Corriere delle Puglie*, Oct. 15, 1920.

12. "Il massacro di S. Giovanni Rotondo. La nostra inchiesta," *Avanti!* Oct. 19, 1920.

13. ACS, MI, DGPS, 1920, b. 103, fasc. *Foggia*, "Relazione sull'eccidio di S. Giovanni Rotondo," Rome, Nov. 2, 1920, signed by Inspector General of Public Security Vincenzo Trani: attachment, transcripts no. 4 (Rev. Giovanni Miscio) and no. 10 (Alfonso Pirro, Popular Party militant).

14. Franzinelli, *Squadristi*, p. 9.

15. See Snowden, *Violence and Great Estates*, pp. 100–102.

16. "Undici morti."

17. Results are drawn from G. B. Guerri, ed., *Rapporto al duce. L'agonia di una nazione nei colloqui tra Mussolini e i federali nel 1942* (1978; Milan: Mondadori, 2002), p. 186.

18. Ibid., telegraph office, San Giovanni Rotondo, telegram from Alfredo Conte to San Severo subprefecture, Oct. 10, 1920.

19. ACS, MI, DGPS, 1920, b. 103, fasc. *Foggia*, telegraph office, San Giovanni Rotondo, telegram from Carabiniere Inspector Giuseppe Galante to San Severo, Oct. 10, 1920.

20. See E. Alessandrone Perona, "La bandiera rossa," in M. Isnenghi, ed., *I luoghi della memoria. Simboli e miti dell'Italia unita* (Rome-Bari: Laterza, 1996), pp. 3003–5. On the events in Siena, Mar. 1920, see E. Gentile, *Storia del partito fascista, 1919–1922. Movimento e milizia* (Rome-Bari: Laterza, 1989), p. 507; for Milan, see Franzinelli, *Squadristi*, p. 44, as well as the correspondence of F. Turati and A. Kuliscioff, *Carteggio*, vol. 5, *Dopoguerra e fascismo (1919–22)*, A. Schiavi, ed. (Turin: Einaudi, 1953), pp. 287 ff.

21. See A. Lyttelton, *The Seizure of Power: Fascism in Italy, 1919–1929* (1973; London: Routledge, 2004); M. Isnenghi, *L'Italia in piazza. I luoghi della vita pubblica dal 1848 ai nostri giorni* (Milan: Mondadori, 1994), pp. 252–54.

22. See S. Caretti, *La rivoluzione russa e il socialismo italiano (1917–1921)* (Pisa: Nistri-Lischi, 1974).

23. Quotations from Gentile, *Storia del partito fascista*, pp. 506 ff.

24. ACS, MI, DGPS, 1920, b. 103, fasc. *Foggia*, "Relazione sull'eccidio."

25. Ibid., attachment, transcript no. 8.

26. For this (and much of what follows), I rely on Vivarelli, *Storia delle origini del fascismo*, vol. 2, pp. 388–423.

27. S. Pivato, "L'anticlericalismo 'religioso' nel socialismo italiano fra Otto e Novecento," *Italia contemporanea* 154 (Mar. 1984), pp. 29–50; Pivato, "Materiali per una storia della religiosità popolare laica," *Movimento operaio e socialista* 10 (1987), pp. 237–49; P. Audenino, *L'avvenire del passato. Utopia e moralità nella sinistra italiana alle soglie del XX secolo* (Milan: Unicopli, 2002).

28. Vivarelli, *Storia delle origini del fascismo*, vol. 2, p. 214.

29. Ibid., p. 707 note.

30. See ACS, MI, DGPS, 1920, b. 103, fasc. *Foggia*, "Relazione sull'eccidio."

31. See F. Molfese, *Storia del brigantaggio dopo l'Unità* (Milan: Feltrinelli, 1964), pp. 20–21.

32. ACS, MI, DGPS, 1920, b. 103, fasc. *Foggia*, "Relazione sull'eccidio," attachment, transcript no. 17/3 (Francesco Guia).

33. Ibid., attachment, no. 16 (deposition-letter).

34. See ibid., attachment, transcript no. 2 (Gennaro Russo, brigadiere).

35. Ibid., attachment, transcript no. 4 (Reverend Giovanni Miscio, Popular Party section leader).

36. See ibid., "Relazione sull'eccidio."

37. See G. Rochat, *Gli arditi della Grande Guerra. Origini, battaglie e miti* (1981; Gorizia: Editrice Goriziana, 1990), pp. 37 ff.

38. ACS, MI, DGPS, 1920, b. 103, fasc. *Foggia*, "Relazione sull'eccidio": attachment, transcript no. 8 (Gigante).

39. Ibid., attachment, transcript no. 12 (Ettore Fiorentino, "landowner, treasurer of the Veterans cooperative").

40. Ibid., attachment, transcript no. 4 (Reverend Miscio).

41. See Snowden, *Violence and Great Estates*, p. 48.

42. ACS, MI, DGPS, 1920, b. 103, fasc. *Foggia*, "Relazione sull'eccidio": attachment, transcript no. 4 (Reverend Miscio).

43. See Lyttelton, *The Seizure of Power*.

44. The figures are in Franzinelli, *Squadristi*, p. 46.

45. ACS, MI, DGPS, 1920, b. 103, fasc. *Foggia*, "Relazione sull'eccidio": attachment, transcript no. 6.

46. U. Aubert, "La nostra inchiesta sulla tragica giornata di San Giovanni Rotondo (dal nostro inviato speciale)," *L'Avvenire delle Puglie*, n.d. (Oct. 18, 1920).

47. "Il massacro di S. Giovanni Rotondo."

48. ACS, MI, DGPS, 1920, b. 103, fasc. *Foggia*, report by Prefect Regard, Foggia, Oct. 20, 1920.

49. Ibid. Two others died later from injuries, bringing the total victims to thirteen.

50. Ibid.

51. On relations between Giolitti and Corradini, see G. De Rosa, *Il Partito popolare italiano* (1966; Rome-Bari: Laterza, 1977), p. 86.

52. Sturzo letter, ACS, MI, DGPS, 1920, b. 103, fasc. *Foggia*.

53. *Inchiesta dell'onorevole Vincenzo Ursi sui tragici fatti di S. Giovanni Rotondo*, ACS, MI, DGPS, 1920, b. 103, fasc. *Foggia*.

54. See L. M. Faccini, *Un poliziotto perbene* (Lerici: Faccini, 2002); although somewhat fictionalized, the book provides useful biographical information.

55. See unsigned article, "L'ispettore generale della P.S. a S. Giovanni Rotondo," *Il Giornale d'Italia*, Oct. 21, 1921.

56. ACS, MI, DGPS, 1920, b. 103, fasc. *Foggia*, "Relazione sull'eccidio" (dated Nov. 2, 1920).

57. See C. E. Gadda (1957), *That Awful Mess on the Via Merulana*, W. Weaver, trans. (New York: New York Review Books, 2007).

58. ACS, MI, DGPS, 1920, b. 103, fasc. *Foggia*, "Relazione sull'eccidio."

59. Ibid.

60. Ibid.

61. See E. Francescangeli, *Gli Arditi del popoli. Argo Secondari e la prima organizzazione antifascista, 1917–1922* (Rome: Odradek, 2000). On the development of the movement in Puglia, see Colarizi, *Dopoguerra e fascismo*, p. 220.

62. See S. Tramontin, *Dalla ribellione all'organizzazione: le leghe bianche e l'opera di G. Corazzin a Treviso, 1910–1925* (Treviso: Tipografia editrice trevigiana, 1982), pp. 65–66.

63. ACS, MI, DGPS, 1920, b. 103, fasc. *Foggia*, "Relazione sull'eccidio" (letter attached to Trani's report, sent by him to Alfredo Conte, Oct. 21, 1920).

64. See *Atti parlamentari*, Chamber of Deputies, Twenty-fifth Legislature, session one, Dec. 4, 1920, question session, pp. 6246–52.

65. See ibid., p. 6247.

66. Ibid., p. 6247–48.

67. Ibid., p. 6250.

68. See Vivarelli, *Storia delle origini del fascismo*, vol. 2, p. 904.

69. For background, see A. L. Cardoza, *Agrarian Elites and Italian Fascism: The Province of Bologna, 1901–1926* (Princeton: Princeton University Press, 1982).

70. See M. Ridolfi, *Le feste nazionali* (Bologna: il Mulino, 2003), p. 149; M. Mondini, "La festa mancata. I militari e la memoria della Grande Guerra, 1918–1923," *Contemporanea. Rivista di storia dell'800 e del'900*, 7, no. 4 (Oct. 2004), pp. 555–78.

71. See N. S. Onofri, *La strage di palazzo D'Accursio. Origine e nascita del fascismo bolognese* (Milan: Feltrinelli, 1980), pp. 260 ff.

72. On Giulio Giordani and Bolognese veteran ultranationalism, led by Angelo Manaresi and the Italian Alpine Club, see A. Pastore, *Alpinismo e storia d'Italia. Dall'Unità alla Resistenza* (Bologna: il Mulino, 2003), pp. 147 ff.

73. See C. Delcroix, *Il secondo olocausto: in commemorazione dell'avv. Giulio Giordani, nel trigesimo della morte: Bologna, Teatro comunale, 21 dicembre 1920*, Associazione nazionale mutilati e invalidi di guerra, Bologna, 1921.

74. See M. Berezin, *Making the Fascist Self: The Political Culture of Interwar Italy* (Ithaca: Cornell University Press, 1997), pp. 196 ff.

75. A. Del Fante, *Giulio Giordani martire del fascismo* (Bologna: Galleri, 1934), p. 45.

76. See chap. 7, pp. 174 ff.

77. See A. Gibelli, *Il popolo bambino. Infanzia e nazione dalla Grande Guerra a Salò* (Turin: Einaudi, 2005), pp. 196 ff.

78. See S. Falasca Zamponi, *Fascist Spectacle. The Aesthetics of Power in Mussolini's Italy* (Berkeley: University of California Press, 1997), pp. 33 ff. See also the valuable reflections of B. Bracco, "I caduti e i mutilati della grande guerra a Milano: retorica della morte e uso politico del corpo," in Bracco, ed., *Combattere a Milano, 1915–1918. Il corpo e la guerra nella capitale del fronte interno* (Milan: Editoriale Il Ponte, 2005), pp. 99–117.

79. On the "mass" adhesion of disabled veterans' association leaders to fascism, see Emilio Lussu's sharp retrospective observations in *Marcia su Roma e dintorni* (1933; Rome: Einaudi, 1945), p. 65.

80. What follows relies on the biographical account (not necessarily reliable) of P. Bruni, *Giuseppe Caradonna e la destra nazionale* (Rome: Serarcangeli, 1996), pp. 108 ff.

81. Ibid., p. 108.

82. See S. Lupo, *Il fascismo. La politica in un regime totalitario* (Rome: Donzelli, 2000), p. 150.

83. The lines echo a World War I tune (*Se non ci conoscete . . .*) popular in many versions in the Ardito and *squadre* movements after the war; see C.

Caravaglios, *I canti delle trincee. Contributo al folklore di querra* (Rome: Leonardo da Vinci, 1930), pp. 308–9.

84. See D. Lajolo, *Il volto umano di un rivoluzionario. La straordinaria avventura di Giuseppe Di Vittorio* (Florence: Vallecchi, 1979), p. 38 note.

85. See Colarizi, *Dopoguerra e fascismo*, pp. 151 ff.; Snowden, *Violence and Great Estates*, pp. 184 ff.

86. See G. Albanese, *La marcia su Roma* (Rome-Bari: Laterza, 2006), p. 88.

87. ACS, MI, DGPS, Direzione generale della Pubblica Sicurezza, 1920, b. 103, fasc. *Foggia*, "Relazione sull'eccidio."

88. See *Atti parlamentari*, Chamber of Deputies, Twenty-fifth Legislature, session one, Dec. 4, 1920, question session, p. 6250 (Mucci).

89. See ibid.

90. The classic study is that of E. Gentile, *Il culto del littorio. La sacralizzazione della politica nell'Italia fascista* (Rome-Bari: Laterza, 1993), pp. 46 ff.

91. I draw on the excellent work of G. Crainz, *Padania. Il mondo dei braccianti dall'Ottocento alla fuga dalle campagne* (Rome: Donzelli, 1994), pp. 183 ff.

92. So one Po Delta *squadrista* recalled later, quoted in M. Isnenghi, *L'Italia in piazza. I luoghi della vita pubblica dal 1848 ai nostri giorni* (Milan: Mondadori, 1994), p. 293.

93. The events are reconstructed in *La storia come identità. I fatti di Sarzana del luglio 1921 nella storiografia nazionale ed europea*, Ippogrifo, Lerici, 2003.

94. See C. Costantini, "I fatti di Sarzana nelle relazioni della Polizia," *Movimento operaio e socialista*, 8, no. 1 (Jan–Mar. 1962), pp. 61–100.

95. Ibid., pp. 92 ff. Renzo De Felice points to the lucidity of Trani's 1921 investigations of Fascist violence in his *Mussolini il rivoluzionario, 1883–1920* (Turin: Einaudi, 1965), pp. 603–4.

96. See Franzinelli, *Squadristi*, p. 127.

4. Holy Man, Holy Office

1. See F. Pieroni Bortolotti, *Francesco Misiano: vita di un internazionalista* (Rome: Editori Riuniti, 1972).

2. As denounced by A. Tasca, *Nascita e avvento del fascismo* (1950; Florence: La Nuova Italia, 1955), p. 260. A glowing account from the Fascist side is in R. Farinacci, *Squadrismo. Dal mio diario della vigilia, 1919–1922* (Rome: Edizioni Ardita, 1933), pp. 64 ff.

3. See G. Fiori, *Il cavaliere dei Rossomori. Vita di Emilio Lussu* (Turin: Einaudi, 1985), pp. 56 ff.

4. Emilio Lussu, *Marcia su Roma e dintorni* (1933; Rome: Einaudi, 1945), p. 28.

5. See F. Chiocci and L. Cirri, *Padre Pio. Storia di una vittima* (Rome: I libri del N., 1967), vol. 1, p. 329.

6. See chap. 2, pp. 58–59.

7. ACDF, Santo Offizio, Dev. V. 1919, 1, *Cappuccini*, P. Pio da Pietrelcina, fasc. 1, doc. 14: *Voto del P. Lemius, Qualificatore del S.O.*, all. 2, pp. 21–22.

8. Ibid., pp. 23–24.

9. See E. Morrica, "L'avventura francescana a S. Giovanni Rotondo. Quel che ne serive uno scettico," *Il Mattino*, June 30, 1919; see chap. 1, pp. 33–34.

10. ACDF, Santo Offizio, Dev. V. 1919, 1, *Cappuccini*, P. Pio da Pietrelcina, fasc. 1, doc. 14: *Voto*, pp. 23–24.

11. Ibid., pp. 25–26.

12. Ibid., all. 3, pp. 26–28.

13. Ibid., doc. 5, letter from Bishop of Foggia to Holy Office, Foggia, July 24, 1920.

14. Ibid., doc. 14, all. 5: *Relazione del P. Provinciale dei Cappuccini di Foggia al P. Generale dell'Ordine, intorno al P. Pio in data 10 ottobre 1919.* (See chap. 2, pp. 40–41.)

15. Ibid., *Voto*, all. 4, p. 29.

16. See M. Gotor, *Chiesa e santità nell'Italia moderna* (Rome-Bari: Laterza, 2004), pp. 110 ff.

17. ACDF, Santo Offizio, Dev. V. 1919, 1, *Cappuccini*, P. Pio da Pietrelcina, fasc. 1, doc. 14: *Voto*, p. 10.

18. See Padre Pio da Pietrelcina, *Epistolario*, vol. 3, *Corrispondenza con le figlie spirituali, (1915–1923)*, Melchiorre de Pobladura and Alessandro da Ripabottoni, eds., Edizioni Padre Pio da Pietrelcina, San Giovanni Rotondo, 2002, pp. 467 ff.

19. ACDF, Santo Offizio, Dev. V. 1919, 1, *Cappuccini*, P. Pio da Pietrelcina, fasc. 1, doc. 14: *Voto*, all. 3, p. 28.

20. See *Annuario pontificio per l'anno 1920*, Tipografia poliglotta vaticana, Rome, 1920, passim.

21. See D. Levasseur, *Histoire ses Missionnaires Oblats de Marie Immaculée. Essai de synthèse*, vol. 2, *1898–1985*, Maison provinciale, Montreal, 1983–86, p. 8.

22. I draw on the persuasive study by G. Daly, *Transcendence and Immanence. A Study in Catholic Modernism and Integralism* (Oxford: Clarendon Press, 1980), pp. 196 ff. It presents incontrovertible evidence that Lemius wrote the encyclical, pp. 232–34.

23. On the *Pascendi*'s impact on the life of the church, see M. Guasco, *Storia del clero in Italia dall'Ottocento a oggi* (Rome-Bari: Laterza, 1997), pp. 153 ff; G. Miccoli, "Intransigentismo, modernismo e antimodernismo: tre risvolti di un'unica crisi," *Ricerche per la storia religiosa di Roma* 8 (1990), pp. 13–38.

24. P. Sabatier, *Life of St. Francis*, L. S. Houghton, trans. (New York: Scribners, 1914).

25. See A. Del Col, *L'Inquisizione in Italia. Dal XII al XXI secolo* (Milan: Mondadori, 2006), pp. 811 ff.

26. See A. Prosperi, *L'Inquisizione romana. Letture e ricerche* (Rome: Edizioni di Storia e Letteratura, 2003), pp. 35 ff. and pp. 229 ff.

27. See A. Prosperi, "L'elemento storico nelle polemiche sulla santità," in G. Zarri, ed., *Finzione e santità tra Medioevo ed età moderna* (Turin: Rosenberg e Sellier, 1991), pp. 88–118; V. Marchetti, "La simulazione di santità nella riflessione medico-legale del sec. XVII," in the same volume, pp. 202–27; A. Prosperi, *Tribunali della coscienza. Inquisitori, confessori, missionari* (Turin:

Einaudi, 1996), pp. 438 ff.; A. Pastore, *Le regole dei corpi. Medicina e disciplina nell'Italia moderna* (Bologna: il Mulino, 2006), pp. 77 ff.

28. See chap. 2, pp. 37–39.

29. ACDF, Santo Offizio, Dev. V. 1919, 1, *Cappuccini*, P. Pio da Pietrelcina, fasc. 1, doc. 14: *Voto*, pp. 3–7.

30. Ibid, pp. 8–13.

31. On the living saint's link with locality, see A. Vauchez, *Sainthood in the Later Middle Ages*, Jean Birrell, trans. (New York: Cambridge University Press, 1997). Many examples of forced transfers are in M. Gotor, *I beati del papa. Santità, Inquisizione e obbedienza in età moderna* (Florence: Olschki, 2002).

32. ACDF, Santo Offizio, Dev. V. 1919, 1, *Cappuccini*, P. Pio da Pietrelcina, fasc. 1, doc. 14: *Voto*, p. 14.

33. Ibid., pp. 14–15.

34. ACDF, Santo Offizio, Dev. V. 1919, 1, *Cappuccini*, P. Pio da Pietrelcina, doc. 15, *Voti e pareri di alcuni consultori*.

35. Rossi is portrayed in the hagiographical study printed by the Carmelite order: F. Della Trinità, *Lane sotto la porpora. La santa vita di un porporato dei nostri giorni: il Cardinale Raffaele Carlo Rossi*, Ordine dei carmelitani scalzi, Rome, 1953.

36. See E. Brambilla, *La giustizia intollerante. Inquisizione e tribunali confessionali in Europa (secoli IV–XVIII)* (Rome: Carocci, 2006), pp. 45 ff.

37. ACDF, Santo Offizio, Dev. V. 1919, 1, *Cappuccini*, P. Pio da Pietrelcina, doc. 21: *Sul P. Pio da Pietrelcina*, pp. 106–7.

38. Ibid., all. 18–24, *Deposizioni del P. Pio da Pietrelcina, Cappuccino*, pp. 117–18 and p. 104, respectively.

39. Ibid., pp. 102–16.

40. Ibid., p. 115.

41. Ibid., pp. 102–17.

42. Ibid., p. 112 and pp. 98–99.

43. Ibid., p. 114.

44. His correspondence and pastoral letters are published in: R. C. Rossi, *Pastore e maestro. Scritti*, V. and V. Bondani, ed. (Milan: Edizioni Ancora, 1971); Rossi, *Epistolario*, V. and V. Bondani, ed. (Rome: Teresianum, 1974–75), two vols.

45. *Pontificale romanum Summorum Pontificum jussu editum a Benedicto XIV et Leone XIII pontificibus maximis recognitum et castigatum* (Turin: Marietti, 1941), pp. 111–12.

46. See V. Lavenia, "Marchio del diavolo," in A. Prosperi and J. Tedeschi, eds., *Dizionario Storico dell'Inquisizione* (Pisa: Edizioni della Scuola Normale Superiore, 2008).

47. ACDF, Santo Offizio, Dev. V. 1919, 1, *Cappuccini*, P. Pio da Pietrelcina, doc. 21: *Sul P. Pio*, pp. 24–38.

48. Ibid., pp. 38–41.

49. Ibid., p. 35.

50. Ibid., p. 19.

51. Ibid., pp. 3–4.

52. Ibid., p. 18.

53. See Prosperi, *L'Inquisizione romana*, p. 232.

54. ACDF, Santo Offizio, Dev. V. 1919, 1, *Cappuccini*, P. Pio da Pietrelcina, doc. 21b: *Lettere e copie di lettere inviate a P. Pio.*

55. Ibid.

56. See M. Bloch, *The Royal Touch; Sacred Monarchy and Scrofula in England and France*, J. E. Anderson, trans. (1924; London: Routledge and Kegan Paul, 1973).

57. See A. Gemelli, "Le guarigioni di Lourdes dinnanzi alla scienza," *La Scuola cattolica*, July 1908, pp. 15–32; Gemelli, *La lotta contro Lourdes. Resoconto stenografico della discussione sostenua alla Associazione Sanitaria Milanese (10–11 gennaio 1910) con note e commenti* (Florence: Libreria editrice fiorentina, 1911).

58. ACDF, Santo Offizio, Dev. V. 1919, 1, *Cappuccini*, P. Pio da Pietrelcina, doc. 21: *Sul P. Pio*, p. 20.

59. Ibid., appendix, *Il P. Benedetto da S. Marco in Lamis, Cappuccino*, pp. 124–25.

60. Ibid., doc. 21: *Sul P. Pio*, p. 16.

61. See J.-C. Schmitt, *Mort d'une hérésie. L'Église et les clercs face aux béguines et aux béghards du Rhin supérieur du XIVe au XVe siècle* (Paris and The Hague: Mouton, 1978), p. 65.

62. The above is based primarily on J. Dalarun, *Robert of Arbrissel: Sex, Sin and Salvation in the Middle Ages*, B. L. Venarde, trans. (Washington: Catholic University of America Press, 2006); J. Coakley, "Friars as Confidants of Holy Women in Medieval Dominican Hagiography," in R. Blumenfeld-Kosinski and T. Szell, eds., *Images of Sainthood in Medieval Europe* (Ithaca: Cornell University Press, 1991), pp. 222–46; C. W. Bynum, *Holy Feast and Holy Fast: The Religious Significance of Food to Medieval Women* (Berkeley and Los Angeles: University of California Press, 1987); A. Prosperi, "Croci nei campi, anime alla porta. Religione popolare e disciplina tridentina nelle campagne padane del '500," in Prosperi, ed., *Il piacere del testo. Saggi e studi per Albano Biondi* (Rome: Bulzoni, 2001), vol. 1, pp. 83–117.

63. ACDF, Santo Offizio, Dev. V. 1919, 1, *Cappuccini*, P. Pio da Pietrelcina, fasc. 1, doc. 21: *Sul P. Pio*, p. 15.

64. Again, readers should consult M. Gotor's masterful study, *I beati del papa*.

65. ACDF, Santo Offizio, Dev. V. 1919, 1, *Cappuccini*, P. Pio da Pietrelcina, fasc. 3, doc. 52 (letter of June 2, 1922).

66. Ibid.

5. A Change of Climate

1. See D. Menozzi, *Il Sacro Cuore. Un culto tra devozione interiore e restaurazione cristiana della società* (Rome: Viella, 2001), pp. 264 ff.; F. De Giorgi, "Forme spirituali, forme simboliche, forme politiche. La devozione al S. Cuore," *Rivista di storia della Chiesa in Italia*, 48, no. 2 (1994), pp. 442–57; P. Di Cori, "Rosso e bianco. La devozione al Sacro Cuore di Gesù nel primo dopoguerra," *Memoria. Rivista di storia delle donne* 5 (1982), pp. 82–107.

2. On the girls' youth organization in Azione Cattolica, see M. Bocci, "Una 'distrazione' storiografica significativa: il caso di Armida Barelli," in *Annali di storia moderna e contemporanea* (Università cattolica del Sacro Cuore) 9 (2003), pp. 429–43. On the importance of Gemelli's vast editorial activities around the review *Vita e Pensiero* and his overall political-religious aims with Pius XI, see esp. G. Rumi, "Profilo culturale della diocesi ambrosiana fra le due guerre," in P. Pecorari, ed., *Chiesa, Azione cattolica e fascismo nell'Italia settentrionale durante il pontificato di Pio XI (1922–1939)* (Milan: Vita e Pensiero, 1979), pp. 321–58.

3. On the well-known dispute between Father Gemelli and Don Sturzo in 1919, see G. De Rosa, *Il Partito popolare italiano* (1966; Rome-Bari: Laterza, 1976), pp. 21–22. More broadly, see G. Vecchio, *I cattolici milanesi e la politica. L'esperienza del Partito popolare (1919–1926)* (Milan: Vita e Pensiero, 1982); G. Sale, *Popolari e destra cattolica al tempo di Benedetto XV* (Milan: Jaca Book, 2006).

4. See E. Gentile, *La Grande Italia. Ascesa e declino del mito della nazione nel ventesimo secolo* (Milan: Mondadori, 1997), pp. 129–30.

5. See A. Gemelli, "Perché i cattolici italiani debbono avere una loro Università" (1919), in Gemelli, *Idee e battaglie per la coltura cattolica*, new edition (Milan: Vita e Pensiero, 1940), pp. 54–60.

6. See G. Miccoli, "Chiesa e società in Italia fra Ottocento e Novecento: il mito della cristianità" (1980), in Miccoli, *Fra mito della cristianità e secolari zzazione* (Casale Monferrato: Marietti, 1985), pp. 85 ff.

7. See G. Gentile, *Discorsi di religione* (1920), fourth edition (Florence: Sansoni, 1957), pp. 9 ff.

8. F. Olgiati, "Mentre s'inaugura l'Università Cattolica del Sacro Cuore," *Rivista del Clero italiano* 2 (1921), p. 531. Don Olgiati's and Father Gemelli's extremely pugnacious ideological stance at the time of the founding of the Catholic University is evident in F. Olgiati, *I nostri giovani ed il coniglismo. Risultati di un questionario* (Milan: Vita e Pensiero, 1922); on Gemelli's concord with Olgiati, beginning prior to the war, see G. Vecchio, "L'Unione giovani cattolici milanesi tra attività religiosa e impegno civile (1906–1915)," in Vecchio, *Alla ricerca del partito. Cultura politica ed esperienze dei cattolici italiani del primo Novecento* (Brescia: Morcelliana, 1987), pp. 81–133.

9. Here I draw on A. Giovagnoli, *La cultura democristiana. Tra Chiesa cattolica e identità italiana, 1918–1948* (Rome-Bari: Laterza, 1991), pp. 88 ff. On the figure of Achille Ratti, see Y. Chiron, *Pié XI. 1857–1939* (Paris: Perrin, 2004).

10. See R. M. Bell and C. Mazzoni, *The Voices of Gemma Galgani. The Life and Afterlife of a Modern Saint* (Chicago: University of Chicago Press, 2002), pp. 186 ff.

11. See Giovagnoli, *La cultura democristiana*, pp. 59 ff.

12. See A. G. Roncalli, *Fiducia e obbedienza. Lettere ai Rettori del Seminario romano*, ed. C. Badalà (Milan: Edizioni S. Paolo, 1999), pp. 247–48 (letter to Monsignor Vincenzo Bugarini, Nov. 11, 1922, detailing his movements in Puglia).

13. More precisely, in his role as commander of the so-called southern column and "inspector general of Puglia and Calabria," Caradonna, at a rally in Naples on Oct. 24, urged the *squadristi* to attack southern cities and personally oversaw the conquest of Foggia; see G. Albanese, *La marcia su Roma* (Rome-Bari: Laterza, 2006), p. 88 and 231 note.

14. See S. Trinchese, "'Servire obbedire e tacere.' L'immagine dell'Italia fascista nell'opinione di Angelo Roncalli," *Storia contemporanea* 20, no. 2 (1989), pp. 216 ff.

15. See chap. 10, pp. 269 ff.

16. According to Monsignor Carlo Maccari's recollection in 1990—Maccari was John XXIII's apostolic visitor to San Giovanni Rotondo in the summer of 1960—Roncalli, returning from Puglia in 1923, told the prefect of the Propaganda Fide, Cardinal Willem Van Rossum, that he had declined to go to San Giovanni, and Van Rossum replied, "You did well not to accept." See C. Maccari, "Relazione al cardinale J. Ratzinger," in *Congregatio de causis Sanctorum. Beatificationis et canonizationis Servi Dei Pii a Pietrelcina sacerdotis professi ofm cap. (Francesco Forgione)*, vol. 4, *Quaestiones selectae*, Tipografia Favia, Bari, 1997, p. 426.

17. See S. Trinchese, "L'accentramento a Roma dell'Opera della Propagazione della Fede. La missione Roncalli-Drehmanns del 1921," in G. Alberigo et al., *Fede tradizione profezia. Studi su Giovanni XXIII e sul Vaticano II* (Brescia: Paideia, 1984), esp. pp. 138–42.

18. See AFSCIRE, Fondo Roncalli, *Corrispondenza*, vol. 72, *Joseph Drehmanns* (esp. letters of Sept. 1922).

19. Joseph Lemius, another actor in the inquisitorial proceedings of 1921–22, was a *consultor* of Propaganda Fide: see *Annuario pontificio per l'anno 1922*, Tipografia poliglotta vaticana, Rome, 1922.

20. A particularly important influence in early twentieth-century Rome was Redentorist Father Francesco Pitocchi: see A. G. Roncalli / Giovanni XXIII, "Testimonianza di don Angelo Roncalli a p. Francesco Pitocchi" (1922), in Roncalli, *Giornale dell'anima* (Rome: Edizioni di Storia e letteratura, 1964), pp. 467–76. See also G. Battelli, "La formazione di Angelo Giuseppe Roncalli. Il rapporto col redentorista Francesco Pitocchi," in Alberigo et al., *Fede tradizione profezia*, esp. pp. 47–67.

21. So Roncalli said, in 1959, about what he had learned in his Bergamo years from Bishop Radini Tedeschi; quoted in G. Battelli, "G. M. Radini Tedeschi e Angelo Roncalli (1905–1914)," in G. Alberigo, ed., *Papa Giovanni* (Rome-Bari: Laterza, 1987), p. 52.

22. See A. G. Roncalli, "Memorie ed appunti 1919," in *Humanitas. Rivista mensile di cultura* 26 (1973), pp. 420–87.

23. H. Heine, "Disputation," Margaret Armour, trans., from *The Works of Heinrich Heine* (New York: E. P. Dutton, 1906), vol. 12, p. 49.

24. See J. Bouflet, *Padre Pio. Des foudre du Saint-Office à la splendeur de la vérité* (Paris: Presses de la Renaissance, 2002), p. 69.

25. *Declaratio*, "Acta Apostolicae Sedis," 15 (1923), p. 356. Minutes and official

copy in ACDF, Santo Offizio, Dev. V. 1919, 1, *Cappuccini*, P. Pio da Pietrelcina, fasc. 3, doc. 51.

26. As referred by the minister general of the Capuchin order, Father Giuseppe Antonio of Persiceto, to the Holy Office secretary, Cardinal Del Val, Nov. 22, 1923, ACDF, Santo Offizio, Dev. V. 1919, 1, *Cappuccini*, P. Pio da Pietrelcina, fasc. 3, doc. 81.

27. Unsigned article attributable to Adelchi Fabroncini, "San Giovanni Rotondo in difesa di padre Pio," *Il Mattino*, June 29–30, 1923.

28. Ibid.

29. On the Caradonna-Starace rivalry, see S. Colarizi, *Dopoguerra e fascismo in Puglia, (1919–1926)* (Rome-Bari: Laterza, 1971), pp. 258 ff. On dissidence within fascism, see A. Lyttelton, *The Seizure of Power: Fascism in Italy, 1919–1929* (1973; London: Routledge, 2004).

30. Unsigned/Fabroncini, "San Giovanni Rotondo in difesa."

31. Published in *Messaggero* of Jan. 23, the photograph, retouched, is reproduced in *Il Calvario di Padre Pio*, Tipografia Suman, Padova, 1978, vol. 1, p. 70.

32. See the unsigned article "Per il trasferimento di Padre Pio a S. Giovanni Rotondo," *Gazzetta di Puglia*, July 3, 1923.

33. See Bouflet, *Padre Pio*, p. 27.

34. G. Castelli, "Perché la Chiesa non ha riconosciuto i pretesi miracoli di padre Pio da Pietralcina," *Gazzetta di Puglia*, July 11, 1923.

35. Unsigned article, Rome, July 20, 1923.

36. Pio da Pietrelcina, *Epistolario*, vol. 4, *Corrispondenza con diverse categorie di persone*, Melchiorre da Pobladura and Alessandro da Ripabottoni, eds., third edition, Edizioni Padre Pio da Pietrelcina, San Giovanni Rotondo, 1998, p. 734 (letter of Aug. 12, 1923).

37. Dated Rome, July 31, 1923, the letter from Father Giuseppe Antonio to Father Cherubino is found in G. Pagnossin, *Il Calvario di Padre Pio*, Tipografia Suman, Padova, 1978, vol. 1, p. 234. The strong personality of Father Giuseppe Antonio of San Giovanni in Persiceto, a theologian influenced by Rosminian philosophy and future archbishop of Modena, is evident in De Giorgi, "Vita culturale tra Ottocento e Novecento. La significativa impronta del rosminianesimo educatore," in G. Pozzi and P. Prodi, eds., *I Cappuccini in Emilia-Romagna. Storia di una presenza*, Centro editoriale dehoniano, Bologna, 2002, pp. 103–4.

38. Dated Ancona, Aug. 4, 1923, the letter is found in Pagnossin, *Il Calvario*, vol. 1, pp. 234–35.

39. Letter to Monsignor Antonio Valbonesi, Aug. 25, 1923, quoted in F. Peloso, *Don Luigi Orione e Padre Pio da Pietrelcina nel decennio della tormenta, 1923–1933* (Milan: Jaca Book, 1999), pp. 24–25.

40. ACS, MI, DGPS, DAGR, 1930–31, busta 316, fasc. *Foggia*, sottofasc. *San Giovanni Rotondo*, "Agitazione contro l'allontanamento di Padre Pio da Pietralcina": letter from Father Giuseppe Antonio of San Giovanni in Persiceto to General De Bono, Rome, Aug. 22, 1923.

41. See R. Allegri, *Padre Pio. Un Santo tra noi* (Milan: Mondadori, 1998), p. 229.

42. Pio da Pietrelcina, *Epistolario*, vol. 4, pp. 398–99 (letter, Aug. 27, 1923).

43. Ibid., p. 399.
44. *Testamento spirituale di Padre Pio*, San Giovanni Rotondo, Aug. 10, 1923 (ibid., p. 988).
45. Dozens of hagiographic accounts of Padre Pio repeat this version of the events.
46. ACS, MI, DGPS, Confinati politici, fascicoli personali, b. 180, *Camilleri Carmelo*: from a report by the local legion commander of the the Royal Carabinieri of Agrigento to high command of Agrigento, Sept. 7, 1931.
47. ACS, MI, DGPS, DAGR, 1930–31, busta 316, fasc. *Foggia*, sottofasc. *San Giovanni Rotondo*, "Agitazione contro l'allontanamento di Padre Pio da Pietralcina," report by prefect, Foggia, Sept. 1, 1923.
48. Ibid.
49. The circular is found in Pagnossin, *Il Calvario*, vol. 1, p. 89. A copy in Latin is filed in ACDF, Santo Offizio, Dev. V. 1919, 1, *Cappuccini*, P. Pio da Pietrelcina, fasc. 4, doc. 93.
50. Ibid. Father Melchiorre of Benisa also specified that the provisions must not be announced publicly in the refectory but "referred prudently" to individuals.
51. Ibid., doc. 103.
52. See M. Canali, *Il delitto Matteotti. Affarismo e politica nel primo governo Mussolini* (Bologna: il Mulino, 1997).
53. See A. M. Banti, *La nazione del Risorgimento. Parentela, santità e onore alle origini dell'Italia unita* (Turin: Einaudi, 2000).
54. See F. Turati, "Il vindice sacrificio di Giacomo Matteotti," in *Il vindice sacrificio di Giacomo Matteotti celebrato da Filippo Turati (27 giugno 1924). La dichiarazione delle opposizioni alla Camera. L'ultimo discorso del martire (Camera dei Deputati, 30 maggio 1924)*, Partito socialista unitario, Rome, 1924, pp. 3–9.
55. See the abundantly documented collection by S. Caretti, ed., *Matteotti. Il mito* (Pisa: Nistri-Lischi, 1994), pp. 185–364. On the Matteotti kidnapping in the collective imagination, see also E. Diemoz, "Il *noir* Matteotti. Lotta politica, vendette private, fantasie romanzesche," *Passato e presente* 23, no. 66 (2005), pp. 39–64.
56. See V. Zaghi, "'Con Matteotti si mangiava': simboli e valori nella genesi di un mito popolare," *Rivista di storia contemporanea* 3 (1990), pp. 432–46; M. Filippa, *La morte contesa. Cremazione e riti funebri nell'Italia fascista* (Turin: Paravia, 2001), pp. 152–54.
57. See G. Matteotti, *Reliquie*, collection edited by M. Guarnieri, preface by C. Treves (Milan: Corbaccio, 1924).
58. See S. Caretti, "Matteotti," in M. Isnenghi, ed., *I luoghi della memoria. Simboli e miti dell'Italia unita* (Rome-Bari: Laterza, 1996), p. 195.
59. On the song, "O tu santo Manganello" (O thou holy Nightstick), see C. Caravaglios, *I canti delle trincee. Contributo al folklore di guerra* (Rome: Leonardo da Vinci, 1930), p. 305.
60. On relations between Malaparte and Dumini even before the Matteotti affair, see G. Mayda, *Il pugnale di Mussolini. Storia di Amerigo Dùmini, sicario di Matteotti* (Bologna: il Mulino, 2004), pp. 126 ff.

61. The most perceptive readings of Malaparte in this period remain L. Mangoni, *L'interventismo della cultura. Intellettuali e riviste del fascismo* (Rome-Bari: Laterza, 1974) and E. Gentile, *Le origini dell'ideologia fascista (1918-1925)* (1974; Bologna: il Mulino, 1996). See also G. Pardini, *Curzio Malaparte. Biografia politica* (Milan and Trento: Luni, 1998), pp. 85 ff.

62. K. Suckert, "Ritratto delle cose d'Italia, degli eroi, del popolo, degli avvenimenti, delle esperienze e delle inquietudini della nostra generazione," in Suckert, *La rivolta dei santi maledetti* (1923), in C. Malaparte, *L'Europa vivente e altri saggi politici (1921-1931)* (Florence: Vallecchi, 1961), pp. 166-67 and p. 201.

63. Ibid., pp. 166, 188, and 202-3, respectively.

64. See W. L. Adamson, "The Culture of Italian Fascism and the Fascist Crisis of Modernity: The Case of 'Il Selvaggio,'" *Journal of Contemporary History* 30 (October 1995), pp. 555-75.

65. See E. Gentile, *Il culto del littorio. La sacralizzazione della politica nell'Italia fascista* (Rome-Bari: Laterza, 1993), pp. 92-94; M. Berezin, *Making the Fascist Self: The Political Culture of Interwar Italy* (Ithaca: Cornell University Press, 1997), pp. 82-99.

66. I owe this observation and what follows to the pioneering work of P. Angelini, "Religiosità popolare," in V. de Grazia and S. Luzzatto, eds., *Dizionario del fascismo*, vol. 2, L–Z (Turin: Einaudi, 2003), pp. 488-94.

67. Essential reading on the complex, ultimately conflictual relationship between Gentile's scholastic approach and the Vatican's neoscholasticism is in G. Verucci, *Idealisti all'Indice. Croce, Gentile e la condanna del Sant'Uffizio* (Rome-Bari: Laterza, 2006).

68. An example, from L. Longanesi, *Vade-Mecum del perfetto fascista, seguito da dieci assiomi per il milite, ovvero Avvisi ideali* (Florence: Vallecchi, 1926), p. 36: "You like following processions and holy tabernacles? Go then, and beat up those Freemasons who are laughing."

69. So D'Annunzio proclaimed in a lecture of 1919, in S. Migliore, *Mistica povertà. Riscritture francescane tra '800 e '900*, Edizioni Collegio San Lorenzo da Brindisi, Istituto storico dei cappuccini, Rome, 2001, p. 326.

70. See A. Fava, "Chiesa e regime nella stampa locale: riti e modelli 'religiosi' della propaganda fascista in Umbria," in A. Monticone, ed., *Cattolici e fascisti in Umbria (1922-1945)* (Bologna: il Mulino, 1978), pp. 247-95; L. Di Nucci, *Fascismo e spazio urbano. Le città storiche dell'Umbria* (Bologna: il Mulino, 1992), passim; F. Bracco and E. Irace, "La memoria e l'immagine. Aspetti della cultura umbra tra Otto e Novecento," in *Storia d'Italia. Le regioni dall'Unità a oggi, L'Umbria*, R. Covino and G. Gallo, eds. (Turin: Einaudi, 1989), pp. 654-56; E. Irace, *Itale glorie* (Bologna: il Mulino, 2003), pp. 209-25.

71. See Migliore, *Mistica povertà*, p. 227.

72. D. Giuliotti and G. Papini, *Carteggio*, vol. 1, *1913-1927*, N. Vian, ed. (Rome: Edizioni di Storia e Letteratura, 1984), p. 342 (letter from Papini to Giuliotti, Aug. 24, 1926) and p. 343 (letter from Giuliotti to Papini, Aug. 27, 1926).

73. See M. Franzinelli, *Il clero del duce, il duce del clero. Il consenso ecclesiastico nelle lettere a Mussolini (1922-1945)* (Ragusa: La Fiaccola, 1998), p. 140.

74. See V. Facchinetti, *Le stimmate di san Francesco d'Assisi: nel 7° centenario del grande miracolo, 1224–1924*, Lega eucaristica, Milan, 1924, pp. 45–78.

75. See A. Gemelli, "Le stimate di S. Francesco nel giudizio della scienza," *Vita e Pensiero* 10 (1924), fasc. 10, pp. 580–603. A slightly different version of the same study is A. Gemelli, "Le affermazioni della scienza intorno alle Stimmate di S. Francesco," in *Studi francescani* 10 (1924), pp. 368–404.

76. Gemelli, "Le stimate di S. Francesco," p. 580.

77. See chap. 2, pp. 46–47.

78. Gemelli, "Le stimate di S. Francesco," p. 584.

79. Ibid., pp. 589–91.

80. Ibid., p. 598.

81. Ibid., pp. 599–603.

82. Ibid., p. 598.

83. Ibid., p. 592 and p. 590, respectively.

84. Ibid., p. 592.

85. Ibid., p. 590.

86. Among the many critical studies, see the lucid analysis of G. Verucci, *La Chiesa cattolica in Italia dall'Unità a oggi* (Rome-Bari: Laterza, 1999), pp. 50 ff.

87. See G. Verucci, "Il XX settembre," in Isnenghi, ed., *I luoghi della memoria*, pp. 99–100.

88. See A. A. Mola, *Storia della Massoneria italiana dalle origini ai nostri giorni* (Milan: Bompiani, 1997), pp. 526 ff.; D. Menozzi, "Liturgia e politica: l'introduzione della festa di Cristo Re," in A. Melloni et al., *Cristianesimo e storia. Saggi in onore di Giuseppe Alberigo* (Bologna: il Mulino, 1996), pp. 607–56.

89. The best source on the coup d'état remains A. Aquarone, *L'organizzazione dello Stato totalitario* (1965; Turin: Einaudi, 1995), pp. 47 ff.

90. See C. Salotti, *I santi ed i beati proclamati nell'anno santo 1925. Panegirici tenuti in Roma in occasione dei tridui solenni* (Turin: Sei, 1927). Also G. Verucci, "I simboli della cultura laica e delle istituzioni civili" (1997), in Verucci, *Cattolicesimo e laicismo nell'Italia contemporanea* (Milan: Angeli, 2001), pp. 226–27.

91. See Franzinelli, *Il clero del duce*, p. 45.

92. See S. Cavazza, *Piccole patrie. Feste popolari tra regione e nazione durante il fascismo* (Bologna: il Mulino, 1997), p. 95.

93. Dated Apr. 22, 1925, Father Bernardo d'Alpicella's letter to Padre Pio is quoted in Bouflet, *Padre Pio*, p. 289.

94. ACS, MI, DGPS, DAGR, 1930–31, busta 316, fasc. *Foggia*, sottofasc. *San Giovanni Rotondo*, "Agitazione contro l'allontanamento di Padre Pio da Pietralcina," letter, May 28, 1925.

95. Ibid., telegram in code, May 29, 1925.

96. Ibid., letter from chief of police to Foggia prefect (*Riservatissimo*), June 24, 1925.

97. See Y. Chiron, *Padre Pio. Le stigmatisé* (1989; Paris: Perrin, 2004), p. 173; L. Peroni, *Padre Pio da Pietrelcina* (Rome: Borla, 1991), pp. 331 ff.

98. As of when this research was concluded in 2007, the Holy Office archive (in what is now the Congregation for the Doctrine of the Faith) was available to researchers only through Pius XI's papacy, that is, until 1939. My research on Padre Pio's inquisitorial file thus necessarily ends at that date. Although the role of the Holy Office in investigating the friar is reported in the press and other sources, mostly hagiographic in intent, a true historical reconstruction must await the time the Vatican opens the records for the era after Pius XI.

99. See, for example, the anonymous editorial note (disputing Father Fredegando of Antwerp) in *Vita e Pensiero*, 14 (1928), p. 725.

100. See Peloso, *Don Luigi Orione e Padre Pio da Pietrelcina*, pp. 107 ff.

101. Dated Oct. 1919 and Aug. 1920, respectively, the two reports by Giorgio Festa to the Capuchin hierarchy are found in Gerardo di Flumeri, ed., *Le stigmate di Padre Pio da Pietrelcina. Testimonianze. Relazioni*, Edizioni Padre Pio da Pietrelcina, San Giovanni Rotondo, 1995, pp. 179–221.

102. Titled "Per amore di verità. Impressioni e deduzioni scientifiche sul Padre Pio da Pietrelcina," dated Apr. 7, 1925, Festa's report to the Holy Office is found in di Flumeri, ed., *Le stigmate di Padre Pio*, pp. 222–73 (quotes on pp. 244–46).

103. I quote from the unsigned article "Il VII Centenario delle stimmate di S. Francesco e la preparazione del centenario della sua beata morte," *La Civiltà cattolica*, LXXVI, 1925, vol. 1, p. 49.

104. Father Gemelli's "Third Report," as it is called, is found in Gerardo di Flumeri, ed., *Il beato padre Pio da Pietrelcina*, Edizioni Padre Pio da Pietrelcina, San Govanni Rotondo, 2001, pp. 428–38. The following quotations come from the original, in ACDF, Santo Offizio, Dev. V. 1919, 1, *Cappuccini*, P. Pio da Pietrelcina, fasc. 5, doc. 131: "Osservazioni sullo scritto: 'Per amore di verità. Impressioni e deduzioni scientifiche sul Padre Pio da Pietralcina del dottor Giorgio Festa,' April 6 1926."

105. See V. Bianchi, "Sudor sanguigno e stigmate religiose," *Rivista di psicologia. Organo della società italiana di psicologia* (Jan.–March 1926), pp. 1–21.

106. G. B. Guerri reconstructs the episode in *Eretico e profeta. Ernesto Buonaiuti, un prete contro la Chiesa* (Milan: Mondadori, 2001), pp. 119–27.

107. E. Buonaiuti, *Lettere ad Arturo Carlo Jemolo*, ed., C. Fantappié, Pubblicazioni degli Archivi di Stato, Rome, 1997, p. 92 (letter of Jan. 16, 1926) and p. 94 (letter of Jan. 23, 1926).

108. "I'm actually more of a heretic than G.(emelli) would like to have people believe": ibid., p. 94, Jan. 23, 1926.

109. A. Gemelli, "Buonaiuti e noi," *Rivista di filosofia neoscolastica* (Jan. 1929), p. 123.

110. The entire affair is brilliantly reconstructed in L. Roscioni, *Lo smemorato di Collegno. Storia italiana di un'identità contesa* (Turin: Einaudi, 2007); here, see pp. 56 ff.

111. A recent appraisal, faith-based and lacking historiographical skill, is A. M. Mischitelli, *Padre Pio e il caso Gemelli* (Foggia: Leone editrice, 2003); also

Mischitelli, *Padre Pio tra polemiche e storia* (Ferrazzano: Edizioni Enne, 2004), pp. 221–84.

112. From a Canella family history, quoted in Roscioni, *Lo smemorato di Collegno*, p. 153.

113. R. O. Collin, *La donna che sparò a Mussolini* (Milan: Rusconi, 1988).

114. See B. Dalla Casa, *Attentato al duce. Le molte storie del caso Zamboni* (Bologna: il Mulino, 2000).

115. Both the background and the quotations are from E. Rossi, *Il manganello e l'aspersorio*, M. Franzinelli, ed. (1958; Milan: Kaos edizioni, 2000), pp. 127 and 130.

116. On the cultural impact of the book, see, among others, L. Passerini, *Mussolini immaginario. Storia di una biografia, 1915–1939* (Rome-Bari: Laterza, 1991), pp. 43 ff.; P. V. Cannistraro and B. R. Sullivan, *Il Duce's Other Woman* (New York: Morrow, 1993), pp. 299–308; S. Urso, *Margherita Sarfatti. Dal mito del "dux" al mito americano* (Venice: Marsilio, 2003).

117. M. Sarfatti, *Dux* (Milan: Mondadori, 1926), p. 297.

118. Ibid., p. 298.

119. B. Mussolini, preface, ibid., p. 7.

120. As Margherita Sarfatti writes in ibid., p. 185. The incident took place on Feb. 23, 1917.

121. On Mussolini's use of his war wounds as propaganda, see L. Passerini, "L'immagine di Mussolini: specchio dell'immaginario e promessa di identità," *Rivista di storia contemporanea*, 14 (1986), pp. 332–33.

122. Sarfatti, *Dux*, pp. 184–85.

123. See B. Bracco, "I caduti e i mutilati della grande guerra a Milano: retorica della morte e uso politico del corpo," in Bracco, ed., *Combattere a Milano, 1915–1918. Il corpo e la guerra nella capitale del fronte interno* (Milan: Editoriale Il Ponte, 2005), p. 103.

124. See C. Delcroix, *Sette santi senza candele* (Florence: Vallecchi, 1925), pp. 7–24.

125. C. Delcroix, *Un uomo e un popolo* (Florence: Vallecchi, 1928), pp. 173–77.

126. See E. H. Kantorowicz, *Laudes Regiae. A Study in Liturgical Acclamations and Mediaeval Ruler Worship* (Berkeley: University of California Press, 1958), pp. 180–86; also G. Agamben, *Il Regno e la Gloria. Per una genealogia teologica dell'economia e del governo* (Vicenza: Neri Pozza, 2007).

127. See C. Fogu, "'Il Duce Taumaturgo': Modernist Rhetorics in Fascist Representations of History," *Representations* 57 (Winter 1997), pp. 24–51; S. Luzzatto, *Il duce taumaturgo*, in Luzzatto, *L'immagine del duce. Mussolini nelle fotografie dell'Istituto Luce* (Rome: Editori Riuniti, 2001), pp. 145–47.

128. See A. Gibelli, *Il popolo bambino. Infanzia e nazione dalla Grande Guerra a Salò* (Turin: Einaudi, 2005), p. 247.

129. See P. G. Zunino, *L'ideologia del fascismo. Miti, credenze e valori nella stabilizzazione del regime* (Bologna: il Mulino, 1985), pp. 122 ff.

130. P. Orano, *Mussolini da vicino* (Rome: Casa editrice Pinciana, 1928), p. 21.

131. On the cult of saints, see Delcroix, *Un uomo e un popolo*, p. 385; on the question of hierarchical power, see B. Giuliano, "Il Fascismo e l'avvenire della coltura," in G. L. Pomba, ed., *La civiltà fascista: illustrata nella dottrina e nelle opere* (Turin: Utet, 1928), p. 207.

132. Delcroix, *Un uomo e un popolo*, p. 12.

6. Lives of the Saint

1. ACDF, Santo Offizio, Dev. V. 1919, 1, *Cappuccini*, P. Pio da Pietrelcina, fasc. 5, doc. 131: "Osservazioni sullo scritto: 'Per amore di verità. Impressioni e deduzioni scientifiche sul Padre Pio da Pietralcina del dottor Giorgio Festa, 6 aprile 1926.'"

2. Ibid.

3. F. Chiocci, *L'uomo che salvò Padre Pio. Vita, avventure e morte di Emanuele Brunatto* (Rome: Adnkronos Libri, 2003).

4. See chap. 1, p. 34.

5. See ACDF, Santo Offizio, Dev. V. 1919, 1, *Cappuccini*, P. Pio da Pietrelcina, fasc. 4, doc. 127, and fasc. 5, doc. 148: the decree placing Brunatto's *Padre Pio* on the Index was published in *L'Osservatore Romano*, Apr. 30, 1926, and in the *Acta Apostolicae Sedis* 18, no. 5 (May 1926), p. 186; that regarding Cavaciocchi's book, ibid., p. 308.

6. G. Cavaciocchi, *Padre Pio da Pietrelcina. Il fascino e la fama mondiale di un umile e grande francescano* (Rome: Casa editrice Giorgio Berlutti, 1924); G. De Rossi [Emanuele Brunatto], *Padre Pio da Pietrelcina* (Rome: Casa editrice Giorgio Berlutti, 1926).

7. As far as I know, the only text devoted to him is the hagiographic portrait by the amateur scholar G. B. Sposetti Corteselli: *Giorgio Berlutti, cuore d'Italia e di Maremma*, Cooperativa Fani Servizi, Viterbo, 2003.

8. See G. Turi, "La 'marcia su Roma' degli intellettuali," in Turi, *Lo Stato educatore. Politica e intellettuali nell'Italia fascista* (Rome-Bari: Laterza, 2002), pp. 29 ff. (See pp. 43–44 on Berlutti's role.)

9. ACS, MI, DGPS, DPP, personal files, 1927–44, busta 114, fasc. *Berlutti Giorgio*: anonymous police source dated Rome, Feb. 11, 1931.

10. Ibid.

11. See B. Mussolini, *Programma di governo. Commento di Giuseppe Bottai* (Rome: Giorgio Berlutti editore, 1922).

12. See B. Mussolini, *Un anno di governo fascista. Discorsi pronunciati alla Camera e al Senato* (Rome: Casa editrice G. Berlutti, n.d. but 1923); Mussolini, *I discorsi agl'italiani* (Rome: Casa editrice G. Berlutti, n.d. but 1924).

13. See, respectively, M. Carli, *La mia divinità* (Rome, Società tipografica G. Berlutti, 1923); A. Finzi, *Discorsi elettorali* (Rome: Giorgio Berlutti editore, n.d. but 1924); G. Acerbo, *I primi tre mesi della rivoluzione fascista* (Rome: Società tipografica G. Berlutti, n.d. but 1923); A. Turati, *Ragioni ideali di vita fascista*, preface by Benito Mussolini (Rome: Giorgio Berlutti editore, 1926).

14. See L. Zambarelli, *Liriche francescane* (Rome: Casa editrice G. Berlutti, 1923); S. M. Cutelli, *I leoni che ridono* (Rome: Casa editrice G. Berlutti, 1923). On Cutelli's contribution to Bottai's theoretical review *Critica fascista*, see A.

J. De Grand, *Bottai e la cultura fascista* (Rome-Bari: Laterza, 1978), pp. 97 and 136; on Cutelli's role as a theorist of racism (and founder between 1929 and '38 of the periodicals *Rivista internazionale di Diritto razziale, La Nobiltà della Stirpe*, and *Il Diritto razzista*), see M. Franzinelli, *L'amnistia Togliatti. 22 giugno 1946: colpo di spugna sui crimini fascisti* (Milan: Mondadori, 2006), pp. 210–12.

15. See V. de Grazia, *The Culture of Consent: Mass Organization of Leisure in Fascist Italy* (New York and London: Cambridge University Press, 1981).

16. See M. L. Betri, *Leggere obbedire combattere. Le biblioteche popolari durante il fascismo* (Milan: Angeli, 1991), pp. 49 and 63; A. Scotto di Luzio, *L'appropriazione imperfetta. Editori, biblioteche e libri per ragazzi durante il fascismo* (Bologna: il Mulino, 1998), pp. 56–58.

17. See G. Longo, *L'Istituto nazionale fascista di cultura. Gli intellettuali tra partito e regime* (Rome: Antonio Pellicani editore, 2000), pp. 51 ff.; G. Turi, *Giovanni Gentile. Una biografia* (Florence: Giunti, 1995), p. 438.

18. See A. F. Formìggini, *Dizionarietto rompitascabile degli Editori italiani, compilato da uno dei suddetti*, Formìggini, Rome, 1928, p. 127. For some details on Berlutti's role in publicizing Mussolini's ideas, see D. De Masi, ed., *Libro e moschetto. Come il fascismo educava alla violenza* (Rome: La Nuova Frontiera, 1972), pp. 7–8.

19. Surprisingly, neither Berlutti nor the Libreria del Littorio are mentioned in M. Galfré, *Il regime degli editori. Libri, scuola e fascismo* (Rome-Bari: Laterza, 2005).

20. Cavaciocchi, *Padre Pio*, pp. 7–8. Cavaciocchi's articles were published in *Messaggero* beginning on Jan. 23, 1924.

21. Memories of that experience are in G. Cavaciocchi, *La compagnia della morte. Ricordi di un volontario della legione Cipriani*, preface by Arturo Labriola (Naples: Croce, 1898). A wider picture of volunteers in the conflict between Greece and Turkey is in G. Oliva, "Illusioni e disinganni del volontariato socialista: la 'legione Cipriani' nella guerra greco-turca del 1897," *Movimento operaio e socialista* 3 (1982), pp. 361–66.

22. See P. V. Cannistraro, *La fabbrica del consenso. Fascismo e mass media* (Rome-Bari: Laterza, 1975); see pp. 74–75 on Cavaciocchi's specific role.

23. Among the many sources, see esp. A. Campi, *Mussolini* (Bologna: il Mulino, 2001); Campi, *Mussolinismo*, in V. De Grazia and S. Luzzatto, ed., *Dizionario del fascismo*, vol. 2, L–Z (Turin: Einaudi, 2003), pp. 200–204.

24. See G. Cavaciocchi, *Mussolini. Sintesi critiche* (Florence: Vallecchi, 1932).

25. See P. J. Geary, *Furta sacra. Thefts of Relics in the Central Middle Ages* (Princeton: Princeton University Press, 1978), pp 10 ff.

26. Here, I draw on M. de Certeau, *Hagiographie*, in *Encyclopaedia universalis*, vol. 9, Encyclopaedia universalis, Paris, 1985, p. 71.

27. Cavaciocchi, *Padre Pio*, pp. 43 ff. (quotes on pp. 54–55).

28. Ibid., pp 19, 22, 77 respectively.

29. Ibid., pp. 30 ff (quote on p. 31).

30. Ibid., pp. 70 and 75.

31. Ibid., pp. 79–80.

32. Ibid., pp. 19–21.

33. Ibid., pp. 32–33.

34. ACS, MI, DGPS, DPP, fascicoli personali, 1927–44, busta 195, fasc. *Brunatto Emanuele*: from source "No. 353" (Vincenzo Bellavia) in turn based on report by subinformer "Pericles" (Pitigrilli), Parigi, Oct. 1, 1936.

35. This information on his early career is open to question insofar as it comes from an "unpublished autobiography" from the hand of Chiocci, *L'uomo che salvò Padre Pio*, pp. 12–14.

36. ACS, MI, DGPS, DAGR, cat. A4, busta 70, fasc. *Brunatto Emanuele*. From a detailed note by military intelligence (SIM), Rome, June 3, 1935.

37. As we shall see below, Brunatto probably had some personal ties to police chief Arturo Bocchini. Documentation in this regard may emerge when the State Archives open Bocchini's personal files, in the process of catalogization while this research was being carried out in 2007.

38. See G. Pagnossin, *Il Calvario di Padre Pio*, Tipografia Suman, Padova, 1978, vol. 1, p. 459.

39. See J. M. De Bujanda, ed., *Index librorum prohibitorum 1600–1966*, vol. 11, (Montreal-Genevae: Médiaspaul-Librairie Droz, 2002), p. 280. The biographical sketch of "De Rossi," however, is erroneous; he is described as a "satirical and comic writer" "born in Rome in 1861"(*sic!*).

40. G. De Rossi, [Emanuele Brunatto], *Padre Pio da Pietrelcina* (Rome: Casa editrice Giorgio Berlutti, 1926), pp. 12 ff. (quote on p. 25).

41. Ibid. (quotes on pp. 63, 137, and 68, respectively).

42. Ibid. (quotes on pp. 87, 134, and 103, respectively).

43. Ibid., pp. 82–86.

44. Ibid., pp. 82–93.

45. Ibid., p. 135.

46. Ibid., p. 77.

47. Ibid., pp. 95 and 77.

48. See F. Peloso, *Don Luigi Orione e Padre Pio da Pietrelcina nel decennio della tormenta, 1923–1933* (Milan: Jaca Book, 1999), pp. 51 ff.

49. Among the many sources, see G. Fragnito, *La Bibbia al rogo. La censura ecclesiastica e i volgarizzamenti della Scrittura* (Bologna: il Mulino, 1997); M. Infelise, *I libri proibiti da Gutenberg all'Encyclopédie* (Rome-Bari: Laterza, 1999); M. Gotor, *I beati del papa. Santità, Inguisizione e obbedienza in età moderna* (Florence: Olschki, 2002); G. Caravale, *L'orazione proibita. Censura ecclesiastica e letteratura devozionale nella prima età moderna* (Florence: Olschki, 2003).

50. Quoted in G. Fragnito, *Proibito capire. La Chiesa e il volgare nella prima età moderna* (Bologna: Il Mulino, 2005), p. 247; see also A. Prosperi, *L'eresia del Libro Grande. Storia di Giorgio Siculo e della sua setta* (Milan: Feltrinelli, 2000), esp. p. 194.

51. See the German theologian Hubert Wolf, *Index. Der Vatikan und die verbotenen Bücher* (Munich: C. H. Beck, 2006).

52. ACDF, Santo Offizio, Dev. V. 1919, 1, *Cappuccini*, P. Pio da Pietrelcina, fasc. 4, doc. 112: attached to Brunatto's memo, titled *P. Pio da Pietrelcina*, is a note in the hand of Cardinal Gasparri, dated June 27, 1925.

53. See Peloso, *Don Luigi Orione e Padre Pio*, pp. 44 ff.

54. See E. Bonora, "I 'beati del papa': note su politica e religione in età postridentina," *Rivista di storia del cristianesimo* 2 (2004), pp. 405–14.

55. See photos of documents in F. Chiocci and L. Cirri, *Padre Pio. Storia di una vittima* (Rome: I libri del No, 1967), vol. 3, pp. 194 and 206.

56. ACDF, Santo Offizio, Dev. V. 1919, 1, *Cappuccini*, P. Pio da Pietrelcina, fasc. 5, doc. 161: letter from De Lai to Monsignor Nicola Canali of the Holy Office, Rome, Jan. 3, 1927.

57. See ACDF, Santo Offizio, Dev. V. 1919, 1, *Cappuccini*, P. Pio da Pietrelcina, fasc. 2-5, passim.

58. ACDF, Santo Offizio, Dev. V. 1919, 1, *Cappuccini*, P. Pio da Pietrelcina, fasc. 6, doc. 177 (communication dated Foggia, Dec. 24, 1928).

59. On the diplomatic front, see F. Margiotta Broglio, *Italia e Santa Sede dalla grande guerra alla Conciliazione*, (Rome-Bari: Laterza, 1966); on culture, G. Turi, *Il mecenate, il filosofo e il gesuita. L'Enciclopedia italiana, specchio della nazione* (Bologna: il Mulino, 2002), pp. 80 ff.; on espionage, M. Franzinelli, *Delatori. Spie e confidenti anonimi: l'arma segreta del regime fascista* (Milan: Mondadori, 2001), pp. 114 ff.

60. See M. Franzinelli, *Il clero del duce, il duce del clero. Il consenso ecclesiastico nelle lettere a Mussolini (1922-1945)* (Ragusa: La Fiaccola, 1998), pp. 76–77.

61. See Father Melchiorre da Benisa, "Litterae de quarto Centenario ab Ordinis approvatione can [onica] celebrando," in *Analecta Ordinis Minorum Capuccinorum* 44 (1928), pp. 3 ff.

62. On Father Facchinetti's favor with the Fascists, see G. Isola, *Abbassa la tua radio, per favore . . . Storia dell'ascolto radiofonico nell'Italia fascista* (Florence: La Nuova Italia, 1990), pp. 143–68

63. See S. Luzzatto, *The Body of Il Duce: Mussolini's Corpse and the Fortunes of Italy* (New York: Metropolitan, 2005); F. Bonacina, *La salma nascosta. Mussolini a Cerro Maggiore dopo piazzale Loreto (1946-1957)*, Comune di Cerro Maggiore, Cerro Maggiore (Milan), 2004.

64. See P. Bruni, *Giuseppe Caradonna e la destra nazionale* (Rome: Serarcangeli, 1996), pp. 108–10.

65. On Caradonna's power, and its limits, as *ras* of Foggia beginning in 1926, see R. Colapietra, *La Capitanata nel periodo fascista (1926-1942)*, Amministrazione provinciale di Foggia, Foggia, 1978, pp. 21 ff.; L. Ponziani, *Il fascismo dei prefetti. Amministrazione e politica nell'Italia meridionale, 1922-1926* (Rome: Donzelli, 1995), pp. 111–12.

66. ACS, MI, DGPS, DAGR, 1930–31, busta 316, fasc. Foggia, sottofasc. San Giovanni Rotondo, *Agitazione contro l'allontanamento di Padre Pio da Pietralcina*: report dated Rome, Apr. 13, 1929.

67. ACS, MI, DGPS, DAGR, busta 316, fasc. Foggia, sottofasc. San Giovanni Rotondo, *Agitazione contro l'allontanamento di Padre Pio da Pietralcina*: Foggia, Apr. 19, 1929.

68. Ibid.

69. The quotations below come from A. Baldini, "Lascia stare i santi," *Corriere della Sera*, June 30, 1925. The article, slightly condensed, is printed as

"Sangiovanni Rotondo" (1925), in Baldini, *Italia di Bonincontro* (Florence: Sansoni, 1940), pp. 152–57.

70. R. Bacchelli, "Colloquio con uno che un giorno sarà forse sugli altari" (1929), in A. Motta, ed., *Scrittori per Padre Pio* (Novara: Interlinea edizioni, 1999), pp. 23–25.

71. See chap. 9, p. 235 ff.

72. On the group of young Trieste natives living in Florence during the flowering of such reviews, see R. Pertici, ed., *Intellettuali di frontiera. Triestini a Firenze (1900–1950)* (Florence: Olschki, 1985). On Spaini's scholarly role, see: A. D'Orsi, *La cultura a Torino tra le due guerre* (Turin: Einaudi, 2000), pp. 127 ff; G. Turi, *Casa Einaudi. Libri uomini idee oltre il fascismo* (Bologna: il Mulino, 1990), pp. 105–6; L. Mangoni, *Pensare i libri. La casa editrice Einaudi dagli anni trenta agli anni sessanta* (Turin: Bollati Boringhieri, 1999), p. 60 and passim. Among his translations: see A. Döblin, *Berlin Alexanderplatz. Storia di Franz Biberkopf,* introduction and Italian translation from the German by Alberto Spaini (Milan: Modernissima, 1930); F. Kafka, *Il processo,* version and preface of *The Trial* by Alberto Spaini (Turin: Frassinelli, 1933). His report on Padre Pio was reworked and republished in the Aug. 13, 1934, issue of *Il Popolo Nuovo. Settimanale fascista* of Foggia, and won that year's Gargano Prize.

73. See A. Ara and C. Magris, *Trieste. Un'identità di frontiera* (Turin: Einaudi, 1982), pp. 56 ff.

74. As he himself recalled in his memoirs; see A. Spaini, *Autoritratto triestino* (Milan: Giordano editore, 1962), pp. 267 ff.

75. A. Spaini, "Visita a Padre Pio, figlio di San Francesco," *Il Resto del Carlino,* May 5, 1931.

76. See A. Spaini, *Il teatro tedesco* (Milan: Treves, 1933).

77. Spaini, "Visita a Padre Pio."

78. Ibid.

79. E. J. Hobsbawm points to such manifestations in *Primitive Rebels: Studies in Archaic Forms of Social Movement in the 19th and 20th Centuries* (Manchester: Manchester University Press, 1959).

80. The tale of Donato Manduzio and the Jews of San Nicandro has been magnificently reconstructed by a French historian of religion in Mesapotamia: Elena Cassin, *San Nicandro: histoire d'une conversion* (Paris: Plon, 1957).

81. See De Bujanda, ed., *Index librorum,* pp. 203 and 280, respectively.

82. A. Bruers, "L'Indice dei libri proibiti," *Gerarchia. Rivista politica* 9, no. 12 (Dec. 1929), p. 1032.

83. ACS, MI, DGPS, DPP, fascicoli personali, 1927–44, busta 114, fasc. *Berlutti Giorgio*: anonymous police source, dated Rome, Aug. 6, 1928. The same police informer criticized Berlutti for his purchase of "an automobile for personal use" (ibid.).

84. See S. Colarizi, *L'opinione degli italiani sotto il regime, 1929–1943* (Rome-Bari: Laterza, 1991), pp. 83 ff.

85. See ACS, MI, DGPS, DPP, Materia, busta 271, fasc. *"Libreria del Littorio": Appunto per S.E. il Capo del Governo,* Feb. 11, 1931.

86. B. Berlutti, *Il cuore d'Italia* (Rome: Libreria del Littorio, 1930), pp. 9 and 235.

87. C. E. Gadda, "Impossibilità di un diario di guerra," *L'Ambrosiano*, Dec. 7, 1931, reprinted in Gadda, *Romanzi e racconti* (Milan: Garzanti, 1988), vol. 1, pp. 136–37.

88. See ACS, MI, DGPS, DPP, Fascicoli personali, 1927–44, busta 114, fasc. *Berlutti Giorgio*: source "N. 35" (Bice Pupeschi), Rome, Aug. 18, 1928.

89. ACDF, Santo Offizio, Dev. V. 1919, 1, *Cappuccini*, P. Pio da Pietrelcina, fasc. 6, doc. 182 (report dated Andria, Jan. 29, 1930).

90. Ibid., doc. 183 (handwritten note to the secretary of the Holy Office, Feb. 6, 1930).

7. Rasputin Reborn

1. A. Spaini, "Visita a Padre Pio, figlio di San Francesco," *Il Resto del Carlino*, May 5, 1931.

2. See ACDF, Santo Offizio, Dev. V. 1919, 1, *Cappuccini*, P. Pio da Pietrelcina, fasc. 7, doc. 201, from a letter to the new secretary, Cardinal Sbarretti (successor to Cardinal Del Val), dated Bologna, Apr. 24, 1931.

3. See F. Morcaldi, "La morte della madre di Padre Pio," *Il Resto del Carlino*, Jan. 30, 1930.

4. See, among others, G. Cavaciocchi, "L'eremo di Padre Pio," *Il Resto del Carlino*, Apr. 8, 1926.

5. See Ego, "Frate Padre Pio da Pietrelcina," *Il Resto del Carlino*, May 1, 1926.

6. See A. Del Fante, *A Padre Pio da Pietrelcina, l'araldo del Signore*, Galleri, Bologna, 1931; Del Fante, *Per la storia. Padre Pio di Pietrelcina, il primo sacerdote stigmatizzato*, Galleri-Tipografia aldina, Bologna, 1932. Apart from the different titles, the books are practically identical. The Holy Office first put Del Fante on the Index on May 22, 1931: see ACDF, Santo Offizio, Dev. V. 1919, 1, *Cappuccini*, P. Pio da Pietrelcina, fasc. 7, doc. 212.

7. Aristarco Scannabue, "L'ultima bestialità di Papini," *Italia laica* 1, no. 1 (Feb. 14, 1922).

8. Bertonte, *I miracoli di Frate Pio*, *Italia laica* 1, no. 5 (Mar. 14, 1922).

9. See A. Del Fante, *Dal dubbio alla fede. A Padre Pio di Pietrelcina*, Galleri, Bologna, 1931.

10. See ACS, MI, DGPS, DAGR, 1930–31, busta 316, fasc. Foggia, sottofasc. San Giovanni Rotondo, *Agitazione contro l'allontanamento di Padre Pio da Pietralcina*: report and telegram from Foggia prefect, Apr. 27 and June 12, 1931.

11. See Y. Chiron, *Padre Pio. Le stigmatisé* (1989; Paris: Perrin, 2004), pp. 195 ff.

12. See ACDF, Santo Offizio, Dev. V. 1919, 1, *Cappuccini*, P. Pio da Pietrelcina, fasc. 6, docc. 191 and 197.

13. Ibid., fasc. 7, doc. 206 (minute dated Apr. 30, 1931).

14. Ibid., doc. 210 (letter to Cardinal Sbarretti dated Como, May 6, 1931). Monsignor Macchi had meanwhile been named bishop of Como.

15. Ibid., doc. 211 (the proposal from the Holy Office is dated May 13, 1931, the papal approval on May 14).

16. See Chiron, *Padre Pio*, p. 190.

17. ACDF, Santo Offizio, Dev. V. 1919, 1, *Cappuccini*, P. Pio da Pietrelcina, fasc. 7, doc. 219 (June 12, 1931).

18. Ibid., doc. 222 (the signatures were collected between June 22 and July 4, 1931).

19. Ibid., fasc. 8, doc. 228 (letter to Cardinal Sbarretti, Sept. 16, 1931).

20. Ibid., fasc. 7, doc. 221 (minute, June 18, 1931).

21. Ibid., doc. 222.

22. See H. Goetz, *Il giuramento rifiutato. I docenti universitari e il regime fascista* (Milan: La Nuova Italia, 2000), pp. 80–81; G. Boatti, *Preferirei di no. Le storie dei dodici professori che si opposero a Mussolini* (Turin: Einaudi, 2001), pp. 268–70.

23. E. Buonaiuti, *La vita allo sbaraglio. Lettere a Missir, 1926–1946*, A. Donini, ed. (Florence: La Nuova Italia, 1980), p. 201 (Rome, June 29, 1931). For background and his friendship with Remo Missir, see L. Bedeschi, *Buonaiuti, il Concordato e la Chiesa* (Milan: il Saggiatore, 1970), p. 343 note.

24. See G. Verucci, *La Chiesa cattolica in Italia dall'Unità a oggi*, Laterza, Rome-Bari, 1999, pp. 60–61.

25. On Buonaiuti and mysticism, see G. B. Guerri, *Eretico e profeta. Ernesto Buonaiuti, un prete contro la Chiesa* (Milan: Mondadori, 2001), pp. 56–57.

26. In particular, Francesco Morcaldi had direct access to Cardinal Rossi, as can be seen from various documents in ACDF, Santo Offizio, Dev. V. 1919, 1, *Cappuccini*, P. Pio da Pietrelcina, fasc. 8, docc. 236 and 247.

27. It was in fact in Istanbul that Monsignor Cesarano was named archbishop of Manfredonia, on Aug. 15, 1931.

28. See A. Giovagnoli, *La cultura democristiana. Tra Chiesa cattolica e identità italiana, 1918–1948* (Rome-Bari: Laterza, 1991), pp. 100–101.

29. See chap. 1, pp. 18 ff.

30. Excellent historiographical background is in P. Sbalchiero, ed., *Dictionnaire des miracles et de l'extraordinaire chrétiens* (Paris: Fayard, 2002).

31. See G. Festa, *Tra i misteri della scienza e le luci della fede*, Arte della stampa, Rome, 1933.

32. ACDF, Santo Offizio, Dev. V. 1919, 1, *Cappuccini*, P. Pio da Pietrelcina, fasc. 8, doc. 239 (letter of Mar. 1, 1932).

33. ACDF, Santo Offizio, Dev. V. 1919, 1, *Cappuccini*, P. Pio da Pietrelcina, fasc. 6, doc. 200.

34. "Pubblicazione sbagliata," *L'Osservatore Romano*, Feb. 17, 1932.

35. See ACS, MI, DGPS, DPP, fascicoli personali, 1927–1944, busta 195, fasc. *Brunatto Emanuele*: source "N. 40" (Virginio Troiani), Rome, June 20, 1931.

36. This entire episode, at times verging on a bizarre caper, can be reconstructed using the documentation in ACDF, Santo Offizio, Dev. V. 1919, 1, *Cappuccini*, P. Pio da Pietrelcina, fasc. 8, docc. 247, 247 bis, 248 (Oct. 18–Nov. 9, 1932).

37. Pio da Pietrelcina, *Epistolario*, vol. 4, *Corrispondenza con diverse categorie di persone*, Melchiorre da Pobladura and Alessandro da Ripabottoni, eds., third edition, Edizioni Padre Pio da Pietrelcina, San Giovanni Rotondo, 1998, pp. 740–41 (letter of Mar. 14–15, 1933).

38. See ACDF, Santo Offizio, Dev. V. 1919, 1, *Cappuccini*, P. Pio da Pietrelcina, fasc. 8, doc. 253.

39. Ibid., doc. 247 bis (letter, Francesco Morcaldi to Capuchin minister general, Oct. 15, 1932).

40. The most complete source on De Luca is L. Mangoni, *In partibus infidelium. Don Giuseppe De Luca: il mondo cattolico e la cultura italiana del Novecento* (Turin: Einaudi, 1989).

41. The twelve-page letter from De Luca to Papini, dated Oct. 28, 1934, is reproduced in part in G. M. Viscardi, "Padre Pio, padre Gemelli e don Giuseppe De Luca, ovvero la santità tra scienza e intelligenza," *Ricerche di storia sociale e religiosa* 63 (2003), pp. 187 ff.

42. Ibid., p. 193.

43. See chap. 10, pp. 282–83.

44. Such was the title of his much-admired article in the Aug. 1934 issue of *Frontespizio*.

45. From L. Mangoni, *L'interventismo della cultura. Intellettuali e riviste del fascismo* (Rome-Bari: Laterza, 1974), p. 266. But see the entire chapter, pp. 197–283.

46. See M. Canali, *Le spie del regime* (Bologna: il Mulino, 2004), pp. 278–79.

47. ACS, MI, DGPS, DPP, fascicoli personali, series B, 1927–44, busta 18 B, fasc. *Pio da Pietralcina" [sic], padre*: source "N. 326" (Cesare Mansueti), dated Rome, Mar. 29, and May 18, 1934.

48. See chap. 6, pp. 159–60.

49. See A. Del Fante, *Savonarola, l'illuminato di Dio*, Galleri, Bologna, 1933; Del Fante, *Le procellarie del futuro. Profezie*, Galleri, Bologna, 1936.

50. See ACDF, Santo Offizio, Dev. V. 1919, 1, *Cappuccini*, P. Pio da Pietrelcina, fasc. 7, doc. 227 (registered by the Holy Office on Oct. 5, 1931). All quotations below refer to this document.

51. I draw here on the fine study by W. A. Christian, *Visionaries. The Spanish Republic and the Reign of Christ* (Berkeley: University of California Press, 1996), pp. 25 and 284.

52. Father Giannantonio's pamphlet is so rare that even the largest libraries in the world show no trace in their electronic catalogs. I was unable to review it and draw the quotation—which appears to come from p. 57 of Giannantonio's text—from Del Fante, *Per la storia*, p. 171. A noted priest and confessor for half a century at the Cathedral of Milan, Father Giannantonio was deported to Flossenburg in 1944 for having helped Jews under the German occupation. See Giannantonio Agosti [da Romallo], *Nei Lager vinse la bontà. Memorie dell'internamento nei campi di eliminazione tedeschi*, Edizioni Missioni estere dei Padri Cappuccini, Milan, 1968.

53. Del Fante, *Per la storia*, p. 169.

54. The quotation is from a letter by Angela Serritelli to Caradonna's wife, announcing that "Cavaliere Morcaldi" would pay her a visit, dated June 20, 1932: in G. Pagnossin, *Il calvario di Padre Pio*, Tipografia Suman, Padova, 1978, vol. 1, p. 600.

55. Pio da Pietrelcina, *Epistolario*, vol. 4, p. 49 (letter, Apr. 2, 1932).

56. See p. 181.

57. ACS, MI, DGPS, DPP, fascicoli personali, 1927–44, busta 195, fasc. *Brunatto Emanuele*: source "N. 40," June 20, 1931. See also ACS, MI, DGPS, DAGR, cat. A4, busta 70, fasc. *Brunatto Emanuele*: source, Questura, Rome, Sept. 2, 1934.

58. A photographic copy of the letter is found in Pagnossin, *Il calvario di Padre Pio*, vol. 1, p. 724.

59. ACS, MI, DGPS, DPP, fascicoli personali, 1927–44, busta 195, fasc. *Brunatto Emanuele*: source "N. 40," June 20, 1931.

60. ACS, MI, DGPS, DPP, fascicoli personali, 1927–44, busta 195, fasc. *Brunatto Emanuele*: source, Prefecture, Bologna, May 5, 1935.

61. ACS, MI, DGPS, DAGR, cat. A4, busta 70, fasc. *Brunatto Emanuele*: War Ministry, Military Intelligence (SIM), Rome, June 3, 1935.

62. Dating from Feb. 1935, the SIM note is attached to the prefect's report of May 5, 1935 (in ACS, MI, DGPS, DPP, fascicoli personali, 1927–44, busta 195, fasc. *Brunatto Emanuele*).

63. Dated June 25, 1935, the letter is reproduced in Pagnossin, *Il calvario di Padre Pio*, vol. 1, p. 747.

64. See C. B. Ruffin, *Padre Pio: The True Story*, Our Sunday Visitor, Huntington, Indiana, 1991, pp. 213 ff.

65. ACS, MI, DGPS, DAGR, cat. A4, busta 70, fasc. *Brunatto Emanuele*: letter, Paris, Mar. 3, 1936.

66. ACS, MI, DGPS, DAGR, cat. A4, busta 70, fasc. *Brunatto Emanuele*: letter, Sept. 20, 1935.

67. Ibid., letter from Paris, Nov. 25, 1935.

68. Letter, July 14, 1935, reproduced in Pagnossin, *Il calvario di Padre Pio*, vol. 1, p. 750.

69. ACS, MI, DGPS, DAGR, cat. A4, busta 70, fasc. *Brunatto Emanuele*: letter from Bologna, Sept. 26, 1935.

70. Ibid., letter from Bologna, Oct. 22, 1935.

71. Undated, his note is reproduced in a photograph in Pagnossin, *Il calvario di Padre Pio*, vol. 1, p. 712.

72. Ibid., p. 712 (letter of Antonio Massa, Mar. 4, 1931).

73. ACS, MI, DGPS, DAGR, cat. A4, busta 70, fasc. *Brunatto Emanuele*: letter from Giovannini to Brunatto, June 21, 1935.

74. Pio da Pietrelcina, *Epistolario*, vol. 4, pp. 746–47.

75. See the classic study by Z. Sternhell, *Ni droite ni gauche. L'idéologie fasciste en France* (Paris: Seuil, 1983).

76. The broader picture is in J.-B. Duroselle, *La décadence, 1932–1939* (Paris: Imprimerie nationale, 1979); S. Berstein, *Histoire du parti radical*, vol. 2, *Crise du radicalisme, 1926–1939* (Paris: Presses de la Fondation nationale des sciences politiques, 1980).

77. ACS, MI, DGPS, DPP, fascicoli personali, 1927–44, busta 195, fasc. *Brunatto Emanuele*: source "N. 353" (Vincenzo Bellavia), with additional information from "N. 373" (Dino Segre, *alias* Pitigrilli): Paris, Oct. 1, 1936.

78. See Canali, *Le spie del regime*, pp. 228 ff. OVRA was so secretive that it has

never been determined exactly what the acronym stood for. The agency's name also echoes the Italian word *piovra*, the long-tentacled octopus.

79. Ibid., pp. 287–89.

80. Ibid., note dated Dec. 4 and Dec. 14, 1935.

81. Ibid., note, May 14, 1936.

82. Ibid., note, Oct. 14, 1936.

83. See J.-P. Cointet, *Pierre Laval* (Paris: Fayard, 1993), pp. 195–201.

84. ACS, Gabinetto, Minculpop, Reports, busta 3, m. 28/A, *Activities of Italo Sulliotti, editor of 'La Nuova Italia,' Paris*: letter from Sulliotti to Major Celso Luciano, chief of staff of the Press and Propaganda Ministry, Jan. 2, 1936. Correspondence from the previous weeks reveals that Sulliotti had speedily communicated the plan by "comrade Brunatto" to Undersecretary Dino Alfieri, who in turn (Nov. 30, 1935) informed chief of police Bocchini.

85. ACS, MI, DGPS, DPP, fascicoli personali, 1927–44, busta 195, fasc. *Brunatto Emanuele*: source "N. 353" (Vincenzo Bellavia), Parigi, May 30, 1936. See also ACS, MI, DGPS, DPP, fascicoli personali, 1927–44, busta 96A, fasc. Sulliotti Italo: source "N. 158" (Valerio Benuzzi), Rome, Feb. 11, 1936, estimates the sum as FF 100,000.

86. According to what Sulliotti told Major Luciano, letter of Jan. 2, 1936.

87. ACS, MI, DGPS, DAGR, cat. A4, busta 70, fasc. *Brunatto Emanuele*: letter, Paris, Jan. 9, 1936.

88. ACS, MI, DGPS, DPP, fascicoli personali, 1927–44, busta 195, fasc. *Brunatto Emanuele*: source "N. 373" (Pitigrilli), Paris, Feb. 8, 1937.

89. Ibid., source "N. 353" (Vincenzo Bellavia), Paris, Oct. 14, 1936.

90. On Pius XI's physical decline (and his spiritual evolution) near the end of his papacy, see E. Fattorini's fundamental work, *Pio XI, Hitler e Mussolini. La solitudine di un papa* (Turin: Einaudi, 2007), pp. 44 ff.

91. ACS, MI, DGPS, DPP, fascicoli personali, 1927–44, busta 195, fasc. *Brunatto Emanuele*: source "N. 353" (Vincenzo Bellavia), Paris, Mar. 22, 1937.

92. Ibid.

93. Ibid.: handwritten letter, dated Paris, Mar. 30, XV (XV being the fifteenth year of Fascist rule).

94. Ibid: source "N. 353" (Vincenzo Bellavia), Paris, Mar. 22, 1937.

95. Ibid.: il capo della Polizia a Sulliotti, Rome, Apr. 5, 1937.

96. Ibid.: letter from Sulliotti to "Commendatore" Bocchini, Budapest, Apr. 23, 1937.

97. Ibid.: chief of police to Pietro Francolini, Rome, Apr. 10, 1937.

98. Ibid.: chief of police to "N. 353" (Vincenzo Bellavia), Rome, July 31, 1937.

99. See J. Bouflet, *Padre Pio. Des foudres du Saint-Office à la splendeur de la vérité* (Paris: Presses de la Rennaissance, 2002), p. 334.

100. See Chiron, *Padre Pio*, pp. 211–12.

101. See Benedetto da San Marco in Lamis, *Piccola pedagogia dello spirito, o Manualetto di direzione delle anime pie in forma epistolare*, Società anonima tipografica, Vicenza, 1935.

102. Letter to Francesco Morcaldi, Paris, June 25 (Pagnossin, *Il calvario di Padre Pio*, vol. 1, p. 747).

103. On the publishing history of *Bread and Wine*, see B. Falcetto, "Vino e pane. Genesi e storia editoriale," in I. Silone, *Romanzi e saggi*, vol. 1, *1927–1944* (Milan: Mondadori, 2000), pp. 1499–1522 (including significant details on the postwar transformation of *Pane e vino* into *Vino e pane* [Wine and Bread], 1955). In those years Giovanni Papini published a poetry collection by the same name: *Pane e vino, con un soliloquio sulla poesia* (Florence: Vallecchi, 1926).

104. I. Silone, *Pane e vino* (Lugano: Nuove edizioni di Capolago, 1937), p. 88.

105. Ibid., p. 89 (the quotation) and pp. 316 ff.

106. See S. Soave, *Senza tradirsi, senza tradire. Silone e Tasca dal comunismo al socialismo cristiano (1900–1940)* (Turin: Nino Aragno editore, 2005), pp. 346 ff; D. Biocca, *Silone. La doppia vita di un italiano* (Milan: Rizzoli, 2005), pp. 197–99.

8. The Sorrows of This World

1. See D. Argentieri, *La prodigiosa storia di Padre Pio, narrata e discussa con 21 fotoincisioni* (Milan: Tarantola, 1951), p. 129.

2. From *Il Resto del Carlino*, Oct. 12, 1939, by G. Barbaci: quoted in Argentieri, *Prodigiosa storia*, pp. 130–31.

3. See J. Bouflet, *Padre Pio. Des foudres du Saint-Office à la splendeur de la vérite* (Paris: Presses de la Renaissance, 2002), p. 346.

4. A. Del Fante, *Se ci avessero creduti*, Galleri, Bologna, 1940, p. 18.

5. For the history of the Vieux-Colombier, see M.-F. Christout, N. Guibert, and D. Pauly, *Théâtre du Vieux-Colombier, 1913–1993* (Paris: Éditions Norma, 1993).

6. E. De Pio, *Frère Soleil. Cinq tableaux de la vie de Saint François d'Assise* (Paris: Jean-Renard, 1942).

7. See ACS, MI, DGPS, DPP, fascicoli personali, 1927–44, busta 195, fasc. *Brunatto Emanuele*: source "N. 353" (Vincenzo Bellavia), July 21, 1937; source "Franco" (Pietro Francolini), May 20, 1938, etc.

8. On the pro-Nazi orientation of the Comité international permanent degli ex combattenti, under Delcroix's influence, see A. Prost, *Les anciens combattants et la société française, 1914–1939* (Paris: Presses de la Fondation nationales des sciences politiques, 1977), vol. 1, pp. 184–85.

9. Extracts from "Informations parlementaires et diplomatiques," sent to Bocchini at Brunatto's request, are found in ACS, MI, DGPS, DPP, fascicoli personali, 1927–44, busta 195, fasc. *Brunatto Emanuele*, attached to a note by "Franco" of Jan. 21, 1938.

10. See ACS, MI, DGPS, DAGR, cat. A4, busta 70, fasc. *Brunatto Emanuele*: letter from Cesare Festa to Antonio Tonelli, Paris, Jan. 25, 1940. Attorney Festa had himself sought to become an informer for chief of police Arturo Bocchini: see ACS, MI, DGPS, DPP, fascicoli personali, 1927–44, busta 500, fasc. *Festa Cesare* (esp. the letter from Festa to Bocchini of Oct. 19, 1938).

11. See ACS, SPD, Carteggio ordinario, fasc. 546.417, *Brunatto Emanuele*: various documents from the Italian embassy in Paris to the press office of the minister for popular culture (Minculpop), Nov. 1942.

12. The "troisième tableau" was a near-literal citation from the *Fioretti*; see De Pio, *Frère Soleil*, pp. 89 ff.

13. An anastatic print copy of the receipt for the deposit, on Banque Italo-Française de Crédit letterhead, is in F. Chiocci and L. Cirri, *Padre Pio. Storia di una vittima* (Rome: I libri del No, 1967), vol. 3, p. 242.

14. F. Chiocci, *L'uomo che salvò Padre Pio. Vita, avventure e morte di Emanuele Brunatto* (Rome: Adnkronos Libri, 2003), p. 97.

15. See chap. 6, p. 156.

16. See the extensive study by P. Sanders, *Histoire du marché noir, 1940–1946* (Paris: Perrin, 2001), esp. pp. 163 ff.

17. Ibid., docc. 13–14 (Aug–Sept. 1941).

18. ACS, MI, DGPS, DAGR, cat. A4, busta 70, fasc. *Brunatto Emanuele*: Supreme Command (SIM) to director of public security, Rome, July 22, 1942.

19. Ibid.

20. The observation is that of one of the most acute scholars of the Occupation, Philippe Burrin: *La France à l'heure allemande, 1940–1944* (Paris: Seuil, 1995), pp. 283 ff.

21. The very best account here is R. Cobb, *French and Germans, Germans and French. A Personal Interpretation of France under Two Occupations, 1914–1918/1940–1944* (Hanover: University Press of New England, 1983).

22. P. Assouline, *Lutetia* (Paris: Gallimard, 2005) offers a fictionalized reconstruction based on scrupulous historical research.

23. AJM, dossier 1531/1990, *Brunatto Emmanuel Louis* (Atteinte à la sûreté extérieure de l'État), fasc. Information, docc. 25 and following.

24. Ibid., doc. 24 (report by Office of Judicial Police to the Paris Prefecture, Mar. 13, 1945), doc. 36 (rapporto dell'*expert-comtable* incaricato di rivedere la contabilità di Brunatto, per conto del Tribunal de la Seine: Parigi, July 17, 1945).

25. Ibid., dossier 1531/1990, *Brunatto Emmanuel Louis* (Atteinte à la sûreté extérieure de l'État), fasc. Information, docc. 4–8 (Jan.–Feb. 1941).

26. Ibid., doc. 36.

27. See Sanders, *Histoire du marché noir*, pp. 194 ff.

28. See AJM, dossier 1531/1990, *Brunatto Emmanuel Louis* (Atteinte à la sûreté extérieure de l'État), fasc. Information, doc. 43 (July 1945).

29. See S. Roffat, *Animation et propagande. Les dessins animés pendant la Seconde Guerre mondiale* (Paris: L'Harmattan, 2005).

30. AJM, dossier 1531/1990, *Brunatto Emmanuel Louis* (Atteinte à la sûreté extérieure de l'État), fasc. Information, doc. 37 (deposition, Court of Justice, Département Seine, Paris, Oct. 25, 1945).

31. ACS, SPD, Carteggio riservato, Rsi, busta 36, fasc. 322, *Brunatto Emanuele*: letter from Marchiandi to Mussolini, Salò, Apr. 4, 1944.

32. G. Papini, "Pagine di diario e di appunti," in Papini, *Scritti postumi* (Milan: Mondadori, 1966), vol. 2, p. 196.

33. Ibid., pp. 218–21 (July 14–22, 1944). The best reconstruction of that stage of Papini's life is in P. G. Zunino, *La Repubblica e il suo passato. Il fascismo dopo il fascismo, il comunismo, la democrazia: le origini dell'Italia contemporanea* (Bologna: il Mulino, 2003), pp. 557 ff.

34. P. Calamandrei, *Diario, 1939–1945*, G. Agosti, ed. (Florence: La Nuova Italia, 1982), p. 422.

35. On the church's historical role as a protective agent for a war-torn Italy ever less defended by the armed forces, see G. De Luna, "L'identità coatta. Gli italiani in guerra (1940–1945)," in *Storia d'Italia*, *Annali*, vol. 18, *Guerra e pace*, W. Barberis, ed. (Turin: Einaudi, 2002), pp. 773 ff.

36. See G. Chianese, *"Quando uscimmo dai rifugi." Il Mezzogiorno tra guerra e dopoguerra (1943–46)* (Rome: Carocci, 2004), pp. 40–43.

37. See C. Bermani, *Spegni la luce che passa Pippo. Voci, leggende e miti della storia contemporanea* (Rome: Odradek, 1996), pp. 159–71; G. Gribaudi, *Guerra totale. Tra bombe alleate e violenze naziste: Napoli e il fronte meridionale, 1940–44* (Turin: Bollati Boringhieri, 2005), pp. 89 ff.

38. See F. Cordella, *San Giuseppe da Copertino e la società del suo tempo: dall'agiografia alla storia, 1603–1663*, Galatina, Congedo, 1997.

39. Calamandrei, *Diario*, p. 94 (Dec. 13, 1942).

40. On this matter, see U. Gentiloni Severi and M. Carli, *Bombardare Roma. Gli Alleati e la "città aperta" (1940–1944)* (Bologna: il Mulino, 2007), pp. 31 ff.

41. See Y. Chiron, *Padre Pio. Le stigmatisé* (1989; Paris: Perrin, 2004), p. 218.

42. L. Bidot, *Padre Pio. La Volonté de Dieu* (Paris: Éditions du Triomphe, 2000).

43. N. Lewis, *Naples '44* (London: Eland, 1989), p. 110. Carlo Fumian brought this source to my attention.

44. See R. Martucci, *Storia costituzionale italiana. Dallo Statuto Albertino alla Repubblica (1848–2001)* (Rome: Carocci, 2002), pp. 199 ff.

45. See A. M. Imbriani, *Gli italiani e il duce. Il mito e l'immagine di Mussolini negli ultimi anni del fascismo (1938–1943)* (Naples: Liguori, 1992), pp. 169 ff.; P. Colombo, *Storia costituzionale della monarchia italiana* (Rome-Bari: Laterza, 2001), pp. 107 ff.

46. See D. I. Kertzer, *Prisoner of the Vatican: The Popes' Secret Plot to Capture Rome* (Boston: Houghton Mifflin, 2004).

47. See F. Margiotta Broglio, *Dalla Conciliazione al giubileo 2000*, in *Storia d'Italia*, *Annali*, vol. 16, *Roma città del papa.Vita civile e religiosa dal giubileo di Bonifacio VIII al giubileo di papa Wojtyla*, L. Fiorani and A. Prosperi, eds. (Turin: Einaudi, 2000), pp. 1174 ff.

48. See L. Scaraffia, "Devozioni di guerra. Identità femminile e simboli religiosi negli anni quaranta," in A. Bravo, ed., *Donne e uomini nelle guerre mondiali* (Rome-Bari: Laterza, 1991), pp. 152–60: E. Fattorini, *Il culto mariano tra Ottocento e Novecento: simboli e devozione. Ipotesi e prospettive di ricerca* (Milan: FrancoAngeli, 1999), pp. 67 ff.

49. A. Del Fante, *Quindici anni dopo la mia prima visita a padre Pio di Pietrelcina: impressioni*, Anonima Arti grafiche, Bologna, 1946, pp. 5–13 (text is dated San Giovanni Rotondo, June 1945).

50. See P. Delfino Sessa, *P. Pio da Pietrelcina* (Genoa: Demos, 1949), pp. 153–55.

51. See P. Bruni, *Giuseppe Caradonna e la destra nazionale* (Rome: Serarcangeli, 1996), pp. 96–97.

52. The *New York Times Magazine* article, July 29, 1956, is quoted in Chiocci and Cirri, *Padre Pio*, vol. 2, p. 25.

53. For an examination of what a miracle means in Christian thought, see P.

Sbalchiero, ed., *Dictionnaire des miracles et de l'extraordinaire chrétiens* (Paris: Fayard, 2002), esp. pp. 531–46.

54. Pio da Pietrelcina, *Epistolario*, vol. 4, *Corrispondenza con diverse categorie di persone*, Melchiorre da Pobladura and Alessandro da Ripabottoni, eds., third edition, Edizioni Padre Pio da Pietrelcina, San Giovanni Rotondo, 1998, p. 644.

55. See Alessandro da Ripabottoni, *Padre Pio da Pietrelcina. Un Cireneo per tutti*, Centro culturale francescano convento Immacolata, Foggia, 1974, pp. 366–71.

56. C. Trabucco, *Il mondo di P. Pio* (Rome: E. Giacomaniello, 1952), pp. 52 ff.

57. See R. D. Edwards, *The Pursuit of Reason. "The Economist," 1843-1993* (Boston: Harvard Business School Press, 1995), esp. pp. 482–85 and pp. 754–64.

58. Her most influential book would be published a few years later: B. Ward, *Faith and Freedom* (New York: Norton, 1954).

59. A typical hagiographical account of these matters in A. Del Fante, *Fatti nuovi. Seguito del volume: "Per la storia. Padre Pio di Pietrelcina, il primo sacerdote stigmatizzato,"* Arti grafiche, Bologna, 1951, pp. 334 ff.

60. Recounted endless times by hagiographers, the story can be read in Alessandro da Ripabottoni, *Padre Pio da Pietrelcina*, pp. 380–81.

61. See UNRRA Italian Mission, *Survey of Italy's Economy*, UNRRA, Rome, 1947: "The Health Situation in 1946," pp. 107 ff.

62. See F. M. Snowden, *The Conquest of Malaria. Italy, 1900–1962* (New Haven: Yale University Press, 2006), pp. 181–97.

63. See S. Luzzi, *Salute e sanità nell'Italia repubblicana* (Rome: Donzelli, 2004), pp. 115 ff.

64. Istituto Luigi Sturzo, Rome, Fondo Giuseppe Spataro (1911–78), *Anno 1945*: "confidential" letter from Montini to De Gasperi.

65. See UNA, UNRRA 1943–49, Pag 4/3.0.14.0.0.2, box 10, *Subect files. Vatican*: mixed correspondence, Oct. 1945–May 1947.

66. On Keeny and his notable role as an American and international civil servant, see J. L., Harper, *America and the Reconstruction of Italy, 1945–1948* (Cambridge: Cambridge University Press, 1986), pp. 91 ff.

67. See UNA, UNRRA 1943–49, Pag 4/3.0.14.0.0.2, box 10, *Subect files. Vatican*: in particular, Jackson helped to organize a visit to Washington by Lodovico Montini at the end of 1946. During the first half of 1947, Jackson mainly dealt with Giovanni Battista Montini on the matter of the fledgling International Refugee Organization.

68. UNA, UNRRA 1943–49, Pag 4/3.0.14.0.0.0.1, box 1, *Italy Chief of Mission. Correspondance with Individuals*: letter from Keeny to Humphrey Gale of the European Regional Office, London, dated Rome, Feb. 25, 1947.

69. ACS, MI, AAI, Presidenza, busta 34, *UNRRA, Pubblicazioni, convenzioni, riunioni 1945–47*: transcript of Keeny-Montini meeting of Jan. 14, 1947, with handwritten corrections by Lodovico Montini.

70. A. Giovagnoli has written of the "dangers" inherent in the powers Prime Minister De Gasperi had granted to Lodovico Montini as president of the

Italian delegation to UNRRA in his *Le premesse della ricostruzione. Tradizione e modernità nella classe dirigente cattolica del dopoguerra*, Nuovo istituto editoriale italiano, Milan, 1982, pp. 295 ff.

71. See UNA, UNRRA 1943–49, Pag 4/3.0.14.0.0.2, box 10, *Subect files. Vatican*: the sole issue was published in Feb. 1946.

72. Ibid., "personal" letter dated Vatican, May 8, 1947.

73. Ibid., reply dated Rome, May 17, 1947.

74. See UNRRA, Supplement to *Il Seminatore*, publication of the Opera Pia Fondazione Vittorino di Camillo, Feb. 1946, p. 5.

75. See ACDF, Santo Offizio, Dev. V. 1919, 1, *Cappuccini*, P. Pio da Pietrelcina, fasc. 10, doc. 371 (Nov. 1941): documentation presently not available for consultation; I learned of its existence from the overall inventory list.

76. Ibid., docc. 357–58 (Mar. 1940).

77. Ibid., doc. 361 (Jan. 31, 1941).

78. Among the extensive literature on the subject, see A. Monticone, "De Gasperi e la scelta politica per la democrazia occidental," in U. Corsini and K. Repgen, eds., *Konrad Adenauer e Alcide De Gasperi: due esperienze di rifondazione della democrazia* (Bologna: il Mulino, 1984), pp. 55–78; P. Craveri, *De Gasperi* (Bologna: il Mulino, 2006), pp. 342–44.

79. "Warning from Italy," *Economist*, Mar. 27, 1948, p. 492.

80. See the "Accordo tra il Governo italiano e l'Amministrazione delle Nazioni Unite per l'assistenza e la riabilitazione sull'uso del Fondo lire supplementare agli Accordi dell'8 marzo 1945 e del 19 gennaio 1946," jointly signed by Keeny and Montini on Nov. 12, 1947: in the *Gazzetta ufficiale della Repubblica italiana* 178 (Aug. 3, 1948), pp. 2787 ff.

81. ACS, MI, AAI, Presidenza, busta 56, *AUSA, Trattati e convenzioni, 1948–1951: Richieste di finanziamento dal Fondo Lire AUSA*, sent to Rome AUSA Mission with note 015146.

82. See, for example, the lively description from the diary of Ambassador Egidio Ortona, in E. Ortona, *Anni d'America*, vol. 1, *La ricostruzione: 1944-1951* (Bologna: il Mulino, 1984), p. 85.

83. On the close relations between Jackson and La Guardia, see UNA, UNRRA 1943–49, Pag 4/3.0.14.0.0.0.1, box 1, *Italy Chief of Mission. Correspondence with Individuals*, various documents; see also Sir R. Jackson, "Foreword," in M. Black, *The Children and the Nations. The Story of UNICEF* (New York: UNICEF, 1986), pp. 8–9.

84. Del Fante, *Fatti nuovi*, pp. 333–34.

85. See his memoirs, published posthumously: F. H. La Guardia, *The Making of an Insurgent: An Autobiography: 1882-1919* (Philadelphia and New York: J. B. Lippincott, 1948), pp. 169–86.

86. What follows draws on the excellent study of S. Gerbi and G. De Luna, "Lettere a Fiorello La Guardia, sindaco di New York," in C. Zadra and G. Fait, eds., *Deferenza rivendicazione supplica. Le lettere ai potenti* (Treviso: Pagus edizioni, 1991), pp. 69–87.

87. See ibid., p. 73. (The entire correspondence is filed in the municipal archives of New York City.)

88. ACS, Presidenza del Consiglio dei Ministri, 1948–50, busta 3973, fasc. 14–16. 17329, *Onoranze a Fiorello La Guardia*: press release, Apr. 9, 1948.

89. In his observations on the AAI-AUSA cooperation, Lodovico Montini, writing in 1950, says little about the criteria by which financing decisions were made and makes no reference to Padre Pio's hospital. See L. Montini, *Giorno per giorno tra i protagonisti di un'epoca. Scritti ed appunti (1944–1970)*, G. Mingoni and C. Del Vico, eds. (Florence: Vallecchi, 1971), pp. 35 ff.

90. See ACS, MI, AAI, Presidenza, busta 56, *AUSA, Trattati e convenzioni, 1948–1951: Richieste di finanziamento*.

91. These events are reconstructed from ACS, Presidenza del Consiglio dei Ministri, 1948–50, busta 3973, fasc. 14–16. 17329, *Onoranze a Fiorello La Guardia*.

92. Ibid., director general of AAI to His Excellency Andreotti, Rome, Aug. 13, 1948.

93. See S. Alpern, *Freda Kirchwey. A Woman of "The Nation"* (Cambridge: Harvard University Press, 1987), pp. 162 ff., and F. Kirchwey, "Journey among Creeds III: Rome and Foggia," *Nation* 167, no. 21 (Nov. 20, 1948).

94. Kirchway, "Journey."

95. Agostino da San Marco in Lamis, *Diario*, third edition, F. Colacelli, ed., Edizioni Padre Pio da Pietrelcina, San Giovanni Rotondo, 2003, pp. 179–80 (Sept. 9, 1948).

96. Ibid., p. 175 (Mar. 31, 1948).

97. Ibid.

98. A. G. Roncalli / Giovanni XXIII, *Anni di Francia*, vol. 1, *Agende del nunzio, 1945–1948*, É. Fouilloux, ed., Istituto per le scienze religiose, Bologna, 2004, p. 219 (Aug. 19, 1946).

99. AFSCIRE, Fondo Roncalli, *Corrispondenza*, vol. 72, *Alcide De Gasperi*.

100. A. G. Roncalli / Giovanni XXIII, *Anni di Francia*, vol. 1, p. 222.

101. Ibid., p. 224 (Sept. 2).

102. Ibid., pp. 248 and 258. The contacts between Roncalli and Brunatto declined in the following year (a single audience with "sig. De Pio" on Mar. 27) but picked up again in 1948.

103. The historical contest is best outlined in P. Novick, *The Resistance Versus Vichy: The Purge of Collaborators in Liberated France* (New York: Columbia University Press, 1968).

104. The sequence of judicial proceedings against Brunatto can be traced in the documents in AJM, dossier 1531/1990, *Brunatto Emmanuel Louis* (Atteinte à la sûreté extérieure de l'État), fasc. "Règlement," buste varie. On the "scandalous"—because so generous—amnesty of Aug. 6, 1953, see S. Gascon, *L'amnistie. De la Commune à la guerre d'Algérie* (Paris: Seuil, 2002), pp. 235 ff.

105. See É. Fouilloux, introduction, in Roncalli / Giovanni XXIII, *Anni di Francia*, vol. 1, pp. xii–xvii.

106. Roncalli / Giovanni XXIII, *Anni di Francia*, vol. 1, p. 64 (June 5, 1945); see also p. 62 (May 30, 1945).

107. See chap. 5, pp. 118–20.

108. See AFSCIRE, Fondo Roncalli, *Corrispondenza*, vol. 70, *Andrea Cesarano*: an extensive, candid correspondence between the two during the 1930s and '40s.
109. Ibid.
110. Ibid.
111. Ibid.
112. See chap. 10, pp. 271 ff.
113. In the version given in *L'Avvenire d'Italia*, for example, the ill-mannered communist agitator from San Marco in Lamis didn't get off merely with colic; he was struck by sudden paralysis.
114. Agostino da San Marco in Lamis, *Diario*, p. 176 (Apr. 30, 1948).
115. On the date of that first visit (sometime between Mar. 29 and Apr. 4, 1948), see S. Campanella, *Il papa e il frate*, Edizioni Padre Pio da Pietrelcina, San Giovanni Rotondo, 2005. Wojtyla's doctoral thesis, completed in June 1948, dealt with Carmelite mysticism: see K. Wojtyla, *La dottrina della fede in S. Giovanni della Croce*, M. Bettetini, ed. (Milan: Bompiani, 2003).

9. The White Hand and the Red

1. See A. Riccardi, "Governo e 'profezia' nel pontificato di Pio XII," in Riccardi, ed., *Pio XII* (Rome-Bari: Laterza, 1984), pp. 31–92. On the personal style of Pius XII, see the portrait in A. Tornielli, *Pio XII. Un uomo sul trono di Pietro* (Milan: Mondadori, 2007).
2. V. Pratolini, "Garofani rossi per Fausto" (*Il Nuovo Corriere*, June 5, 1947), in Pratolini, *Cronache dal Giro d'Italia (maggio-giugno 1947)* (Milan: La Vita Felice, 1995), pp. 68–71.
3. See A. Del Fante, *Fatti nuovi. Seguito del volume: "Per la storia. Padre Pio di Pietrelcina, il primo sacerdote stigmatizzato,"* Arti grafiche, Bologna, 1951, p. 51, where he quotes from *Stadio*, June 6, 1947.
4. See S. Pivato, *Sia lodato Bartali. Ideologia, cultura e miti dello sport cattolico (1936–1948)* (Rome: Edizioni Lavoro, 1985); D. Marchesini, *Coppi e Bartali* (Bologna: il Mulino, 1998).
5. See D. Marchesini, *L'Italia del Giro d'Italia* (Bologna: il Mulino, 1996), pp. 206 ff.
6. An astute reconstruction of the political-cultural circumstances is in P. G. Zunino, *La Repubblica e il suo passato. Il fascismo dopo il fascismo, il comunismo, la democrazia: le origini dell'Italia contemporanea* (Bologna: il Mulino, 2003), pp. 705 ff.
7. A. Lingua, *Ho visto padre Pio da Pietrelcina: diario di tre fortunati viaggi a S. Giovanni Rotondo*, Tip. G. Mondino, Fossano, n.d. (1950), pp. 5 and 28.
8. Ibid., p. 5.
9. Nuvolari's wins in the most famous Italian road race date to the early 1930s: see D. Marchesini, *Cuori e motori. Storia delle Mille Miglia, 1927–1957* (Bologna: il Mulino, 2001), pp. 82 ff.
10. Quoted in A. Santini, *Nuvolari* (1983) (Milan: Rizzoli, 1987), pp. 260–61. (I thank Daniele Marchesini for this reference.)

11. F. Fano, "Padre Pio nascose le stimmate nelle maniche del saio francescano," *Momento Sera*, Sept. 28, 1947.

12. See D. Argentieri, *La prodigiosa storia di Padre Pio, narrata e discussa con 21 fotoineisioni* (Milan: Tarantola, 1951), p. 129.

13. See prologue, p. 2.

14. R. Mutinelli, ed., *Ritorno di padre Rebora. Testimonianze ed inediti*, Longo, Rovereto, 1991, p. 76.

15. Quoted in U. Muratore, *Clemente Rebora. Santità soltanto compie il canto* (Cinisello Balsamo: Edizioni San Paolo, 1997).

16. See C. Rebora, *Curriculum vitae* (Milan: All'insegna del pesce d'oro, 1955); Rebora, *Canti dell'infermità* (Milan: All'insegna del pesce d'oro, 1956) and a second, amplified edition in 1957.

17. Quoted in Muratore, *Clemente Rebora*, p. 346.

18. See Del Fante, *Fatti nuovi*, pp. 175–78 and 254–58.

19. Along with other hagiographic accounts cited in these notes, see L. Patri, *Cenni biografici su padre Pio da Pietrelcina*, Edizioni San Francesco, San Giovanni Rotondo, 1951; G. V. M., *La storia di padre Pio (da Pietrelcina a S. Giovanni Rotondo)*, Officine grafiche italiane, Rome, 1955.

20. The Abresch postcard was frequently placed (or glued) between the pages of devotional works.

21. Lingua, *Ho visto padre Pio*, p. 15.

22. Ibid., pp. 15 and 28.

23. R. Barthes, "The Iconography of the Abbé Pierre" (1957), in Barthes, *Mythologies*, Annette Lavers, trans. (London: Jonathan Cape, 1972).

24. On the beard as icon, see S. Bulgari, "Il segno della barba," in P. Magli, G. Manetti, and P. Violi, eds., *Semiotica: storia, teoria, interpretazione. Saggi intorno a Umberto Eco* (Milan: Bompiani, 1992), pp. 425–41.

25. See U. Lucas and T. Agliani, "Tra Miss Italia e Padre Pio. Società e fotogiornalismo dal dopoguerra ai nostri giorni," in *L'Italia del Novecento. Le fotografie e la storia*, G. De Luna, G. D'Autilia, and L. Criscenti, eds., vol. 2, *La società in posa* (Turin: Einaudi, 2006), pp. 365–66.

26. Quoted in D. Freedberg, *The Power of Images: Studies in the History and Theory of Response* (Chicago: University of Chicago Press, 1989), p. 440.

27. See N. N. Perez, ed., *Revelation: Representations of Christ in Photography* (London: Merrell, 2003).

28. See G. Didi-Huberman, "The Index of the Absent Wound (Monograph of a Stain)," *October* 29 (1994), p. 65. Also, on the cultural roots of the matter, H. Belting, *La vera immagine di Cristo* (Turin: Bollati Boringhieri, 2007).

29. See chap. 2, p. 41, and chap. 1, p. 32.

30. I quote from the typescript "Ricordo della visita a Padre Pio del Dott. Giovanni Santucci," dated Naples, Oct. 1957, from a private family archive.

31. G. Tomaselli, *Storia di un frate (Padre Pio)*, Scuola grafica salesiana, Palermo, 1968, p. 80.

32. C. Trabucco, *Il mondo di Padre Pio*, Giacomaniello, Rome, 1952, p. 120. (Most of this material was published in *Popolo* between 1950 and 1952).

33. On the role played by Vergani in 1930s Italian journalism, see G. Licata, *Storia del "Corriere della Sera"* (Milan: Rizzoli, 1976), pp. 253 ff.

34. O. Vergani, "Da trent'anni sanguinano le stimmate di Padre Pio," *Corriere della Sera*, Apr. 9, 1950.

35. O. Vergani, "Da Milano per vedere me? Serviva di più un'Ave Maria," *Corriere della Sera*, Apr. 10, 1950.

36. Ibid.

37. Ibid.

38. For the cultural background, see A. Cappabianca, *Il cinema e il sacro* (Recco-Genoa: Le Mani, 1998), pp. 56–57.

39. L. Bedeschi, *Carlo Campanini imparò l'umorismo da Padre Pio*, cited in Del Fante, *Fatti nuovi*, pp. 178–82.

40. See T. De Mauro, ed., *Grande dizionario italiano dell'uso* (Turin: Utet, 1999), vol. 4, p. 228.

41. See S. Boesch Gajano, *Santità, culti, agiografia, Temi e prospettive* (Rome: Viella, 1997), pp. 38 ff.

42. The most acute account of the period is G. Crainz, *Storia del miracolo italiano. Culture, identità, trasformazioni fra anni cinquanta e sessanta* (Rome: Donzelli, 1996).

43. Vergani, "Da Milano per vedere me?"

44. See A. Casellato, "Santi e madonne per l'Italia del boom. Lettere a Gigliola Cinquetti e papà Cervi," in A. Iuso and Q. Antonelli, eds. *Scrivere agli idoli: la scrittura popolare negli anni Sessanta e dintorni a partire dalle 150.000 lettere a Gigliola Cinquetti* (Trento: Fondazione Museo Storico del Trentino, 2007).

45. See F. De Santis, *Padre Pio* (Milan: Longanesi, 1966). The author was the Vatican expert for *Corriere della Sera*.

46. See Del Fante, *Fatti nuovi*, pp. 17–182 and 183–342, respectively.

47. De Monticelli, *I prodigi di Padre Pio*.

48. See S. Luzzatto, *The Body of Il Duce: Mussolini's Corpse and the Fortunes of Italy* (New York: Metropolitan, 2005), pp. 172–76.

49. De Monticelli, "I prodigi di Padre Pio."

50. Ibid.

51. Ibid.

52. See Agostino da San Marco in Lamis, *Diario*, third edition, F. Colacelli, ed., Edizioni Padre Pio da Pietrelcina, San Giovanni Rotondo, 2003, pp. 171 (June 27, 1947) and ff.

53. According to P. Delfino Sessa, *P. Pio da Pietrelcina* (Genoa: Demos, 1949), p. 207.

54. Quoted in R. Allegri, *Padre Pio. Il santo dei miracoli* (Milan: Mondadori, 2002), pp. 400–401.

55. See E. D'Ercole, "Guarisce senza saperlo," *Nuova Stampa Sera*, Oct. 15, 1950; E. D'Ercole, "Anche Genova ha un 'mago,'" *Corriere Mercantile*, Nov. 16, 1950.

56. See L. Garibaldi, "Guarisco i malati per ordine di Padre Pio," *Gente*, Jan. 18, 1971.

57. G. Palumbo, "Ho guarito il fratello di Padre Pio," *Eva Express*, Aug. 5, 1974.

58. Trabucco, *Il mondo di Padre Pio*, pp. 36–44.

59. De Monticelli, "I prodigi di Padre Pio."

60. Trabucco, *Il mondo di Padre Pio*, pp. 26 ff.

61. See D. Lajolo, *Il volto umano di un rivoluzionario. La straordinaria avventura di Giuseppe Di Vittorio* (Florence: Vallecchi, 1979), pp. 43 and 113.

62. F. Chiocci and L. Cirri, *Padre Pio. Storia di una vittima* (Rome: I libri del No, 1967), vol. 1, p. 309.

63. Ibid.

64. Patri, *Cenni biografici*, p. 6.

65. See *Suprema Sacra Congregatio Sancti Officii. Decretum Proscriptio Librorum*, Feria 4, die 23 iulii 1952, *L'Osservatore Romano*, Aug. 3, 1952.

66. "A proposito di un Decreto del Sant'Offizio," *L'Osservatore Romano*, Aug. 4–5, 1952.

67. See chap. 5, pp. 127–28.

68. C. Camilleri, *Padre Pio da Pietrelcina. Nella vita, nel mistero, nel prodigio*, Società tipografica Leonardo da Vinci, Città di Castello, 1952, pp. 85–88.

69. ACS, MI, DGPS, Confinati politici, fascicoli personali, busta 180, *Camilleri Carmelo*: letter from Camilleri to Mussolini, Rome, July 22, 1937.

70. See M. Franzinelli, *I tentacoli dell'Ovra, Agenti, collaboratori e vittime della polizia politica fascista* (Turin: Bollati Boringhieri, 1999), p. 81.

71. My reconstruction is based on documents in ACS, MI, DGPS, Confinati politici, fascicoli personali, busta 180; and in ACS, MI, DGPS, Divisione Polizia politica, fascicoli personali, 1927–44, busta 222, fasc. *Camilleri dr. Carmelo*.

72. See ACS, MI, DGPS, Confinati politici, fascicoli personali, b. 180, *Camilleri Carmelo*: letter from Camilleri to chief of police, from the Tremiti Islands, May 30, 1939.

73. See C. Camilleri, "Storia dell'attentato di piazza Giulio Cesare a Milano," in *Ordine pubblico*, Jan. 31 and Mar. 31, 1953. E. Rossi, *La pupilla del duce. L'Ovra* (Parma: Guanda, 1956) drew on Camilleri's arguments.

74. See C. Camilleri, *Polizia in azione. Incursione nel mondo che ho combattuto*, Editoriale ordine pubblico, Rome, 1958.

75. Camilleri, *Padre Pio*, pp. 145–46.

76. See E. Magrì, *Un italiano vero: Pitigrilli* (Milan: Baldini and Castoldi, 1999), pp. 164 ff.; M. Giovana, *Giustizia e Libertà in Italia. Storia di una cospirazione antifascista, 1929-1937* (Turin: Bollati Boringhieri, 2005), pp. 356 ff.

77. See Pitigrilli, *Pitigrilli parla di Pitigrilli* (Milan: Sonzogno, 1949), pp. 171–77.

78. A. Di Legge and V. Epifano, *Padre Pio da Pietrelcina, primo cavaliere del bene* (Caserta: Cisca, 1951), p. 10.

79. Ibid., p. 12.

80. ACS, MI, DGPS, Confinati politici, fascicoli personali, busta 359, *Di Legge Antonio*: report from Lazio command, Royal Carabinieri, Feb. 1, 1928.

81. Ibid.: letter from Di Legge to Mussolini, from Lipari, Jan. 30, 1928. On the

discovery of Matteotti's body, see G. Capecelatro and F. Zaina, *La banda del Viminale* (Milan: il Saggiatore, 1996), pp. 77 ff.

82. See A. Di Legge, *La città di Priverno, antica capitale dei Volsci: cenni storici*, Scuola tipografica antoniana, Ferentino, 1934; Di Legge, *Storia delle corporazioni. Preistoria, Roma antica, alto e basso Medio evo, Rinascimento, epoca moderna, secolo del lavoro, universalità di Roma*, Giudici, Clusone, 1936.

83. Sent from Rome, the letter is in ACS, MI, DGPS, DPP, fascicoli personali, 1927–44, busta 155, fasc. *Bombacci Nicola*.

84. ACS, MI, CPC, b. 1794, *Di Legge Antonio*: letter from Rome Questura to director of Public Security, July 11, 1940.

85. See M. Canali, *Le spie del regime* (Bologna: il Mulino, 2004), pp. 533–35.

86. Quoted in F. Chiocci and L. Cirri, *Padre Pio*, vol. 1, p. 615.

87. I take the quotes above (and below) from G. Piovene, *Viaggio in Italia* (1957; Milan: Baldini and Castoldi, 1993), pp. 761–64.

88. See S. Luzzatto, *L'immagine del duce. Mussolini nelle fotografie dell'Istituto Luce* (Rome: Editori Riuniti, 2001), p. 145; also S. Gerbi, *Tempi di malafede. Una storia italiana tra fascismo e dopoguerra: Guido Piovene ed Eugenio Colorni* (Turin: Einaudi, 1999), pp. 102 ff.

89. Piovene, *Viaggio in Italia*, pp. 764–66.

90. Ibid., p. 765.

91. F. Chiocci and L. Cirri offer photographic reproductions of these newspaper clippings in *Padre Pio*, vol. 3, pp. 250–51.

92. See A. Vauchez, *Sainthood in the Later Middle Ages*, Jean Birrell, trans. (New York: Cambridge University Press, 1997). Other fundamental works on this theme include G. Pomata, *La promessa di guarigione. Malati e guaritori in Antico Regime. Bologna XVI–XVIII secolo* (Rome-Bari: Laterza, 1994); G. Fiume, ed., "Guarigioni mirabili," special issue of *Quaderni storici* 112, no. 1 (2003). An anthropological angle is in V. Lanternari, "Le terapie carismatiche. Medicina popolare e scienza moderna," *La ricerca folklorica*. (Oct. 1983; special issue titled "La medicina popolare in Italia"), pp. 85 ff.

93. I draw on C. Gallini's impeccable research, "Lourdes e la medicalizzazione del miracolo," *La ricerca folklorica* 29 (Apr. 1994), pp. 83–94; Gallini, *Il miracolo e la sua prova. Un etnologo a Lourdes* (Naples: Liguori, 1998). See also the fine study by R. Harris, *Lourdes. Body and Spirit in the Secular Age* (London: Penguin, 1999), esp. pp. 325 ff.

94. See J.-M Sallmann, *Naples et ses saints á l'âge barogue (1540–1750)* (Paris: Presses universitaires de France, 1994), p. 375.

95. See Pio da Pietrelcina, *Epistolario*, vol. 3, *Corrispondenza con le figlie spirituali (1915-1923)*, Melchiorre da Pobladura and Alessandro da Ripabottoni, eds., Edizioni Padre Pio da Pietrelcina, San Giovanni Rotondo, 2002.

96. For a positive interpretation of this conviction, see G. Pasquale, *Padre Pio. Sperare oltre il soffrire* (Milan: Jaca Book, 2003), esp. pp. 49 ff.; for a negative one, see A. Pascale, "Digli di smettere di baciarmi" (preface to the Italian edition of *The Missionary Position: Mother Teresa in Theory and Practice*) and C. Hitchens, *La posizione della missionaria. Teoria e pratica di Madre Teresa*, trans. E. Kampmann (Rome: minimum fax, 1997), pp. 7–16.

97. Two different emphases are in G. Cosmacini, *Gemelli* (Milan: Rizzoli 1985), pp. 275 ff; and M. Bocci, *Agostino Gemelli rettore e francescano. Chiesa, regime, democrazia* (Brescia: Morcelliana, 2003), pp. 78–79 and 612–13.

98. See P. Pombeni, *Il gruppo dossettiano e la fondazione della democrazia italiana (1938–1948)* (Bologna: il Mulino, 1979); E. Galavotti, *Il giovane Dossetti. Gli anni della formazione, 1913–1939* (Bologna: il Mulino, 2006), pp. 149–222.

99. See ACDF, Santo Offizio, Dev. V. 1919, 1, *Cappuccini*, P. Pio da Pietrelcina, fasc. 1, Inventario generale 1919–56, doc. 439 (Oct. 27, 1947), doc. 481 (Oct. 1, 1951), etc.

100. For his critical remarks in *Settimana Incom*, 1952, see E. Malatesta, *Aiutatemi tutti a portare la croce*, Pratiche editrice, Milan, 2002, p. 203.

101. See J. Bouflet, *Padre Pio. Des foudres du Saint-Office à la splendeur de la vérité* (Paris: Presses de la Renaissance, 2002), pp. 377 ff.

102. On the origins of the IOR, see J. F. Pollard, *Money and the Rise of the Modern Papacy: Financing the Vatican, 1850–1950* (Cambridge: Cambridge University Press, 2005).

103. Anastatic copies of Padre Pio's request and Pius XII's reply (dated Apr. 4, 1957) are in Chiocci and Cirri, *Padre Pio*, vol. 3, pp. 255–59.

104. Quotations from Agostino da San Marco in Lamis, *Diario*, pp. 220–22 (Feb. 10 to Nov. 18, 1958).

10. A Straw Idol

1. See A. Tornielli, *Pius XII. Un uomo sul trono di Pietro* (Milan: Mondadori, 2007), pp. 567–68.

2. See P. Niehans, *La sénéscence et le rajeunissement* (Paris: Vigot, 1937).

3. See A. Paravicini Bagliani, *Il corpo del papa* (Turin: Einaudi, 1994), p. xviii and passim.

4. See J. Cornwell, *Hitler's Pope: The Secret History of Pius XII* (London: Viking/Penguin, 1999).

5. See G. Verucci, *La Chiesa cattolica in Italia dall'Unità a oggi* (Rome-Bari: Laterza, 1999), p. 69.

6. "Taccuino," in *Il Mondo*, Oct. 28, 1958.

7. See A. Melloni, *Il Conclave. Storia di un'istituzione* (Bologna: il Mulino, 2001), pp. 106, 118, 181.

8. This photo magazine was timed to the appearance in cinemas of the newsreels by the same name: see A. Sainati, ed., *La Settimana Incom. Cinegiornali e informazione negli anni '50* (Turin: Lindon, 2001).

9. V. Lojacono, "Padre Pio predisse il papato a Roncalli," *La Settimana Incom illustrata*, Aug. 22, 1959.

10. See Agostino da San Marco in Lamis, *Diario*, third edition, F. Colacelli, ed., Edizioni Padre Pio da Pietrelcina, San Giovanni Rotondo, 2003, pp. 224–28 (June 8 to Oct. 22, 1959).

11. F. Morcaldi, *San Giovanni Rotondo nella luce del francescanesimo*, Edizioni Mantilli, Parma 1960, p. 53.

12. Agostino da San Marco in Lamis, *Diario*, p. 227 (Sept. 8, 1959). See also *La*

Madonna e Padre Pio. Pubblicazione speciale dell'Apostolato della Madonna di Fatima in Italia in occasione della beatificazione di Padre Pio, Centro di Fatima, Rome, 1999.

13. See P. Apolito, *Il cielo in terra. Costruzioni simboliche di un'apparizione mariana* (Bologna: il Mulino, 1992), pp. 153–68; Apolito, *La religione degli italiani* (Rome: Editori Riuniti, 2001), pp. 25 ff.; E. Fattorini, *Il culto mariano tra Ottocento e Novecento: simboli e devozione. Ipotesi e prospettive di ricerca*, (Milan: Franco Angeli, 1999), pp. 67 ff.

14. I quote from a note by Father Agostino dated 1915, *Diario*, p. 47.

15. See A. Del Fante, *Fatti nuovi. Seguito del volume: "Per la storia. Padre Pio di Pietrelcina, il primo sacerdote stigmatizzato,"* Arti grafiche, Bologna, 1951, p. 90 and passim.

16. See W. A. Christian, "Religious Apparitions and the Cold War in Southern Europe," in E. R. Wolf, ed., *Religion, Power and Protest in Local Communities: The Northern Shore of the Mediterranean* (Berlin-Amsterdam: Mouton, 1984), pp. 239–66.

17. See L. Scaraffia, "Devozioni di guerra. Identità femminile e simboli religiosi negli anni quaranta," in A. Bravo, ed., *Donne e uomini nelle guerre mondiali* (Rome-Bari: Laterza, 1991), pp. 152–60.

18. On relations between Padre Pio and the Piacenza clairvoyant Rosa Quattrini ("Mamma Rosa"), see W. A. Christian, "Holy People in Peasant Europe," *Comparative Studies in Society and History* 15 (1973), pp. 106–14.

19. On the global spread of Marian visionaries in the second half of the twentieth century, see W. A. Christian, "Believers and Seers: The Expansion of an International Visionary Culture," in D. Albera, A. Blok, and C. Bromberger, eds., *L'anthropologie de la Méditerranée/Anthropology of the Mediterranean* (Paris: Maisonneuve and Larose, 2001).

20. See R. Pierri, *Il quarto segreto di Fátima* (Milan: Kaos edizioni, 2003), p. 129.

21. See Fattorini, *Il culto mariano*, p. 84.

22. See Christian, "Holy People," p. 109.

23. According to E. Bianchi, "L'eloquenza della santità. Appunti sulla spiritualità di papa Giovanni XXIII," in *Un cristiano sul trono di Pietro. Studi storici su Giovanni XXIII*, Servitium, Gorle (Bergamo), 2003, pp. 277–88.

24. Both quotations (from Roncalli's diaries) are in E. Galavotti, "I giorni del patriarca Roncalli," in *Rivisitare Giovanni XXIII. Atti del colloquio internazionale di Bologna (1–3 giugno 2003)*, E. Galavotti, ed., *Cristianesimo nella storia* 25, no. 2 (2004), pp. 433–56.

25. "Per la difesa della fede. Istruzione religiosa," *Bollettino ecclesiatico della Diocesi di Vittorio Veneto* 48, no. 2 (Feb. 1960). An anastatic copy of this document is found in F. Chiocci and L. Cirri, *Padre Pio. Storia di una vittima* (Rome: I libri del No, 1967), vol. 3, p. 443.

26. See J. Bouflet, *Padre Pio. Des foudres du Saint-Office à la splendeur de la vérité* (Paris: Presses de la Renaissance, 2002), pp. 390–94.

27. Ibid., pp. 377 ff.

28. On the use of the confessional in Borromean Milan, see the excellent study

by W. De Boer, *The Conquest of the Soul: Confession, Discipline and Public Order in Counter-Reformation Milan* (Leiden: Brill, 2001). The quotation comes from a text of 1575.

29. See Del Fante, *Fatti nuovi*, pp. 13–14.

30. See Bouflet, *Padre Pio*, pp. 403 ff.

31. Quoted in G. Alberigo and A. Melloni, eds., *Beatificationis et canonizationis Servi Dei Ioannis Papae XXIII Summi Pontificis (1881–1963), Biografia documentata*, Pars 4, Tipografia Guerra, Rome, 1995, p. 2842.

32. This seems to have been true as far back as when he began to confide his inner feelings to his *Giornale dell'anima*: see G. De Rosa, "Angelo Roncalli e Radini Tedeschi," appendix to *Giovanni XXIII. Linee per una ricerca storica* (Rome: Edizioni di storia e letteratura, 1965), p. 57.

33. Alberigo and Melloni, eds., *Beatificationis et canonizationis*, pp. 2928 and 2932.

34. AFSCIRE, Fondo Roncalli, *Scritti del Servo di Dio*, vol. XI-127, entry, June 25, 1960.

35. See the testimony of his personal assistant, Monsignor Loris Capovilla, quoted in E. Galavotti, *Appunti per una storia del processo di canonizzazione di Giovanni XXIII*, in *Un cristiano sul trono di Pietro. Studi storici su Giovanni XXIII* (Gorle, BG: Servitium/Fondazione per le scienze religiose Giovanni XXIII di Bologna, 2003), p. 308.

36. AFSCIRE, Fondo Roncalli, *Scritti del Servo di Dio*, vol. XI-127, entry, June 25, 1960.

37. Ibid.

38. A first account of Monsignor Maccari's apostolic visit and its consequences is in M. Tosatti, *Quando la Chiesa perseguitava Padre Pio* (Casale Monferrato: Piemme, 2005).

39. See Maccari's report of Nov. 27, 1990, to Cardinal Joseph Ratzinger, prefect of the Congregation for the Doctrine of the Faith, in Congregatio de causis Sanctorum, *Beatificationis et canonizationis Servi Dei Pii a Pietrelcina sacerdotis professi ofm cap. (Francesco Forgione)*, vol. 4, *Quaestiones selectae*, Tipografia Favia, Bari, 1997, pp. 419–42.

40. Alberigo and Melloni, eds., *Beatificationis et canonizationis*, p. 2938 (from John XXIII's daybook, July 19, 1960).

41. Long portions of this appear in Congregatio de causis Sanctorum, *Beatificationis et canonizationis*, pp. 103–41.

42. Ibid., pp. 160–61 (Maccari's diary, Sept. 3 1960).

43. Ibid., pp. 162–69 (July 31–Sept. 5, 1960).

44. Quotations, like those that follow, are from Monsignor Maccari's report of Nov. 5, 1960: ibid., pp. 117–21.

45. Ibid., pp. 127–30.

46. Ibid., pp. 131–32.

47. Ibid., pp. 133–34.

48. Ibid., pp. 134–37.

49. Ibid., p. 138.

50. Ibid.

51. Ibid., p. 141.

52. *Giudizio del S. Officio sulla Visita Ap. Di Mons. Maccari*; quote, ibid., pp. 363–64.

53. Diary of Monsignor Maccari, p. 171 (Sept. 19, 1960).

54. Giovanni XXIII, *Lettere, 1958–1963*, L. F. Capovilla, ed. (Rome: Edizioni di Storia e Letteratura, 1978), p. 159 (Aug. 16, 1959).

55. Quote from the daybook of John XXIII in Alberigo and Melloni, eds., *Beatificationis et canonizationis*, p. 2949.

56. See Paravicini Bagliani, *Il corpo del papa*, pp. 28–37.

57. AFSCIRE, Fondo Roncalli, *Corrispondenza*, vol. 70, *Andrea Cesarano* (from Manfredonia, Nov. 18, 1960).

58. A copy of Brunatto's letter is reproduced in Chiocci and Cirri, *Padre Pio*, vol. 3, pp. 557–61.

59. Ibid., p. 561.

60. See E. Malatesta, *L'ultimo segreto di Padre Pio* (Casale Monferrato: Piemme, 2002), pp. 169 ff.

61. See F. Chiocci, *L'uomo che salvò Padre Pio. Vita, avventure e morte di Emanuele Brunatto* (Rome: Adnkronos Libri, 2003), pp. 117–25.

62. L. Montesi, "Padre Pio tradito," *Epoca*, Oct. 16, 1960.

63. Mino Caudana published twenty-two articles about Padre Pio in *Il Tempo* in May and June 1957; Luciano Cirri wrote about him in *Il Borghese* mostly in the spring of 1963; Francobaldo Chiocci in *Il Tempo* beginning in 1962–63, and then extensively in 1967.

64. See L. Cirri, *Padre Pio e i papponi di Dio* (Milan: Edizioni del Borghese, 1963); Chiocci and Cirri, *Padre Pio.*; F. Chiocci, *I nemici di padre Pio* (Rome: Edizioni Reporter, 1968); F. Chiocci, *Padre Pio non è morto* (Rome: Gallo Rosso, 1968).

65. Quotations are drawn from two titles: E. Malatesta, *Aiutatemi tutti a portare la Croce. La biografia definitiva di Padre Pio da Pietrelcina* (Milan: Pratiche, 2002); R. Allegri, *Padre Pio. Il santo dei miracoli* (Milan: Mondadori, 2002). Each of these authors wrote a half dozen books about Padre Pio.

66. See S. Boesch Gajano, *Santità, culti, agiografia. Temi et prospettive* (Rome: Viella, 1997), pp. 38–39.

67. Useful reflections on these issues are in L. Lanna and F. Rossi, *Fascisti immaginari. Tutto quello che c'è da sapere sulla destra* (Florence: Vallecchi, 2003), pp. 233–37.

68. See Luzzatto, *The Body of Il Duce: Mussolini's Corpse and the Fortunes of Italy* (New York: Metropolitan, 2005), pp. 117 ff.

69. See M. Caudana, *Il figlio del fabbro* (Rome: CEN, 1960).

70. See F. Chiocci, *Donna Rachele* (Rome: Ciarrapico editore, 1983). On Brunatto, see Chiocci, *L'uomo che salvò Padre Pio.*

71. Ten articles by Pisanò appeared in the Milanese weekly *Secolo XX* in the spring and summer of 1960.

72. A series of Berlutti's articles was published in *Secolo d'Italia* in Oct. 1960. See also G. Berlutti, *Noi crediamo nel Duce* (Rome: Unione editoriale d'Italia,

1941); Berlutti, *Ritorno all'amore sulle orme di Gesù*, Carabba, Lanciano, 1944.

73. See chap. 6, pp. 182–84. And in 1953, writing in *La Casa Sollievo della Sofferenza*, bulletin of the Opera di Padre Pio, De Luca didn't rule out the supernatural explanation for Padre Pio's stigmata: See G. M. Viscardi, "Padre Pio, padre Gemelli e don Giuseppe De Luca, ovvero la santità tra scienza e intelligenza," *Ricerche di storia sociale e religiosa* 63 (2003), pp. 207–11.

74. G. De Luca, "Dove io, di carnevale, chiedo alla Madonna un miracolo," *L'Osservatore Romano*, Feb. 11, 1962, reprinted in De Luca, *Bailamme, ovverosia pensieri del sabato sera* (Brescia: Morcelliana, 1963), pp. 281 ff.

75. See R. Guarnieri, *Don Giuseppe De Luca. Tra cronaca e storia* (1974; Cinisello Balsamo: Edizioni Paoline, 1991), p. 114. On the ties between Roncalli and Don De Luca, see G. De Rosa, "Erudizione ecclesiastica e pietà in Angelo Roncalli e Giuseppe De Luca," in De Rosa, *Tempo religioso e tempo storico. Saggi e note di storia sociale e religiosa dal Medioevo all'età contemporanea* (Rome: Edizioni di Storia e Letteratura, 1987), vol. 1, pp. 267–301.

76. De Luca, "Dove io, di carnevale," p. 283.

77. See chap. 8, pp. 216 ff.

78. Quotations from Tosatti, *Quando la Chiesa*, pp. 174–75.

79. See Malatesta, *L'ultimo segreto*, pp. 45 ff.

80. Dated San Giovanni Rotondo, Nov. 23, 1968, Father Carmelo's report is published in its entirety in ibid., pp. 45–52.

81. See P. Camporesi, *Il sugo della vita. Simbolismo e magia del sangue* (1988; Milan: Mondadori, 1993), p. 61.

82. See P. Brown, *The Cult of the Saints: Its Rise and Function in Latin Christianity* (Chicago: University of Chicago Press, 1982).

83. I quote from the report of Father Carmelo of San Giovanni in Galdo, in Malatesta, *L'ultimo segreto*, pp. 50–51.

84. R. Barthes, "The Iconography of the Abbé Pierre" (1957), in Barthes, *Mythologies*, Annette Lavers, trans. (London: Jonathan Cape, 1972).

Epilogue. May 2, 1999

1. I. Silone, *L'avventura di un povero cristiano* (Milan: Mondadori, 1968), p. 166.

2. See W. A. Christian, *Local Religion in Sixteenth Century Spain* (Princeton: Princeton University Press, 1981).

3. I draw on M. de Certeau, *Hagiographie*, in *Encyclopaedia universalis*, vol. 9, Encyclopaedia universalis, Paris 1985, pp. 69–72.

4. The most reliable guide to these matters is A. Vauchez, *Sainthood in the Later Middle Ages*, Jean Birrell, trans. (New York: Cambridge University Press, 1997); Vauchez, *Saints, prophètes et visionnaires. Le pouvoir du surnaturel au Moyen Âge* (Paris: Albin Michel, 1999).

5. See P. Post, *The Modern Saint: An Exploration of Sacral Interferences*, in M. Poorthuis and J. Schwartz, eds., *Saints and Role Models in Judaism and Christianity* (Leiden and Boston: Brill, 2004), pp. 398–403.

6. See J.-C. Schmitt, ed., *Les saints et les stars. Le texte agiographique dans la culture populaire* (Paris: Beauchesne, 1983).

7. See P. Apolito, *Internet e la Madonna. Sul visionarismo religioso in Rete* (Milan: Feltrinelli, 2002), pp. 155 ff.

8. A chronology of Karol Wojtyla's relations with Padre Pio appears in S. Campanella, *Il papa e il frate*, Edizioni Padre Pio da Pietrelcina, San Giovanni Rotondo, 2005.

9. See C. Frugoni, *Vita di un uomo: Francesco d' Assisi* (Turin: Einaudi, 1995), p. 121.

10. John Paul II's address is reprinted in full in Gerardo di Flumeri, *Il beato padre Pio da Pietrelcina*, Edizioni Padre Pio da Pietrelcina, San Giovanni Rotondo, 2001, pp. 471–74 (quotation on p. 472).

11. The sermon in full appears in ibid., pp. 483–86 (quotation on p. 484).

12. See, for comparison, the perspectives of F. De Palma, "La santità postconciliare: considerazioni statistiche, tipologiche e sociologiche per una storia delle canonizzazioni," in F. Scorza Barcellona, ed., *Santi del Novecento: storia, agiografia, canonizzazioni* (Turin: Rosenberg e Sellier, 1998), pp. 49–82; M. Politi, "L'inflazione dei santi," *MicroMega* 3 (1999), pp. 201–10; A. Melloni, "La duttilità dei santi. Note sulla canonizzazione di Padre Pio," *il Mulino* 4, (2002), pp. 679–86.

13. See A. Tornielli, *Il segreto di Padre Pio e Karol Wojtyla* (Casale Monferrato: Piemme, 2006), pp. 110–19. In 1990, a leading American scholar called the beatification of Padre Pio the Catholic Church's most important such cause in the last two centuries: see K. L. Woodward, *Making Saints: How the Catholic Church Determines Who Becomes a Saint and Who Doesn't* (New York: Touchstone, 1990).

14. See T. J. Dandelet, *Spanish Rome, 1500–1700* (New Haven and London: Yale University Press, 2001), pp. 171–85.

15. See M. Ranchetti, *Non c'è più religione. Istituzione e verità nel cattolicesimo italiano del Novecento* (Milan: Garzanti, 2003), pp. 11 ff.

16. See E. Arosio, "Il miracolo di Renzo Piano," *L'espresso*, Oct. 24, 2002, p. 170.

17. G. G. Merlo, *Nel nome di san Francesco. Storia dei frati Minori e del francescanesimo sino agli inizi del XVI secolo* (Padua: Editrici Francescane, 2003), pp. 391–92.

18. See C. McKevitt, "San Giovanni Rotondo and the Shrine of Padre Pio," in J. Eade and M. Salinow, eds., *Contesting the Sacred: The Anthropology of Christian Pilgrimage* (Urbana and Chicago: University of Illinois Press, 2000), p. 78.

19. Paul VI was speaking in the Vatican, on Feb. 20, 1971, to the "definitor general" of the Capuchin Order.

20. See P. J. Margry, "Merchandising and Sanctity: The Invasive Cult of Padre Pio," *Journal of Modern Italian Studies* 7, no. 1 (2002), pp. 94 ff.

21. See M. Cucco, "Come se Padre Pio vivesse ancora," *Famiglia cristiana* 38, (Sept. 29, 1978), p. 49; S. Contenta, "Padre Pio's Kitsch e Conflict," *Toronto Star*, June 15, 2003.

22. See P. Apolito, *La religione degli italiani* (Rome: Editori Riuniti, 2001), p. 27.

On the Web site www.cultodellaforza.it, a disturbing example of how modern-day Nazi sentiments can meld with the cult of Padre Pio.

23. G. Buccini, "Due 'angeli,' un po' di gasolio. Così si è salvato il piccolo Nicolò," *Corriere della Sera*, Sept. 29, 2003.

24. See R. Cri, "Veglia il cadavere del figlio, poi muore," *La Stampa*, Feb. 3, 2003.

25. See F. Caccia, "Non vivrò senza gambe, fatemi morire," *Corriere della Sera*, June 8, 2004.

26. See A. Garibaldi, "Sorelline adottate dalla nonna. 'Dove sono mamma e papà'?" *Corriere della Sera*, Nov. 22, 2004.

27. See A. Cazzullo, "Il paese dei campanili nel sacrario ritrovato," *Corriere della Sera*, Nov. 18, 2003.

28. See N. Ammaniti, *The Crossroads* (London: Canongate, 2009). Other novelists who draw on Padre Pio's appeal in contemporary Italy: A. Busi, *Seminar on Youth*, Stuart Hood, trans. (New York: Farrar, Straus and Giroux, 1989); A. Pascale, *La città distratta* (Turin: Einaudi, 2001) p. 77; P. Di Stefano, *Aiutami tu* (Milan: Feltrinelli, 2005), p. 167.

29. Ammaniti, *The Crossroads*.

30. A. Capurso, "E io so a che santo votarmi," *Sette: Magazine del Corriere della Sera*, Apr. 29, 2004, p. 61.

31. See G. A. Stella, "Il telerosario dei politici," *Corriere della Sera*, Jan. 13, 2005.

32. See F. Verderami, "I timori di Francesco e la lezione di Ciriaco," *Corriere della Sera*, May 6, 2006.

33. See A. Cazzullo, "Bondi, coordinatore mistico. 'Berlusconi è bontà e purezza,'" *Corriere della Sera*, Oct. 25, 2003; Cazzullo, "Lasciatemi qui, sono un mito anche per i comunisti, Viaggio a Retequattro," *Corriere della Sera*, Dec. 17, 2003.

34. See Stella, "Il telerosario dei politici" *La vera storia italiana*, Movimento politico Forza Italia, Rome, 2006, p. 42.

35. See C. A. Viano, *Le imposture degli antichi e i miracoli dei moderni* (Turin: Einaudi, 2005), pp. 143 ff.

36. See C. De Gregorio, *Non lavate questo sangue* (Rome-Bari: Laterza, 2001); G. Chiesa, *G8/Genova* (Turin: Einaudi, 2001).

37. Quoted in F. Caffarena and C. Stiaccini, eds., *Fragili, resistenti. I messaggi di piazza Alimonda e la nascita di un luogo di identità collettiva* (Milan: Terre di mezzo, 2005), p. 90.

ACKNOWLEDGMENTS

It is impossible to name here all who have aided and supported me in the years of research. But I would like to thank those without whom this book could not have been written, none of whom, needless to say, share any responsibility for its contents.

At the Vatican, Monsignor Alejandro Cifres offered me the greatest courtesy at the archive of the Congregation for the Doctrine of the Faith. At the State Archives in Rome, I was the beneficiary not only of the helpfulness of the staff but of the guidance of a very generous colleague, Mauro Canali. At the Monte dei Cappuccini library in Turin, Silvia Ciliberti supplied me with excellent research facilities. At the Fondazione per le Scienze Religiose in Bologna, my colleagues Alberto Melloni and Enrico Galavotti encouraged my research in every way. In Puglia, I was able to rely on the help of and dialogue with Fernando Orsini and Giuseppe Florio. Discovering Padre Pio's adopted land with them made the experience all the more fascinating.

A part of the book was written in the United States, in the marvelously protected atmosphere of the Remarque Institute at New York University. I'd like to express my gratitude to Tony Judt and Jair Kessler for making my stay in New York so pleasant.

In Turin, between the Faculty of Letters and Philosophy, and the offices of Einaudi, I was lucky enough to be able to discuss my draft with two unusually perceptive readers: Giovanni De Luna and Andrea Romano. In Rome, I found in Stefano Chiodi the ideal interlocutor with whom to work out the iconographic issues of the Padre Pio affair.

His eye, trained in the history of art, helped me see into things otherwise opaque to my gaze.

Miguel Gotor and Gabriele Pedullà, by now permanent comrades in intellectual adventure, offered so much help for so long that I can't help but feel the book is as much theirs as mine (except for its defects). And Gabriele's hospitality in Rome made my every stay there a celebration.

Finally, I'd like to remember two historians, two friends, who were with me when this project began but did not live long enough to see its conclusion. This book is dedicated to the memory of Cesare Mozzarelli and Paolo Viola.

❖

My list of thanks would not be complete without a mention of those who made the American edition possible. Above all, Sara Bershtel, who once again believed in me and took a chance that this Italian story might interest faraway readers overseas. Also—more than ever—Frederika Randall, who translated *Padre Pio* with the same enviable assurance and the same fine sensitivity that she applied to *The Body of Il Duce*. And finally, Grigory Tovbis, the editor whose sharp eye and deft hand offered definitive proof that an author with Metropolitan Books is fortunate indeed.

INDEX

ABOUT THE AUTHOR

SERGIO LUZZATTO is the author of numerous books on French and Italian history, including *The Body of Il Duce: Mussolini's Corpse and the Fortunes of Italy.* He is a professor of modern history at the University of Turin, Italy, and a regular contributor to the leading Italian daily *Il Sole 24 Ore.*